WHAT THE
BIBLE SAYS...
about
THE
TABERNACLE
(ITS MESSAGE FOR TODAY)

WHAT THE
BIBLE SAYS...
about
THE
TABERNACLE
(ITS MESSAGE FOR TODAY)

Leadership Ministries Worldwide
Chattanooga, TN

What The Bible Says About The Tabernacle is written for God's people to use both in their personal lives and in their teaching. The purpose of the copyright is to prevent the illegal reproduction, misuse, and abuse of the material.

May our Lord bless us all as we live, preach, teach, and write for Him, fulfilling His great commission to live righteous and godly lives and to make disciples of all nations.

Please address all requests for information or permission to:
Leadership Ministries Worldwide
PO Box 21310
Chattanooga TN 37424-0310
Ph.# (423) 855-2181   FAX (423) 855-8616   E-Mail info@outlinebible.org
http://www.outlinebible.org

Library of Congress Catalog Card Number: 97-075959
International Standard Book Number: 978-1-57407-125-2

PRINTED IN THE U.S.A.

PUBLISHED BY LEADERSHIP MINISTRIES WORLDWIDE

3   4   5   6   7   08   09   10   11   12

DEDICATED

To all the men and women of the world who preach and teach the Gospel of our Lord Jesus Christ and to the Mercy and Grace of God

- Demonstrated to us in Christ Jesus our Lord.

  "In whom we have redemption through His blood, the forgiveness of sins, according to the riches of His grace." (Ep.1:7)

- Out of the mercy and grace of God His Word has flowed. Let every person know that God will have mercy upon him, forgiving and using him to fulfill His glorious plan of salvation.

  "For God so loved the world, that he gave His only begotten Son, that whosoever believeth in Him should not perish, but have everlasting life. For God sent not his son into the world to condemn the world, but that the world through him might be saved." (Jn.3:16-17)

  "For this is good and acceptable in the sight of God our Saviour; who will have all men to be saved, and to come unto the knowledge of the truth." (1 Ti.2:3-4)

  3/08

What the Bible Says About the Tabernacle...

is written for God's servants to use in their study, teaching, and preaching of God's Holy Word...

- to share the Word of God with the world.
- to help believers, both ministers and laypersons, in their understanding, preaching, and teaching of God's Word.
- to do everything we possibly can to lead men, women, boys, and girls to give their hearts and lives to Jesus Christ and to secure the eternal life that He offers.
- to do all we can to minister to the needy of the world.
- to give Jesus Christ His proper place, the place the Word gives Him. Therefore, no work of Leadership Ministries Worldwide—no Outline Bible Resources—will ever be personalized.

THE TABERNACLE....

TABLE OF CONTENTS

Part One: The Tabernacle, Its Blueprint and Priesthood: The True Way to Approach and Worship God (Exodus 25:1-31:18)

Part Two: The Tabernacle, Its Construction and Dedication: The People Obey God (Exodus 35:1-40:38)

Part Three: The Tabernacle and Ark in the Old Testament: A Devotional Study

Part Four: The Tabernacle and Ark in the New Testament: A Devotional Study

Part Five: Resource Chart Section

"Go ye therefore, and teach all nations"
(Mt.28:19)

PART I

THE TABERNACLE, ITS BLUEPRINT AND PRIESTHOOD: THE TRUE WAY TO APPROACH AND WORSHIP GOD
(Exodus 25:1–31:18)

If a people were ever to experience a high moment, this was the perfect moment. Never before had a people been so privileged as Israel. Never before had God so blessed a people. Just imagine a people who had recently experienced so much:

⇒ The Israelites had just been liberated, set free after 400 years of slavery. They were now free—free at last.

⇒ Their nation was being born, the nation of Israel. They were soon to be given a homeland, their very own country, the land of Canaan that is known today as Palestine.

⇒ Moreover, and just as important as any of the above events, the Israelites had been chosen by God to be His followers, the people of God.

They had been chosen to be God's witnesses to the other nations of the earth, witnessing that there is only One true and living God. In fact, during these very days Moses had been up on Mount Sinai face to face with God. God had given him the civil and religious laws that were to form the Israelites into a nation and govern them as a people. We know from the record of Exodus chapters 19–31 that God had just completed giving Moses three things: the Ten Commandments, the civil and religious laws, and the instructions for constructing the Tabernacle, the place where God's very own presence was to dwell in a very special way upon earth. Moses had come down from the mountain and shared all with the people, forming them into a nation ruled by law, the laws that had actually been given by God Himself. Now the people were ready to begin their final march to the promised land. They were ready to begin their march except for one thing: building the house of God, the Tabernacle. The Tabernacle was to be the place where God's presence would dwell and guide His people in a very special way as they marched to the promised land. The building of the Tabernacle was to be one of the most joyful and momentous occasions in the history of Israel.

The Tabernacle was the worship center of the Israelites during their *wilderness wanderings* or *wilderness journeys*. The *wilderness wanderings* stretched from the day of Israel's liberation from slavery over to the day of Israel's entrance into the promised land. The Tabernacle was actually a large, beautiful, portable tent, built so it could be easily pitched and taken down. Several facts need to be noted before studying the Scriptures that actually cover the Tabernacle.

1

1. The Tabernacle was the worship center of the Israelites for a long, long time: almost *five hundred years* from Moses to David—until Solomon's temple was built.

2. A large portion of God's Holy Word is dedicated to the Tabernacle: *thirty-seven entire chapters*. Thirteen chapters in the book of Exodus discuss the Tabernacle and its priesthood. Eighteen chapters of Leviticus center on the sacrificial system of the Tabernacle. Two chapters of Deuteronomy are set aside for the study of the Tabernacle. In the New Testament, the Tabernacle is discussed in four of the thirteen chapters in the book of Hebrews, over 30% of the entire book.

3. The Tabernacle was the worship center for the Israelites, but it was also used by God as a great object lesson, as a great teaching tool. The Tabernacle was full of symbols, types, pictures, and shadows that point to spiritual truths for the believer. The symbolism of the Tabernacle is significant, very significant. However in looking at symbolic meanings, we must be careful to guard against the extreme of so many interpreters.

> ⇒ There are well-known and respected commentaries that find specific meanings for everything mentioned in the Tabernacle. Often, it seems that these commentaries are making an attempt to force a meaning upon a particular term.
>
> ⇒ At the other end of the interpretation spectrum, there are just as many respected commentaries that focus only on the historical purpose of the Tabernacle. These commentaries acknowledge very few, if any, symbolic teachings from the Tabernacle.

What are we to make of these two extremes? It is the duty of every believer and sincere Bible scholar to be true to God's Word. The Bible is full of symbols, pictures, and shadows waiting to be studied and taught without having to make them up. It will be our goal...

- to allow the Bible to speak for itself
- to allow Scripture to interpret Scripture
- to draw out useful, significant, and practical application
- to study, with the Holy Spirit as our guide, the design that God showed Moses

4. God's Holy Spirit inspired Moses to write down *everything* that God's people would need in order to know how God wanted to be approached and worshipped. The Tabernacle and its priesthood were teaching tools for almost five hundred years. The Tabernacle was a picture, an object lesson, the focal point of life for God's people—from the time of Moses until Solomon's Temple. The people of that time could only faintly appreciate the message, the reality that stood behind the symbols and shadows. Israel had to settle for an abstract, imperfect Tabernacle that was made with human hands. The believer today has a much better perspective of the great plan of redemption that was spelled out in the Tabernacle. We are no longer limited to a mere shadow of the Tabernacle and its priesthood; we have the reality of the Tabernacle's message, the very Person to whom the Tabernacle pointed, the Lord Jesus Christ, the Savior and Redeemer of the world.

> **"Which are a shadow of things to come; but the body is of Christ"** **(Col.2:17).**
>
> **"Who serve unto the example and shadow of heavenly things, as Moses was admonished of God when he was about to make the tabernacle: for, See, saith he, that thou make all things according to the pattern showed to thee in the mount" (He.8:5).**
>
> **"It was therefore necessary that the patterns of things in the heavens should be purified with these; but the heavenly things themselves with better sacrifices than these. For Christ is not entered into the holy places made with hands, which are the figures of the true; but into heaven itself, now to appear in the presence of God for us....So Christ was once offered to bear the sins of many; and unto them that look for him shall he appear the second time without sin unto salvation" (He.9:23-24, 28).**
>
> **"For the law having a shadow of good things to come, and not the very image of the things, can never with those sacrifices which they**

offered year by year continually make the comers thereunto perfect. For then would they not have ceased to be offered? because that the worshippers once purged should have had no more conscience of sins. But in those sacrifices there is a remembrance again made of sins every year. For it is not possible that the blood of bulls and of goats should take away sins. Wherefore when he cometh into the world, he saith, Sacrifice and offering thou wouldest not, but a body hast thou prepared me....Then said he, Lo, I come to do thy will, O God. He taketh away the first, that he may establish the second. By the which will we are sanctified through the offering of the body of Jesus Christ once for all. And every priest standeth daily ministering and offering oftentimes the same sacrifices, which can never take away sins: But this man, after he had offered one sacrifice for sins for ever, sat down on the right hand of God" (He.10:1-5, 9-12).

5. The Tabernacle symbolizes or pictures three major things. The symbols and pictures will be clearly seen as each portion of Scripture is studied.
   a. The Tabernacle symbolizes or pictures the ministry of Jesus Christ. The materials used to construct the Tabernacle are pictures of God's redemption in Jesus Christ. The various furnishings show God's great plan of salvation for the repentant sinner. The Tabernacle of Moses reveals every aspect of Jesus Christ and His work as the Word who became flesh and dwelt (*tabernacled*) among us (Jn.1:14).
   b. The Tabernacle symbolizes or pictures the ministry of the church. The Tabernacle was a worship center in which God dwelt, and the Tabernacle stood as a witness to the world. So does the church. God's presence and witness dwell within the church in two ways:
   ⇒ God's Spirit dwells within believers.

   > "What? know ye not that your body is the temple of the Holy Ghost which is in you, which ye have of God, and ye are not your own? For ye are bought with a price: therefore glorify God in your body, and in your spirit, which are God's" (1 Co.6:19-20).

   ⇒ God's Spirit dwells among believers—within the very presence of believers—when two or three of them gather together.

   > "For where two or three are gathered together in my name, there am I in the midst of them" (Mt.18:20).
   > "Know ye not that ye [plural, referring to the church, the body or assembly of believers] are the temple of God, and that the Spirit of God dwelleth in you?" (1 Co.3:16).
   > "In whom ye [plural, the body of believers] also are builded together for an habitation of God through the Spirit" (Ep.2:22).

   c. The Tabernacle symbolizes or pictures the Christian believer, the person who *truly* follows God. The Tabernacle was the dwelling place for God's presence upon earth, standing as a strong witness to the LORD. The believer—his body—is the very temple of God, the sanctuary and dwelling place for the presence and witness of God upon earth.

   > "I in them, and thou in me, that they may be made perfect in one; and that the world may know that thou hast sent me, and hast loved them, as thou hast loved me" (Jn.17:23).
   > "What? know ye not that your body is the temple of the Holy Ghost which is in you, which ye have of God, and ye are not your own? For ye are bought with a price: therefore glorify God in your body, and in your spirit, which are God's" (1 Co.6:19-20).

"And what agreement hath the temple of God with idols? for ye are the temple of the living God; as God hath said, I will dwell in them, and walk in them; and I will be their God, and they shall be my people" (2 Co.6:15).

"I am crucified with Christ: nevertheless I live; yet not I, but Christ liveth in me: and the life which I now live in the flesh I live by the faith of the Son of God, who loved me, and gave himself for me" (Ga.2:20).

"To whom God would make known what is the riches of the glory of this mystery among the Gentiles; which is Christ in you, the hope of glory" (Col.1:27).

"Your life is hid with Christ in God" (Col.3:3).

The excellent Bible expositor Stephen Olford says this about the Tabernacle's parallel to the Christian believer:

> *In a remarkable way, the entire person of the Christian represents the three compartments of the Tabernacle. The body corresponds to the outer court: it is the outer and visible part of our personality; it is the place of sacrifice and cleansing (see Romans 12:1-2; 1 John 1:7,9). The soul answers to the holy place, and therefore is that aspect of our personality which worships and enjoys fellowship with other believers, eating at the table, walking in the light, and interceding in prayer. The spirit speaks of the believer's inner holy of holies—the deepest hidden life, the individual and personal communion of one sheltered under the blood (John 4:23; Romans 1:9); it is the place of spiritual victory. As such, the Tabernacle speaks of the whole ministry of the New Testament Christian.[1]*

6. There was the great purpose of the Tabernacle. The purpose of the Tabernacle was at least twofold.

   a. Its short-term purpose was to build God a sanctuary where God might be worshipped and be able to live among His people.

> "And let them make me a sanctuary; that I may dwell among them" (Ex.25:8).
>
> "And there I will meet with thee, and I will commune with thee from above the mercy seat, from between the two cherubims which are upon the ark of the testimony, of all things which I will give thee in commandment unto the children of Israel" (Ex.25:22).

   b. The long-term purpose of the Tabernacle was to arouse God's people to look at the promised Messiah. The promised Messiah would come and fulfill every picture of the Tabernacle within Himself. Through the life of Jesus Christ, God's people would no longer have to settle for a pattern made with human hands. Jesus Christ is the true Tabernacle who came to *tabernacle*—camp out, dwell, live among—His people.

> "And the Word was made flesh, and dwelt [tabernacled] among us, (and we beheld his glory, the glory as of the only begotten of the Father,) full of grace and truth" (Jn.1:14).
>
> "God, who at sundry times and in divers manners spake in time past unto the fathers by the prophets, Hath in these last days spoken unto us by his Son, whom he hath appointed heir of all things, by whom also he made the worlds; Who being the brightness of his glory, and the express image of his person, and

---

[1] Stephen Olford. *The Tabernacle, Camping With God.* (Neptune, NJ: Loizeaux Brothers, 1971), p.23.

upholding all things by the word of his power, when he had by himself purged our sins, sat down on the right hand of the Majesty on high" (He.1:1-3).

7. The word *tabernacle* (mishkan) means dwelling place, a tent, a place of habitation, a residence. The root word means to *pitch a tent*. The picture of the tabernacle is graphic:
    ⇒ God literally pitched His tent, the tabernacle, among His people, the Israelites.
    ⇒ Jesus Christ pitched His tent, the tabernacle of His body, and He lived and dwelt among us.

8. The message of the tabernacle is graphically illustrated by the excellent expositor Stephen Olford. He says:

> *The message of the tabernacle...can be summed up in a twofold proposition:*
> *God's appearance to man in grace.*
> *Man's approach to God in faith.*
> *It is of very great significance that in giving the instructions for the construction of the tabernacle, God begins with the ark and concludes with the brazen altar; whereas in the use of the tabernacle, man commences with the brazen altar and moves through to the holy of holies and ark of the covenant. That is the Christian gospel.*
> *Christianity is unique in that it is the only religion which claims that God has taken the initiative in revealing Himself to man. All other religions describe man's search after God. But having revealed Himself to man by leaving His throne and humbling Himself unto death—even the death of the cross—God has effected a plan of salvation for man to approach Him by faith. That simple way of salvation is beautifully illustrated in seven steps, which we shall consider in more detail later.*
> *For the present, let us note that the penitent sinner who comes by faith there is:*
> *a. The Way of Introduction - The gate of the outer court. Jesus said: "Enter ye in at the strait gate...because strait is the gate, and narrow is the way, which leadeth unto life" (Matthew 7:13-14).*
> *b. The Way of Reconciliation - the brazen altar. "God was in Christ, reconciling the world unto Himself....For He hath made Him to be sin for us, who knew no sin; that we might be made the righteousness of God in Him" (2 Corinthians 5:19, 21).*
> *c. The Way of Separation - the laver. Speaking to His disciples Jesus said: "He that is washed needeth not save to wash his feet, but is clean every whit" (John 13:10). Later He said: "Now ye are clean through the word which I have spoken unto you" (John 15:3).*
> *d. The Way of Illumination - the golden candlestick. Jesus said: "I am the light of the world: he that followeth Me shall not walk in darkness, but shall have the light of life" (John 8:12).*
> *e. The Way of Satisfaction - the table of showbread. Jesus said: "I am the bread of life: he that cometh to Me shall never hunger; and he that believeth on Me shall never thirst" (John 6:35).*
> *f. The Way of Intercession - the altar of incense. "By Him therefore let us offer the sacrifice of praise to God continually, that is, the fruit of our lips giving thanks to His name" (Hebrews 13:15).*
> *g. The Way of Communion - the ark of the covenant. "Truly our fellowship is with the Father, and with His Son Jesus Christ" (1 John 1:3).*[2]

---

[2] Stephen Olford. *The Tabernacle, Camping With God*, pp.23-25.

**PLEASE NOTE THE
RESOURCE CHART SECTION**

The following charts on the Tabernacle are in the Resource Chart Section at the back of this book. This is to keep from interrupting a person's study of the Scripture outlines and commentary. A study of the Charts will help the reader more fully grasp the meaning of the Tabernacle.

Chart 1: **THE PICTURE OF THE BELIEVER'S LIFE IN THE TABERNACLE**

Chart 2: **HOW CHRIST FULFILLED THE SYMBOLISM OF THE TABERNACLE**

Chart 3: **HOW CHRIST FULFILLED THE SYMBOLISM OF THE PRIESTHOOD**

CHAPTER ONE

The Materials Needed to Construct the Tabernacle: God's Call to Stewardship, to Give from a Willing Heart (Exodus 25:1-9)

Contents

The Materials Needed to Construct the Tabernacle: God's Call to Stewardship, to Give from a Willing Heart (Exodus 25:1-9)

1. The architect of the Tabernacle: God Himself
2. The supplier of the materials: The people
  a. Were to bring an offering
  b. Were to give willingly
 	
3. The materials listed
  a. Gold, silver, & bronze
 	
  b. Blue, purple, & scarlet yarn, fine threaded linen, & goat hair
  c. Ram skins dyed red
  d. Badger (sea cow) skins
	And the LORD spake unto Moses, saying,
	2 Speak unto the children of Israel, that they bring me an offering: of every man that giveth it willingly with his heart ye shall take my offering.
	3 And this is the offering which ye shall take of them; gold, and silver, and brass,
	4 And blue, and purple, and scarlet, and fine linen, and goats' hair,
	5 And rams' skins dyed red, and bad-
		gers' skins, and shittim wood,
		6 Oil for the light, spices for anointing oil, and for sweet incense,
		7 Onyx stones, and stones to be set in the ephod, and in the breastplate.
		8 And let them make me a sanctuary; that I may dwell among them.
		9 According to all that I show thee, after the pattern of the tabernacle, and the pattern of all the instruments thereof, even so shall ye make it.
			e. Acacia wood
			f. Oil for light
			g. Spices for the anointing oil & for incense
			h. Onyx stones
			i. Gems to be set in the priest's ephod & breastpiece
			4. The purpose: To build a sanctuary so that God could dwell among His people
			5. The plan & design of the Tabernacle: Dictated by God—God alone determines how a person is to approach Him

A place to meet God—this is one of the dire needs of man. When man is bombarded with the painful trials and sufferings of life, he needs the help that only God can give. He needs the help of God in facing the moments of...

- loneliness and despair
- emptiness and restlessness
- accident and disease
- suffering and pain
- hunger and thirst
- hopelessness and helplessness
- unemployment and poverty
- temptation and sin
- aging and dying

Man needs the presence and assurance of God all throughout life. He needs the security of God, to know that God loves and cares for him, that God is looking after him. But even more basic than all this, man needs the peace and reconciliation of God. Man needs to know that his sins are forgiven, that God accepts him and is going to receive him into heaven, that God is going to give him eternal life.

God knows that man has these needs. Therefore, God established a very special place for His people...

- a place where He could live among His people
- a place where a special manifestation of His presence would dwell
- a place where His people could come to Him for worship and help

That place was the Tabernacle. This is the focus of this passage: *The Materials Needed to Construct the Tabernacle: God's Call to Stewardship, to Give from a Willing Heart,* Ex.25:1-9.

I.   The architect of the Tabernacle: God Himself (v.1).
II. The supplier of the materials: the people (v.2).
III. The materials listed (vv.3-7).
IV. The purpose: to build a sanctuary so that God could dwell among His people (v.8).
V.   The plan and design of the Tabernacle: dictated by God—God alone determines how a person is to approach Him (v.9).

I. The Architect of the Tabernacle Was God Himself (v.1).

When planning and constructing a building, the most important person is the architect. The architect is the person...

- who is the master builder
- who knows the science, rules, and principles of buildings and architecture
- who dreams and lays out the plan for the building
- who designs and works out the structure for the building
- who oversees and looks after the construction
- who inspects and approves the building

More than anyone else, the architect is responsible for the construction of a building. He determines whether a building stands or falls, functions or fails, is problem-free or loaded with problems, lasts or quickly needs repairs, brings joy to the users or arouses disappointment.

The Tabernacle was so important—so desperately needed by God's people—that God Himself chose to be the architect of the Tabernacle. He could not leave the design and structure of the Tabernacle in the hands of men. Why? Because the Tabernacle was to be...

- His dwelling place among men, the very place where God's presence was to be manifested among His people
- the special place where people would come to worship God
- the special place where people would learn about God

Only God knew what kind of building He needed and wanted for the manifestation of His presence, what kind of building He needed to receive man's worship, what kind of building He needed to teach people about Himself. No man knew. Therefore, God Himself had to be the architect of the Tabernacle.

> "For this man [Christ Jesus] was counted worthy of more glory than Moses, inasmuch as he who hath builded the house hath more honour than the house" (He.3:3; see Ro.11:33).
> "One thing have I desired of the LORD, that will I seek after; that I may dwell in the house of the LORD all the days of my life, to behold the beauty of the LORD, and to inquire in his temple" (Ps.27:4; see Ps.122:1).
> "And many people shall go and say, Come ye, and let us go up to the mountain of the LORD, to the house of the God of Jacob; and he will teach us of his ways, and we will walk in his paths: for out of Zion shall go forth the law, and the word of the LORD from Jerusalem" (Is.2:3).

II. The Materials to Build the Tabernacle Were Supplied by the People (v.2).

Moses was to take up offerings from the people, and the people were to give willingly and generously. The word for *offering* (terumah) has the idea of a present, a gift that is given sacrificially; the giving of a special gift, a valuable, costly gift.

Remember: just several months before, the Israelites had been slaves in Egypt where they had been enslaved for about 400 years. As slaves, they had earned and accumulated little if any wealth. But now they had enough to give offerings to build the Tabernacle. Where had their wealth come from? From the Egyptians. Right before God had freed the Israelites from Egypt, He had stirred within the Egyptians a desperate desire to get rid of the Israelites. The Egyptians' desperation ran so deep that they were willing to pay the Israelites just to get rid of them, willing to pay them in gold and silver and other goods that would help the Israelites as they journeyed to the promised land of Canaan (Ex.11:2; 12:35-36). God had seen to it that the needs of His people were met. Thus they were now able to give offerings to build the Tabernacle.

The point is this: God had provided for the people. What they had was due to Him: they had money—gold, silver, and possessions—because God had moved upon the Egyptians to give them wealth. Now, they were to give some of the wealth back to Him:

⇒ give willingly and sacrificially
⇒ give valuable, costly gifts

Thought
Note several important lessons.

a) Ultimately everything belongs to God. All that we have has come from Him.

> **"For every beast of the forest is mine, and the cattle upon a thousand hills" (Ps.50:10).**
> **"The silver is mine, and the gold is mine, saith the LORD of hosts" (Hag.2:8).**

b) The greatest thing we can give God is an undivided heart, totally yielded to Him.

> **"No man can serve two masters: for either he will hate the one, and love the other; or else he will hold to the one, and despise the other. Ye cannot serve God and mammon [money]" (Mt.6:24; see Mt.6:19-21).**
> **"And he said to [them] all, If any [man] will come after me, let him deny himself, and take up his cross daily, and follow me" (Lu.9:23).**

c) Every person has something to offer to God. No matter how little a person may have, he has something that he can give to God.

> **"They gave after their ability unto the treasure of the work threescore and one thousand drams of gold, and five thousand pound of silver, and one hundred priests' garments" (Ezr. 2:69).**
> **"And there came a certain poor widow, and she threw in two mites, which make a farthing. And he [Jesus] called [unto him] his disciples, and saith unto them, Verily I say unto you, That this poor widow hath cast more in, than all they which have cast into the treasury" (Mk.12:42-43).**
> **"Then the disciples, every man according to his ability, determined to send relief unto the brethren which dwelt in Judaea" (Ac.11:29).**

d) We are to share with those who are in need.

> **"And all that believed were together, and had all things common; And sold their possessions and goods, and parted them to all men, as every man had need" (Ac.2:44-45).**
> **"I have showed you all things, how that so labouring ye ought to support the weak, and to remember the words of the Lord Jesus, how he said, It is more blessed to give than to receive" (Ac.20:35; see Lu.18:18-25).**

e) We are to give sacrificially, to give willingly and cheerfully.

> **"Every man according as he purposeth in his heart, so let him give; not grudgingly, or of necessity: for God loveth a cheerful giver" (2 Co.9:7; see Acts 4:34-35).**
> **"Every man shall give as he is able, according to the blessing of the LORD thy God which he hath given thee" (De.16:17).**

III. The Materials for the Tabernacle Are Clearly Listed (vv.3-7).

The materials for the Tabernacle are clearly listed. But note this fact first: throughout Scripture the Tabernacle and its materials are said to be full of rich symbolism, pointing in particular to Christ. Because of this...

- some writers strain to see a symbolic meaning or some type in everything
- other writers ignore and fail to point out the symbolism and types

When looking at symbolism and types, it is always most important to be true to Scripture. The Scripture must never be strained nor stretched to give some meaning that is not there. But on the other hand we must not be stubborn or opinionated when people see some symbolic meaning or type that is not specifically mentioned in Scripture. We must always keep this fact in mind: when a person looked at the Tabernacle, God wanted His people to think about certain spiritual truths. When a person saw the valuable metals and materials and the beautiful colors, God wanted the person's mind to focus upon spiritual things. There is, therefore, a richness of meaning and symbolism in the Tabernacle that is sometimes clear, although it is not specifically spelled out by Scripture. When the symbolic meaning is clear, it points the person to Christ and spiritual truth. Now, note the materials that were to be used in building the Tabernacle.

1. There was gold, silver, and bronze (v.3).
   a. Gold is a symbol of value, of the greatest and most precious value that can be possessed. In Scripture it is a symbol of the great value of the LORD Himself, of His Person, His righteousness, and His mercy.

> **"I counsel thee to buy of me gold [righteousness] tried in the fire, that thou mayest be rich; and white raiment, that thou mayest be clothed, and that the shame of thy nakedness do not appear; and anoint thine eyes with eyesalve, that thou mayest see" (Re.3:18).**
> **"And thou shalt make a mercy seat of pure gold: two cubits and a half shall be the length thereof, and a cubit and a half the breadth thereof" (Ex.25:17).** (Remember, the Mercy Seat sat upon the ark of God itself, which represented the throne of God, the very place where the presence and mercy of God were symbolized as flowing out to God's people. The point: gold is the symbol of the great value of the LORD Himself, of His righteousness and His mercy.)

   b. Silver is a symbol of redemption, of the soul being ransomed by the atonement money.

> "When thou takest the sum of the children of Israel after their number, then shall they give every man a ransom for his soul unto the LORD, when thou numberest them; that there be no plague among them, when thou numberest them. This they shall give, every one that passeth among them that are numbered, half a shekel [a silver coin] after the shekel of the sanctuary: (a shekel is twenty gerahs:) an half shekel shall be the offering of the LORD....And thou shalt take the atonement money of the children of Israel, and shalt appoint it for the service of the tabernacle of the congregation; that it may be a memorial unto the children of Israel before the LORD, to make an atonement for your souls" (Ex.30:12-13, 16; see Nu.18:16).

c. Bronze or copper is a symbol of the death of Christ, of His bearing the judgment of sin for man. This is seen in the brazen altar, the place where the lamb was slain as the sacrificial offering on behalf of the people.

> "And thou shalt make his pans to receive his ashes, and his shovels, and his basons, and his fleshhooks, and his firepans: all the vessels [for the altar] thou shalt make of brass" (Ex.27:3).

2. There was blue, purple, and scarlet yarn and fine linen (v.4). This combination of colors was the main color scheme used in the Tabernacle. These main colors are mentioned about twenty-five times in the book of *Exodus* alone.

a. Blue is the color of the heavens above; therefore, it is said to be the symbol of the heavenly character of Christ.

> "For such an high priest became us, who is holy, harmless, undefiled, separate from sinners, and made higher than the heavens" (He.7:26).

b. Purple is the color of royalty; therefore, it is a symbol of Christ as the King of kings and LORD of lords.

> "And they clothed him with purple, and platted a crown of thorns, and put it about his head, And began to salute him, Hail, King of the Jews!" (Mk.15:17-18).
> "And he hath on his vesture and on his thigh a name written, KING OF KINGS, AND LORD OF LORDS" (Re.19:16).

c. Scarlet (red) symbolizes sacrifice, picturing the entire scene of sacrifice and redemption. Jesus Christ is the Lamb of God, the One sacrificed to take away the sins of man.

> "For if the blood of bulls and of goats, and the ashes of an heifer sprinkling the unclean, sanctifieth to the purifying of the flesh: How much more shall the blood of Christ, who through the eternal Spirit offered himself without spot to God, purge your conscience from dead works to serve the living God?" (He.9:13-14).
> "For when Moses had spoken every precept to all the people according to the law, he took the blood of calves and of goats, with water, and scarlet wool, and hyssop, and sprinkled both the book, and all the people, Saying, This is the blood of the testament which God hath enjoined unto you" (He.9:19-20).
> "So Christ was once offered to bear the sins of many; and unto them that look for him shall he appear the second time without sin unto salvation" (He.9:28; see He.9:23).

d. White linen symbolizes purity and righteousness, the purity, righteousness, and holiness of God and the purity and righteousness demanded by God.

> **"And to her was granted that she should be arrayed in fine linen, clean and white: for the fine linen is the righteousness of saints" (Re.19:8).**
> **"He that overcometh, the same shall be clothed in white raiment [righteousness]; and I will not blot out his name out of the book of life, but I will confess his name before my Father, and before his angels" (Re.3:5; see Re.3:18; 4:4).**
> **"After this I beheld, and, lo, a great multitude, which no man could number, of all nations, and kindreds, and people, and tongues, stood before the throne, and before the Lamb, clothed with white robes [righteousness], and palms in their hands" (Re.7:9).**

3. There was *goat hair* (izzim) (v.4) which was to be used for the tent's covering (see Ex.26:7). These curtains of goat hair were most likely black in color. A set of eleven curtains were joined together to make one great covering for the tent. There seems to be a direct symbolism between the goat hair and Christ's relationship to sin, pointing to Christ as the sin-bearer appointed by God to bear the sins of the world. Stephen Olford comments about the significance of the goat in Scripture:

> *..the goat, in Scripture, is mentioned in connection with the sin offering and sinners. We read: "Take ye a kid of the goats for a sin offering" (Leviticus 9:3). "Take...two kids of the goats for a sin offering" on the great Day of Atonement (Leviticus 16:5-28). "One kid of the goats for a sin offering unto the LORD shall be offered' (Numbers 28:15). "He shall separate them one from another, as a shepherd divideth his sheep from the goats"—representing the saved and the unsaved at the judgment of the nations (Matthew 25:32). So it is fairly clear that the tent of goat's hair speaks of the Lord Jesus as the divine Sin-bearer.[1]*

Thought
Jesus Christ became the *scapegoat* for the world. Instead of allowing the sting of sin to rest upon sinners, Jesus Christ offered Himself as a Sacrifice, as the Substitute and Savior of the world, as the sin-bearer for the sins of all people of all generations.

> **"Therefore will I divide him a portion with the great, and he shall divide the spoil with the strong; because he hath poured out his soul unto death: and he was numbered with the transgressors; and he bare the sin of many, and made intercession for the transgressors" (Is.53:12).**
> **"Who gave himself for our sins, that he might deliver us from this present evil world, according to the will of God and our Father" (Ga.1:4).**
> **"So Christ was once offered to bear the sins of many; and unto them that look for him shall he appear the second time without sin unto salvation" (He.9:28; see 1 Pe.2:24; 1 Jn.3:5; Re.1:5).**

4. There were ram skins dyed red (v.5). *The Expositor's Bible Commentary* describes these ram skins as *"skins that had all the wool removed and then were dyed red; it was like our morocco leather."* [2] The purpose of these tanned ram skins was to provide a protective covering for the tent. It was layered between the goat hair and the badger (or sea cow) skins. (For more discussion, see Chapter Thirteen, Ex.36:19.)

---

1   Stephen Olford. *The Tabernacle, Camping With God,* pp.80-81.
2   Frank E. Gaebelein. *The Expositor's Bible Commentary*, Vol. 2. (Grand Rapids, MI: Zondervan Publishing House, 1990), p.453.

5. There were badger (sea cow) skins (v.5). The source of this outer covering for the Tabernacle probably came from the Red Sea.[3] This durable, weather-resistant skin was the ideal choice to protect the tent from the hot sun, the drenching rains, and the piercing dust storms that swept across the desert.

6. There was acacia wood (v.5). Acacia or Shittim was an area in the plains of Moab, slightly northeast of the Dead Sea. Acacia wood came from a tree that flourished in the wilderness. Acacia was an extremely hard wood that was a mixture of brown and orange in color. During the period of the Old Testament, the tree was very plentiful as it grew in groves next to fast-moving bodies of water. It was the craftsman's prime choice for furniture because of its durability. The Septuagint (the Greek translation of the Hebrew Old Testament) translates acacia as *incorruptible* wood.

Thought

In a world filled with corruption, Jesus Christ is the only person who is incorruptible. As the acacia tree speaks of durability and strength, Jesus Christ is the perfect picture of durability and strength. Jesus Christ is the only Man strong enough...

- to live a sinless life and take away our sins
- to defeat sin and death on the Cross

> **"And ye know that he was manifested to take away our sins; and in him is no sin" (1 Jn.3:5).**
>
> **"Who his own self bare our sins in his own body on the tree, that we, being dead to sins, should live unto righteousness: by whose stripes ye were healed" (1 Pe.2:24).**

7. There was oil for light (v.6). The oil was made by crushing the olives from olive trees. The oil would be needed to provide continuous light for the sanctuary with the golden lampstand (see Chapter Six, Ex.27:20). Throughout Scripture, the olive tree is a symbol of fulness and fruitfulness, a choice tree among people. Thus the oil is a symbol of the fullness and fruitfulness of God's Spirit, a symbol of the anointing of God's Spirit.

> **"But the anointing [Holy Spirit] which ye have received of him abideth in you, and ye need not that any man teach you: but as the same anointing teacheth you of all things, and is truth, and is no lie, and even as it hath taught you, ye shall abide in him" (1 Jn.2:27).**
>
> **"But the olive tree said unto them, Should I leave my fatness, wherewith by me they honour God and man, and go to be promoted over the trees?" (Jud.9:9; see Ps.52:8).**
>
> **"The LORD called thy name, A green olive tree, fair, and of goodly fruit: with the noise of a great tumult he hath kindled fire upon it, and the branches of it are broken" (Je.11:16; see Ho.14:6).**

8. There were spices for the anointing oil and for incense (v.6. See Chapter Ten, Ex.30:22-25 for the list of ingredients that made the anointing oil. See Ex.30:34-38 for the four spices used in making the incense.)

9. There were onyx stones (v.7). These were semi-precious stones. The color of these stones is uncertain. The Scripture is clear on their purpose: they were to be used on the priests' ephod and breastpiece. (See Chapter Seven, Ex.28:6-25 for more discussion on the purpose of these stones.) The Hebrew word for *onyx* (shoh-ham) comes from a root word meaning a flashing forth of splendor. The names of the twelve tribes of Israel were to be inscribed on the two onyx stones. The picture is this: in God's eyes, His people shine forth in splendor, as precious gems.

10. There were gems to be set in the priests' ephod and breastpiece (v.7).

---

3   Frank E. Gaebelein. *The Expositor's Bible Commentary*, Vol. 2, p.453.

IV. God Had One Main Purpose for Building the Tabernacle, That He Might Dwell in a Very Special Way Among His People (v.8).

The word *sanctuary* (miqdash) means a holy place, a hallowed place, a place sanctified or set apart for God. God wanted the Tabernacle to be a holy, hallowed place...

- a place sanctified or set apart for God
- a place looked upon as being where God dwelt in a very special way
- a place where God could live in a special way among His people
- a place where God met with people and people with God
- a place where people worshipped God, received the forgiveness of God, and committed their lives to God

Note that God took the initiative to build a relationship with Israel. God longs to be with His people, to fellowship and commune with them. How can He do this? By planning a special place where He can meet with people and people can come to meet with Him. In dealing with the ancient Israelites, that place was the Tabernacle, the sanctuary.

Thought
The believer's body is now the temple, the sanctuary of God. We are therefore to sanctify, to set apart, our bodies to live holy and righteous lives. Our bodies are to be fit sanctuaries, "holy places" in which the Spirit of God can live.

> **"Know ye not that ye are the temple of God, and that the Spirit of God dwelleth in you? If any man defile the temple of God, him shall God destroy; for the temple of God is holy, which temple ye are" (1 Co.3:16-17; see 1 Co.3:23).**
> **"What? know ye not that your body is the temple of the Holy Ghost which is in you, which ye have of God, and ye are not your own? For ye are bought with a price: therefore glorify God in your body, and in your spirit, which are God's" (1 Co.6:19-20).**
> **"Having therefore these promises, dearly beloved, let us cleanse ourselves from all filthiness of the flesh and spirit, perfecting holiness in the fear of God" (2 Co.7:1; see Le.11:45; Lu.1:74-75; He.12:14; 1 Pe.1:15-16).**

V. The Pattern or Model of the Tabernacle Was Dictated by God (v.9).

God alone determines how a person is to approach Him. This is the first time the word *tabernacle* is used in Scripture. The word *tabernacle* (mishkan) means a dwelling place, a habitation, a residence, a tent. The picture is that of God's pitching His tent among His people and living in a very special way with them. Note that the Tabernacle is God's tent, God's residence. The point is emphatic: since the Tabernacle is His residence, He alone has the right to plan and design the Tabernacle with all its furnishings. This is exactly what this verse says: "I will show you"—show you the plan and design.

Thought
The application is clear: the Tabernacle was the place where a person approached God, where a person came to meet God. God alone determines how a person is to approach Him. There is only one approach, only one way to God: that way is through His Son, the Lord Jesus Christ.

> **"Jesus saith unto him, I am the way, the truth, and the life: no man cometh unto the Father, but by me" (Jn.14:6; see Jn.3:16-18; 6:68; 8:24; 10:9).**
> **"Neither is there salvation in any other: for there is none other name under heaven given among men, whereby we must be saved" (Ac.4:12).**

TYPES, SYMBOLS, AND PICTURES
(Exodus 25:1-9)

Historical Term	Type or Picture (Scriptural Basis)	Life Application for Today's Believer	Biblical Application for Today's Believer
Badger (sea cow) skins (Ex.25:5)	*The badger skins acted as a protective shield for the Tabernacle. This outer covering gave protection against the windswept desert sands, the beating sun, and the occasional rains. The protection of the badger skins against the harsh wilderness symbolized a protective separation from the world.* **"And he made a covering for the tent** *of* **rams' skins dyed red, and a covering** *of* **badgers' skins above** *that"* **(Ex.36:19).**	a. Jesus Christ protects the believer from the world. Christ protects us from the elements of... • fear • guilt • sin • evil • death • loneliness • emptiness b. Jesus Christ is our protective separation from the world. Jesus Christ protects us from the world's perils and temptations. Jesus Christ protects us... • by sanctifying us, setting us apart to God • by sanctifying us with His Word • by watching over us with loving eyes • by surrounding us with His presence	*"And be not conformed to this world: but be ye transformed by the renewing of your mind, that ye may prove what is that good, and acceptable, and perfect, will of God" (Ro.12:2).* *"I have given them thy word; and the world hath hated them, because they are not of the world, even as I am not of the world. I pray not that thou shouldest take them out of the world, but that thou shouldest keep them from the evil. They are not of the world, even as I am not of the world. Sanctify them through thy truth: thy word is truth" (Jn.17:14-17).* *"If ye were of the world, the world would love his own: but because ye are not of the world, but I have chosen you out of the world, therefore the world hateth you" (Jn.15:19).* *"No man that warreth entangleth himself with the affairs of this life; that he may please him who hath chosen him to be a soldier" (2 Ti.2:4).* *"Love not the world, neither the things that are in the world. If any man love the world, the love of the Father is not in him" (1 Jn.2:15).*

Historical Term	Type or Picture (Scriptural Basis)	Life Application for Today's Believer	Biblical Application for Today's Believer
Onyx stones (Ex.25:7)	*The onyx stones were placed in the ephod that was worn by the High Priest as he ministered to the LORD in the Tabernacle. The onyx stones symbolized the High Priest's representing and carrying the name of God's people before the LORD as their mediator and intercessor.* **"Onyx stones, and stones to be set in the ephod, and in the breastplate" (Ex.25:7).**	⇒ In God's eyes, His people shine forth in splendor, as precious, priceless gems. Jesus Christ, our great High Priest, always intercedes for us and carries the names of believers before God. But a person must bring his needs to Christ in order for Christ to act as his Mediator before God.	*"Wherefore he is able also to save them to the uttermost that come unto God by him, seeing he ever liveth to make intercession for them" (He.7:25).* *"Seeing then that we have a great high priest, that is passed into the heavens, Jesus the Son of God, let us hold fast our profession. For we have not an high priest which cannot be touched with the feeling of our infirmities; but was in all points tempted like as we are, yet without sin. Let us therefore come boldly unto the throne of grace, that we may obtain mercy, and find grace to help in time of need" (He.4:14-16).* *"Since thou wast precious in my sight, thou hast been honourable, and I have loved thee" (Is.43:4).* *"Now therefore, if ye will obey my voice indeed, and keep my covenant, then ye shall be a peculiar treasure unto me above all people: for all the earth is mine" (Ex.19:5).* *"For the LORD hath chosen Jacob unto himself, and Israel for his peculiar treasure" (Ps.135:4).*

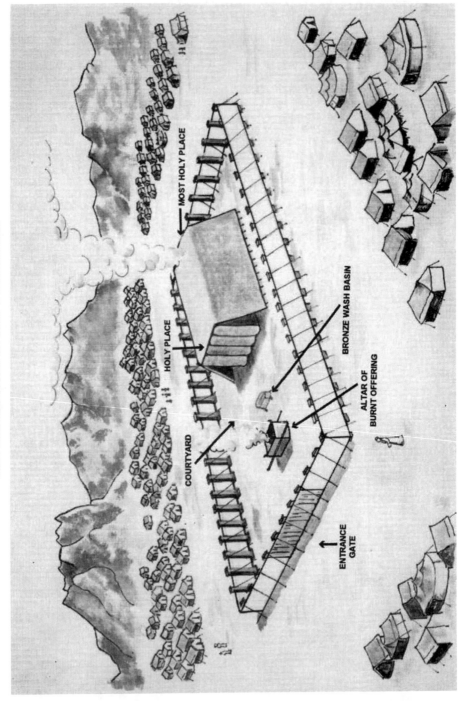

THE TABERNACLE IN THE WILDERNESS

THE TABERNACLE

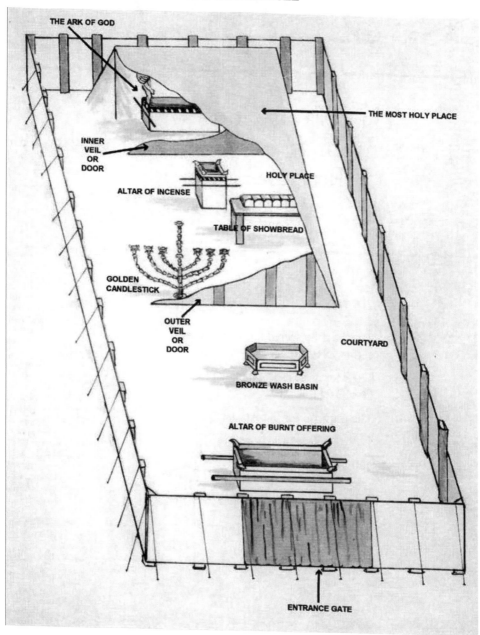

The Ark or Chest of God: The Symbol of the Very Throne and Presence of God (Exodus 25:10-22)

Contents

The Ark or Chest of God:
The Symbol of the Very Throne
and Presence of God
(Exodus 25:10-22)

1. The Ark, the sacred throne & chest of God Himself	10 And they shall make an ark of shittim wood: two cubits and a half shall be the length thereof, and a cubit and a half the breadth thereof, and a cubit and a half the height thereof.	15 The staves shall be in the rings of the ark: they shall not be taken from it.
a. To make it of acacia wood		
b. To make it 3¾' x 2¼' x 2¼' (1.1 meters by .07 meters by .07 meters)		16 And thou shalt put into the ark the testimony which I shall give thee.
c. To overlay it with pure gold (inside & out) & to use a pure gold molding	11 And thou shalt overlay it with pure gold, within and without shalt thou overlay it, and shalt make upon it a crown of gold round about.	17 And thou shalt make a mercy seat of pure gold: two cubits and a half shall be the length thereof, and a cubit and a half the breadth thereof.
d. To cast four gold rings & attach them to the four corners of the Ark	12 And thou shalt cast four rings of gold for it, and put them in the four corners thereof; and two rings shall be in the one side of it, and two rings in the other side of it.	18 And thou shalt make two cherubims of gold, of beaten work shalt thou make them, in the two ends of the mercy seat. 19 And make one cherub on the one end, and the other cherub on the other end: even of the mercy seat shall ye make the cherubims on the two ends thereof.
e. To make two poles of acacia wood & overlay them with gold	13 And thou shalt make staves of shittim wood, and overlay them with gold.	20 And the cherubims shall stretch forth their wings on high, covering the mercy seat with their wings, and their faces shall
f. To insert the poles into the gold rings on the Ark for the purpose of carrying it: The poles were never to be removed	14 And thou shalt put the staves into the rings by the sides of the ark, that the ark may be borne with them.	g. To put the Testimony of God, the Ten Commandments, into the Ark (see v.21) **2. The Mercy Seat or Atonement Cover for the Ark** a. To make it of pure gold b. To make it 3¾' long by 2¼' wide (1.1 meters by .07 meters) c. To make two cherubim at the two ends of the Mercy Seat 1) To be made by hammering out the gold 2) To hammer out one cherub at one end of the Mercy Seat & the other cherub at the other end 3) To spread the wings of the cherubim upward, overshadowing the Mercy Seat 4) To have the cherubim facing

each other, look-ing toward the Mercy Seat	look one to another; toward the mercy seat shall the faces of the cherubims be. 21 And thou shalt put the mercy seat above upon the ark; and in the ark thou shalt put the testimony that I shall give thee. 22 And there I will	meet with thee, and I will commune with thee from above the mercy seat, from between the two cherubims which are upon the ark of the testimony, of all things which I will give thee in command-ment unto the chil-dren of Israel.	mandments) was kept, the place for special instruction
d. To place the Mercy Seat on top of the Ark			b. To be the place where God met with His people
3. The purpose for the Ark			c. To be the place where God's mercy was symbolized
a. To be the place where God's testi-mony (the 10 Com-			d. To be the place where God would instruct & guide His people

Most of us have a place, or would like to have a place, where we can get all alone and be quiet, a place where we can think, work through problems, meditate, or pray. The place may be some room, an office, a corner, a porch, a backyard, an alley, a field, a for-est—it does not matter where. It is hallowed, meaningful ground to us.

The Tabernacle was something like this to the Israelite believer. The Tabernacle was to be the place—the very special place—where God's people came to meet Him, seek-ing...

- His presence
- His forgiveness
- His guidance

- His help
- His strength

This is what this passage is all about: it spells out the most important piece of furniture in the Tabernacle, that of the Ark of God, the symbol of the very presence and throne of God (1 S.4:4; 2 S.6:2). More than anything else, the Ark of God pictured the presence of God, His glory and mercy. The Tabernacle drew people to approach God for help; but it was knowing that the Ark of God, God's holy presence, sat in the midst of the Tabernacle that especially drew them. This is the subject of this important passage: *The Ark or Chest of God: the Symbol of the Very Throne of God*, Ex.25:10-22.

I. The Ark, the sacred throne and chest of God Himself (vv.10-16).
II. The Mercy Seat or Atonement Cover for the Ark (vv.17-21).
III. The purpose for the Ark (vv.21-22).

I. There Were the Instructions to Build the Ark of God, the Sacred Throne and Chest of God Himself (vv.10-16).

The Ark was the most important piece of furniture in the Tabernacle. The Ark was to represent...

- the throne and presence of God Himself (1 S.4:4; 2 S.6:2)
- the Mercy Seat of God
- the place where the testimony of God, the Ten Commandments, was kept

Nothing could be any more important to the people than the Ark of God. Why? Be-cause it was to be the very place where God Himself was to meet with them. God would rule and instruct them, have mercy and forgive them, guide and help them—all from the Ark. As they walked day by day through the *wilderness journey*, He would take care of them as they marched toward the promised land of God. The Ark of God was to become the most precious meeting place between God and His dear people. It was to be hallowed and holy ground, a very special place. This was to be especially true to the believer who loved God and was faithful in his worship of God.

The Ark was the centerpiece of the Tabernacle. Every part of the Tabernacle and every piece of furniture pointed toward and focused attention upon the Ark of God, the very place where God focused His presence. As long as the Tabernacle existed—in fact, up until Solomon's temple—God focused His presence upon the Ark of the Covenant. This is the reason the room where it was kept is called the *Holy of Holies* or *The Most Holy Place*.

Historically, the Ark of God was the most important piece of furniture to the Israelites. Its significance is emphasized in that it is mentioned over 200 times in the Bible. The Ark is called different names throughout Scripture:

⇒ The Ark (Ex.25:14)

⇒ The Ark of the LORD (1 S.4:6)

⇒ The Ark of God (1 S.4:18)

⇒ The Ark of the Testimony (referring to the great testimony of God given to man, the Ten Commandments) (Ex.25:22)

⇒ The Ark of the Covenant of God (referring to the great covenant of God made with man, the Ten Commandments) (Jud.20:27)

⇒ The Ark of the LORD God (1 K.2:26)

Now note the instructions for building the Ark, how detailed they are. The plan and design were exact, precise.

1. The Ark was to be made of acacia wood (v.10): a hard, durable wood, resistant to weather and insects.

2. The Ark was to be a box-like or chest-like structure: 3¾' long x 2¼' wide x 2¼' high (1.1 meters by .07 meters by .07 meters) (v.10).

3. The Ark was to be overlaid with pure gold both inside and out, and it was to have a gold molding around the rim (v.11).

4. The Ark was to have four gold rings attached to its four lower corners at the base of the ark (v.12).

5. The Ark was to have two strong poles made of acacia wood overlaid with gold (v.13).

6. The poles were to be slid into the gold rings on the Ark for the purpose of carrying it (v.14). And note: once inserted, the poles were never to be removed. They were a permanent part of the Ark of God.

7. The *Testimony of God*, the stone tablets of God's covenant (the Ten Commandments), was to be placed into the Ark.

Thought 1.
The one thing we need throughout life is the presence of God. We need:

⇒ God's care and love

⇒ God's guidance and help

⇒ God's mercy and forgiveness

⇒ God's rule and instructions

> **"And, behold, I am with thee, and will keep thee in all places whither thou goest, and will bring thee again into this land; for I will not leave thee, until I have done that which I have spoken to thee of" (Ge.28:15; see Ex.33:14; Jos.1:5).**
>
> **"When thou passest through the waters, I will be with thee; and through the rivers, they shall not overflow thee: when thou walkest through the fire, thou shalt not be burned; neither shall the flame kindle upon thee" (Is.43:2).**
>
> **"Lo, I am with you alway, [even] unto the end of the world. Amen" (Mt.28:20; see Jn.14:18; He.13:5).**

Thought 2.
There are three arks mentioned in Scripture, and all three were used by God to save His people.

a) There was *Noah's ark*, the ark that God used to save Noah and his family from the terrible judgment of the flood. (See Ge.7:1-9.)

b) There was *Moses' ark*, the ark that God used to save baby Moses from the holocaust launched by Pharaoh against the newborn babies of the Israelites. (See Ex.2:1-10.)

c) There was the Ark of God, the Ark of the Covenant, that had the Mercy Seat sitting on top of it. The mercy of God was pictured (symbolized) as flowing out upon God's people, flowing out from the Mercy Seat. Salvation flowed out to the people from the presence and mercy of God, from the Mercy Seat and Ark of God.

"And thou shalt put the mercy seat above upon the ark...And there I will meet with thee, and I will commune with thee from above the mercy seat, from between the two cherubims which are upon the ark of the testimony, of all things which I will give thee in commandment unto the children of Israel" (Ex.25:21-22).

"And it shall come to pass, that whosoever shall call on the name of the Lord shall be saved" (Ac.2:21).

"For whosoever shall call upon the name of the Lord shall be saved" (Ro.10:13; see Tit.2:11-13).

"The Lord is not slack concerning his promise, as some men count slackness; but is longsuffering to us, not willing that any should perish, but that all should come to repentance" (2 Pe.3:9).

II. There Was the Mercy Seat or Atonement Cover for the Ark (vv.17-21).

The Hebrew word for *Mercy Seat* (kapporeth) means *covering* or *atonement*. The idea is that of the covering of sins, of atonement or reconciliation being made possible by the mercy of God. Forgiveness and reconciliation were made possible because the blood of the sacrifice (propitiation) was sprinkled upon the Mercy Seat once a year on the Day of Atonement.

The root word for *Mercy Seat* or *Atonement Cover* (kapporeth) comes from *kaphar* which means...

- to cover
- to make atonement, to reconcile
- to appease, placate, cancel, annul

- to cleanse, forgive, pardon, purge away, put off

This root word has a rich meaning in relation to the Mercy Seat.[1] It is at the Mercy Seat...

- that God covers man's sin
- that God cleanses, forgives, pardons, purges away, and puts off man's sin
- that God makes atonement and reconciles man to Himself
- that God's wrath is appeased, placated, canceled, annulled

The importance of the Mercy Seat in picturing the mercy of God cannot be overstressed. Various commentators say this:

The Pulpit Commentary says:

> *The truth is that kapporeth...never [has] any other sense than that of covering, or forgiving sins.*[2]

---

[1] James Strong. *Strong's Exhaustive Concordance of the Bible.* (Nashville, TN: Thomas Nelson, Inc., 1990), #3722, 3727.

[2] *Pulpit Commentary, Vol.1, Exodus.* Edited by H.D.M. Spence & Joseph S. Exell. (Grand Rapids, MI: Eerdmans Publishing Company, 1950), p.249.

The Expositor's Bible Commentary says:

> The verb that lies behind the noun "atonement" in the expression "atonement cover" (v.17) means 'to ransom or deliver by means of a substitute....The LXX [Greek Septuagint Version] has "propitiatory covering" or "Mercy Seat," as does Hebrews 9:5 (NIV mg.). This place of expiating the sins of mankind is an adumbration [sketchy picture] of Christ's propitiatory work...and is at the heart of our worship of the one who died for us.[3]

The NIV Study Bible says:

> atonement. *Reconciliation, the divine act of grace whereby God draws to himself and makes "at one" with him those who were once alienated from him. In the OT, the shed blood of sacrificial offerings effected atonement (see Lev 17:11 and note); in the NT, the blood of Jesus, shed once for all time, does the same (see Ro 3:25; 1Jn 2:2). atonement cover. See NIV text note; see also Lev 16:2 and note. That God's symbolic throne was capped with an* atonement *cover signified his great mercy toward his people—only such a God can be revered (see Ps 130:3-4).[4]*

F.B. Huey, Jr. says:

> *"Mercy seat" comes from a word that means "to cover," hence "to provide reconciliation, atonement."[5]*

Matthew Henry says:

> The mercy seat was the covering of the ark or chest, made of solid gold, exactly to fit the dimensions of the ark, v.17, 21. This propitiatory covering, as it might well be translated, was a type of Christ, the great propitiation, whose satisfaction fully answers the demands of the law, covers our transgressions, and comes between us and the curse we deserve. Thus he is the end of the law for righteousness.[6]

Maxie Dunnam says:

> The rendered "mercy seat" really means "a covering." This makes special reference to the forgiveness and covering of transgression and sin by the slain blood of the lamb. The same word occurs in the Greek in the New Testament, where we are told by the apostle Paul that the Father sent Christ to be a propitiation through faith, by His blood and in the passing over of sin.
>
> But now the righteousness of God apart from the law is revealed, being witnessed by the Law and the Prophets, even the righteousness of God, through faith in Jesus Christ, to all and on all who believe. For there is no difference; for all have sinned and fall short of the glory of God, being justified freely by His grace through the redemption that is in Christ Jesus, whom God set forth as a propitiation by His blood, through faith, to demonstrate His righteousness, because in His forbearance God had passed over the sins that were previously committed...." Rom. 3:21-25
>
> We might translate that 25th verse in this fashion: "The redemption that is in Christ Jesus whom God set forth to be a mercy seat."

---

3   Frank E. Gaebelein. *The Expositor's Bible Commentary*, Vol. 2, p.455.

4   *The NIV Study Bible*. (Grand Rapids, MI: The Zondervan Corporation, 1985), p.123.

5   F.B. Huey, Jr. *A Study Guide Commentary, Exodus*. (Grand Rapids, MI: Zondervan Publishing House, 1977), p.107.

6   Matthew Henry, *Matthew Henry's Commentary*, Vol. 1. (Old Tappan, NJ: Fleming H. Revell Co., n.d.), pp.383-384.

Isn't that a beautiful term? A seat of mercy. Is there a more beautiful term in our language? Let it hang on your lip—mercy—mercy—mercy. More than that, be immersed in the meaning of it, for that is the constant stream of love flowing from God—abundant mercy. Not wrath, not judgment, not indignation, but mercy is pouring forth from the eternal fountain in the heart of God.

I'm not saying that there's not judgment. I'm not saying that God does not get indignant with our sloppy response to His call. I'm not saying that there isn't the demand of holiness and the expression of wrath in the character of God. I'm saying what the Bible says, that even before we reach that pinnacle of revelation as to who God is—Jesus Christ hanging on a cross—we have the eternal mercy seat to show us God's nature.[7]

Paul the apostle says this:

"Whom God hath set forth to be a propitiation through faith in his blood, to declare his righteousness for the remission of sins that are past, through the forbearance of God" (Ro.3:25).

John the apostle says:

"Herein is love, not that we loved God, but that he loved us, and sent his Son to be the propitiation [atonement] for our sins" (1 Jn.4:10).

Note the plan and design for constructing the Mercy Seat or Atonement Cover. Keep in mind that it was to be placed on top of the Ark, that it was to serve both as a *lid* to the Ark or Chest and as the Mercy Seat for God's Holy Presence.
1. The Mercy Seat was to be made of pure gold (v.17).
2. The Mercy Seat was to be oblong: the very same size as the Ark itself: 3¾' long x 2¼' wide (v.17).
3. There were to be two cherubim at the two ends of the Mercy Seat (vv.18-20). The cherubim symbolized God's justice. Stephen F. Olford says this:

We meet them first in the very early chapters of the Bible, placed at the east of the Garden of Eden with a 'flaming sword which turned every way, to keep the way of the tree of life' (Genesis 3:24). It is true that the progressive revelation gives us more light on them, as we see them appearing again in such books as the prophecy of Ezekiel, and later the Revelation, but essentially they are messengers of judgment. Here on the mercy seat they stand poised to strike, were it not for the blood-sprinkled mercy seat.[8]

Note how the Mercy Seat was to be made:
⇒ To make it of pure gold
⇒ To make it 3¾' long by 2¼' wide (1.1 meters by .07 meters)
⇒ To make two cherubim at the two ends of the Mercy Seat
⇒ To be made by hammering out the gold
⇒ To hammer out one cherub at one end of the Mercy Seat and the other cherub at the other end
⇒ To spread the wings of the cherubim upward overshadowing the Mercy Seat
⇒ To have the cherubim facing each other, looking toward the Mercy Seat

4. The Mercy Seat was to be placed on top of the Ark (v.21).

---

7   Maxie Dunnam. The *Preacher's Commentary on Exodus.* (Nashville, TN: Word Publishing, 1987, 2003), p.314.
8   Stephen F. Olford. *The Tabernacle, Camping with God*, p.139.

Thought

Our sin has separated us from God. There is a great gulf between God and man, a gulf so vast that it keeps us from reaching God. That gulf is sin. And sin condemns us to death. But there is hope, one hope: the *mercy of God.* This is the very reason God designed the Mercy Seat of the Ark, to proclaim the great *mercy of God.* Scripture says:

a) The mercy of God saves us.

> **"Not by works of righteousness which we have done, but according to his mercy he saved us, by the washing of regeneration, and renewing of the Holy Ghost; Which he shed on us abundantly through Jesus Christ our Saviour; That being justified by his grace, we should be made heirs according to the hope of eternal life" (Tit.3:5-7).**

> **"But God, who is rich in mercy, for his great love wherewith he loved us, Even when we were dead in sins, hath quickened us together with Christ, (by grace ye are saved)....For by grace are ye saved through faith; and that not of yourselves: it is the gift of God: Not of works, lest any man should boast" (Ep.2:4-5, 8-9).**

b) The mercy of God demands repentance for salvation.

> **"And rend your heart, and not your garments, and turn unto the Lord your God: for he is gracious and merciful, slow to anger, and of great kindness, and repenteth him of the evil" (Joel 2:13).**

c) The mercy of God is poured out upon those who fear Him.

> **"But the mercy of the Lord is from everlasting to everlasting upon them that fear him, and his righteousness unto children's children" (Ps.103:17).**

> **"I am a companion of all them that fear thee, and of them that keep thy precepts. The earth, O Lord, is full of thy mercy: teach me thy statutes" (Ps.119:63-64).**

d) The mercy of God sent His Son, Jesus Christ, to become the merciful and faithful High Priest, to make atonement for sin, and to deliver us from death.

> **"Forasmuch then as the children are partakers of flesh and blood, he also himself likewise took part of the same; that through death he might destroy him that had the power of death, that is, the devil; And deliver them who through fear of death were all their lifetime subject to bondage. For verily he took not on him the nature of angels; but he took on him the seed of Abraham. Wherefore in all things it behoved him to be made like unto his brethren, that he might be a merciful and faithful high priest in things pertaining to God, to make reconciliation for the sins of the people" (He.2:14-17).**

e) The mercy of God forgives our sin.

> **"Who is a God like unto thee, that pardoneth iniquity, and passeth by the transgression of the remnant of his heritage? he retaineth not his anger for ever, because he delighteth in mercy" (Mi.7:18).**

f) The mercy of God delivers us from the consuming trials of life day by day.

> **"It is of the LORD's mercies that we are not consumed, because his compassions fail not. They are new every morning: great is thy faithfulness" (La.3:22-23).**

g) The mercy of God invites us to approach God in order to receive mercy and find help in time of need.

> **"Let us therefore come boldly unto the throne of grace, that we may obtain mercy, and find grace to help in time of need" (He.4:16).**

h) The mercy of God has no end; it reaches above the heavens.

> **"For thy mercy is great above the heavens: and thy truth reacheth unto the clouds" (Ps.108:4).**

III. There Were Four Purposes for the Ark of God (vv.21-22).

Note how clearly God spelled out why He had planned and designed the Ark of the Covenant.

1. The Ark of God was to hold God's testimony, the two tablets of the covenant, that is, the Ten Commandments (v.21). The Ten Commandments are a very special covenant between God and man, the basic laws that are to govern man's life and society. So far as laws are concerned, above all man is to keep the Ten Commandments. Therefore, they were to be preserved and secured, contained in the very throne of God Himself. They were to be under His watchful care.

There were several other items kept in the Ark as well. These are not covered in this particular passage of Scripture, but they are noted here because this is the most complete and detailed coverage of the Ark of God.

a. There was the golden pot of the Manna.

> **"Which had the golden censer, and the ark of the covenant overlaid round about with gold, wherein was the golden pot that had manna, and Aaron's rod that budded, and the tables of the covenant" (He.9:4).**
> **"And Moses said unto Aaron, Take a pot, and put an omer full of manna therein, and lay it up before the Lord, to be kept for your generations. As the Lord commanded Moses, so Aaron laid it up before the Testimony, to be kept" (Ex.16:33-34; see Ex.16:11-31; Nu.11:1-9).**

b. There was Aaron's rod or staff that budded.

> **"Which had the golden censer, and the ark of the covenant overlaid round about with gold, wherein was the golden pot that had manna, and Aaron's rod that budded, and the tables of the covenant" (He.9:4; see Nu. Chapters 16 and 17).**

c. There was the Book of the Covenant (most likely the civil law of God).

> **"And he took the book of the covenant, and read in the audience of the people: and they said, All that the Lord hath said will we do, and be obedient" (Ex.24:7).**
> **"That Moses commanded the Levites, which bare the ark of the covenant of the Lord, saying, Take this book of the law, and put it in the side of the ark of the covenant of the Lord your God, that it may be there for a witness against thee" (De.31:25-26).**

2. The Ark was to be the place—the very special place—where God met with His people (v.22). In a very special way, God's presence dwelt above the Ark of the Covenant. The people knew this. Therefore, when they needed a special sense of God's presence—when they needed to feel a special closeness to God—they knew where to go. They could go to the Tabernacle, the ground surrounding the Tabernacle, to worship and seek forgiveness by offering sacrifice to the Lord.

Keep in mind that only the High Priest could enter the Holy of Holies and actually stand before the Ark of God. Moreover, he could only do this once a year on the Day of Atonement, when he offered the sacrifice for sins on behalf of all the people. However, the people did have access to God—access to a deep sense of God's presence—by coming to the ground surrounding the Tabernacle and offering a sacrifice or giving an offering to God.

The Tabernacle presented a graphic, vivid picture of God's Holy presence and, no doubt, aroused a deep, deep sense of God's presence within the believers who truly believed and loved God. Genuine believers would have visited the holy, hallowed ground often in order to meet God: to experience a deep sense of His holy presence and to seek His guidance and help.

3. The Ark was to be the place of mercy, the place where God's mercy was clearly pictured (v.22). Once a year on the Day of Atonement, the High Priest was to offer sacrifice and sprinkle the blood of the victim upon the Mercy Seat. The people were to learn this: they were to learn all about the Mercy Seat and the blood sprinkled upon it. They were to learn that the blood made atonement for their sins, reconciled them to God. They were to learn that the mercy of God was to be showered upon them because of the blood, because they believed and trusted the blood of the sacrifice to cover their sins. This was one of the great lessons to be learned, one of the purposes for the Ark of God.

Thought

There are two meaningful pictures seen in the Mercy Seat that covered the Ark of God.

a) There is the picture that points toward the finished work of Christ. The High Priest was never allowed to sit on the Mercy Seat, no matter how tired or weary he became. In fact, the priests were always working when in the Tabernacle. Their priestly work was never finished: they were continually offering sacrifice and ministering. But this was not true with Jesus Christ. When Jesus Christ offered Himself as the Perfect Sacrifice to God, His work was finished. His sacrifice for the sins of people was perfect: no other sacrifice was ever needed. Therefore, Christ was able to sit down on the right hand of God's throne. This is exactly what Scripture says:

> **"And every priest standeth daily ministering and offering oftentimes the same sacrifices, which can never take away sins: But this man, after he had offered one sacrifice for sins for ever, sat down on the right hand of God" (He.10:11-12; see Ro.6:10).**
>
> **"Which he wrought in Christ, when he raised him from the dead, and set him at his own right hand in the heavenly places" (Ep.1:20).**
>
> **"And being found in fashion as a man, he humbled himself, and became obedient unto death, even the death of the cross. Wherefore God also hath highly exalted him, and given him a name which is above every name: That at the name of Jesus every knee should bow, of things in heaven, and things in earth, and things under the earth" (Ph.2:8-10; see Re.5:12-13).**

b) There is the picture that points toward God's mercy covering the law. No person can keep the law, not perfectly. And perfection is required in order to live in God's holy presence. How then can we ever become acceptable to God, be allowed to live in heaven with Him? By His mercy. God's mercy has been given us through His Son, the Lord Jesus Christ. God gave His Son to be the *Perfect Sacrifice* for our sins. The mercy of God shown us in Jesus Christ covers the law, that is, covers our sin, our failure to keep the law. When we trust Jesus Christ as our Savior, the mercy of God covers all the law—all the accusations of the law against us, all our failure to keep the law, all the guilt that gnaws at our hearts and convicts us.

"Therefore by the deeds of the law there shall no flesh be justified in his sight: for by the law is the knowledge of sin. But now the righteousness of God without the law is manifested, being witnessed by the law and the prophets; Even the righteousness of God which is by faith of Jesus Christ unto all and upon all them that believe: for there is no difference" (Ro.3:20-22; see Ro.3:23-25; 5:20-21).

"But when the fulness of the time was come, God sent forth his Son, made of a woman, made under the law, To redeem them that were under the law, that we might receive the adoption of sons" (Ga.4:4-5; see Ga.3:22-26; Col.2:13-14).

4. The Ark was to be the place where God would instruct and guide His people (v.22). The Ark was to be the symbol of the throne of God. His divine presence was apparently to be manifested in a very special way right above the empty space of the Mercy Seat, right between the cherubim. From that position, God promised to speak to His people, to give them His commandments, instructions, and guidance.

When God's people needed help or guidance, they were to come to the Tabernacle. The Tabernacle was to become very, very special to God's people. Special because it was where God's presence was manifested in a very significant way. It was the place where they would be able to seek God's special care and help, His direction and guidance. No matter what the pain or suffering was—no matter how terrible the trial—God was ready and able to help His dear believer.

"For we have not an high priest which cannot be touched with the feeling of our infirmities; but was in all points tempted like as we are, yet without sin. Let us therefore come boldly unto the throne of grace, that we may obtain mercy, and find grace to help in time of need" (He.4:15-16).

"But if from thence thou shalt seek the LORD thy God, thou shalt find him, if thou seek him with all thy heart and with all thy soul" (De.4:29; see 2 Chr.7:14).

"For this God is our God for ever and ever: he will be our guide even unto death" (Ps.48:14).

"Thou shalt guide me with thy counsel, and afterward receive me to glory" (Ps.73:24; see Ps.105:4; Is.55:6).

TYPES, SYMBOLS, AND PICTURES
(Exodus 25:10-22)

Historical Term	Type or Picture (Scriptural Basis)	Life Application for Today's Believer	Biblical Application for Today's Believer
Acacia wood (Ex.25:10)	Acacia wood was a hard, durable wood that was resistant to insects and harsh weather. Acacia flourished in the wilderness and speaks of the incorruptibility and perfection of Jesus Christ. "And they shall make an ark of shittim [acacia] wood: two cubits and a half shall be the length thereof, and a cubit	⇒ In a world filled with corruption, Jesus Christ is the One who is the perfect picture of durability and strength, the only One who is incorruptible. Therefore, the believer should build his life upon Jesus Christ, the only foundation that will stand the test of time. ⇒ The believer should	"For other foundation can no man lay than that is laid, which is Jesus Christ" (1 Co.3:11). "Now therefore ye are no more strangers and foreigners, but fellowcitizens with the saints, and of the household of God; and are built upon the foundation of the apostles and prophets, Jesus Christ himself being the chief corner

Historical Term	Type or Picture (Scriptural Basis)	Life Application for Today's Believer	Biblical Application for Today's Believer
	and a half the breadth thereof, and a cubit and a half the height thereof" (Ex.25:10).	call upon Christ for help in time of need and for strength in time of temptation.	*stone; in whom all the building fitly framed together groweth unto an holy temple in the Lord" (Ep.2:19-21).* *"For we have not an high priest which cannot be touched with the feeling of our infirmities; but was in all points tempted like as we are, yet without sin" (He. 4:15).*
The Ark or Chest (Ex.25:10-22; 40:20) See also Ex.35:12; 37:1-5; 39:35; 40:3, 20-21	*The Ark was the very special place where God's Holy presence was manifested.* *a. The Ark was the symbol of God's presence. A very special manifestation of God's presence dwelt right above the Ark, right between the two cherubim.*	What the Ark of the Covenant taught: a. God reveals His presence to believers in a very special way: When people need a special sense of God's presence — when they need to feel a special closeness to God — they can go directly into the presence of God. How is this possible? Because of Jesus Christ. Jesus Christ opened the way into God's presence through His great sacrifice.	 *"Having therefore, brethren, boldness to enter into the holiest by the blood of Jesus, by a new and living way, which he hath consecrated for us, through the veil, that is to say, his flesh; and having an high priest over the house of God" (He.10:19-22).* *"For Christ also hath once suffered for sins, the just for the unjust, that he might bring us to God, being put to death in the flesh, but quickened by the Spirit" (1 Pe.3:18).* *"I love them that love me; and those that seek me early shall find me" (Pr. 8:17).*
	b. The Mercy Seat sat on top of the Ark; therefore, the Ark was a symbol of God's mercy.	b. God covers our lives with His mercy: • Believers are to understand that the blood shed upon the cross makes atonement for their sins, that the blood reconciles them to God. Believers are to	*"But the mercy of the LORD is from everlasting to everlasting upon them that fear him, and his righteousness unto children's children" (Ps.103:17).* *"But God, who is rich in mercy, for his great love wherewith*

Historical Term	Type or Picture (Scriptural Basis)	Life Application for Today's Believer	Biblical Application for Today's Believer
		learn that the mercy of God is to be showered upon them because of the blood, because they believe and trust the blood of the sacrifice (Jesus Christ) to cover their sins.	*he loved us, Even when we were dead in sins, hath quickened us together with Christ, (by grace ye are saved;) And hath raised us up together, and made us sit together in heavenly places in Christ Jesus"* (Ep.2:4-6).
	c. The Ark was the symbol of the very throne of God. It was the place where the people sought the guidance and instruction of God.	c. God instructs and guides His people from His heavenly throne. From that position, God speaks to His people, gives them His commandments, instructions, and guidance; therefore, when God's people need help or guidance, they are to come directly to the throne of mercy, to come and find grace to help in time of need.	*"I will instruct thee and teach thee in the way which thou shalt go: I will guide thee with mine eye"* (Ps.32:8; see Ps.25:9). *"For we have not an high priest which cannot be touched with the feeling of our infirmities; but was in all points tempted like as we are, yet without sin. Let us therefore come boldly unto the throne of grace, that we may obtain mercy, and find grace to help in time of need"* (He.4:15-16).
	d. The Ark was the symbol of God's Law, holding the Ten Commandments.	d. God gave the Ten Commandments so we would know how to live and relate to God and to one another—so we would know how to build a just and peaceful society.	*"For this is the love of God, that we keep his commandments: and his commandments are not grievous"* (1 Jn.5:3). *"Righteousness exalteth a nation: but sin is a reproach to any people"* (Pr.14:34).
	e. The Ark was the symbol of Christ, of the very presence of God's personally fulfilling every picture of the Ark. Remember, the word "tabernacle" means to dwell, to abide in the midst of.	e. How Christ fulfilled the symbolism of the Ark of God: • Jesus Christ promises to be with His people always.	*"Lo, I am with you alway, even unto the end of the world. Amen"* (Mt.28:20; see Mt.18:20).

Historical Term	Type or Picture (Scriptural Basis)	Life Application for Today's Believer	Biblical Application for Today's Believer
	"And they shall make an ark of shittim wood: two cubits and a half shall be the length thereof, and a cubit and a half the breadth thereof, and a cubit and a half the height thereof" (Ex.25:10).	• Jesus Christ sacrificed Himself, shed His blood in order to have mercy upon us and to cleanse us from our sins.	"*Who his own self bare our sins in his own body on the tree, that we, being dead to sins, should live unto righteousness: by whose stripes ye were healed*" (1 Pe. 2:24; see 1 Pe.3:18; Re.1:5).
	"And he took and put the testimony into the ark, and set the staves on the ark, and put the mercy seat above upon the ark" (Ex.40:20).	• Jesus Christ kept the Law of the covenant that was kept in the Ark, kept the Law perfectly, without sin.	"*For we have not an high priest which cannot be touched with the feeling of our infirmities; but was in all points tempted like as we are, yet without sin*" (He.4:15; see He.7:26).
Gold (Ex.25:17)	*A symbol of value, of the greatest worth there is: A symbol of the LORD Himself, of His deity and righteousness.* "And thou shalt make a mercy seat of pure gold: two cubits and a half shall be the length thereof, and a cubit and a half the breadth thereof" (Ex.25:17).	⇒ Jesus Christ is the greatest and most precious value that can be possessed. He is more precious and more valuable than gold. Above all else, a person should strive to have Jesus Christ in his life.	"*For what is a man profited, if he shall gain the whole world, and lose his own soul? or what shall a man give in exchange for his soul?*" (Mt.16:26). "*Thanks be unto God for his unspeakable gift*" (2 Co.9:15).
The Mercy Seat (Ex.25:17-21; 25:22) See also Ex.; 35:12; 37:6-9; 39:35; 40:3, 20	*The Mercy Seat covered the Ark and symbolized at least three things:* *a. The Mercy Seat symbolized the very mercy of God Himself.*	What the Mercy Seat taught: a. God is not only holy and righteous, He is also merciful. God is the Sovereign Creator and Majesty who rules in mercy as well as in righteousness and holiness. The Mercy Seat symbolized that God has mercy upon all who truly come to Him, who truly believe and follow Him.	"*Who is a God like unto thee, that pardoneth iniquity, and passeth by the transgression of the remnant of his heritage? he retaineth not his anger for ever, because he delighteth in mercy*" (Mi.7:18; see Joel 2:13).

Historical Term	Type or Picture (Scriptural Basis)	Life Application for Today's Believer	Biblical Application for Today's Believer
	b. The Mercy Seat symbolized that God covered the Law with His mercy: Remember, the law (the Ten Commandments) was kept in the Ark under the Mercy Seat. The mercy of God covers the law and its charges against people, covers the transgressions of every person who trusts in Jesus Christ.	b. There was the picture that pointed to God's mercy covering the law. No person can keep the law, not perfectly. And perfection is required in order to live in God's holy presence. How then can we ever become acceptable to God, be allowed to live in heaven with Him? By His mercy. God's mercy has been given us through His Son, the Lord Jesus Christ. God gave His Son to be the *Perfect Sacrifice* for our sins. The mercy of God shown us in Jesus Christ covers the law, covers our sin, our failure to keep the law. When we trust Jesus Christ as our Savior, the mercy of God covers all the law—all the accusations of the law against us, all our failure to keep the law, all the guilt that gnaws at our hearts and convicts us.	*"Blessed be the God and Father of our Lord Jesus Christ, which according to his abundant mercy hath begotten us again unto a lively hope by the resurrection of Jesus Christ from the dead"* (1 Pe. 1:3). *"For as many as are of the works of the law are under the curse: for it is written, Cursed is every one that continueth not in all things which are written in the book of the law to do them. But that no man is justified by the law in the sight of God, it is evident: for, The just shall live by faith. And the law is not of faith: but, The man that doeth them shall live in them. Christ hath redeemed us from the curse of the law, being made a curse for us: for it is written, Cursed is every one that hangeth on a tree"* (Ga.3:10-13).
	c. The Mercy Seat symbolized the finished work of Christ. The High Priest was never allowed to sit on the Mercy Seat, no matter how tired or weary he became. In fact, the priests were always working when in the Tabernacle. Their priestly work was never finished: they were continually	c. When Jesus Christ offered Himself as the Perfect Sacrifice to God, His work was finished. His sacrifice for the sins of people was perfect: no other sacrifice was ever needed. Therefore, Christ was able to sit down on the right hand of God's throne. Believers no longer have to offer sacrifices to God to atone	*"For all have sinned, and come short of the glory of God; Being justified freely by his grace through the redemption that is in Christ Jesus: Whom God hath set forth to be a propitiation [covering, sacrifice] through faith in his blood, to declare his righteousness for the remission of sins that are past, through the forbearance of*

Historical Term	Type or Picture (Scriptural Basis)	Life Application for Today's Believer	Biblical Application for Today's Believer
	offering sacrifice and ministering. "And thou shalt make a mercy seat of pure gold: two cubits and a half shall be the length thereof, and a cubit and a half the breadth thereof" (Ex.25:17). "And there I will meet with thee, and I will commune with thee from above the mercy seat, from between the two cherubims which *are* upon the ark of the testimony, of all *things* which I will give thee in commandment unto the children of Israel" (Ex.25:22).	for their sins. Christ has already satisfied God's requirement. It is because of the mercy of God in the sacrifice of His Son that we are cleansed once and for all from our sins.	*God" (Ro.3:23-25).* *"And every priest standeth daily ministering and offering oftentimes the same sacrifices, which can never take away sins: But this man, after he had offered one sacrifice for sins for ever, sat down on the right hand of God" (He.10:11-12).* *"And being found in fashion as a man, he humbled himself, and became obedient unto death, even the death of the cross. Wherefore God also hath highly exalted him, and given him a name which is above every name: That at the name of Jesus every knee should bow, of things in heaven, and things in earth, and things under the earth" (Ph.2:8-10).*

THE ARK AND MERCY SEAT

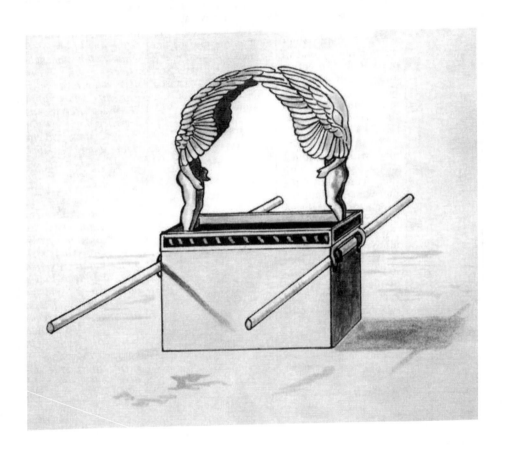

CHAPTER THREE

The Table of Showbread:
The Symbol of God Himself
as the Bread of Life
(Exodus 25:23-30)

Contents

The Table of Showbread: The Symbol of God Himself as the Bread of Life (Exodus 25:23-30)

1. The Table's design & materials a. To make it of acacia wood b. To make it 3' long & 1½' wide & 2¼' high (.9 meters x .5 meters x .7 meters) c. To overlay it with pure gold & make a gold molding d. To make a 3" gold border or trim e. To make four gold rings 1) Attach them to the four corners where the	23 Thou shalt also make a table of shittim wood: two cubits shall be the length thereof, and a cubit the breadth thereof, and a cubit and a half the height thereof. 24 And thou shalt overlay it with pure gold, and make thereto a crown of gold round about. 25 And thou shalt make unto it a border of an hand breadth round about, and thou shalt make a golden crown to the border thereof round about. 26 And thou shalt make for it four rings of gold, and put the rings in the four cor- ners that are on the	four feet thereof. 27 Over against the border shall the rings be for places of the staves to bear the ta- ble. 28 And thou shalt make the staves of shittim wood, and overlay them with gold, that the table may be borne with them. 29 And thou shalt make the dishes thereof, and spoons thereof, and covers thereof, and bowls thereof, to cover withal: of pure gold shalt thou make them. 30 And thou shalt set upon the table show- bread before me al- way.	legs are 2) Place them close to the border or rim to hold the poles for carry- ing the table f. To make the poles of acacia wood & overlay them with gold: To be used to carry the table g. To make the dishes, plates, pic- tures, & bowls of gold: To be used in the offerings **2. The Table's pur- pose: To give the bread as an offer- ing of thanksgiv- ing & of depend- ence upon God**

The gnawing pain of hunger, the need to feed oneself, is one of the strongest drives that a person has. As long as a person's hunger is fed, he can go on about his normal life. However if food is withheld for a long time, the body starves to death. Without food, a person becomes sick and eventually dies. Now note: physical hunger is a picture of spiritual hunger. When a person senses spiritual hunger, he seeks to satisfy that hunger. Spiritual hunger is a normal thing: God made the human heart to hunger and thirst after Him. But spiritual hunger becomes abnormal when man tries to satisfy his hunger with the things of the world...

- illicit sex
- partying
- sensual pleasures
- excessive possessions
- position and power
- money and property
- recognition and fame
- alcohol and drugs
- food and drink

The hunger of the human heart can be met by God and by God alone. This is what the Table of the Showbread is all about: it points a person to God as the provision of life, as the One who provides whatever is necessary to meet the hunger of man. This is the much

needed lesson of this passage: *The Table of Showbread: The Symbol of God Himself as the Bread of Life*, Ex.25:23-30.
  I.   The Table's design and materials (vv.23-29).
  II. The Table's purpose: to give the bread as an offering of thanksgiving and of dependence upon God (v.30).

I. There Was the Design and Materials of the Table (vv.23-29).

The second piece of furniture to be built was the Table of Showbread. The word *showbread* (paneh) literally means two things:
  ⇒ The *Bread of the Face,* referring to the face of God. The showbread was bread placed before the very face of God Himself.
  ⇒ The *Bread of the Presence,* referring to the presence of God. The showbread was bread placed in the very presence of God Himself.

The showbread is also called the *Holy Bread* or the *Consecrated Bread* (1 S.21:4-6). Obviously the Table of Showbread was the table upon which the bread of thanksgiving and dependence was placed. Note that the Table was not to sit in the Holy of Holies: it was to be placed in the Holy Place right outside the inner curtain of the Holy of Holies. It was to sit, so to speak, right before the presence and face of God, which was behind the inner curtain. There was only one piece of furniture in the Holy of Holies: the Ark of God which symbolized the very throne of God itself. The arrangement of furniture in the two sanctuaries was to be this:

THE HOLY OF HOLIES OR THE MOST HOLY PLACE	THE HOLY PLACE
The Ark of God with the Mercy Seat (25:10-22)	The Table of Showbread (25:23-30) The Lampstand (25:31-40) The Altar of Incense (30:1-10)

Now note that the design for the Table of Showbread was planned by God Himself. The design was exact, precise.
1. The table was to be made of acacia wood: a hard and durable wood, resistant to insects, disease, and weather (v.23).
2. The table was to be quite small: 3' long & 1½' wide & 2¼' high (.9 meters x .5 meters x .7 meters) (v.23).
3. The table was to be overlaid with pure gold and have a gold molding running around it (v.24).
4. The table was to have a rim three inches wide around the top with a gold molding around it (v.25).
5. The table was to have four gold rings attached to the four corners where the legs were: to support the poles for carrying the table (vv.26-27).
6. The poles to carry the table were to be made of acacia wood and be overlaid with gold (v.28).
7. The table's plates and dishes were to be made of gold as well as the pitchers and bowls to be used in pouring out drink offerings (v.29).

II. The Table's Purpose Was to Hold the Showbread, to Present the Showbread before the Face of God, to Present It as an Offering of Thanksgiving and of Dependence upon God (v.30).

In order to get a complete picture of the showbread table, it is helpful to look at the Scripture that describes the showbread itself:

"And thou shalt take fine flour, and bake twelve cakes thereof: two tenth deals shall be in one cake. And thou shalt set them in two rows, six on a row, upon the pure table before the LORD. And thou shalt put pure frankincense upon each row, that it may be on the bread for a memorial, even an offering made by fire unto the LORD. Every sabbath he shall set it in order before the LORD continually, being taken from the children of Israel by an everlasting covenant. And it shall be Aaron's and his sons'; and they shall eat it in the holy place: for it is most holy unto him of the offerings of the LORD made by fire by a perpetual statute" (Le.24:5-9).

⇒ Twelve loaves of bread were to be made (v.5).
⇒ The loaves were to be made of choice flour, three quarts each (v.5).
⇒ The loaves were to be arranged in two rows of six each (v.6).
⇒ Some frankincense was to be sprinkled over each row and burned in place of the bread as *an offering* (v.7).
⇒ The bread was to be changed every Sabbath day (v.8).
⇒ The bread was to be laid out in behalf of the people as *an offering*, as a continuing part of the covenant (v.8).
⇒ The bread was to be eaten by the priest, but only in a holy place, for the bread was an *offering made to the Lord* (v.9).

Now note the significant facts about the bread: twelve loaves of bread were to be made and they were to be presented to God as an offering. Where were they to be presented? On the Table of Showbread, in the very presence of God Himself, right before His face. The meaning and symbolism are obvious.

1. The twelve loaves of showbread represented an offering from each tribe of Israel, an offering of thanksgiving to God. Each tribe was represented as thanking God for the bread and food He provided, for meeting their physical needs.

"When thou hast eaten and art full, then thou shalt bless the LORD thy God for the good land which he hath given thee" (De.8:10; see Ps.100:4).
"And when he [Paul] had thus spoken, he took bread, and gave thanks to God in presence of them all: and when he had broken it, he began to eat" (Ac.27:35; see 1 Th.5:18).

2. The twelve loaves also represented the people's dependence upon God. Note that the loaves sat in God's presence, before His very face (v.30). The people were to acknowledge their dependence upon God, acknowledge that they needed His provision. They needed His watchful eye upon the bread, upon them as His followers. They needed Him to continue to provide their bread and food, continue to look after and care for them. Their dependence upon God as the Provision of life was symbolized in the showbread as well as their offering of thanksgiving.

3. The twelve loaves also acknowledged the people's trust of God (v.30). By setting the bread before God, they were declaring their belief and trust that He would continue to meet their needs, both physical and spiritual needs.

"Blessed [are] they which do hunger and thirst after righteousness: for they shall be filled" (Mt.5:6).
"But seek ye first the kingdom of God, and his righteousness; and all these things shall be added unto you" (Mt.6:33; see Jn.3:27; 15:5).
"But my God shall supply all your need according to his riches in glory by Christ Jesus" (Ph.4:19).
"But I am poor and needy; yet the Lord thinketh upon me: thou art my help and my deliverer; make no tarrying, O my God" (Ps.40:17; see Ps.107:9; 136:25-26).

4. The showbread also pointed to Jesus Christ as the Bread of Life. Scripture declares that He is the Living Bread who came *out of* heaven to satisfy the hunger of a person's soul.

> **"And Jesus said unto them, I am the bread of life: he that cometh to me shall never hunger; and he that believeth on me shall never thirst" (Jn.6:35; see Jn.6:33; 6:48).**
>
> **"This is the bread which cometh down from heaven, that a man may eat thereof, and not die. I am the living bread which came down from heaven: if any man eat of this bread, he shall live for ever: and the bread that I will give is my flesh, which I will give for the life of the world" (Jn.6:50-51; see Jn.6:58).**

5. The showbread pointed to God Himself as the nourishment that man really needs. Far too often man tries to live his life apart from God's provision and presence. The culture of today says...

- have it your way—where man is self-exalted
- do it your way—where man is making his own path in life
- go it alone—where man is cut off from the very One he needs

There is nothing that can replace man's need for God. It is God and God alone who truly nourishes and satisfies the hungry soul of man.

> **"The Lord is my shepherd; I shall not want. He maketh me to lie down in green pastures: he leadeth me beside the still waters. He restoreth my soul: he leadeth me in the paths of righteousness for his name's sake. Yea, though I walk through the valley of the shadow of death, I will fear no evil: for thou art with me; thy rod and thy staff they comfort me. Thou preparest a table before me in the presence of mine enemies: thou anointest my head with oil; my cup runneth over. Surely goodness and mercy shall follow me all the days of my life: and I will dwell in the house of the Lord for ever" (Ps.23:1-6; see Ps.132:15; 31:19; Is.26:9).**
>
> **"But my God shall supply all your need according to his riches in glory by Christ Jesus" (Ph.4:19; see 2 Chr.15:15; Lu.6:21).**
>
> **"Blessed [are] they which do hunger and thirst after righteousness: for they shall be filled" (Mt.5:6).**

6. The showbread pointed to the great need of people for the bread of God's presence and worship. A constant diet of unhealthy things will cause a person to become sick and unhealthy, things such as...

lust	dissension	impurity	strife
pride	laziness	enmities	outbursts of anger
apathy	disputes	envy	drunkenness
sorcery	immorality	gossip	slothfulness
jealousy	idolatry	sensuality	carousing

The bread of God's presence and worship is the only thing that will cause the soul to be healthy.

> **"Bless the Lord, O my soul: and all that is within me, bless his holy name. Bless the Lord, O my soul, and forget not all his benefits: Who forgiveth all thine iniquities; who healeth all thy diseases; Who redeemeth thy life from destruction; who crowneth thee with lovingkindness and tender mercies; Who satisfieth thy mouth with good things; so that thy youth is renewed like the eagle's" (Ps.103:1-5; see De.30:9; Ps.36:8; 73:25-26).**
>
> **"Wherefore do ye spend money for that which is not bread? and your labour for that which satisfieth not? hearken diligently unto me, and eat ye that which is good, and let your soul delight itself in fatness" (Is.55:2; see Re.2:7; 2:17).**

7. The showbread pointed to the bread that we all desperately need, the bread...
- that satisfies the hunger of our hearts
- that supplies our needs
- that provides for us
- that nourishes fellowship among us (see 1 Jn.1:3; Re.3:20)

Note what Jesus Christ, the Son of God Himself, said about this bread:
⇒ It is "the true bread."

> **"Then Jesus said unto them, Verily, verily, I say unto you, Moses gave you not that bread from heaven; but my Father giveth you the true bread from heaven" (Jn.6:32).**

⇒ It is "the living bread," the bread that causes a person to live forever.

> **"I am the living bread which came down from heaven: if any man eat of this bread, he shall live for ever: and the bread that I will give is my flesh, which I will give for the life of the world" (Jn.6:51).**

⇒ It is "the bread of God."

> **"For the bread of God is he which cometh down from heaven, and giveth life unto the world" (Jn.6:33).**

⇒ It is "the bread of life."

> **"And Jesus said unto them, I am the bread of life: he that cometh to me shall never hunger; and he that believeth on me shall never thirst" (Jn.6:35).**
> **"I am that bread of life" (Jn.6:48).**

Note what the disciples said about this bread:

> **"Then said they unto him, Lord, evermore give us this bread" (Jn.6:34).**

8. The showbread pointed to the spiritual needs of man. This is seen in that the showbread sat in the Tabernacle itself, the very place where spiritual needs were met. This truth was dictated by both God and His Son, the Lord Jesus Christ.

> **"And he [God] humbled thee, and suffered thee to hunger, and fed thee with manna, which thou knewest not, neither did thy fathers know; that he might make thee know that man doth not live by bread only, but by every word that proceedeth out of the mouth of the Lord doth man live" (De.8:3).**
> **"But he [Jesus Christ] answered and said, It is written, Man shall not live by bread alone, but by every word that proceedeth out of the mouth of God" (Mt.4:4).**

TYPES, SYMBOLS, AND PICTURES
(Exodus 25:23-30)

Historical Term	Type or Picture (Scriptural Basis)	Life Application for Today's Believer	Biblical Application for Today's Believer
The Table of Showbread (Ex.25:23-30;	*The purpose for the Table of Showbread was to be able to set the showbread before God.*	What the Table of Showbread taught: God is the only One who can satisfy the	*"But my God shall supply all your need according to his riches in glory by*

Historical Term	Type or Picture (Scriptural Basis)	Life Application for Today's Believer	Biblical Application for Today's Believer
40:22-23) See also Ex.35:13; 37:10-16; 39:36; 40:4, 22-23	*The Table of Showbread is the Symbol of God Himself as the Bread of Life. The showbread pointed to God Himself as the nourishment that a person really needs. Note that the loaves sat in God's presence, before His very face. The people were to acknowledge their dependence upon God, acknowledge that they needed His provision. They needed His watchful eye upon the bread, upon them as His followers. They needed Him to continue to provide their bread and food, to continue to look after and care for them. By setting the bread before God, they were declaring their belief and trust that He would continue to meet their needs.* **"Thou shalt also make a table of shittim wood: two cubits shall be the length thereof, and a cubit the breadth thereof, and a cubit and a half the height thereof"** (Ex.25:23). **"And he put the table in the tent of the congregation, upon the side of the tabernacle northward, without the vail. And he set the bread in order upon it before the LORD; as the LORD had commanded Moses"** (Ex. 40:22-23).	spiritual hunger in a person's soul. God knows what a person needs in order to thrive; therefore God provides and cares for us, feeds the hunger of the believer's soul. Far too often, a person tries to live his life apart from God's provision and presence. But Scripture declares that Christ is the Living Bread that came *out of* heaven to satisfy the hunger of a person's soul. If a person attempts to satisfy his soul in any other way, the results will be empty and unsatisfying. Note this fact as well: God promises to meet the physical needs as well as the spiritual needs of the believer—if the believer will truly seek the kingdom of God and His righteousness above all else.	*Christ Jesus"* (Ph.4:19; see Ps.23). *"Thou preparest a table before me in the presence of mine enemies: thou anointest my head with oil; my cup runneth over"* (Ps.23:5). *"Oh how great is thy goodness, which thou hast laid up for them that fear thee; which thou hast wrought for them that trust in thee before the sons of men!" (Ps. 31:19).* *"Trust in the LORD, and do good; so shalt thou dwell in the land, and verily thou shalt be fed" (Ps.37:3).* *"I am that bread of life" (Jn.6:48).* *"For the bread of God is he which cometh down from heaven, and giveth life unto the world" (Jn.6:33).* *"And Jesus said unto them, I am the bread of life: he that cometh to me shall never hunger; and he that believeth on me shall never thirst" (Jn.6:35).* *"But seek ye first the kingdom of God, and his righteousness; and all these things shall be added unto you" (Mt.6:33).*

THE TABLE OF SHOWBREAD

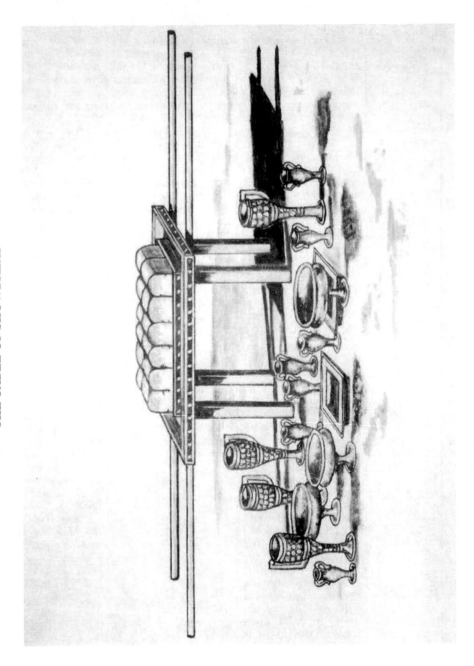

CHAPTER FOUR

The Gold Lampstand, the Symbol of God Himself as the Light of the World (Exodus 25:31-40)

Contents

I.   The design and materials (vv.31-39).   47

II. The strict instructions and warning: to be made according to the pattern, the plan and design of God Himself (v.40).   48

The Gold Lampstand,
the Symbol of God Himself
as the Light of the World
(Exodus 25:31-40)

1. The design & materials
a. To be made of pure gold, hammered out as one piece
  1) The center stem
  2) The branches with their flower-like cups, buds, & blossoms
b. To have six branches
  1) Three branches on each side
 	
  2) Each branch with its three cups shaped like almond flowers with buds & blossoms
 	
c. To have a center stem with four similar almond flower-like cups with buds & blossoms
	31 And thou shalt make a candlestick of pure gold: of beaten work shall the candlestick be made: his shaft, and his branches, his bowls, his knops, and his flowers, shall be of the same. 32 And six branches shall come out of the sides of it; three branches of the candlestick out of the one side, and three branches of the candlestick out of the other side: 33 Three bowls made like unto almonds, with a knop and a flower in one branch; and three bowls made like almonds in the other branch, with a knop and a flower: so in the six branches that come out of the candlestick. 34 And in the candlestick shall be four bowls made like unto almonds, with their knops and their flowers.	35 And there shall be a knop under two branches of the same, and a knop under two branches of the same, and a knop under two branches of the same, according to the six branches that proceed out of the candlestick. 36 Their knops and their branches shall be of the same: all it shall be one beaten work of pure gold. 37 And thou shalt make the seven lamps thereof: and they shall light the lamps thereof, that they may give light over against it. 38 And the tongs thereof, and the snuffdishes thereof, shall be of pure gold. 39 Of a talent of pure gold shall he make it, with all these vessels. 40 And look that thou make them after their pattern, which was showed thee in the mount.

		d. To have one blossom under each pair of branches e. To hammer out the gold flower buds & branches as one piece with the Lampstand f. To make seven lamps for the Lampstand & set them so they would reflect light forward g. To make lamp snuffers & trays of pure gold to use with the lampstand h. To use 75 pounds of pure gold in the construction **2. The strict instructions & warning: To be made according to the pattern, the plan & design of God Himself**

Spiritual darkness—is it a reality? Does it exist? Whether or not man acknowledges or recognizes it, spiritual darkness does indeed exist. Spiritual darkness is prevalent throughout the world. In every nation and every culture, millions of men and women are stumbling about in the darkness of this world. They are attempting to find the way through life on their own, yet they are stumbling about and falling ever more deeply into the abyss. Their hearts are crying out for some direction, some leading. But what they need—what we all need—is not the direction and leadership of the world but the light of God. We need a clear picture showing us how to reach God and giving us the assurance that we are acceptable to God. We need a clear picture showing us how to secure the fullness of life.

Yet the fullness of life is being missed by so many of us. Furthermore, the deep down assurance, the absolute certainty that we will live with God eternally, is missing. God knows this. God knows...

- that man's heart is blind and lacks assurance
- that man is short, ever so short, in experiencing the fullness of life
- that man needs the way to God lit and lit brightly
- that man can never reach God unless God gives him light and shows him the way

This is what this passage is all about. This is: *The Gold Lampstand, the Symbol of God Himself as the Light of the World,* Ex.25:31-40.

   I.   The design and materials (vv.31-39).
   II.   The strict instructions and warning: to be made according to the pattern, the plan and design of God Himself (v.40).

I. The Third Piece of Furniture Was the Lampstand (vv.31-39).

The Lampstand was probably the most beautiful and ornate furniture in the Tabernacle. It was the first thing that captured the attention of the ministering priests as they entered the Sanctuary. Just imagine the experience of the priests who entered this room. The sense of smell quickly picked up the sweet scent of incense that filled the Holy Place. As the priests peered into the room without windows, a beautiful glow illuminated the Table of Showbread, the Altar of Incense, and the gold Lampstand. A sense of reverence and awe would have swept over their being as it would over any person entering such an atmosphere in the Holy Place of God.

The design and materials of the Lampstand were exact and precise (25:31-39). Again, God Himself designed the Lampstand. Human creativity had no part in designing this Lampstand, no part in designing anything in the Tabernacle. No person knew the perfect way to approach God; no person knew perfectly how to please God in his worship. God and God alone knew how He was to be approached and worshipped. Therefore, God and God alone had to design the Lampstand and the other furnishings that were to be used in worshipping Him.

1. The Lampstand was to be made of pure gold, hammered out as one piece (v.31). The entire Lampstand was to be of one piece of gold: the base and center stem, the flower-like lamp cups, buds, and blossoms.

2. The Lampstand was to have six branches (vv.32-38).
   ⇒   Three branches were to be on each side (v.32).
   ⇒   Each branch was to have three cups shaped like almond flowers with buds and blossoms (v.33).

3. The Lampstand was to have four similar flower-like cups, one flower bud under each pair of branches (v.34).
4. The Lampstand was to have one blossom or bud under each pair of branches (v.35). All this means that the total number of ornaments was 69. Imagine 69 ornaments on one Lampstand. What beauty and splendor must have attracted the eye of the priest as he entered the Holy Place and saw the glowing, flickering flames arising from the seven light holders (six branches and the center stem). The impact of these ornaments can be better seen when glanced at in a chart:

BRANCH NUMBER	ORNAMENT #1: CUPS	ORNAMENT #2: BUDS	ORNAMENT #3: BLOSSOMS	TOTAL ORNAMENTS
#1 on the left side: 3 sets	3 Cups (gebia)	3 Buds (kaph-torim)	3 Blossoms (perahehah)	9
#2 on the left side: 3 sets	3 Cups (gebia)	3 Buds (kaph-torim)	3 Blossoms (perahehah)	9
#3 on the left side: 3 sets	3 Cups (gebia)	3 Buds (kaph-torim)	3 Blossoms (perahehah)	9
Central shaft: 4 sets	4 Cups (gebia)	7 Buds (kaph-torim)	4 Blossoms (perahehah)	15
#1 on the right side: 3 sets	3 Cups (gebia)	3 Buds (kaph-torim)	3 Blossoms (perahehah)	9
#2 on the right side: 3 sets	3 Cups (gebia)	3 Buds (kaph-torim)	3 Blossoms (perahehah)	9
#3 on the right side: 3 sets	3 Cups (gebia)	3 Buds (kaph-torim)	3 Blossoms (perahehah)	9
				TOTAL: 69

5. The decorations (flower buds) and branches were to be hammered out as one piece with the stem (v.36).

6. The seven lamps were to be made for the Lampstand and set so they would reflect the light forward (v.37).

7. The lampsnuffers and trays were to be made of pure gold to use with the lampstand (v.38).

8. The Lampstand and the accessories would require 75 pounds of pure gold (v.39).

II. The Lampstand Was to Be Made According to the Pattern, the Plan and Design of God Himself (v.40).

Note the strict instructions and warning given by God: this was a warning to Israel and to all succeeding generations as well, a warning that the Tabernacle and its furnishings...

- were only types of the real salvation and worship of God
- were only symbolic of how a person was to approach and worship God

A person must be sure, very sure, that he does not miss this truth, the reality lying behind the type and symbol. As Scripture says, these things were only shadows of good things to come:

> **"For the law having a shadow of good things to come, and not the very image of the things, can never with those sacrifices which they offered year by year continually make the comers thereunto perfect" (He.10:1).**

What are the types and symbols, the shadows, the pictures seen in the Lampstand? There are at least four.

1. The Lampstand taught that a person needs light and illumination in order to know God and serve God. There were no windows and no opening (other than a closed door) within the Holy Place. The Holy Place would have been in complete darkness without the Lampstand. It was the Lampstand that gave light and illuminated the Holy Place so that the priests could serve God. Therefore, the light of the Lampstand...

- symbolized the need of man for light and illumination in order to know and serve God

2. The Lampstand pictured God's people (Israel) as the light of the world, as God's witnesses to the world. This is emphasized by Scripture itself:

> "Ye are the light of the world. A city that is set on an hill cannot be hid" (Mt.5:14).
>
> "For so hath the Lord commanded us, saying, I have set thee to be a light of the Gentiles, that thou shouldest be for salvation unto the ends of the earth" (Ac.13:47; see Is.42:6; Zec.4:1-6).
>
> "For ye were sometimes darkness, but now are ye light in the Lord: walk as children of light" (Ep.5:8; see Ph.2:15).

3. The Lampstand pointed to Jesus Christ as the Light of the world.

> "In him [Jesus Christ] was life; and the life was the light of men" (Jn.1:4).
>
> "Then spake Jesus again unto them, saying, I am the light of the world: he that followeth me shall not walk in darkness, but shall have the light of life" (Jn.8:12; see Jn.12:35, 46; 2 Co.4:6; Re.21:23; Is.9:2).

4. The Lampstand pointed to God as the Light of the world, the Light that shows man how to approach and worship Him. It was God who planned and designed the Lampstand, who showed the Israelites exactly how to approach and worship Him. He does the same for us.

> "The Lord is my light and my salvation; whom shall I fear? the Lord is the strength of my life; of whom shall I be afraid?" (Ps.27:1; see Ps.84:11; Is.60:20; Mi.7:8).
>
> "This then is the message which we have heard of him, and declare unto you, that God is light, and in him is no darkness at all. If we say that we have fellowship with him, and walk in darkness, we lie, and do not the truth: But if we walk in the light, as he is in the light, we have fellowship one with another, and the blood of Jesus Christ his Son cleanseth us from all sin" (1 Jn.1:5-7; Re.22:5).

Thought

Jesus Christ is the true Lampstand. Christ came into the world to give light and illumination so that we might know and serve God. As the Light of the world, Christ fulfills the symbolism of the Lampstand. Christ and Christ alone is able to bring people out of the darkness of sin and death, giving them the light of salvation and eternal life.

a) The light of Christ is the true light, the only true light.

> "The same [John the Baptist] came for a witness, to bear witness of the Light, that all men through him might believe. He was not that Light, but was sent to bear witness of that Light. That [Jesus Christ] was the true Light, which lighteth every man that cometh into the world" (Jn.1:7-9).

b) The light of Jesus Christ shines in the darkness and brings life to people.

> "In him was life; and the life was the light of men. And the light shineth in darkness; and the darkness comprehended it not [can never extinguish it]" (Jn.1:4-5).

c) The light of Christ will keep people out of darkness and give them light.

> "Then spake Jesus again unto them, saying, I am the light of the world: he that followeth me shall not walk in darkness, but shall have the light of life" (Jn.8:12).

d) The light of Christ is the only way for believing men to escape the darkness.

> **"I am come a light into the world, that whosoever believeth on me should not abide in darkness" (Jn.12:46).**

e) The light of Christ brings the believer out of darkness into the marvelous light of God.

> **"But ye are a chosen generation, a royal priesthood, an holy nation, a peculiar people; that ye should show forth the praises of him who hath called you out of darkness into his marvelous light" (1 Pe.2:9).**

f) The light of Christ is the only way a man can see and find his way to the Father.

> **"Jesus saith unto him, I am the way, the truth, and the life: no man cometh unto the Father, but by me" (Jn.14:6).**

g) The light of Christ gives light to those who are spiritually asleep and dead.

> **"Wherefore he saith, Awake thou that sleepest, and arise from the dead, and Christ shall give thee light" (Ep.5:14).**

h) The light of Christ brings life and immortality to people.

> **"But is now made manifest by the appearing of our Saviour Jesus Christ, who hath abolished death, and hath brought life and immortality to light through the gospel" (2 Ti.1:10).**

i) The light of Christ makes people the children of light.

> **"Then Jesus said unto them, Yet a little while is the light with you. Walk while ye have the light, lest darkness come upon you: for he that walketh in darkness knoweth not whither he goeth. While ye have light, believe in the light, that ye may be the children of light. These things spake Jesus, and departed, and did hide himself from them" (Jn.12:35-36).**

j) The light of Christ shines in the heart of the believer.

> **"For God, who commanded the light to shine out of darkness, hath shined in our hearts, to give the light of the knowledge of the glory of God in the face of Jesus Christ" (2 Co.4:6).**

k) The light of Christ is in the world.

> **"As long as I am in the world, I am the light of the world" (Jn.9:5).**

l) The light of Christ has no darkness at all.

> **"This then is the message which we have heard of him [Christ], and declare unto you, that God is light, and in him is no darkness at all" (1 Jn.1:5).**

m) The light of Christ will be the only light needed for the new Jerusalem.

> **"And the city had no need of the sun, neither of the moon, to shine in it: for the glory of God did lighten it, and the Lamb is the light thereof. And the nations of them which are saved shall walk in the light of it: and the kings of the earth do bring their glory and honour into it" (Re.21:23-24).**

TYPES, SYMBOLS, AND PICTURES
(Exodus 25:31-40)

Historical Term	Type or Picture (Scriptural Basis)	Life Application for Today's Believer	Biblical Application for Today's Believer
The Gold Lampstand (Ex.25:31-40; 40:24) See also Ex.27:20-21; 35:14; 37:17-24; 39;37; 40:4, 25	*The Gold Lampstand provided the only light in the Holy Place. In the absence of light, darkness would have kept the priest from serving the LORD. The priest would have been helpless without light, unable to see his way, having to blindly feel his way around the Sanctuary. Thus the Lampstand pictures at least four things:*		
	a. The Lampstand symbolized God as the Light of the World.	a. The Lampstand pointed to God as the Light of the world, the Light that shows a person how to approach and worship Him. It was God who planned and designed the Lampstand, who showed the Israelites exactly how to approach and worship Him. He does the same for us.	*"The LORD is my light and my salvation; whom shall I fear? the LORD is the strength of my life; of whom shall I be afraid?" (Ps.27:1).* *"This then is the message which we have heard of him, and declare unto you, that God is light, and in him is no darkness at all" (1 Jn.1:5; see Ps.84:11).*
	b. The Lampstand symbolized Jesus Christ as the Light of the World.	b. Jesus Christ is the true Lampstand. Christ came into the world to give light and illumination so that we might know and serve God. As the Light of the world, Christ fulfills the symbolism of the Lampstand. Christ and Christ alone is able to bring people out of	*"The same [John the Baptist] came for a witness, to bear witness of the Light, that all men through him might believe. He was not that Light, but was sent to bear witness of that Light. That [Jesus Christ] was the true Light, which lighteth every man that cometh into the world" (Jn.1:7-9; see Jn.1:4-5).*

Historical Term	Type or Picture (Scriptural Basis)	Life Application for Today's Believer	Biblical Application for Today's Believer
		the darkness of sin and death, giving them the light of salvation and life, life now and forever.	*"I am come a light into the world, that whosoever believeth on me should not abide in darkness"* *(Jn.12:46; see Jn.14:6; 2 Co.4:6).*
	c. The Lampstand symbolized believers, God's people, as the light of the world.	c. Believers are called to be the light of the world: they are to shine as God's witness to the world. In a world that is filled with darkness, God has placed His light in the hearts of His people. Every believer has the great responsibility to walk in the light so the world might see a witness of God's light.	*"Ye are the light of the world. A city that is set on an hill cannot be hid" (Mt.5:14).* *"For ye were sometimes darkness, but now are ye light in the Lord: walk as children of light" (Ep.5:8).*
	d. The Lampstand symbolized the Word of God, His Word that enables a person to know and serve God. **"And thou shalt make a candlestick of pure gold: of beaten work shall the candlestick be made: his shaft, and his branches, his bowls, his knops, and his flowers, shall be of the same" (Ex.25:31).** **"And he put the candlestick in the tent of the congregation, over against the table, on the side of the tabernacle southward" (Ex.40:24).**	d. The believer must have light, the light of God's Word, in order to know God and serve God. The Word of God provides the believer light... • when he needs direction • when he needs wisdom • when he needs comfort • when he needs correction • when he needs anything from the infinite counsel of God.	*"Thy word is a lamp unto my feet, and a light unto my path" (Ps.119:105).* *"For the commandment is a lamp; and the law is light; and reproofs of instruction are the way of life" (Pr. 6:23).* *"All scripture is given by inspiration of God, and is profitable for doctrine, for reproof, for correction, for instruction in righteousness" (2 Ti. 3:16).*

THE GOLDEN LAMSTAND

The Tabernacle Itself: The Symbol of God's Dwelling Among His People and of Man's Need to Approach God Exactly as God Dictates (Exodus 26:1-37)

Contents

The Tabernacle Itself: The Symbol of God's Dwelling Among His People and of Man's Need to Approach God Exactly as God Dictates (Exodus 26:1-37)

1. **It was to be a tent constructed of four coverings**
   a. The 1st covering of fine linen: Pictured purity & righteousness
      1) The design: 10 curtains with cherubim
      2) The size
         * Each was to be about 42' long x 6' wide

         * Two groups of five curtains each were to be stitched together to make two long sets of curtains
      3) The loops & clasps to join & fasten the curtains together
         * To be blue material
         * To be sewed along the edges

         * To sew 50 loops on each curtain

Moreover thou shalt make the tabernacle with ten curtains of fine twined linen, and blue, and purple, and scarlet: with cherubim of cunning work shalt thou make them.
2 The length of one curtain shall be eight and twenty cubits, and the breadth of one curtain four cubits: and every one of the curtains shall have one measure.
3 The five curtains shall be coupled together one to another; and other five curtains shall be coupled one to another.
4 And thou shalt make loops of blue upon the edge of the one curtain from the selvedge in the coupling; and likewise shalt thou make in the uttermost edge of another curtain, in the coupling of the second.
5 Fifty loops shalt thou make in the one curtain, and fifty loops shalt thou

make in the edge of the curtain that is in the coupling of the second; that the loops may take hold one of another.
6 And thou shalt make fifty taches of gold, and couple the curtains together with the taches: and it shall be one tabernacle.
7 And thou shalt make curtains of goats' hair to be a covering upon the tabernacle: eleven curtains shalt thou make.
8 The length of one curtain shall be thirty cubits, and the breadth of one curtain four cubits: and the eleven curtains shall be all of one measure.
9 And thou shalt couple five curtains by themselves, and six curtains by themselves, and shalt double the sixth curtain in the forefront of the tabernacle.
10 And thou shalt make fifty loops on the edge of the one curtain that is out

* To make 50 gold clasps: To fasten the curtains together, making the tabernacle a single tent
   b. The 2nd covering of goat hair: Pictured the need for a sin offering & for cleansing (Nu. 28:15; Le.16)
      1) The number: 11 curtains
      2) The size: Each was to be about 45' long x 6'wide

      * Five to be joined together into one set & six into another set
      * The 6th curtain: To be folded double at the front of the tent
      3) The loops & clasps
         * To sew 50 loops along

the edge of both curtains

- To make 50 bronze clasps: For fastening the curtains together, making the tabernacle a single tent

4) The extra half sheet length of this first covering
  - To hang down at the rear of the tabernacle
  - To hang 18" extra over the sides of the tabernacle: To completely cover it

c. The 3rd covering of ram skins dyed red: Pictured the blood

d. The 4th covering of leather: Pictured a protective separation from the world

2. It was to be a tent hanging over wood framing (acacia wood): Symbolized stability, support, a strong foundation

a. The size of each framing board: 15' long x 2¼' wide with two pegs set parallel to each other (for hooking to the base)

most in the coupling, and fifty loops in the edge of the curtain which coupleth the second.

11 And thou shalt make fifty taches of brass, and put the taches into the loops, and couple the tent together, that it may be one.

12 And the remnant that remaineth of the curtains of the tent, the half curtain that remaineth, shall hang over the backside of the tabernacle.

13 And a cubit on the one side, and a cubit on the other side of that which remaineth in the length of the curtains of the tent, it shall hang over the sides of the tabernacle on this side and on that side, to cover it.

14 And thou shalt make a covering for the tent of rams' skins dyed red, and a covering above of badgers' skins.

15 And thou shalt make boards for the tabernacle of shittim wood standing up.

16 Ten cubits shall be the length of a board, and a cubit and a half shall be the breadth of one board.

17 Two tenons shall there be in one board, set in order one against another: thus shalt thou make for all the boards of the tabernacle.

18 And thou shalt make the boards for the tabernacle, twenty boards on the south side southward.

19 And thou shalt make forty sockets of silver under the twenty boards; two sockets under one board for his two tenons, and two sockets under another board for his two tenons.

20 And for the second side of the tabernacle on the north side there shall be twenty boards:

21 And their forty sockets of silver; two sockets under one board, and two sockets under another board.

22 And for the sides of the tabernacle westward thou shalt make six boards.

23 And two boards shalt thou make for the corners of the tabernacle in the two sides.

24 And they shall be coupled together beneath, and they shall be coupled together above the head of it unto one ring: thus shall it be for them both; they shall be for the two corners.

25 And they shall be eight boards, and their sockets of silver, sixteen sockets; two sockets under one board, and two sockets under another board.

26 And thou shalt make bars of shittim wood; five for the

b. The framing

1) To make a wall, a frame of 20 boards on the south side
  - A foundation of 40 silver sockets or bases, 2 under each board
  - Joined together by pegs

2) To make a wall frame of 20 boards on the north side: A foundation of 40 silver sockets, 2 sockets under each board

3) To make a wall frame on the west of six boards

4) To make a framing post of two boards for each corner
  - Joined together at the bottom
  - Joined together at the top, fitted into a single ring
  - A total of 8 board frames & a foundation of 16 silver sockets, 2 under each board

5) To make durable crossbars (acacia wood)

• 5 crossbars for the south	boards of the one side of the tabernacle,	ets of silver. 33 And thou shalt hang up the vail under the taches, that thou mayest bring in thither within the vail the ark of the testimony: and the vail shall divide unto you between the holy place and the most holy.	c. The purpose for the inner veil: To shield the ark of the testimony (covenant) from all else 1) To separate the Holy Place from the Most Holy Place
• 5 crossbars for the north • 5 crossbars for the west	27 And five bars for the boards of the other side of the tabernacle, and five bars for the boards of the side of the tabernacle, for the two sides westward.		
• A center crossbar running from end to end in the middle of the frames	28 And the middle bar in the midst of the boards shall reach from end to end.	34 And thou shalt put the mercy seat upon the ark of the testimony in the most holy place.	2) To separate the Mercy Seat from all else: Pictured separation, no access; man's desperate need for mercy
6) To cover the crossbars with gold & to make gold rings to hold the crossbars	29 And thou shalt overlay the boards with gold, and make their rings of gold for places for the bars: and thou shalt overlay the bars with gold.	35 And thou shalt set the table without the vail, and the candlestick over against the table on the side of the tabernacle toward the south: and thou shalt put the table on the north side.	• From the table: To be placed on the north side • From the lamp-stand: To be placed on the south side
c. The strict instructions: To be exact—to build exactly according to plan, exactly as the design dictated	30 And thou shalt rear up the tabernacle according to the fashion thereof which was showed thee in the mount.	36 And thou shalt make an hanging for the door of the tent, of blue, and purple, and scarlet, and fine twined linen, wrought with needlework.	4. **It was to be a tent with an outer curtain, a screen-like entrance: Symbolized the door into God's presence**
3. **It was to be a tent with a very special inner curtain, an inner veil: Symbolized God's majestic holiness & man's separation from God**	31 And thou shalt make a vail of blue, and purple, and scarlet, and fine twined linen of cunning work: with cherubims shall it be made:		a. An entrance of great beauty & craftsmanship
a. A veil of great beauty & skill		37 And thou shalt make for the hanging five pillars of shittim wood, and overlay them with gold, and their hooks shall be of gold: and thou shalt cast five sockets of brass for them.	b. The hanging frame 1) Make gold hooks & 5 posts overlaid with gold
b. To hang with gold hooks on 4 posts of durable wood (acacia): Posts to stand on 4 silver sockets or bases	32 And thou shalt hang it upon four pillars of shittim wood overlaid with gold: their hooks shall be of gold, upon the four sock-		2) Make 5 bronze bases for them

Note the magnitude of the following statement: the great Creator of the Universe—the Sovereign Lord and Majesty of all—wants to dwell among His people. God wants to dwell in a world...

- where many people ignore and scorn Him
- where many people curse and deny Him
- where many people have allowed evil to run rampant in their lives
- where people have even killed His Son, His one and only Son, the Lord Jesus Christ

This is the picture revealed in the Tabernacle: God wants to live among people. The Tabernacle shows us that God has taken steps to give man a personal relationship with

Himself. In having the Tabernacle built, God was declaring that He wanted to live and establish a permanent, eternal relationship with man. But it is important to note:

⇒ God was not cheapening Himself by coming to dwell among His people.

⇒ God was not demeaning His holy character by associating with sinful men.

⇒ God was not compromising His greatness by coming down to live with people.

The truth is this: by coming to earth to live with people, God was revealing His great compassion and love for people. In fact, God was teaching His people two basic truths through the Tabernacle:

1. God loved His people and wanted to be with them, wanted to dwell and live among them.

2. God had to be approached by His people in the right way, exactly as God dictated.

God's master plan to dwell with His people was revealed to Moses in this chapter. The design of the Tabernacle was a plan of great beauty and craftsmanship. The Tabernacle would soon become the most ornate portable place of worship in the world, designed by God Himself.

In seeking to understand the Tabernacle, we must do exactly what Stephen Olford, the excellent expositor of Scripture, says:

> *In seeking to interpret the Tabernacle, we must not dogmatize but humbly follow the method of the Holy Spirit as illustrated in the Epistle to the Hebrews. Referring there to the Tabernacle and the priesthood, He speaks of the "shadow of heavenly things" (Hebrews 8:5); "the patterns of things in the heavens" (Hebrews 9:23); "the figures of the true" (Hebrews 9:24); "a shadow of good things to come" (Hebrews 10:1). Thus it is clear that the Tabernacle was intended to signify spiritual realities. In other words, in the Tabernacle we see shadows, patterns, and figures of heavenly or spiritual things that are revealed in Christ.*[1]

The Tabernacle itself is the subject of this most important passage of Scripture. This is: *The Tabernacle Itself: The Symbol of God's Dwelling Among His People and of Man's Need to Approach God Exactly as God Dictates*, Ex.26:1-37.

    I.   It was to be a tent constructed of four coverings (vv.1-14).

    II.   It was to be a tent hanging over wood framing (acacia wood): symbolized stability, support, a strong foundation (vv.15-30).

    III. It was to be a tent with a very special inner curtain, an inner veil: symbolized God's majestic holiness and man's separation from God (vv.31-35).

            It was to be a tent with an outer curtain, a screen-like entrance: symbolized the

    IV. door into God's presence (vv.36-37).

I. The Tabernacle Was a Tent Constructed of Four Coverings That Were to Serve as the Roof and Sides of the Tabernacle (vv.1-14).

1. The first covering was made of ten linen curtains that served as the inside ceiling and walls (vv.1-6). This inner covering would be what the priests would see as they ministered in the Holy Place and in the Most Holy Place. To behold such a striking beauty was the greatest of privileges, a privilege that no one else would have. Each trip inside the Tabernacle was an experience beyond description. It was a trip into the presence of the God of Abraham, Isaac, and Jacob, into the presence of the LORD God Himself (Jehovah, Yahweh). The curtains symbolized purity and righteousness. The priest who entered into the Tabernacle never lost sight of God's character. As he looked up and studied the curtains, he saw the blue, purple, and scarlet yarn—all twisted and sewn together to make the linen. He knew what the colors meant: the blue represented the heavenly nature of God, the purple His kingly nature, and the scarlet His humility in receiving and accepting

---

[1] Stephen F. Olford. *The Tabernacle, Camping with God*, pp.21-22.

man through sacrifice. The priest was bound to be caught up in the worship of God, in all that God is.

Moreover, as he worshipped God, the priest knew that his feeble act of worship was focused upon the One who was perfectly pure and absolutely righteous. As the priest gazed about the Holy Place, the light from the Lampstand illuminated the beautiful linen walls and ceiling, the Table, the Altar of Incense, and the Lampstand itself. Everything in the Sanctuary magnified God's glory and made even the most prideful man take note of how small he was when in the presence of a pure and righteous God. Note the facts about these unique curtains:

a. The design of cherubim was embroidered on each curtain (v.1). With a background color of blue, purple, and scarlet, the curtains were without doubt breathtaking.

b. The size of each curtain was to be about 42 feet long by 6 feet wide (v.2). Two groups of five curtains each were to be stitched together to make two sets of long curtains (v.3).

c. The loops and clasps to join and fasten the curtains together were to be made of blue material and sewn along the edges (v.4). A total of 50 loops were to be sewn on each curtain (v.5). The curtains were fastened together by making 50 gold clasps that were inserted through the connecting loops. This made the Tabernacle a single tent (v.6).

Thought 1.
Jesus Christ fulfilled the symbolism of these inner curtains by being the perfect embodiment of purity and righteousness.

a) Jesus Christ is the righteousness of believers just as the fine linen is a symbol of righteousness.

> **"And to her was granted that she should be arrayed in fine linen, clean and white: for the fine linen is the righteousness of saints" (Re.19:8).**
>
> **"But of him are ye in Christ Jesus, who of God is made unto us wisdom, and righteousness, and sanctification, and redemption" (1 Co.1:30).**
>
> **"For he hath made him to be sin for us, who knew no sin; that we might be made the righteousness of God in him" (2 Co.5:21).**
>
> **"But now the righteousness of God without the law is manifested, being witnessed by the law and the prophets; Even the righteousness of God which is by faith of Jesus Christ unto all and upon all them that believe: for there is no difference" (Ro.3:21-22).**

b) Jesus Christ is righteous and pure, without sin.

> **"For we have not an high priest which cannot be touched with the feeling of our infirmities; but was in all points tempted like as we are, yet without sin" (He.4:15; see He.7:26; 2 Co.5:21).**
>
> **"Forasmuch as ye know that ye were not redeemed with corruptible things, as silver and gold, from your vain conversation received by tradition from your fathers; but with the precious blood of Christ, as of a lamb without blemish and without spot" (1 Pe.1:18-19; see 1 Jn.3:5).**

c) Jesus Christ loves righteousness.

> **"Thou [the Messiah] lovest righteousness, and hatest wickedness: therefore God, thy God, hath anointed thee with the oil of gladness above thy fellows" (Ps.45:7).**

d) Jesus Christ is the Righteous Branch.

> **"Behold, the days come, saith the Lord, that I will raise unto David a righteous Branch, and a King shall reign and prosper, and shall execute judgment and justice in the earth" (Je.23:5).**

Thought 2.
Whenever a believer enters into the presence of God, he is to focus upon two facts:
a) The fact that God is pure and righteous.

> **"According to thy name, O God, so is thy praise unto the ends of the earth: thy right hand is full of righteousness" (Ps.48:10; see Ps.97:2).**
> **"The Lord is righteous in all his ways, and holy in all his works" (Ps.145:17).**
> **"In his days Judah shall be saved, and Israel shall dwell safely: and this is his name whereby he shall be called, THE LORD OUR RIGHTEOUSNESS" (Je.23:6).**

b) The fact that God demands righteousness, that any person who approaches and worships God must live a righteous life.

> **"For I say unto you, That except your righteousness shall exceed [the righteousness] of the scribes and Pharisees, ye shall in no case enter into the kingdom of heaven" (Mt.5:20).**
> **"Awake to righteousness, and sin not; for some have not the knowledge of God: I speak this to your shame" (1 Co.15:34).**

2. The second covering was made of goat hair. This covering symbolized the need for the sin offering and for cleansing (vv.7-13). It is significant that this outer curtain of goat hair was laid on top of the inner curtain. If the inner curtain is symbolic of purity and righteousness, then the place for the goat hair is most appropriate. It clearly pictures that a person's sins must be forgiven before he can approach the righteousness of God. The picture is this: as God gave Moses the pattern for the Tabernacle, it is important to note the sequence: from the inside out.
  ⇒ The first covering of linen: speaks of purity and righteousness.
  ⇒ The second covering of goat skin: speaks of the need for a sin offering and cleansing in order to approach the righteousness of God

Most likely, this goatskin covering was black in color (see Song of Solomon 1:5). This covering of goat hair was coarse to touch, unlike the soft fine linen of the inner curtains. Contrasted with the beautiful blue, purple, and scarlet curtain that was embroidered with cherubim, the curtains of goat hair were not very appealing to view. Sin is never a pretty picture, but the curtains of goat hair speak of sacrifice, the fact that God forgives our sins through the blood of the sacrifice.

These are the facts that apply to the covering of goat hair:
  a. The number of the curtains was eleven (v.7).
  b. The size of each curtain was to be about 45 feet long by 6 feet wide (v.8). Five of the curtains were to be joined together into one set and six curtains into another set. The sixth curtain was to be folded double at the front of the tent (v.9).
  c. The loops and clasps fastened the curtains together, making the curtains a single covering for the tent or Tabernacle. Note the instructions:
    ⇒ to sew 50 loops along the edge of both curtains
    ⇒ to make 50 bronze clasps for fastening the curtains together (vv.10-11)

  d. The extra half-sheet length of this first covering was to hang down at the rear of the Tabernacle (v.12). The goat hair curtain was to hang 18 inches over the sides of the Tabernacle.

Thought

The Lord Jesus Christ is the One who took the blackness of sin upon Himself. He became the sin-offering for the sins of His people. (See page 64, DEEPER STUDY # 1, *Goats—Sin Offering*, for more discussion.)

> **"Yet it pleased the Lord to bruise him; he hath put him to grief: when thou shalt make his soul an offering for sin, he shall see his seed, he shall prolong his days, and the pleasure of the Lord shall prosper in his hand" (Is.53:10; see Is.53:12; 2 Co.5:21).**
>
> **"Who gave himself for our sins, that he might deliver us from this present evil world, according to the will of God and our Father" (Ga.1:4; see Ep.5:2).**
>
> **"Who his own self bare our sins in his own body on the tree, that we, being dead to sins, should live unto righteousness: by whose stripes ye were healed" (1 Pe.2:24; see Re.1:5).**

3. The third covering of ram skins symbolized the sacrificial blood (v.14). The ram skins had the wool removed and were then dyed red. Red, of course, is symbolic of the sacrificial blood.

Thought

The third covering of ram skins points to the sacrifice of Jesus Christ and His shed blood for sinners.

a) It is by the blood of Jesus Christ that our sins are forgiven.

> **"For this is my blood of the new testament, which is shed for many for the remission of sins" (Mt.26:28).**

b) It is by the blood of Jesus Christ that He has purchased us.

> **"Take heed therefore unto yourselves, and to all the flock, over the which the Holy Ghost hath made you overseers, to feed the church of God, which he hath purchased with his own blood" (Ac.20:28).**

c) It is by the blood of Jesus Christ that we are justified.

> **"Much more then, being now justified by his blood, we shall be saved from wrath through him" (Ro.5:9).**

d) It is by the blood of Jesus Christ that our consciences are purged from dead works.

> **"How much more shall the blood of Christ, who through the eternal Spirit offered himself without spot to God, purge your conscience from dead works to serve the living God?" (He.9:14).**

e) It is by the blood of Jesus Christ that we are cleansed from all sin.

> **"But if we walk in the light, as he is in the light, we have fellowship one with another, and the blood of Jesus Christ his Son cleanseth us from all sin" (1 Jn.1:7).**

f) It is by the blood of Jesus Christ that we are freed from the power of sin.

> **"And from Jesus Christ, who is the faithful witness, and the first begotten of the dead, and the prince of the kings of the earth. Unto him that loved us, and washed us from our sins in his own blood" (Re.1:5).**

4. The outside covering was the covering of leather or of seal skins (v.14). The outer covering of leather was symbolic of a protective separation from the world.[2] It was the covering that kept the Tabernacle safe from the elements of the weather and the wilderness: the scorching sun, the torrential rains, the wind-blasted sand, and the wild animals. Moving from campsite to campsite, the Tabernacle obviously took a constant beating. The covering of leather protected the Tabernacle from the outside, from the elements of the world. In simple terms, it kept the bad things out (the world) and the good things in (the worship of God). Today, there are many things that the believer needs in order to have protective separation from the world.

Thought 1.
The outer covering of leather is a picture of separation, of being protected from the world and the things in the world.
a) The believer needs protection from the pleasures of the world.

> "Love not the world, neither the things that are in the world. If any man love the world, the love of the Father is not in him. For all that is in the world, the lust of the flesh, and the lust of the eyes, and the pride of life, is not of the Father, but is of the world" (1 Jn.2:15-16).

b) The believer needs protection from the unclean thing.

> "Therefore if any man be in Christ, he is a new creature: old things are passed away; behold, all things are become new. And all things are of God, who hath reconciled us to himself by Jesus Christ, and hath given to us the ministry of reconciliation" (2 Co.5:17-18).

c) The believer needs protection from the course or the path of the world.

> "And you hath he quickened, who were dead in trespasses and sins; Wherein in time past ye walked according to the course of this world, according to the prince of the power of the air, the spirit that now worketh in the children of disobedience" (Ep.2:1-2).

d) The believer needs protection from the cares of the world.

> "Therefore take no thought, saying, What shall we eat? or, What shall we drink? or, Wherewithal shall we be clothed? (For after all these things do the Gentiles seek:) for your heavenly Father knoweth that ye have need of all these things. But seek ye first the kingdom of God, and his righteousness; and all these things shall be added unto you. Take therefore no thought for the morrow: for the morrow shall take thought for the things of itself. Sufficient unto the day [is] the evil thereof" (Mt.6:31-34).
> "He also that received seed among the thorns is he that heareth the word; and the care of this world, and the deceitfulness of riches, choke the word, and he becometh unfruitful" (Mt.13:22).

e) The believer needs protection from evil associations.

> "But now I have written unto you not to keep company, if any man that is called a brother be a fornicator, or covetous, or an idolater, or a railer, or a drunkard, or an extortioner; with such an one no not to eat" (1 Co.5:11).

---

[2] Frank E. Gaebelein. *The Expositor's Bible Commentary*, Vol. 2, p.459.

"Be ye not unequally yoked together with unbelievers: for what fellowship hath righteousness with unrighteousness? and what communion hath light with darkness?" (2 Co.6:14).

"Thou shalt not follow a multitude to do evil; neither shalt thou speak in a cause to decline after many to wrest judgment" (Ex.23:2; see Ps.1:1; Pr.4:14; 24:1).

Thought 2.
Jesus Christ fulfilled the symbolism of the outer cover. Jesus Christ is our protective separation from the world, its perils and temptations, and from the coming wrath of God against sin and the evil of the world.
a) Jesus Christ protects us by saving us from the wrath of God against sin and evil.

"For God so loved the world, that he gave his only begotten Son, that whosoever believeth in him should not perish, but have everlasting life" (Jn.3:16).
"Much more then, being now justified by his blood, we shall be saved from wrath through him" (Ro.5:9).
"Who gave himself for our sins, that he might deliver us from this present evil world, according to the will of God and our Father" (Ga.1:4).

b) Jesus Christ protects us by sanctifying us, setting us apart unto God.

"But of him are ye in Christ Jesus, who of God is made unto us wisdom, and righteousness, and sanctification, and redemption" (1 Co.1:30).
"If a man therefore purge himself from these, he shall be a vessel unto honour, sanctified, and meet for the master's use, and prepared unto every good work" (2 Ti.2:21).
"Wherefore Jesus also, that he might sanctify the people with his own blood, suffered without the gate" (He.13:12; see 1 Pe.1:2).

c) Jesus Christ protects us by sanctifying us with His Word.

"I have given them thy word; and the world hath hated them, because they are not of the world, even as I am not of the world. I pray not that thou shouldest take them out of the world, but that thou shouldest keep them from the evil. They are not of the world, even as I am not of the world. Sanctify them through thy truth: thy word is truth" (Jn.17:14-17).

d) Jesus Christ protects us with His watchful eyes.

"For the eyes of the Lord run to and fro throughout the whole earth, to show himself strong in the behalf of them whose heart is perfect toward him. Herein thou hast done foolishly: therefore from henceforth thou shalt have wars" (2 Chr.16:9).

e) Jesus Christ protects us by surrounding us.

"As the mountains are round about Jerusalem, so the Lord is round about his people from henceforth even for ever" (Ps.125:2).

f) Jesus Christ protects us, even the hairs upon our head.

"But there shall not an hair of your head perish" (Lu.21:18).

DEEPER STUDY # 1
(Ex.26:7-13) **Goats—Sin Offering**: throughout Scripture, the goat is pictured as an animal used in the sin offering.

> "And he shall take of the congregation of the children of Israel two kids of the goats for a sin offering, and one ram for a burnt offering" (Le.16:5; see Le.4:23-24; 4:28; 5:6; 9:15; 10:16-17; 16:7-10).
> "Then shall he kill the goat of the sin offering, that is for the people, and bring his blood within the vail, and do with that blood as he did with the blood of the bullock, and sprinkle it upon the mercy seat, and before the mercy seat" (Le.16:15; see Le.16:18; 16:20-22; 16:26-27).
> "Neither by the blood of goats and calves, but by his own blood he entered in once into the holy place, having obtained eternal redemption for us. For if the blood of bulls and of goats, and the ashes of an heifer sprinkling the unclean, sanctifieth to the purifying of the flesh: How much more shall the blood of Christ, who through the eternal Spirit offered himself without spot to God, purge your conscience from dead works to serve the living God?" (He.9:12-14; see He.9:19; 10:4).

II. The Tabernacle Was to Be a Tent Hanging Over Wood Framing (Acacia Wood) (vv.15-30).

The curtains and coverings would have been useless without the wood framing. The wood framing had a very practical purpose: to support the curtains and coverings. Instead of a solid wall of gold-covered boards, it is most likely that the Tabernacle was built like a trellis. A solid wall of boards would have blocked the inner linen curtains from being seen by the priests. Note the facts about the wood framing:
1. The size of each framing board was 15 feet long by 2¼ feet wide with two pegs set parallel to each other for hooking to the base (vv.15-17).
2. The framing consisted of the following items with instructions:
   a. To make a wall, a frame of 20 boards on the south side (v.18). On the south side there was a foundation of 40 silver sockets or bases, two under each board which were joined together by pegs (v.19).
   b. To make a wall, a frame of 20 boards on the north side (v.20). Like the south side, the north side was to have a foundation of 40 silver sockets, two sockets under each board (v.21). Each one of the silver sockets required about 75 pounds of silver. Why did God want the foundation built of silver? Why not gold or bronze? Because silver is a symbol of the atonement: of reconciliation, ransom, or redemption. The silver was collected by taking up an offering that is actually called *atonement money* (Ex.30:11-16; 38:25-28). Each Israelite man gave *atonement money* in the form of silver. Each man gave the same amount of silver—rich and poor, famous and unknown, educated and uneducated. (See outline and notes—Chapter Ten, Ex.30:11-16; see Chapter Fifteen, Ex.38:25-28 for a more detailed study on the atonement money.)

   Thought
   The silver in the Tabernacle would be an ever-present reminder of man's need for atonement: for reconciliation with God, for redemption. The foundation of the Tabernacle would be a foundation of silver. This pictured a glorious truth: the foundation of the believer is to be redemption, reconciliation with God through His Son the LORD Jesus Christ. The great need for the foundation of redemption is clearly seen by looking at Israel's experience.
   ⇒ The Tabernacle was firmly planted in the shifting sands of the desert (a symbol of the world and the shifting sands of a worldly foundation).

> **"Therefore whosoever heareth these sayings of mine, and doeth them, I will liken him unto a wise man, which built his house upon a rock: And the rain descended, and the floods came, and the winds blew, and beat upon that house; and it fell not: for it was founded upon a rock" (Mt.7:24-25).**

⇒ The Tabernacle was firmly planted under God's direction and care as He led His people from campsite to campsite.

> **"Trust in the Lord with all thine heart; and lean not unto thine own understanding. In all thy ways acknowledge him, and he shall direct thy paths" (Pr.3:5-6).**

⇒ The Tabernacle was firmly planted in God's ability to save helpless men.

> **"For when we were yet without strength, in due time Christ died for the ungodly" (Ro.5:6).**

c. To make a wall frame of six boards on the west (v.22).
d. To make a framing post of two boards for each corner (v.23)...
   - joined together at the bottom
   - joined together at the top, fitting into a single ring (v.24)
   - having a total of eight board frames and a foundation of sixteen silver sockets, two under each board (v.25)

e. To make durable crossbars (acacia wood). There were to be...
   - 5 crossbars for the south (v.26)
   - 5 crossbars for the north (v.27)
   - 5 crossbars for the west (v.27)

The exact design as to how these crossbars were arranged on each of the three walls is unknown. What is known is that the center crossbar was to run from end to end in the middle of the frames (v.28).
f. To cover the crossbars with gold and to make gold rings to hold the crossbars (v.29). The 15 crossbars served as a means of stability to the wood framing. Without the support of the crossbars, the Tabernacle would have been at the mercy of every contrary wind. The Scripture gives no reason why God wanted five crossbars for each wall. What we do know and can apply in a most practical way is the purpose of the crossbars: to give stability and support.

Thought
The stability and support of the crossbars picture the stability and support that Jesus Christ gives each believer.
a) Jesus Christ is our support, our eternal refuge.

> **"The eternal God is thy refuge, and underneath are the everlasting arms: and he shall thrust out the enemy from before thee; and shall say, Destroy them" (De.33:27).**

b) Jesus Christ holds us, sustains us with His right hand.

> **"Thou hast also given me the shield of thy salvation: and thy right hand hath holden me up, and thy gentleness hath made me great" (Ps.18:35).**

c)   Jesus Christ strengthens us, holds us up.

"Fear thou not; for I am with thee: be not dismayed; for I am thy God: I will strengthen thee; yea, I will help thee; yea, I will uphold thee with the right hand of my righteousness" (Is.41:10).

d)   Jesus Christ delivers us.

"And the Lord shall deliver me from every evil work, and will preserve me unto his heavenly kingdom: to whom be glory for ever and ever. Amen" (2 Ti.4:18).

e)   Jesus Christ preserves us, those who are faithful.

"O love the Lord, all ye his saints: for the Lord preserveth the faithful, and plentifully rewardeth the proud doer" (Ps.31:23).

3.   The instructions were to be exact: the Tabernacle was to be built exactly according to plan, exactly as God's design dictated (v.30). God's plan is reinforced once again. No shortcuts were to be taken. No materials were to be replaced by other materials. No dimensions were to be adjusted. No man-made suggestions were to be submitted. The Tabernacle had to be built *exactly* as God commanded.

"This book of the law shall not depart out of thy mouth; but thou shalt meditate therein day and night, that thou mayest observe to do according to all that is written therein: for then thou shalt make thy way prosperous, and then thou shalt have good success" (Jos.1:8).
"Not every one that saith unto me, Lord, Lord, shall enter into the kingdom of heaven; but he that doeth the will of my Father which is in heaven" (Mt.7:21; see Jn.14:21).
"If ye keep my commandments, ye shall abide in my love; even as I have kept my Father's commandments, and abide in his love....Ye are my friends, if ye do whatsoever I command you" (Jn.15:10, 14; see Ac.5:29).

III. The Tabernacle Was to Be a Tent with a Very Special Inner Curtain or Door, an Inner Veil (vv.31-35).

The *inner curtain* or *veil* symbolized God's majestic holiness and man's terrible separation from God. This special curtain or veil was made just like the inner covering of the Tabernacle that covered the Holy Place and the Most Holy Place. Note the facts as they are described by the Scripture:
1.   It was a veil of great beauty made with remarkable skill (v.31). Like the inner curtain, it was made of fine linen. The same striking colors of blue, purple, and scarlet were a part of this veil. The embroidered cherubim were also worked into this veil.
2.   It was to hang with gold hooks on four posts of durable wood (acacia). The posts were to stand on four silver sockets or bases (v.32).
3.   The purpose for the inner veil was basically to shield the ark of God's presence from all else.
    a.   The inner veil was to separate the Holy Place from the Most Holy Place (v.33). The Most Holy Place symbolized the very presence of God Himself, His majestic holiness and righteousness. The veil protected all from the light of His perfection which no man can approach.

"Who only hath immortality, dwelling in the light which no man can approach unto; whom no man hath seen, nor can see: to whom be honour and power everlasting. Amen" (1 Ti.6:16).

b. The inner veil was to separate the Mercy Seat from all else. The veil symbolized the holiness of God, separation from the presence of God (v.34). Note what was to be separated from the Mercy Seat in the Most Holy Place:

⇒ The Table of Showbread: the table was to be placed on the north side in the Holy Place (v.35).
⇒ The Lampstand: the Lampstand was to be placed opposite the table on the south side (v.35).

Why was this necessary? The separation of the Mercy Seat from all else symbolized man's terrible separation from God, that man has no access to God, none whatsoever—not apart from God's mercy. God's mercy is an absolute essential if man's approach to God is to be acceptable. How do we know that God has mercy upon us? Because He sent His Son into the world...

• as the Bread of Life (pictured by the Table of Showbread. See outline and notes—Chapter Three, Ex.25:23-30 for more discussion.)
• as the Light of the World (pictured by the Lampstand. See outline and notes—Chapter Four, Ex.25:31-40 for more discussion.)

Note that the initiative for salvation (approaching God) is pictured as being taken by God and God alone. God reaches out in mercy, providing the bread of life and the light of the world. God reaches out from the Mercy Seat that sits in the Most Holy Place.

The *inner veil* is rich in symbolism as it speaks of Jesus Christ. Jesus Christ fulfilled the symbolism of the inner veil. Christ and Christ alone is the way to God, the way to know God and to experience the presence, fellowship, and communion of God. Remember what happened to the inner veil of the temple when Jesus Christ died on the cross: it was torn from top to bottom, symbolizing that God Himself acted, took the initiative, and tore the veil. The heavenly veil that kept man out of God's presence was torn by Christ when He suffered and died on the cross. We now have eternal access into the presence of God. The inner veil pictures at least the following lessons to the believer:

⇒ Fellowship and communion with God Himself is the supreme act of worship.
⇒ God is holy and righteous, far, far removed from man and his world—totally set apart and separated from the pollution and uncleanness of man.
⇒ God must be approached ever so carefully—in reverence, awe, and fear.
⇒ There is only one way to God, only one door into His presence.

> "And, behold, the veil of the temple was rent in twain from the top to the bottom; and the earth did quake, and the rocks rent" (Mt.27:51; see Mk.15:38; Lu.23:45; He.6:19; 9:3).
> "Having therefore, brethren, boldness to enter into the holiest by the blood of Jesus, By a new and living way, which he hath consecrated for us, through the veil, that is to say, his flesh; And having an high priest over the house of God" (He.10:19-21).

IV. The Tabernacle Was to Be a Tent With an Outer Curtain, a Screen-like Entrance (vv.36-37).

The center curtain symbolized the door into God's presence. This curtain divided the Holy Place from the courtyard of the Tabernacle. Note the facts:

1. It was an entrance of great beauty and craftsmanship (v.36). This curtain was identical to the inner curtain with one exception: there were no cherubim embroidered into the curtain.

2. The hanging frame was slightly different from that of the inner curtain's hanging frame.

a. There were to be gold hooks and five posts overlaid with gold (v.37). The inner curtain was hung on four posts overlaid with gold (see v.32).

b. There were to be five bronze bases or sockets for the posts (v.37). The poles for the inner curtain required only four bases of silver (see v.32). Note the change of metals for the bases from silver to bronze. Why? Most likely because sin offerings were made at the bronze altar, and before a person can offer acceptable worship, he must first deal with his sins. There at the bronze altar, his sins were judged by God and God's wrath was satisfied. This is the foundation of man's worship, the blood that cleanses a person from sin. Therefore, the foundation sockets for the entrance to the Tabernacle were made of bronze: all to symbolize the need for cleansing in order to worship God. Simply stated, until a man has been forgiven for his sins, he can never enter into the presence of God. Once blood has been shed, man is invited to come and worship God.

Thought
Jesus Christ fulfilled the symbolism of this outer curtain. With His shed blood, He invites men to come through the door and worship God. The way to a deeper knowledge of God, to the deeper things of God, is through the Lord Jesus Christ and through Him alone. The lessons of the outer veil are these:

a) A person cannot just rush into the presence of a holy God; he cannot show disrespect to a holy God.

b) There is only one way into the presence of God.

> **"I am the door: by me if any man enter in, he shall be saved, and shall go in and out, and find pasture" (Jn.10:9).**
> **"Jesus saith unto him, I am the way, the truth, and the life: no man cometh unto the Father, but by me" (Jn.14:6; see Acts 4:12; Ro.5:2).**
> **"For there is one God, and one mediator between God and men, the man Christ Jesus; Who gave himself a ransom for all, to be testified in due time" (1 Ti.2:5-6).**

c) There is a deeper knowledge of God: there is much more to knowing and experiencing God's presence than just making sacrifice and receiving forgiveness of sins. Remember: offerings for sin were made at the brazen altar in the courtyard. But there was more than this in knowing and worshipping God, more than just receiving forgiveness of sins. There was worship in the Holy Place and even in the inner sanctuary or Most Holy Place.

> **"And this is life eternal, that they might know thee the only true God, and Jesus Christ, whom thou hast sent" (Jn.17:3).**
> **"But of him are ye in Christ Jesus, who of God is made unto us wisdom, and righteousness, and sanctification, and redemption" (1 Co.1:30).**
> **"But speaking the truth in love, may grow up into him in all things, which is the head, even Christ" (Ep.4:15; see Ph.3:10; He.6:1).**
> **"As newborn babes, desire the sincere milk of the word, that ye may grow thereby: if so be ye have tasted that the Lord is gracious" (1 Pe.2:2-3; see 2 Pe.1:4-7).**
> **"But grow in grace, and in the knowledge of our Lord and Saviour Jesus Christ. To him be glory both now and forever" (2 Pe.3:18).**

THE TABERNACLE OF MOSES

SECTION OF THE TABERNACLE	WHAT IS TAUGHT	HOW CHRIST FULFILLED THE SYMBOLISM
The Sanctuary of the Tabernacle	What the Sanctuary (the walls and roof) taught: ⇒ There are different forms of worship, certain steps to take in approaching God.	How Christ fulfilled the symbolism of the Sanctuary (the walls and roof): *"By whom [Christ] also we have access by faith into this grace*

SECTION OF THE TABERNACLE	WHAT IS TAUGHT	HOW CHRIST FULFILLED THE SYMBOLISM
	⇒ There are some initial steps to take in approaching God before one approaches Him in the most intimate worship. ⇒ God is righteous and holy and completely separate from man, even from the religious who move about and minister in walls of religion. ⇒ God must be approached in reverence and awe and ever so carefully by men, even by the religious who are involved in His service.	*wherein we stand, and rejoice in hope of the glory of God" (Ro.5:2).* *"For through him we both have access by one Spirit unto the Father" (Ep.2:18).* *"In whom we have boldness and access with confidence by the faith of him" (Ep.3:12).* *"Let us draw near with a true heart in full assurance of faith, having our hearts sprinkled from an evil conscience, and our bodies washed with pure water" (He.10:22).* *"Wherefore we receiving a kingdom which cannot be moved, let us have grace [of our Lord Jesus Christ], whereby we may serve God acceptably with reverence and godly fear" (He. 12:28).*
The Outer Veil or Curtain Door (The Holy Place, The First Room, or Outer Sanctuary)	What the Outer Veil or Curtain Door taught: ⇒ A person cannot just rush into the presence of God. God is holy; therefore; a person cannot show disrespect to a holy God. ⇒ There is only one way into the deeper things of God. ⇒ There is a deeper knowledge of God—much more to knowing and experiencing God's presence, much more than just making sacrifice and receiving forgiveness of sins. (Remember: offerings for sin were made at the brazen altar in the courtyard. But there was more than this, more than forgiveness of sins. More was necessary to really know and worship God. There was worship in the Holy Place and even in the inner sanctuary of God's presence, that is, in the Most Holy Place or the Holy of Holies.)	How Christ fulfilled the symbolism of the outer veil: ⇒ The way to a deeper knowledge of God, to the deeper things of God, is through the Lord Jesus Christ and through Him alone. *"And this is life eternal, that they might know thee the only true God, and Jesus Christ, whom thou hast sent" (Jn.17:3).* *"But of him are ye in Christ Jesus, who of God is made unto us wisdom, and righteousness, and sanctification, and redemption" (1 Co.1:30).* *"But speaking the truth in love, may grow up into him in all things, which is the head, even Christ" (Ep.4:15).* *"That I may know him, and the power of his resurrection, and the fellowship of his sufferings, being made conformable unto his death" (Ph.3:10).* *"Therefore leaving the principles of the doctrine of Christ, let us go on unto perfection; not laying again the foundation of repentance from dead works, and of faith toward God" (He.6:1).* *"As newborn babes, desire the sincere milk of the word, that ye may grow thereby: if so be ye have tasted that the Lord is gracious" (1 Pe.2:2-3).*

SECTION OF THE TABERNACLE	WHAT IS TAUGHT	HOW CHRIST FULFILLED THE SYMBOLISM
The Inner Veil or Curtain Door, The Holy of Holies, or the Most Holy Place (The Inner Room or Inner Sanctuary)	What the Inner Veil or Curtain Door taught: ⇒ Fellowship and communion with God Himself is the supreme act of worship. ⇒ God is holy and righteous, far, far removed from man and his world—totally set apart and separated from the pollution and uncleanness of man. ⇒ God must be approached ever so carefully—in reverence, awe, and fear. ⇒ There is only one way to God, only one door into His presence.	How Christ fulfilled the symbolism of the veil: ⇒ Christ and Christ alone is the way to God, to knowing God and to experiencing the presence, fellowship, and communion of God. *"Wherefore in all things it behooved him to be made like unto his brethren, that he might be a merciful and faithful high priest in things pertaining to God, to make reconciliation for the sins of the people" (He. 2:17).* *"Seeing then that we have a great high priest, that is passed into the heavens, Jesus the Son of God, let us hold fast our profession. For we have not an high priest which cannot be touched with the feeling of our infirmities; but was in all points tempted like as we are, yet without sin" (He.4:14-15; see He.6:19-20; 9:24; 10:19-20).*

TYPES, SYMBOLS, AND PICTURES
(Exodus 26:1-37)

Historical Term	Type or Picture (Scriptural Basis)	Life Application for Today's Believer	Biblical Application for Today's Believer
Fine-threaded Linen (Ex.26:1)	*Fine linen is clean and white; therefore, the linen symbolized the purity and righteousness of God. This fact is spelled out in Scripture:* **"Moreover thou shalt make the tabernacle *with* ten curtains *of* fine twined linen, and blue, and purple, and scarlet: *with* cherubims of cunning work shalt thou make them" (Ex.26:1).** **"And to her was granted that she should be arrayed in fine linen, clean and white: for the fine linen is the righteousness of saints" (Re.19:8).**	a. God's righteousness is... • totally pure • totally righteous • totally holy b. The believer must strive to be more godly in all his ways, to be pure and righteous and holy... • in his heart (see Ps.24:4; Mt.5:8; 1 Ti.1:5) • in his soul (see 1 Pe. 1:22) • in his religion (see Js.1:27)	*"He that overcometh, the same shall be clothed in white raiment; and I will not blot out his name out of the book of life, but I will confess his name before my Father, and before his angels" (Re.3:5).* *"I counsel thee to buy of me gold tried in the fire, that thou mayest be rich; and white raiment, that thou mayest be clothed, and that the shame of thy nakedness do not appear; and anoint thine eyes with eyesalve, that thou mayest see" (Re.3:18; see Re. 4:4; 7:9).*

Historical Term	Type or Picture (Scriptural Basis)	Life Application for Today's Believer	Biblical Application for Today's Believer
Blue (Ex.26:1)	*Blue, of course, is the color of the sky; therefore, blue is a symbol of the heavenly Person of Christ.* **"Moreover thou shalt make the tabernacle *with* ten curtains *of* fine twined linen, and blue, and purple, and scarlet: *with* cherubims of cunning work shalt thou make them"** (Ex.26:1).	a. Jesus Christ is the great High Priest... • who is made higher than the heavens • who is highly exalted • who has a name higher than any other being b. When a person looks upward toward the beautiful blue sky, he should remember... • to exalt Christ for who He is, for His deity • to praise and worship Christ for what He has done • to lift up prayers of intercession and supplication to the great High Priest, Jesus Christ	*"For such an high priest became us, who is holy, harmless, undefiled, separate from sinners, and made higher than the heavens"* *(He.7:26).* *"Wherefore God also hath highly exalted him, and given him a name which is above every name" (Ph.2:9).* *"He that cometh from above is above all: he that is of the earth is earthly, and speaketh of the earth: he that cometh from heaven is above all" (Jn.3:31).* *"Being made so much better than the angels, as he hath by inheritance obtained a more excellent name than they" (He.1:4; see Re.22:13; Jn.8:42).*
The Inner Curtains in the Sanctuary (Ex.26:1-6; 36:8-9) See also Ex.35:11; 36:8-13; 39:33; 40:19	*The Inner Curtains in the Sanctuary symbolized purity and righteousness. The Inner Curtains were made of brilliant colors and embroidered cherubim. Glancing at these, the High Priest was able to picture how pure, how holy, how perfect and righteous God is. The beauty and splendor of the Inner Curtains in the Sanctuary caused the High Priest to stand in awe of God's holy perfection.* **"Moreover thou shalt make the tabernacle with ten curtains of fine twined linen, and blue, and purple, and scarlet: with cherubims of**	What the Inner Curtains in the Sanctuary taught: a. God is righteous, holy, and completely distinct from any other being. In fact, God is so righteous and holy that there is a great gulf separating man from God. That gulf is caused by sin, by our coming so short of God's glory. It is sin that has caused the great divide and that makes God unapproachable. Man desperately needs someone, a mediator, who can bridge the great gulf or divide to God. That Someone, that Mediator, is Jesus Christ.	*"For there is one God, and one mediator between God and men, the man Christ Jesus; Who gave himself a ransom for all, to be testified in due time" (1 Ti.2:5-6; see 2 Co.5:21; Ro.5:2; Ep.3:12).* *"And for this cause he is the mediator of the new testament, that by means of death, for the redemption of the transgressions that were under the first testament, they which are called might receive the promise of eternal inheritance" (He.9:15).* *"For Christ is not entered into the holy places made with hands, which are the figures of the true; but*

Historical Term	Type or Picture (Scriptural Basis)	Life Application for Today's Believer	Biblical Application for Today's Believer
	cunning work shalt thou make them" (Ex.26:1). "And every wise hearted man among them that wrought the work of the tabernacle made ten curtains *of* fine twined linen, and blue, and purple, and scarlet: *with* cherubims of cunning work made he them. The length of one curtain *was* twenty and eight cubits, and the breadth of one curtain four cubits: the curtains *were* all of one size" (Ex.36:8-9).	b. God must be approached in reverence and awe and ever so carefully by men, even by the religious who are involved in His service.	*into heaven itself, now to appear in the presence of God for us" (He.9:24).* *"My little children, these things write I unto you, that ye sin not. And if any man sin, we have an advocate with the Father, Jesus Christ the righteous: And he is the propitiation for our sins: and not for ours only, but also for the sins of the whole world" (1 Jn.2:1-2).* *"Let all the earth fear the LORD: let all the inhabitants of the world stand in awe of him" (Ps.33:8; see Ps. 89:7; 4:4).* *"Wherefore we receiving a kingdom which cannot be moved, let us have grace, whereby we may serve God acceptably with reverence and godly fear" (He.12:28; see 1 Pe. 1:17; Ps.33:8; 89:7; Hab.2:20).*
Goat Hair Covering (Ex.26:7)	*The covering of goat hair symbolized the need for the sin offering and for cleansing. The goat blood was shed, then its hair was used to cover the inner curtain (which symbolized righteousness).* *On the Day of Atonement, Aaron cast lots to decide which of the two goats brought as offerings should be sacrificed as a sin offering for the people. After killing one goat and sprinkling its blood on the altar, Aaron then returned to*	a. Jesus Christ became the *scapegoat* for the world (the One who carried the blackness of sin away from the camp, see Le.16:5-28). b. Instead of allowing the sting of sin to rest upon sinners, Jesus Christ offered Himself up as the Sacrifice, as the Substitute and Savior of the world. A person has to approach God through the shed blood of Christ before he is counted righteous.	*"And one kid of the goats for a sin offering unto the LORD shall be offered, beside the continual burnt offering, and his drink offering" (Nu.28:15).* *"Therefore will I divide him a portion with the great, and he shall divide the spoil with the strong; because he hath poured out his soul unto death: and he was numbered with the transgressors; and he bare the sin of many, and made intercession*

Historical Term	Type or Picture (Scriptural Basis)	Life Application for Today's Believer	Biblical Application for Today's Believer
	the live goat and laid both his hands upon its head. Aaron transferred the sin and wickedness of the Israelites to the goat's head. The live goat was then led outside the camp and turned loose. **"And thou shalt make curtains *of* goats' *hair* to be a covering upon the tabernacle: eleven curtains shalt thou make" (Ex. 26:7).**	A person's sin must be forgiven before he can approach the righteousness of God.	*for the transgressors" (Is.53:12).* *"Who gave himself for our sins, that he might deliver us from this present evil world, according to the will of God and our Father" (Ga.1:4).* *"So Christ was once offered to bear the sins of many; and unto them that look for him shall he appear the second time without sin unto salvation" (He.9:28; see 1 Pe.2:24; 1 Jn.3:5; Re.1:5)*
Ram Skins Dyed Red (Ex.26:14)	*Red, the color of blood, was dyed into the ram's skin, symbolizing the sacrificial blood of Christ* **"And thou shalt make a covering for the tent *of* rams' skins dyed red, and a covering above *of* badgers' skins" (Ex. 26:14).**	⇒ A person must recognize that it is by the blood of Jesus Christ... • that he is cleansed from all sin • that his sins are forgiven • that he is freed from the power of sin • that He has been redeemed • that he is justified • that his conscience is purged from dead works	*"How much more shall the blood of Christ, who through the eternal Spirit offered himself without spot to God, purge your conscience from dead works to serve the living God?" (He.9:14; see Mt.6:28; Acts 20:28; Ro. 5:9).* *"But if we walk in the light, as he is in the light, we have fellowship one with another, and the blood of Jesus Christ his Son cleanseth us from all sin" (1 Jn.1:7).*
The Framework of the Tabernacle (the posts, bases, boards, and crossbars) (Ex.26:15-30; 36:31-33) See also Ex.36:20-34; 40:2, 17-18	*The Framework of the Tabernacle supported all the curtains and coverings. The foundation of the Tabernacle was firmly planted against the shifting sands of the desert (a symbol of the world and its wilderness). Without the support of the Framework, these hangings would have been useless; therefore, the Framework symbolized the picture of the stability and support that Jesus*	⇒ By dying upon the cross and redeeming a person from his sins, Christ became the foundation of redemption for every believer. Christ is our support and stability, our assurance and security. However, a person must call upon Christ in order to receive the benefit of His support and stability. These blessings are not offered to those who	*"Forasmuch as ye know that ye were not redeemed with corruptible things, as silver and gold, from your vain conversation received by tradition from your fathers; But with the precious blood of Christ, as of a lamb without blemish and without spot" (1 Pe. 1:18-19).* *"Being confident of this very thing, that he which hath begun a good work in you*

Historical Term	Type or Picture (Scriptural Basis)	Life Application for Today's Believer	Biblical Application for Today's Believer
	Christ gives the believer. "And thou shalt make boards for the tabernacle of shittim wood standing up. Ten cubits shall be the length of a board, and a cubit and a half shall be the breadth of one board. Two tenons shall there be in one board, set in order one against another: thus shalt thou make for all the boards of the tabernacle" (Ex.26:15). "And he made bars of shittim wood; five for the boards of the one side of the tabernacle, And five bars for the boards of the other side of the tabernacle, and five bars for the boards of the tabernacle for the sides westward. And he made the middle bar to shoot through the boards from the one end to the other" (Ex.36:31-33).	curse, reject, and deny Christ.	*will perform it until the day of Jesus Christ" (Ph.1:6).* *"For I know whom I have believed, and am persuaded that he is able to keep that which I have committed unto him against that day" (2 Ti. 1:12).* *"And the Lord shall deliver me from every evil work, and will preserve me unto his heavenly kingdom: to whom be glory for ever and ever. Amen" (2 Ti. 4:18).* *"Now unto him that is able to keep you from falling, and to present you faultless before the presence of his glory with exceeding joy, To the only wise God our Saviour, be glory and majesty, dominion and power, both now and ever. Amen" (Jude 24-25).*
The Inner Curtain or Veil (Ex.26:31-35; 36:35-36) See also Ex.35:12; 36:35-36; 39;34; 40:3, 21	*The Inner Veil divided the Most Holy Place from the Holy Place. Remember that the Ark of God, the very presence of God Himself, sat in the Most Holy Place. God used the Inner Veil to draw a clear line of separation between Himself and a person, between His holiness and man's sin. Thus the Inner Veil symbolized at least five things:* *a. The Inner Veil symbolized the great separation between God and man.*	What the Inner Veil or Curtain Door taught: a. God is holy and righteous, far, far removed from man and his world—	 *"If I regard iniquity in my heart, the Lord will not hear me" (Ps.66:18).*

Historical Term	Type or Picture (Scriptural Basis)	Life Application for Today's Believer	Biblical Application for Today's Believer
		totally set apart and separated from the pollution and uncleanness of man.	*"And there is none that calleth upon thy name, that stirreth up himself to take hold of thee: for thou hast hid thy face from us, and hast consumed us, because of our iniquities" (Is.64:7; see Ho.5:6).*
	b. The Inner Veil symbolized that God must be approached ever so carefully.	b. God must be approached ever so carefully—in reverence, awe, and fear.	*"And if ye call on the Father, who without respect of persons judgeth according to every man's work, pass the time of your sojourning here in fear" (1 Pe.1:17; see De.10:12; Ec.12:13; Hab.2:20).*
	c. The Inner Veil symbolized that there is only one way into God's presence.	c. There is only one door into God's presence—that door is Jesus Christ.	*"Jesus saith unto him, I am the way, the truth, and the life: no man cometh unto the Father, but by me" (Jn.14:6; see Jn.3:16; 6:68; Ac.4:12).*
	d. The Inner Veil symbolized the entrance into fellowship and communion with God.	d. God rewards those who diligently seek Him and who enter into His presence. He rewards them with the most wonderful fellowship and communion imaginable—with God Himself.	*"And it came to pass, that, while they communed together and reasoned, Jesus himself drew near, and went with them....And they said one to another, Did not our heart burn within us, while he talked with us by the way, and while he opened to us the scriptures?" (Lu.24:15, 32).* *"God is faithful, by whom ye were called unto the fellowship of his Son Jesus Christ our Lord" (1 Co.1:9; see He.11:6; 1 Jn. 1:3; Re.3:20; Je.33:3).*
	e. The Inner Veil symbolized the great need of man for a	e. Jesus Christ fulfilled the symbolism of the Inner Veil.	*"And, behold, the veil of the temple was rent in twain from the*

Historical Term	Type or Picture (Scriptural Basis)	Life Application for Today's Believer	Biblical Application for Today's Believer
	Savior, a Savior who could tear down the wall that separated man from God. "And he made a vail *of* blue, and purple, and scarlet, and fine twined linen: *with* cherubims made he it of cunning work. And he made thereunto four pillars *of* shittim *wood*, and overlaid them with gold: their hooks *were of* gold; and he cast for them four sockets of silver" (Ex.36:35-36).	Remember what happened to the inner veil of the temple when Christ died on the cross: it was torn from top to bottom, symbolizing that God Himself acted, took the initiative, and tore the veil. The heavenly veil that kept a person out of God's presence was torn by Christ when He suffered and died on the cross. We now have eternal access into the presence of God. The door into God's presence is wide open.	*top to the bottom; and the earth did quake, and the rocks rent" (Mt.27:51; see Mk. 15:38; He.2:17; 4:14-15).* *"[Christ] entereth into that within the veil; wither the forerunner is for us entered, even Jesus" (He. 6:19-20; see He.9:24).* *"Having therefore, brethren, boldness to enter into the holiest by the blood of Jesus, by a new and living way, which he hath consecrated for us, through the veil, that is to say, his flesh" (He.10:19-20).*
The Outer Veil or Curtain Door (The Holy Place: The First Room or Outer Sanctuary) (Ex.26:36-37; 36:37-38) See also Ex.35:15; 39:38; 40:6, 29	*The Outer Veil shielded the Sanctuary (i.e., the Holy Place and the Most Holy Place) from the activity of the Courtyard. The Veil prevented people from seeing into the Holy Place to see the worship of God taking place inside the Sanctuary. God has dictated that any worship of Him must be done by coming into His presence, by entering the Holy Place through the Outer Veil, a symbol of the only entrance into God's presence.* "And thou shalt make an hanging for the door of the tent, of blue, and purple, and scarlet, and fine twined linen, wrought with needlework. And thou shalt make for the hanging five pillars of shittim wood, and overlay them	What the Outer Veil or Curtain Door taught: a. The Outer Veil pointed to Jesus Christ as the Way, the entrance into God's presence. Jesus Christ fulfilled the symbolism of this outer curtain. With His shed blood, He invites men to come through the door and worship God. b. Not just any person can come into the presence of God. Nor can a believer come into God's presence, into a deeper knowledge of God, in just any manner. God has spelled out exactly how He expects us to approach Him:	*"Then said Jesus unto them again, Verily, verily, I say unto you, I am the door of the sheep....I am the door: by me if any man enter in, he shall be saved, and shall go in and out, and find pasture" (Jn.10:7, 9).* *"Jesus saith unto him, I am the way, the truth, and the life: no man cometh unto the Father, but by me" (Jn.14:6; see Acts 4:12; Ro.5:2; Ep. 2:8; Mt.7:14).* *"And this is life eternal, that they might know thee the only true God, and Jesus Christ, whom thou hast sent" (Jn.17:3; see Ph.3:10; 1 Co. 1:30).* *"But speaking the truth in love, may grow up into him in all things, which is the*

Historical Term	Type or Picture (Scriptural Basis)	Life Application for Today's Believer	Biblical Application for Today's Believer
	with gold, and their hooks shall be of gold: and thou shalt cast five sockets of brass for them" (Ex.26:36-37). "And he made an hanging for the tabernacle door *of* blue, and purple, and scarlet, and fine twined linen, of needlework; And the five pillars of it with their hooks: and he overlaid their chapiters and their fillets with gold: but their five sockets *were of* brass" (Ex.36:37-38).	through His Son, Jesus Christ. The way to a deeper knowledge of God, to the deeper things of God, is through the Lord Jesus Christ and through Him alone.	*head, even Christ" (Ep.4:15).* *"Study to show thyself approved unto God, a workman that needeth not to be ashamed, rightly dividing the word of truth" (2 Ti.2:15; see He.6:1).* *"As newborn babes, desire the sincere milk of the word, that ye may grow thereby: if so be ye have tasted that the Lord is gracious" (1 Pe.2:2-3).*

CHAPTER SIX

The Altar of Burnt Offering, the Court of the Tabernacle, and the Lampstand: All Symbolizing the True Way to Approach God (Exodus 27:1-21)

Contents

The Altar of Burnt Offering, the Court of the Tabernacle, and the Lampstand: All Symbolizing the True Way to Approach God (Exodus 27:1-21)

1. **The Altar of Burnt Offering: Symbolized the need for atonement, for reconciliation with God**
   a. To make of acacia wood: 7½' x 7½' x 4½' high
   b. To make a horn at each of the four corners: Make all one piece
   c. To overlay the altar with bronze
   d. To make all utensils of bronze
      1) Ash buckets & shovels
      2) Basins & meat hooks
      3) Fire pans
   e. To make a bronze grate
      1) Make four bronze rings for each corner
      2) Place the grate under the ledge, half way up the altar
   f. To make poles of acacia wood
      1) Overlay the poles with bronze
      2) Insert the poles into the rings on each side to carry the altar
   g. To make the altar hollow
   h. The strict instructions: To build the altar exactly as designed
2. **The Courtyard of the Tabernacle: Symbolized that God can be approached**
   a. The mandate: Build the Courtyard
   b. The south side
      1) To be 150' of linen curtains
      2) To make 20 posts that fit into 20 bronze bases
      3) To make silver hooks & bands attached to the posts
   c. The north side
      1) To be 150' of curtains
      2) To have 20 posts that fit into 20 bronze bases

And thou shalt make an altar of shittim wood, five cubits long, and five cubits broad; the altar shall be foursquare: and the height thereof shall be three cubits. 2 And thou shalt make the horns of it upon the four corners thereof: his horns shall be of the same: and thou shalt overlay it with brass. 3 And thou shalt make his pans to receive his ashes, and his shovels, and his basons, and his fleshhooks, and his firepans: all the vessels thereof thou shalt make of brass. 4 And thou shalt make for it a grate of network of brass; and upon the net shalt thou make four brasen rings in the four corners thereof. 5 And thou shalt put it under the compass of the altar beneath, that the net may be even to the midst of the altar. 6 And thou shalt make staves for the altar, staves of shittim wood, and overlay them with brass. 7 And the staves shall be put into the rings, and the staves shall be upon the two sides of the altar, to bear it. 8 Hollow with boards shalt thou make it: as it was showed thee in the mount, so shall they make it. 9 And thou shalt make the court of the tabernacle: for the south side southward there shall be hangings for the court of fine twined linen of an hundred cubits long for one side: 10 And the twenty pillars thereof and their twenty sockets shall be of brass; the hooks of the pillars and their fillets shall be of silver. 11 And likewise for the north side in length there shall be hangings of an hundred cubits long, and his twenty pillars and their twenty

3) To have silver hooks and boards	sockets of brass; the hooks of the pillars and their fillets of silver.	their hooks shall be of silver, and their sockets of brass.
d. The west end	12 And for the breadth of the court	18 The length of the court shall be an hundred cubits, and the breadth fifty every where, and the height five cubits of fine twined linen, and their sockets of brass.	h. The summary
1) To be 75' of curtains	on the west side shall be hangings of		1) The Courtyard: To be 150' x 75' with 7½' high curtain walls
2) To set 10 posts into 10 bases	fifty cubits: their pillars ten, and their sockets ten.		• To be made of fine linen
e. The east end	13 And the breadth of the court on the	19 All the vessels of the tabernacle in all the service thereof, and all the pins thereof, and all the pins of the court, shall be of brass.	• To have bronze bases supporting the walls
1) To be 75' long	east side eastward shall be fifty cubits.		2) The articles used in the work of the Tabernacle, including the tent pegs: Must be bronze
2) To include the entrance to the Courtyard, flanked by two curtains	14 The hangings of one side of the gate shall be fifteen cubits: their pillars three, and their sockets three.		
• Each to be 22½' long	15 And on the other side shall be hangings fifteen cubits:	20 And thou shalt command the children of Israel, that they bring thee pure oil olive beaten for the light, to cause the lamp to burn always.	**3. The Lampstand of the Tabernacle: Symbolized that the way into God's presence is always open**
• Each to be supported by three posts set into three bases	their pillars three, and their sockets three.		a. A command
f. The entrance itself: Make a curtain 30' long	16 And for the gate of the court shall be an hanging of		1) To provide pure olive oil to keep the light burning continually
• To be of fine linen	twenty cubits, of blue, and purple, and	21 In the tabernacle of the congregation without the vail, which is before the testimony, Aaron and his sons shall order it from evening to morning before the LORD: it shall be a statute for ever unto their generations on the behalf of the children of Israel.	2) To place the Lampstand outside the inner curtain of the most Holy Place
• To be decorated, embroidered in blue, purple, & scarlet yarn	scarlet, and fine twined linen, wrought with needlework:		3) To keep the lamps burning in the LORD's presence day & night
• To be attached to four posts set in four bases	and their pillars shall be four, and their sockets four.		b. The great significance of this command: To be a permanent law—kept by all generations
g. The posts of the Courtyard: To be connected by silver bands & hooks	17 All the pillars round about the court shall be filleted with silver;		

In the beginning of time, when God created the first man and woman (Adam and Eve), there were no barriers between God and man. Man had a continuous, unbroken fellowship with God. Man obeyed God, obeyed Him perfectly. God was able to provide everything man needed, able to meet every need of man. But then it happened: man sinned, disobeyed, and rebelled against God. Man squandered the most important thing in the world: the care, fellowship, and guidance of God. At that very moment, the door into God's holy presence slammed shut. Man was banned from entering into God's presence and was destined to be separated from God forever.

But God had a plan for redemption, a plan that would allow man back into His presence again. It was a plan that took years to fulfill; nevertheless, God worked to carry out His plan down through the centuries. One of the first stages of God's plan was revealed in the construction of the Tabernacle. Through the Tabernacle, God allowed the Priests to stand in His presence for the people. But God's people were still far removed from experiencing the close, intimate presence of God, for they could not approach God personally. They had to approach Him through a mediator. But note: the Tabernacle was only a shadow of greater things to come. In God's perfect timing, He planned to send into the world the One Person who could open the door into God's presence, the One Person who could give open access to God anytime, anywhere. That Person is Jesus Christ. Christ alone is the way into God's presence. It is Jesus Christ who cut the path whereby sinful man can once again walk in the presence of God. It is Jesus Christ who fulfilled the symbolism as the door, the door that only He can open. Christ is the only door into the presence of God. This is the emphasis of this section of Scripture. This is: *The Altar of Burnt Offering, the Court of the Tabernacle, and the Lampstand: All Symbolizing the True Way to Approach God*, Ex.27:1-21.

- I.   The Altar of Burnt Offering: symbolized the need for atonement, for reconciliation with God (vv.1-8).
- II. The Courtyard of the Tabernacle: symbolized that God can be approached (vv.9-19).
- III. The Lampstand of the Tabernacle: symbolized that the way into God's presence is always open (vv.20-21).

I. The Altar of Burnt Offering Sat in the Courtyard of the Tabernacle (vv.1-8).

The altar symbolized the need for atonement, for reconciliation with God. As the believer entered into the great Tabernacle of God, the first thing he saw was the Altar of Burnt Offering. It was, no doubt, the focus of attention for all worshippers who entered the Tabernacle. But note: it was an altar for God's people only. The Altar of Burnt Offering was not for the use of anyone outside the family of God. The altar was where God met with His people—a people who needed to atone for their sins. This bronze altar must have been breathtaking to the observer. Blazing with a red hot fire, the altar was surrounded by priests who tended the constant sacrifices. The massive structure could not be ignored. Every man who entered through the gate had to acknowledge its presence, and the altar symbolized the need for atonement, for reconciliation with God through the sacrificial blood of the animal, the animal that was substituted for the life of the offerer. We must always remember this truth: before any man can have a relationship with God, he must come to grips with his need for atonement, for reconciliation with God through the sacrificial blood of the Savior, Jesus Christ. These are the facts of this sanctified altar:

1. The altar was to be made of acacia wood with the following dimensions: it was to be a square altar that was 7½ feet wide by 7½ feet long by 4½ feet high (v.1). Like the other parts of the Tabernacle, acacia wood was chosen for its hardness and its durability. The wood was harder than oak or hickory. Modern wood products like plywood and particle board would have quickly become useless rubbish and ashes in comparison to acacia wood.

Thought
An atonement that does not last, a reconciliation with God that is not enduring, is of no value at all. The philosophies of the world offer many cheap alternatives to becoming right with God. The world teaches that a person can approach God and become acceptable to God...

- by doing the best he can
- by keeping the rules and rituals of religion
- by belonging to a certain religion or church and being faithful
- by believing in the god worshipped by all religions, who is said to be the same god no matter what he may be called
- by following certain men who claim to be prophets of God

The brazen altar declares a different message. Atonement, reconciliation with God—the forgiveness of sin—is necessary in order to approach and become acceptable to God. Man needs a Savior, a Savior who will sacrifice Himself for man. No person can approach God apart from the Savior. The life of the pure, perfect sacrifice has to be given and substituted for man. Blood has to be shed and substituted in order for man to stand acceptable before God. This is the only way of salvation, and Jesus Christ fulfills the message and symbol of the brazen altar.

> **"The next day John seeth Jesus coming unto him, and saith, Behold the Lamb of God, which taketh away the sin of the world" (Jn.1:29).**
>
> **"For if the blood of bulls and of goats, and the ashes of an heifer sprinkling the unclean, sanctifieth to the purifying of the flesh: How much more shall the blood of Christ, who through the eternal Spirit offered himself without spot to God, purge your conscience from dead works to serve the living God?" (He.9:13-14).**
>
> **"And almost all things are by the law purged with blood; and without shedding of blood is no remission. It was therefore necessary that the patterns of things in the heavens should be purified with these; but the heavenly things themselves with better sacrifices than these. For Christ is not entered into the holy places made with hands, which are the figures of the true; but into heaven itself, now to appear in the presence of God for us: Nor yet that he should offer himself often, as the high priest entereth into the holy place every year with blood of others; For then must he often have suffered since the foundation of the world: but now once in the end of the world hath he appeared to put away sin by the sacrifice of himself. And as it is appointed unto men once to die, but after this the judgment: So Christ was once offered to bear the sins of many; and unto them that look for him shall he appear the second time without sin unto salvation" (He.9:22-28; see Mt.26:28).**
>
> **"Forasmuch as ye know that ye were not redeemed with corruptible things, as silver and gold, from your vain conversation [behavior, conduct] received by tradition from your fathers; But with the precious blood of Christ, as of a lamb without blemish and without spot" (1 Pe.1:18-19).**
>
> **"But if we walk in the light, as he is in the light, we have fellowship one with another, and the blood of Jesus Christ his Son cleanseth us from all sin" (1 Jn.1:7).**

2. The altar was to be made with a horn at each of the four corners, made of one piece (v.2). The horns of the altar were symbolic of several truths.
   a. The horns symbolized the altar's *atoning power*, symbolized the fact that God accepted the sacrifice as a substitute for the believer making the offering. This is seen in the ritual of the sacrifice: some of the blood was put on the horns before the rest was poured out at the base of the altar (Ex.29:12; Le.4:7, 18, 25, 30, 34; 8:15; 9:9; 16:18).
   b. The horns symbolized God's *power and strength*.

> **"The adversaries of the LORD shall be broken to pieces; out of heaven shall he thunder upon them: the LORD shall judge the ends of the earth; and he shall give strength unto his king, and exalt the horn of his anointed" (1 S.2:10; see Jos.6:4-6; Ps.75:10).**
>
> **"For thou art the glory of their strength: and in thy favour our horn shall be exalted" (Ps.89:17).**
>
> **"But my faithfulness and my mercy shall be with him: and in my name shall his horn be exalted" (Ps.89:24; see Ps.148:14).**

   c. The horns symbolized God's *salvation*.

"And Aaron shall make an atonement upon the horns of it once in a year with the blood of the sin offering of atonements: once in the year shall he make atonement upon it throughout your generations: it is most holy unto the LORD" (Ex.30:10; see Le.8:15; 16:18; 1 S. 2:1; Ps.118:27).

"And hath raised up an horn of salvation for us in the house of his servant David" (Lu.1:69).

d. The horns symbolized God's *protection, security, sanctuary, help.*

"The God of my rock; in him will I trust: he is my shield, and the horn of my salvation, my high tower, and my refuge, my saviour; thou savest me from violence" (2 S.22:3; see Ps.18:2).

"And Adonijah feared because of Solomon, and arose, and went, and caught hold on the horns of the altar" (1 K.1:50).

"Then tidings came to Joab: for Joab had turned after Adonijah, though he turned not after Absalom. And Joab fled unto the Tabernacle of the LORD, and caught hold on the horns of the altar" (1 K.2:28).

3. The altar was to be overlaid (covered) with bronze (v.2). Overlaying the altar with bronze was an absolute necessity to prevent its consumption by the blazing fires that burned continuously upon the altar. And God was clear in His instructions: the fire must never be allowed to go out.

"The fire shall ever be burning upon the altar; it shall never go out" (Le.6:13).

It is interesting to note God's scientific wisdom in planning the altar, the fact that the altar was built to withstand the tremendous heat. Stephen Olford comments:

The wood overlaid with brass [bronze] constituted a fireproof combination. Only comparatively recently has it been discovered by scientists what an ingenious, fire-resisting invention is hard wood overlaid with copper and hermetically [airtight] sealed. How wonderfully this combination speaks of the Person of our Lord Jesus Christ, who endured the fires of Calvary without being consumed; like the bush which Moses saw in the wilderness which burned with fire but was not destroyed (Exodus 3:1-5). Peter, quoting from Psalm 16, expresses this plainly in his Pentecostal sermon when he declares: 'Thou wilt not...suffer thine Holy One to see corruption' (Ac.2:27).[1]

Thought
Jesus Christ is the only person who could have endured the cross. He and He alone is the *perfect sacrifice.* Anyone else would have been consumed instantly, consumed by the blazing wrath of God's judging sin.

"And the Word [the Son of God] was made flesh, and dwelt among us, (and we beheld his glory, the glory as of the only begotten of the Father,) full of grace and truth" (Jn.1:14; see 2 Co.5:21; He.4:15).

"For such an high priest became us, who is holy, harmless, undefiled, separate from sinners, and made higher than the heavens" (He.7:26).

"Forasmuch as ye know that ye were not redeemed with corruptible things, as silver and gold, from you vain conversation

---

[1] Stephen Olford. *The Tabernacle, Camping With God,* p.93-94.

received by tradition from your fathers; but with the precious blood of Christ, as of a lamb without blemish and without spot" (1 Pe.1:18-19).

4. All of the utensils were to be made of bronze (v.3):
    a. The ash buckets and shovels. The buckets were used to carry the ashes from the altar to a place outside the camp (Le.6:10-11). The shovels were apparently used to collect the burned out embers from the altar.
    b. The basins and meat hooks. The basins were used to collect the blood of the sacrifice which was either sprinkled inside the Sanctuary or poured out at the base of the altar. The meat hooks were most likely three-pronged forks that adjusted the sacrifice upon the altar.
    c. The fire pans. The fire pans held the living coals of the divine fire whenever the altar was being cleaned or moved from campsite to campsite (see Le.6:13; 9:24). The fire pans were also used to carry hot coals from the altar of incense inside the Holy Place (see Le.10:1; 16:12).
5. A bronze grate was to be made (vv.4-5). Special instructions were given for its construction:
    a. Make four bronze rings for each corner.
    b. Place the grate under the ledge, half way up the altar (v.5).
6. Two poles were to be made of acacia wood. They were to be overlaid with bronze. These poles were then inserted into the four rings when the altar was carried (vv.6-7).
7. The altar was to be made hollow (v.8).
8. Note the strict instructions: the altar was to be built exactly as designed (v.8).

Thought 1.
What kind of altar would man have designed? What kind of altar would man build to secure the favor of God, to become acceptable to God? Man's altar would be...

- an altar of religion and ritual
- an altar that allowed doing one's own thing
- an altar of works and good deeds
- an altar that allowed going one's own way
- an altar of doing good and feeling good
- an altar of self-help and self-esteem
- an altar of money and gifts
- an altar of ego-boosters and self-image
- an altar that requires no sacrifice

Thank God He did not trust the design of the altar to man. But He assigned this great task to His Son, the Lord Jesus Christ, who is the Lamb of God.

"In burnt offerings and sacrifices for sin thou hast had no pleasure. Then said I, Lo, I come (in the volume of the book it is written of me,) to do thy will, O God. Above when he said, Sacrifice and offering and burnt offerings and offering for sin thou wouldest not, neither hadst pleasure therein; which are offered by the law; Then said he, Lo, I come to do thy will, O God. He taketh away the first, that he may establish the second. By the which will we are sanctified through the offering of the body of Jesus Christ once for all" (He.10:6-10; see Ep.5:2; Ph.2:8; Jn.3:16; 1 Pe.3:18).

Thought 2.
The Altar of Burnt Offering taught several things:
- ⇒ Substitutionary sacrifice is necessary for the forgiveness of sins.
- ⇒ There is no forgiveness without the shedding of the blood of the sacrifice.
- ⇒ There is no way to approach God—to be saved—other than through the death of a substitute.

Jesus Christ fulfilled the symbolism of the bronze altar.
a) It is Jesus Christ who is the Lamb of God.

> **"The next day John seeth Jesus coming unto him, and saith, Behold the Lamb of God, which taketh away the sin of the world!" (Jn.1:29).**

b) It is Jesus Christ who is the Lamb brought to the slaughter.

> **"He was oppressed, and he was afflicted, yet he opened not his mouth: he is brought as a lamb to the slaughter, and as a sheep before her shearers is dumb, so he openeth not his mouth" (Is.53:7).**

c) It is Jesus Christ who is the Passover Lamb sacrificed for us.

> **"Purge out therefore the old leaven, that ye may be a new lump, as ye are unleavened. For even Christ our passover is sacrificed for us" (1 Co.5:7).**

d) It is Jesus Christ who gave His life as a ransom.

> **"[I] give my life a ransom for many" (Mk.10:45).**

e) It is Jesus Christ who laid down His life for us.

> **"Hereby perceive we the love of God, because he laid down his life for us: and we ought to lay down our lives for the brethren" (1 Jn.3:16).**

II. The Courtyard of the Tabernacle Symbolized That God Can Be Approached (vv.9-19).

The Courtyard served several purposes, all of which were important in the building of the Tabernacle. Remember the overall purpose of the Tabernacle: to be a place where God could dwell with *His* people, a place where people could approach and worship God. The Courtyard served as a hedge between the outside world and the presence of a holy God. A clear line was drawn between the world and God's presence.

The Courtyard was a guard against any unlawful approach. The Tabernacle of God was the holiest site on earth, and not just anyone could enter its sanctified grounds. Only believers, true believers, were to enter. The Courtyard was a protection against wild animals wandering into the Tabernacle. The Courtyard revealed one clear and distinct truth: the only way to enter God's presence is through *one* entrance, *one* gate or door. These are the facts about the Courtyard:

1. The mandate was to build the Courtyard (v.9). God wanted to ensure the safety of the holy furnishings of the Tabernacle by having His people build a protective hedge around the Tabernacle.

2. The south side was to be built with these exact specifications (vv.9-10):
    - ⇒ to be 150 feet of linen curtains
    - ⇒ to make 20 posts to fit into 20 bronze bases
    - ⇒ to make silver hooks and bands attached to the posts

3. The north side was to be built with these exact specifications (v.11):
    - ⇒ to be 150 feet of linen curtains
    - ⇒ to make 20 posts to fit into 20 bronze bases
    - ⇒ to make silver hooks and bands attached to the posts

4. The west end was to be built with these exact specifications (v.12):
    - ⇒ to be 75 feet of curtains
    - ⇒ to set 10 posts into 10 bases

5. The east end was also to be 75 feet long (v.13). Included in the east end was the one and only Courtyard entrance, but note: the entrance (door) to the Tabernacle was large, large enough to receive any person. The entrance was flanked by two curtains. Note their specifications:

⇒ to be 22½ feet long
⇒ to be supported by 3 posts set into 3 bases (vv.14-15)

6. The entrance (door) was to be constructed with one door and only one door (v.16). The curtain was to be 30 feet long and was to be made of fine linen. This curtain was to be decorated, embroidered in blue, purple, and scarlet yarn—the same set of brilliant colors throughout the inner curtains of the sanctuary. The curtain was to be attached to 4 posts set in 4 bases.

7. The posts of the Courtyard were to be connected by silver bands and hooks (v.17).

8. The summary reinforces what has just been revealed to Moses (vv.18-19):
   a. The Courtyard was to be 150 feet by 75 feet with 7½ foot curtain walls made of fine linen. These walls were to be supported by bronze bases.
   b. The articles used in the work of the Tabernacle, including the tent pegs, had to be bronze.

Thought 1.
The walls of the Courtyard teach at least three lessons:
   ⇒ The walls of linen symbolized the righteousness and holiness of God. He is so righteous and holy, so white and pure, that He is set apart from the world.
   ⇒ When a person looks at God, he must see that God dwells in righteousness and holiness. When a person looked at the walls, he was to be reminded that God was holy.
   ⇒ When a person approaches God, he must approach Him in reverence and awe, adoration and worship. He must praise and thank God that God allows him to enter His presence.

Jesus Christ fulfilled the symbolism of the walls of the Courtyard. Jesus Christ is the righteousness of God.

> **"But now the righteousness of God without the law is manifested, being witnessed by the law and the prophets; Even the righteousness of God which is by faith of Jesus Christ unto all and upon all them that believe: for there is no difference" (Ro.3:21-22).**
>
> **"For he hath made him to be sin for us, who knew no sin; that we might be made the righteousness of God in him" (2 Co.5:21).**

Thought 2.
The door or gate into the Tabernacle taught at least two things:
   ⇒ There is only one way to enter God's presence; there are not many ways as most men think and practice.
   ⇒ God has to be approached if a man wishes to live eternally. No person shall ever live with God unless he approaches God exactly as God dictates.

Jesus Christ fulfilled the symbolism of the door or gate.
   ⇒ Jesus Christ is the door, the only door, into God's presence. A man has to approach God through Jesus Christ, through Him and Him alone.

> **"I am the door: by me if any man enter in, he shall be saved, and shall go in and out, and find pasture" (Jn.10:9).**

   ⇒ Jesus Christ is the way, the only way, that a man can approach and come to the Father.

> **"Jesus saith unto him, I am the way, the truth, and the life: no man cometh unto the Father, but by me" (Jn.14:6).**

III. The Lampstand of the Tabernacle Symbolized That the Way into God's Presence Is Always Open (vv.20-21).

Placed in the Holy Place, the Lampstand was the vessel that illuminated the priest's view. Without the Lampstand, the tent would have been a dark, unknown mystery. For the human heart, darkness causes...

- stumbling about
- fear
- confusion
- helplessness
- hopelessness
- false teaching
- false worship
- loneliness
- emptiness

The Lampstand illuminated the way into God's presence, showed people how to walk into His presence. Note the instructions:

1. A command was given to provide pure olive oil to keep the light burning continually (v.20). The lamp of God was to give brilliant, bright, pure light. The source of this light was from the pure olive oil. The oil came from unripened olives that were beaten not crushed. Olives that were beaten or pounded apparently produced a light that was smokeless (or with very little smoke). The Lampstand was to be placed right outside the inner curtain of the Most Holy Place (v.21). This Lampstand was to provide its light continually in the presence of the LORD, both day and night. To keep this command required the constant attention of the priests who would trim the wicks and replenish the olive oil.

2. Note: this command was to be a permanent law—kept by all generations (v.21). This is significant: God's light is for all generations, for every man, woman, and child throughout history.

⇒ When the light of God is hidden from men, the darkness brings destruction and death.

⇒ When God's light is shielded from the acts of sinful men, their hearts become hardened.

⇒ When God's light is extinguished, people follow after false gods.

This is not only a command for Israel, this is also a command for believers today. The light of God must be kept burning or else the world will be lost in darkness.

Thought 1.
Jesus Christ is the true light and His light is never extinguished. His light is always burning...

- to show a person how to approach God and secure His approval
- to show a person how to face the trials of life, no matter how severe they may be
- to show a person how to solve the serious problems of life

> **"In him was life; and the life was the light of men" (Jn.1:4).**
> **"That was the true Light, which lighteth every man that cometh into the world" (Jn.1:9).**
> **"Then spake Jesus again unto them, saying, I am the light of the world: he that followeth me shall not walk in darkness, but shall have the light of life" (Jn.8:12; see 2 Co.4:6; Re.21:23; 22:5).**

Thought 2.
Throughout Scripture oil is a symbol of the Holy Spirit. We must be filled with God's Spirit so people of the world can see Christ and His great love for them. The challenge for every believer is to have a life marked by the fulness of God's Spirit.

a) The believer who is filled with God's Spirit bears a strong witness of love, joy, and peace.

> **"And be not drunk with wine, wherein is excess; but be filled with the Spirit" (Ep.5:18).**
> **"But the fruit of the Spirit is love, joy, peace, longsuffering, gentleness, goodness, faith, meekness, temperance: against such there is no law" (Ga.5:22-23).**

b) The believer who is filled with God's Spirit is a light for all the world to see.

"**Ye are the light of the world. A city that is set on an hill cannot be hid**" **(Mt.5:14).**
"**That ye may be blameless and harmless, the sons of God, without rebuke, in the midst of a crooked and perverse nation, among whom ye shine as lights in the world**" **(Ph.2:15).**

THE TABERNACLE OF MOSES

SECTION OF THE TABERNACLE	WHAT IS TAUGHT	HOW CHRIST FULFILLED THE SYMBOLISM
The Brazen Altar in the Courtyard, 27:1-8	What the altar taught: ⇒ Substitutionary sacrifice is necessary for the forgiveness of sins. ⇒ There is no forgiveness without the shedding of the blood of a sacrifice. ⇒ There is no way to approach God — to be saved — other than through the death of a substitute.	Jesus Christ fulfilled the symbolism of the brazen altar: He sacrificed Himself for us. By His sacrifice our sins are forgiven and we become acceptable to God. *"[I] give my life a ransom for many" (Mk.10:45; see Is.53:7).* *"The next day John seeth Jesus coming unto him, and saith, Behold the Lamb of God, which taketh away the sin of the world!" (Jn.1:29; see 1 Co.5:7; 1 Pe.1:19; 1 Jn.3:16).*
The Walls of the Tabernacle, 27:9-19	What the Walls taught: ⇒ The wall of white linen symbolized the righteousness and holiness of God. He is so righteous and holy, so white and pure, that He is set apart from the world. ⇒ When a person looks at God, he must see that He dwells in righteousness and holiness. (When a person looked at white walls, he was to be reminded that God was holy.) ⇒ When a person approaches God, he must approach Him in reverence and awe, adoration and worship. He must praise and thank God that God allows him to enter His presence.	Jesus Christ fulfilled the symbolism of the Walls: Jesus Christ secured righteousness for us and He makes us acceptable to God, makes it possible for us to approach God in His righteousness. *"For he hath made him to be sin for us, who knew no sin; that we might be made the righteousness of God in him" (2 Co.5:21).* *"And that ye put on the new man [Christ], which after God is created in righteousness and true holiness" (Ep.4:24).* *"And have put on the new man, which is renewed in knowledge after the image of him that created him" (Col.3:10).*
The Only Door or Gate into the Tabernacle, 27:16	What the Door or Gate taught: ⇒ There is only one way to enter God's presence; there are not many ways as most men think and practice.	Jesus Christ fulfilled the symbolism of the Door or Gate: ⇒ Jesus Christ is the door, the only door, that a man can enter to be saved. ⇒ Jesus Christ is the way, the only way, that a man can come to the Father.

SECTION OF THE TABERNACLE	WHAT IS TAUGHT	HOW CHRIST FULFILLED THE SYMBOLISM
	⇒ God has to be approached if a man wishes to live eternally. No person will ever live with God unless he approaches God exactly as God dictates.	*"I am the door: by me if any man enter in, he shall be saved, and shall go in and out, and find pasture" (Jn.10:9).* *"Jesus saith unto him, I am the way, the truth, and the life: no man cometh unto the Father, but by me" (Jn.14:6).*

TYPES, SYMBOLS, AND PICTURES
(Exodus 27:1-21)

Historical Term	Type or Picture (Scriptural Basis)	Life Application for Today's Believer	Biblical Application for Today's Believer
The Horns of the Altar (Ex.27:2) See also The Altar of Burnt Offering—Ex.27:1-8; 35:16; 38:1-7; 39:39; 40:6, 29 See also The Altar of Incense—Ex.30:1-10; 35:15; 37:25-29; 39:38; 40:5, 26-27	*The Altar of Burnt Offering and the Altar of Incense both had horns on each corner. In the whole of Scripture, the horns of both altars are symbolic of four different things:* *a. The horn throughout Scripture is symbolic of power and strength. Therefore, the Horns of the Altar are symbolic of God's power and strength.* **"But my faithfulness and my mercy shall be with him: and in my name shall his horn be exalted" (Ps.89:24).** **"But my horn shalt thou exalt like the horn [power] of an unicorn: I shall be anointed with fresh oil" (Ps.92:10).** **"There will I make the horn [power] of David to bud: I have ordained a lamp for mine anointed" (Ps. 132:17).** *b. The Horns of the Altar are symbolic of the sacrificial and*	a. God alone has the power and strength to deliver His people through all the trials and temptations of life. b. Today, God accepts the sacrifice of Jesus Christ as the	*"And he said, The LORD is my rock, and my fortress, and my deliverer" (2 S.22:2; see Ps.18:17).* *"I sought the LORD, and he heard me, and delivered me from all my fears" (Ps.34:4).* *"For thou hast delivered my soul from death: wilt not thou deliver my feet from falling, that I may walk before God in the light of the living?" (Ps.56:13).* *"And even to your old age I am he; and even to hoar [gray] hairs will I carry you: I have made, and I will bear; even I will carry, and will deliver you" (Is.46:4; see 2 Co.1:10).* *"And Aaron shall make an atonement upon the horns of it*

Historical Term	Type or Picture (Scriptural Basis)	Life Application for Today's Believer	Biblical Application for Today's Believer
	atoning (reconciling) power of the altar. This is seen in that the altar was the place of sacrifice.	substitute for the believer's offering. Jesus Christ Himself is the atoning (reconciling) power that reconciles the believer to God. But note: a person must first call upon the name of the LORD to receive this atoning, reconciling power.	*once in a year with the blood of the sin offering of atonements: once in the year shall he make atonement upon it throughout your generations: it is most holy unto the LORD" (Ex.30:10; see Le.17:11).* *"And not only so, but we also joy in God through our Lord Jesus Christ, by whom we have now received the atonement" (Ro. 5:11).*
	c. The Horns of the Altar are symbolic of God's salvation.	c. God's salvation can be experienced by every person who cries out to the LORD and who pleads for salvation (see Ex.30:10; Ps. 118:27; Lu.1:69).	*"The LORD is my light and my salvation; whom shall I fear? the LORD is the strength of my life; of whom shall I be afraid?" (Ps.27:1; see Ps.37:39).* *"Behold, God is my salvation; I will trust, and not be afraid: for the LORD JEHOVAH is my strength and my song; he also is become my salvation" (Is.12:2; see Zep.3:17).*
	d. The Horns of the Altar are symbolic of God's protection, security, sanctuary, and help **"And thou shalt make the horns of it upon the four corners thereof: his horns shall be of the same: and thou shalt overlay it with brass" (Ex.27:2).**	d. God has promised to hold His people close to His heart and to watch over them, to lead and guide them as they journey to the promised land of heaven. God has promised to provide everything that His dear people need (see 2 S.22:3; Ps.18:2; 1 K.2:28).	*"Thou art my hiding place; thou shalt preserve me from trouble; thou shalt compass me about with songs of deliverance" (Ps.32:7; see 2 S.22:3; 27:5).* *"In the fear of the LORD is strong confidence: and his children shall have a place of refuge" (Pr.14:26; see Pr.18:10).*
Brass (bronze or copper) (Ex.27:2-3)	*Brass was the only metal durable enough to withstand the consuming fires upon the altar. Brass is a symbol of Jesus Christ. Jesus Christ is the only*	⇒ A person can never imagine the magnitude of God's wrath against sin. Nor can any person bear His wrath. Therefore, it is essential that an	*"And his feet like unto fine brass, as if they burned in a furnace; and his voice as the sound of many waters" (Re.1:15).* *"But he was*

Historical Term	Type or Picture (Scriptural Basis)	Life Application for Today's Believer	Biblical Application for Today's Believer
	Person able to bear the consuming fire of God's judgment against sin, the only Person able to bear the judgment of sin for a person. **"And thou shalt make the horns of it upon the four corners thereof: his horns shall be of the same: and thou shalt overlay it with brass. And thou shalt make his pans to receive his ashes, and his shovels, and his basons, and his fleshhooks, and his firepans: all the vessels thereof thou shalt make** *of* **brass" (Ex.27:2-3).**	individual call upon Christ to bear the wrath of coming judgment against him. No person will escape eternal damnation unless he genuinely turns to Christ.	*wounded for our transgressions, he was bruised for our iniquities: the chastisement of our peace was upon him; and with his stripes we are healed"* *(Is.53:5).* *"But we see Jesus, who was made a little lower than the angels for the suffering of death, crowned with glory and honour; that he by the grace of God should taste death for every man" (He.2:9).*
The Courtyard Walls (Ex.27:9-19) See also Ex.35:17; 36:20-34; 38:9-20; 39:33, 40; 40:8, 33	*The Courtyard Walls were walls of linen. Throughout Scripture, fine linen is described as clean and white, speaking of the righteousness of God.* *The Courtyard Walls symbolized the righteousness and holiness of God. God is so holy and righteous, so white and pure, that He is set apart—totally set apart—from the world.* **"The length of the court** *shall be* **an hundred cubits, and the breadth fifty every where, and the height five cubits** *of* **fine twined linen, and their sockets** *of* **brass" (Ex.27:18).**	What the Courtyard Walls taught: ⇒ When a person looks at God, he is to remember that God is holy, that God dwells in righteousness and holiness. Therefore, when a person approaches God, he must approach Him in reverence and awe, adoration and worship. He must praise and thank God that God allows him to enter His presence.	*"Exalt the LORD our God, and worship at his holy hill; for the LORD our God is holy" (Ps.99:9).* *"That he would grant unto us, that we being delivered out of the hand of our enemies might serve him without fear, In holiness and righteousness before him, all the days of our life" (Lu.1:74-75).* *"Having therefore these promises, dearly beloved, let us cleanse ourselves from all filthiness of the flesh and spirit, perfecting holiness in the fear of God" (2 Co.7:1).* *"By him therefore let us offer the sacrifice of praise to God continually, that is, the fruit of our lips giving thanks to his name" (He.13:15; see 1 Pe.2:9).*

Historical Term	Type or Picture (Scriptural Basis)	Life Application for Today's Believer	Biblical Application for Today's Believer
The Door or Gate (Ex.27:16) See also 35:17; 38:18-19; 39:40; 40:33	*There was an opening to the Tabernacle Courtyard. It was a Door that was clearly marked and accessible to any person, large or small, rich or poor who would accept the invitation to enter. However, there was only one Door to enter God's presence. The Door or Gate symbolized at least two things:*	What the Door or Gate taught:	
	a. *The Veil or Door symbolized the great invitation of God, that God invites a person to enter His presence. But note: there is only one door, only one entrance into God's presence.*	a. There is only one way, one door, to enter God's presence. Jesus Christ is that door. There are not many ways as most men think and practice.	*"I am the door: by me if any man enter in, he shall be saved, and shall go in and out, and find pasture" (Jn.10:9; see Ro.5:2).* *"Having therefore, brethren, boldness to enter into the holiest by the blood of Jesus, By a new and living way, which he hath consecrated for us, through the veil, that is to say, his flesh" (He.10:19-20).*
	b. *The Door symbolized that God has to be approached exactly as God dictates.* **"And for the gate of the court shall be an hanging of twenty cubits, of blue, and purple, and scarlet, and fine twined linen, wrought with needlework: and their pillars shall be four, and their sockets four" (Ex.27:16).**	b. God has to be approached exactly as He dictates. No person will ever live with God unless he approaches God in the right way, through His Son, the Lord Jesus Christ.	*"Jesus saith unto him, I am the way, the truth, and the life: no man cometh unto the Father, but by me" (Jn.14:6).* *"For through him [Christ] we both have access by one Spirit unto the Father" (Ep.2:18).* *"Then said Jesus unto them again, Verily, verily, I say unto you, I am the door of the sheep" (Jn.10:7).*
Oil for light (Ex.27:20-21)	*The Priest was to tend to the Lampstand and keep it supplied with oil so the light would never burn out. The oil symbolized the Holy Spirit, the presence of*	⇒ God has promised that the Holy Spirit would always be present with His people, always leading and guiding them to the true	*"And I will put my spirit within you, and cause you to walk in my statutes, and ye shall keep my judgments, and do them" (Eze.36:27).*

Historical Term	Type or Picture (Scriptural Basis)	Life Application for Today's Believer	Biblical Application for Today's Believer
	the Holy Spirit in the life of the follower of God. "And thou shalt command the children of Israel, that they bring thee pure oil olive beaten for the light, to cause the lamp to burn always. In the tabernacle of the congregation without the vail, which *is* before the testimony, Aaron and his sons shall order it from evening to morning before the LORD: *it shall be* a statute for ever unto their generations on the behalf of the children of Israel" (Ex.27:20-21).	light of Jesus Christ. The Holy Spirit will... • show a person how to approach God and secure His approval • show a person how to face the trials of life, no matter how severe they may be • show a person how to solve the serious problems of life	*"And I will pray the Father, and he shall give you another Comforter, that he may abide with you for ever; Even the Spirit of truth; whom the world cannot receive, because it seeth him not, neither knoweth him: but ye know him; for he dwelleth with you, and shall be in you"* (Jn.14:16-17). *"But if the Spirit of him that raised up Jesus from the dead dwell in you, he that raised up Christ from the dead shall also quicken your mortal bodies by his Spirit that dwelleth in you....For as many as are led by the Spirit of God, they are the sons of God"* (Ro.8:11, 14; see Ro. 8:9; 1 Co. 6:19-20; Ps.23:5; He. 1:9; Js.5:14).

CHAPTER SEVEN

The Garments of the Priests:
The Symbol of Bringing Dignity and Honor to the Name of God
(Exodus 28:1-43)

Contents

The Garments of the Priests:
The Symbol of Bringing Dignity and Honor to the Name of God
(Exodus 28:1-43)

1. The call of the priests
a. The source of the call: God—God Himself called Aaron & his sons
b. The purpose of the call
  1) To set the priests apart from all other people
  2) To serve God
c. The symbol of the High Priests' special call: His clothing—to stir dignity & honor for God's call
  1) Skilled people were appointed to make the special garments
 	
  2) The garments
    • A chestpiece or breast-piece
    • An ephod
    • A robe
    • A woven tunic
    • A turban
    • A sash
	And take thou unto thee Aaron thy brother, and his sons with him, from among the children of Israel, that he may minister unto me in the priest's office, even Aaron, Nadab and Abihu, Eleazar and Ithamar, Aaron's sons. 2 And thou shalt make holy garments for Aaron thy brother for glory and for beauty. 3 And thou shalt speak unto all that are wise hearted, whom I have filled with the spirit of wisdom, that they may make Aaron's garments to consecrate him, that he may minister unto me in the priest's office. 4 And these are the garments which they shall make; a breastplate, and an ephod, and a robe, and a broidered coat, a mitre, and a girdle: and they shall make holy garments for Aaron thy brother, and his sons, that he may minister unto	me in the priest's office. 5 And they shall take gold, and blue, and purple, and scarlet, and fine linen. 6 And they shall make the ephod of gold, of blue, and of purple, of scarlet, and fine twined linen, with cunning work. 7 It shall have the two shoulderpieces thereof joined at the two edges thereof; and so it shall be joined together. 8 And the curious girdle of the ephod, which is upon it, shall be of the same, according to the work thereof; even of gold, of blue, and purple, and scarlet, and fine twined linen. 9 And thou shalt take two onyx stones, and grave on them the names of the children of Israel: 10 Six of their names on one stone, and the other six names of the rest on the other stone,	3) The materials
			  • Yarn: Gold, blue, purple, & scarlet
			  • Fine linen
			2. The ephod: A sleeveless, coat-like garment
			a. The materials
			  1) Yarn: Gold, blue, purple, & scarlet
			  2) Fine linen
			b. The design
			  1) To be in two pieces, front & back, joined by two straps at the shoulder
			  2) To have a sash or waistband: Made of the same materials
			
			  3) To take two onyx stones & engrave Israel's tribes on them
			
			    • Six names on one stone & six names on the other stone: In the

Outline:

order of their birth
- Engrave just as a gemcutter engraves a seal
- Mount the stones in gold settings

- Fasten the stones to the shoulder pieces of the ephod

c. The purpose of the ephod & stones: To symbolize that the priest represented & carried the name of God's people before the LORD

d. The design continued
1) Make all settings gold
2) Make two chains of pure gold: Attach to the settings

1. The breastpiece or chestpiece: A pouch-like garment used to determine God's will

a. The basic materials: The same as the ephod garment

b. The design
1) To be 9" square, folded double, forming a pouch

2) To attach four rows of precious stones on it

Scripture:

according to their birth. 11 With the work of an engraver in stone, like the engravings of a signet, shalt thou engrave the two stones with the names of the children of Israel: thou shalt make them to be set in ouches of gold. 12 And thou shalt put the two stones upon the shoulders of the ephod for stones of memorial unto the children of Israel: and Aaron shall bear their names before the LORD upon his two shoulders for a memorial. 13 And thou shalt make ouches of gold; 14 And two chains of pure gold at the ends; of wreathen work shalt thou make them, and fasten the wreathen chains to the ouches. 15 And thou shalt make the breastplate of judgment with cunning work; after the work of the ephod thou shalt make it; of gold, of blue, and of purple, and of scarlet, and of fine twined linen, shalt thou make it. 16 Foursquare it shall be being doubled; a span shall be the length thereof, and a span shall be the breadth thereof. 17 And thou shalt set in it settings of stones, even four rows of stones: the first row shall be a sardius, a topaz, and a carbuncle: this shall be the first row. 18 And the second row shall be an emerald, a sapphire, and a diamond. 19 And the third row a ligure, an agate, and an amethyst. 20 And the fourth row a beryl, and an onyx, and a jasper: they shall be set in gold in their inclosings. 21 And the stones shall be with the names of the children of Israel, twelve, according to their names, like the engravings of a signet; every one with his name shall they be according to the twelve tribes. 22 And thou shalt make upon the breastplate chains at the ends of wreathen work of pure gold. 23 And thou shalt make upon the breastplate two rings of gold, and shalt put the two rings on the two ends of the breastplate. 24 And thou shalt put the two wreathen chains of gold the two rings which are on the ends of the breastplate. 25 And the other two ends of the two wreathen chains thou shalt fasten in the two ouches, and put them on the shoulderpieces of the ephod before it. 26 And thou shalt make two rings of gold, and thou shalt

Notes:

- The 1st row of stones
- The 2nd row of stones
- The 3rd row of stones
- The 4th row of stones
- To set the stones in gold
- To number 12 stones, one for each of the 12 tribes of Israel
- To engrave the names of the 12 tribes on the stones as a seal

3) To attach the chestpiece to the ephod
- Make braided chains of pure gold
- Make two gold rings: Attach to the top corners of the chestpiece—for the gold cords to go through—tie the cords to the gold settings on the shoulder pieces of the ephod garment

- Make two more gold rings: Attach to the

other two ends of the chest-piece—on the inside next to the ephod garment

• Make two other gold rings: Attach to the ephod garment near the sash

• Tie the rings of the chest-piece to the rings of the ephod with blue cord: To hold the two securely together

c. The purpose for the chestpiece

1) To symbolize that the High Priest represented & carried the names of God's people upon his heart, that he represented them before the Lord continually

2) To hold the urim & thummim (probably two stones or lots) next to the High Priest's heart: Symbolized the High Priest's seeking God's will for the people

4. The robe of the ephod: A long, sleeveless, solid blue robe

put them upon the two ends of the breastplate in the border thereof, which is in the side of the ephod inward. 27 And two other rings of gold thou shalt make, and shalt put them on the two sides of the ephod underneath, toward the forepart thereof, over against the other coupling thereof, above the curious girdle of the ephod. 28 And they shall bind the breastplate by the rings thereof unto the rings of the ephod with a lace of blue, that it may be above the curious girdle of the ephod, and that the breastplate be not loosed from the ephod. 29 And Aaron shall bear the names of the children of Israel in the breastplate of judgment upon his heart, when he goeth in unto the holy place, for a memorial before the LORD continually. 30 And thou shalt put in the breastplate of judgment the Urim and the Thummim; and they shall be upon Aaron's heart, when he goeth in before the LORD: and Aaron shall bear the judgment of the children of Israel upon his heart before the LORD continually. 31 And thou shalt make the robe of the ephod all of blue.

32 And there shall be an hole in the top of it, in the midst thereof: it shall have a binding of woven work round about the hole of it, as it were the hole of an habergeon, that it be not rent. 33 And beneath upon the hem of it thou shalt make pomegranates of blue, and of purple, and of scarlet, round about the hem thereof; and bells of gold between them round about: 34 A golden bell and a pomegranate, a golden bell and a pomegranate, upon the hem of the robe round about. 35 And it shall be upon Aaron to minister: and his sound shall be heard when he goeth in unto the holy place before the LORD, and when he cometh out, that he die not. 36 And thou shalt make a plate of pure gold, and grave upon it, like the engravings of a signet, HOLINESS TO THE LORD. 37 And thou shalt put it on a blue lace, that it may be upon the mitre; upon the forefront of the mitre it shall be. 38 And it shall be upon Aaron's forehead, that Aaron may bear the iniquity of the holy things, which the children of Israel shall hallow in all their holy gifts; and

a. Make an opening for the head in the center: Reinforce the opening with a woven collar so it will not tear

b. Make pomegranates out of yarn: Blue, purple, scarlet yarn

1) Attach them to the hem of the robe with gold bells between them

2) Alternate the pomegranates & bells

c. The symbolic purpose:

1) To sound forth the intercessory ministry of the High Priest

2) To sound forth the acceptance of the offering of the High Priest, that he had not been stricken dead

5. **The gold medallion worn on the turban (a headdress cloth or cap)**

a. To be engraved with these words: HOLY TO THE LORD

b. To be attached to the front of the turban by a blue cord

c. The purpose

1) To symbolize that the High Priest bore the guilt for the shortcomings & errors of the people

2) To symbolize that the people must seek the acceptance of a holy God	it shall be always upon his forehead, that they may be accepted before the LORD.	them, and sanctify them, that they may minister unto me in the priest's office.	then ordained
6. The final instructions governing the clothing	39 And thou shalt embroider the coat of fine linen, and thou shalt make the mitre of fine linen, and thou shalt make the girdle of needlework.	42 And thou shalt make them linen breeches to cover their nakedness; from the loins even unto the thighs they shall reach:	e. The linen underclothing
a. The turban & tunic (a long coat-like garment): Make of fine linen			1) To be worn next to the body, covering the priest from the waist to the thigh
b. The sash (worn around the waist): To be embroidered	40 And for Aaron's sons thou shalt make coats, and thou shalt make for them girdles, and bonnets shalt thou make for them, for glory and for beauty.	43 And they shall be upon Aaron, and upon his sons, when they come in unto the tabernacle of the congregation, or when they come near unto the altar to minister in the holy place; that they bear not iniquity, and die: it shall be a statute for ever unto him and his seed after him.	2) Always to be worn when serving God
c. The clothing for the other priests 1) To be tunics, sashes, & headdresses			3) The purpose: Modesty & purity
2) The purpose: To set them apart for dignity & respect	41 And thou shalt put them upon Aaron thy brother, and his sons with him; and shalt anoint them, and consecrate		• To cover their nakedness • To keep from arousing God's anger & judgment against immodesty & immorality
d. The priests were to be clothed in the special garments,			

Respect, dignity, and honor are virtues missing in today's society. Few people show respect and honor to others, even to those in the highest positions of rule and authority. Tragically, the reason is often because those in authority live such deceptive and immoral lives. They destroy the honor due their position.

This must never be so with the people of God. Whatever believers do reflects upon the name of God. And God deserves the highest respect, the highest dignity and honor. Therefore, believers must live lives that demand respect, dignity, and honor. When people look upon a believer, the life of the believer must point people to God, to God's willingness to forgive and help them. The believer's life must stir people to respect and honor God. This is the subject of this passage: *The Garments of the Priests: The Symbol of Bringing Dignity and Honor to the Name of God,* Ex. 28:1-43.

I. The call of the priests (vv.1-5).
II. The ephod: a sleeveless, coat-like garment (vv.6-14).
III. The breastpiece or chestpiece: a pouch-like garment used to determine God's will (vv.15-30).
IV. The robe of the ephod: a long, sleeveless, solid blue robe (vv.31-35).
V. The gold medallion worn on the turban (a headdress cloth or cap) (vv.36-38).
VI. The final instructions governing the clothing (vv.39-43).

I. There Was the Call of the Priests (vv.1-5).

God called and set apart Aaron and his sons to serve Him in a special way. God selected these men from the masses of humanity to serve Him and Him alone. Note the details of this call:

1. The source of the call was God. God Himself called Aaron and his sons (v. 1). It was God who took the initiative and did the calling. The idea to serve God as a priest did not come from Moses nor from Aaron and his sons. The idea was God's alone. When God calls a person, any person, it is...

- God who *makes* the choice
- God who *equips* His choice
- God who *empowers* His choice
- God who *sends forth* His choice

2. The purpose of the call was to set the priests apart from all other people, to set them apart so they could serve God. Note: the call was given so they could "serve God as priests" (v.1). Scripture says that their work included five activities:

⇒ They were to offer gifts and sacrifices for sin.

"For every high priest taken from among men is ordained for men in things pertaining to God, that he may offer both gifts and sacrifices for sins" (He.5:1).
"Who needeth not daily, as those high priests, to offer up sacrifice, first for his own sins, and then for the people's: for this he did once, when he offered up himself" (He.7:27).

⇒ They were to show compassion for the ignorant and for people who go astray.

"Who can have compassion on the ignorant, and on them that are out of the way; for that he himself also is compassed with infirmity" (He.5:2).

⇒ They were to teach the people.

"And Ezra the priest brought the law before the congregation both of men and women, and all that could hear with understanding, upon the first day of the seventh month....And Nehemiah, which is the Tirshatha, and Ezra the priest the scribe, and the Levites that taught the people, said unto all the people, This day is holy unto the LORD your God; mourn not, nor weep. For all the people wept, when they heard the words of the law" (Ne.8:2, 9).

⇒ They were to be representatives of God, mediators between God and man.

"And he shall bring his trespass offering unto the LORD, a ram without blemish out of the flock, with thy estimation, for a trespass offering, unto the priest: And the priest shall make an atonement for him before the LORD: and it shall be forgiven him for any thing of all that he hath done in trespassing therein" (Le.6:6-7).
"For on that day shall the priest make an atonement for you, to cleanse you, that ye may be clean from all your sins before the LORD" (Le.16:30).

⇒ They were to pray and make strong intercession for the people.

"Aaron shall bear their names [of God's people] before the LORD upon his two shoulders for a memorial" (Ex.28:12).
"And they truly were many priests [who made intercession], because they were not suffered to continue by reason of death: But this man, because he continueth ever, hath an unchangeable priesthood. Wherefore he is able also to save them to the uttermost that come unto God by him, seeing he ever liveth to make intercession for them" (He.7:23-25).

Thought

The greatest privilege in all the world is to be called by God to serve God. Note what Scripture says about God's call.

a) The call of God is made possible because of the gospel.

> "Whereunto he called you by our gospel, to the obtaining of the glory of our Lord Jesus Christ" (2 Th.2:14).

b) The call of God is a call to salvation, a holy calling, not based upon a man's ministry but upon God's very own purpose.

> "Who hath saved us, and called us with an holy calling, not according to our works, but according to his own purpose and grace, which was given us in Christ Jesus before the world began" (2 Ti.1:9).

c) The call of God is a heavenly calling.

> "Wherefore, holy brethren, partakers of the heavenly calling, consider the Apostle and High Priest of our profession, Christ Jesus" (He.3:1).

d) The call of God is a call to the kingdom and glory of God, His eternal glory.

> "But the God of all grace, who hath called us unto his eternal glory by Christ Jesus, after that ye have suffered a while, make you perfect, stablish, strengthen, settle you" (1 Pe.5:10).
> "That ye would walk worthy of God, who hath called you unto his kingdom and glory" (1 Th.2:12).

e) The call of God involves a glorious hope.

> "The eyes of your understanding being enlightened; that ye may know what is the hope of his calling, and what the riches of the glory of his inheritance in the saints" (Ep.1:18).

f) The call of God requires a person to walk worthy of God.

> "That ye would walk worthy of God, who hath called you unto his kingdom and glory" (1 Th.2:12).

g) The call of God demands faithfulness, personal responsibility.

> "I therefore, the prisoner of the Lord, beseech you that ye walk worthy of the vocation wherewith ye are called" (Ep.4:1).
> "Moreover it is required in stewards, that a man be found faithful" (1 Co.4:2).

h) The call of God demands careful diligence.

> "Wherefore the rather, brethren, give diligence to make your calling and election sure: for if ye do these things, ye shall never fall" (2 Pe.1:10).

i) The call of God is a high calling, the ultimate goal for life.

> "I press toward the mark for the prize of the high calling of God in Christ Jesus" (Ph.3:14).

j) The call of God is unique, personal, individual, one of a kind.

> **"For ye see your calling, brethren, how that not many wise men after the flesh, not many mighty, not many noble, are called" (1 Co.1:26).**

3. The symbol of the High Priest's special call was his clothing (vv.2-5). The purpose of his clothing was to stir dignity and honor for God's call and for the Priestly office. The charge was to make holy garments for a man who would personally minister to a holy God. Note the special instructions for making these holy garments:
  a. Skilled people were appointed to make the special garments (v.3). Note that they were equipped for their work by God Himself, equipped with special wisdom and ability.
  b. The garments were...
   - a chestpiece or breastpiece
   - a robe
   - a turban
   - an ephod
   - a woven tunic
   - a sash (v.4)

  c. The materials used were gold thread embroidered into the garments and multicolored yarn (blue, purple, and scarlet) that was spun and made a part of the garments along with fine linen (v.5).

Thought
When the High Priest *put on* these holy garments, it lent dignity to his work. In the same sense, when the believer *puts on holy garments,* it also lends dignity to his work for the Lord.
  ⇒ The believer is to put on Christ.

> **"For as many of you as have been baptized into Christ have put on Christ" (Ga.3:27).**

  ⇒ The believer is to put on the new man.

> **"And that ye put on the new man, which after God is created in righteousness and true holiness" (Ep.4:24).**
> **"And have put on the new man, which is renewed in knowledge after the image of him that created him" (Col.3:10).**

  ⇒ The believer is to put on the armor of God, the whole armor.

> **"Put on the whole armour of God, that ye may be able to stand against the wiles of the devil" (Ep.6:11).**

  ⇒ The believer is to put on the armor of light.

> **"The night is far spent, the day is at hand: let us therefore cast off the works of darkness, and let us put on the armour of light" (Ro.13:12).**

  ⇒ The believer is to put on love.

> **"And above all these things put on charity, which is the bond of perfectness" (Col.3:14).**

  ⇒ The believer is to put on compassion, kindness, humility, gentleness, and patience.

"Put on therefore, as the elect of God, holy and beloved, bowels of mercies, kindness, humbleness of mind, meekness, longsuffering" (Col.3:12).

⇒ The believer is to put on incorruption and immortality.

"For this corruptible must put on incorruption, and this mortal must put on immortality. So when this corruptible shall have put on incorruption, and this mortal shall have put on immortality, then shall be brought to pass the saying that is written, Death is swallowed up in victory" (1 Co.15:53-54).

II. There Was the Ephod, a Sleeveless, Coat-like Garment (vv.6-14).

This was the first garment to be made.

1. The ephod was made of the following materials: gold thread made from thin gold sheets cut into thin, thread-like wires (see Ex.39:3); yarn that was blue, purple, and scarlet (v.6); and fine linen.
2. The design of the ephod was spelled out with these instructions:
    a. It was to be in two pieces, front and back, joined by two straps at the shoulder (v.7).
    b. It was to have a sash or waistband that was made of the same materials (v.8).
    c. It was to have two onyx stones that had Israel's 12 tribes engraved on them (v.9). Six names were to be engraved on each stone in the order of their birth (v.10). Each stone was to be engraved just as a gem-cutter engraves a seal (v.11). The maker of the ephod was to mount the stones in gold settings and then fasten the stones to the shoulder pieces of the ephod (vv.11-12).
3. The purpose of the ephod and stones was to symbolize that the priest represented and carried the name of God's people before the Lord as their *mediator and intercessor* (v.12).
4. The design for the ephod continued with two final points of instruction:
    a. To make all settings gold (v.13).
    b. To make two chains of pure gold and attach these to the settings (v.14).

Thought

Jesus Christ is the One who represents and carries the name of every believer before the LORD God. Jesus Christ is our *Mediator and Intercessor.* No matter what our burden, no matter how heavy or terrifying the burden may be, we can cast it upon Christ. Christ will relieve us, strengthen us, give us peace and rest from the burden. The heavy burdens of the soul need to be freely cast upon His strong, never-failing shoulders. There is no burden that can ever weigh Him down.

"Come unto me, all ye that labour and are heavy laden, and I will give you rest. Take my yoke upon you, and learn of me; for I am meek and lowly in heart: and ye shall find rest unto your souls. For my yoke is easy, and my burden is light" (Mt.11:28-30; see Ro.8:34).

"Wherefore in all things it behooved him to be made like unto his brethren, that he might be a merciful and faithful high priest in things pertaining to God, to make reconciliation for the sins of the people. For in that he himself hath suffered being tempted, he is able to succour them that are tempted" (He.2:17-18; see He.4:15-16).

"Wherefore he is able also to save them to the uttermost that come unto God by him, seeing he ever liveth to make intercession for them" (He.7:25; see 1 Pe.5:7).

III. There Was the Breastpiece or Chestpiece, a Pouch-like Garment Used to Determine God's Will (vv.15-30).

The breastpiece was an ornate, square piece of cloth made of the same materials as the ephod. These are the instructions as to how it was to be made:

1. The basic materials were the same as the ephod garment (v.15).
2. The design of the breastpiece or chestpiece is outlined for simplicity:
   a. To be 9" square, folded double, forming a pouch (v.16).
   b. To have attached 4 rows of precious stones on it, which numbered a total of 12 (vv.17-20). Each one of the 12 stones was attached to a gold setting (v.21). The 12 stones represented the 12 tribes of Israel and were identified by engraving the names of the 12 tribes on the stones as a seal (v.21).
   c. To attach the chestpiece to the ephod—permanently (vv.22-28).
      • Make braided chains of pure gold (v.22)
      • Make 2 gold rings: attach to the top corners of the chestpiece—for the gold cords to go through—tie the cords to the gold settings on the shoulder pieces of the ephod garment (vv.23-25)
      • Make 2 more gold rings: attach to the other 2 ends of the chestpiece—on the inside next to the ephod garment (v.26)
      • Make 2 other gold rings: attach to the ephod garment near the sash (v.27)
      • Tie the rings of the chestpiece to the rings of the ephod with blue cord: to hold the 2 securely together (v.28)

3. The purpose for the chestpiece or breastpiece was twofold (vv.29-30):
   a. To symbolize that the High Priest represented and carried the names of God's people upon his heart, that he represented them before the LORD continually (v.29).

   #### Thought
   Jesus Christ knows us by name, everyone of us. Christ does not know us as a number, a statistic, or a program goal. He knows each one of us individually and personally. This means that Jesus Christ cares for us. He cares about the trials, temptations, and sufferings that afflict us.

   > "Fear not: for I have redeemed thee, I have called thee by thy name; thou art mine" (Is.43:1).
   > "Casting all your care upon him; for he careth for you" (1 Pe.5:7).
   > "But I am poor and needy; yet the LORD thinketh upon me: thou art my help and my deliverer; make no tarrying, O my God" (Ps.40:17; see Is.41:10).
   > "When thou passest through the waters, I will be with thee; and through the rivers, they shall not overflow thee: when thou walkest through the fire, thou shalt not be burned; neither shall the flame kindle upon thee" (Is.43:2).

   b. The second purpose of the chestpiece was to hold the urim and thummim (probably two stones or lots) next to the High Priest's heart (v.30). This symbolized the High Priest's seeking God's will for the people. The Hebrew word for *urim* is uncertain. It means either *lights* or *curse*. *Thummim* means perfection. What these two stones looked like and how they were used is not known. Some scholars feel they were used as dice or lots, that they were cast upon the ground with a decision's being made based upon which stone turned up a certain way. However, this seems unlikely; it is just contrary to the way God works throughout Scripture. God reveals His will. He does not base it upon the turn of stones like dice. Perhaps *The Expositor's Bible Commentary* is closer to the truth:

Perhaps they only symbolized the special revelation open to the high priest rather than being the necessary means of achieving that information.[1]

Imagine the scene as the High Priest entered into the Holy Place. The urim and thummim reminded him and the people that God would speak, giving His direction to His people. The High Priest was there on behalf of the people of God; therefore, God would hear and answer him. God would make His will and direction known to the High Priest. How? God would speak and move upon the heart of the High Priest.

Thought
We are to pray and seek God's face for the needs of others. The world reels under the weight of suffering and evil, of death and judgment to come. The only hope is God. God's help is needed. We must therefore seek His face, seek Him day and night.

> **"Seek the LORD and his strength, seek his face continually" (1 Chr.16:11; see De.4:29; Ps.91:15; Is.55:6).**
>
> **"And it shall come to pass, that before they call, I will answer; and while they are yet speaking, I will hear" (Is.65:24; see Je.33:3).**
>
> **"And I say unto you, Ask, and it shall be given you; seek, and ye shall find; knock, and it shall be opened unto you" (Lu.11:9; see Lu.18:1).**
>
> **"Praying always with all prayer and supplication in the Spirit, and watching thereunto with all perseverance and supplication for all saints" (Ep.6:18).**

IV. There Was the Robe of the Ephod, a Long, Sleeveless, Solid Blue Robe (vv.31-35).

These are the instructions that were given:
1. Make an opening for the head in the center. The opening was to be reinforced with a woven collar so it would not tear (v.32).
2. Make pomegranates out of yarn in the colors of blue, purple, and scarlet (v.33). These pomegranates of yarn were attached to the hem of the robe with gold bells between them. The pattern was a pomegranate and a bell alternated at the hem of the robe (v.34).
3. The symbolic purpose of the robe was twofold:
   a. The first symbol was to sound forth the *intercessory ministry* of the High Priest (v.35). Before the High Priest could minister before the LORD, he had to slip on this robe. After he was fully dressed in the priestly garments, the tinkling of the bells marked his every step. The sound of the bells told the people where he was as he carried their names before the LORD. As he ministered in their behalf, they could follow his intercessory ministry as he moved about the various rituals of worship. As he carried out a particular ritual, the people would obviously meditate and pray over the truth symbolized by the ritual. The pomegranate fruit, traditionally known for its beautiful flower and fertility, symbolized the beauty and fruitfulness of the priest's intercessory ministry.
   b. The second symbol was to sound forth a wonderful fact: that *God accepted the offering* of the High Priest, that he had not been stricken dead (v.35). The sound of the bells let the people know that he was alive and ministering on their behalf. Every time the High Priest went into the Holy Place, there was always the chance that his offering would not be acceptable to God. When a Holy God is approached by an unholy offering, death is always the final consequence (always spiritual death; sometimes physical death).

---

[1] Frank E. Gaebelein. *Expositor's Bible Commentary*, Vol.2, p.467.

Thought 1.
Jesus Christ is the great High Priest who fulfills the intercessory ministry of the High Priest. Jesus Christ intercedes for us at the throne of God, and His intercessory ministry never stops.

⇒ Jesus Christ makes intercession for us at the right hand of God.

> **"Who is he that condemneth? It is Christ that died, yea rather, that is risen again, who is even at the right hand of God, who also maketh intercession for us" (Ro.8:34).**

⇒ Jesus Christ lives forever and makes intercession for those He has saved.

> **"Wherefore he is able also to save them to the uttermost that come unto God by him, seeing he ever liveth to make intercession for them" (He.7:25).**

⇒ Jesus Christ makes intercession for the sinner.

> **"Therefore will I divide him a portion with the great, and he shall divide the spoil with the strong; because he hath poured out his soul unto death: and he was numbered with the transgressors; and he bare the sin of many, and made intercession for the transgressors" (Is.53:12).**

⇒ Jesus Christ makes intercession for those who are weak and ready to fail.

> **"But I have prayed for thee, that thy faith fail not: and when thou art converted, strengthen thy brethren" (Lu.22:32).**

⇒ Jesus Christ makes intercession even for His enemies.

> **"Then said Jesus, Father, forgive them; for they know not what they do. And they parted his raiment, and cast lots" (Lu.23:34).**

⇒ Jesus Christ makes intercession for the church, for all believers throughout all generations.

> **"I pray for them: I pray not for the world, but for them which thou hast given me; for they are thine" (Jn.17:9).**

Thought 2.
Jesus Christ offered Himself to God in five significant ways:
a) Jesus Christ offered Himself as the perfect offering of righteousness, as the Just for the unjust.

> **"For Christ also hath once suffered for sins, the just for the unjust, that he might bring us to God, being put to death in the flesh, but quickened by the Spirit" (1 Pe.3:18).**

b) Jesus Christ offered Himself as the perfect sacrifice, as the Lamb of God.

> **"The next day John seeth Jesus coming unto him, and saith, Behold the Lamb of God, which taketh away the sin of the world" (Jn.1:29).**

c) Jesus Christ offered Himself as the perfect High Priest, as the One who intercedes for man.

> **"But this man, because he continueth ever, hath an unchangeable priesthood. Wherefore he is able also to save them to the uttermost that come unto God by him, seeing he ever liveth to make intercession for them" (He.7:24-25).**

d) Jesus Christ offered Himself as the resurrected Savior, as the One who lives forevermore.

> **"For I delivered unto you first of all that which I also received, how that Christ died for our sins according to the scriptures; And that he was buried, and that he rose again the third day according to the scriptures" (1 Co.15:3-4; see 1 Th.4:16-17).**

e) Jesus Christ offered Himself as the exalted Lord, as the One who is seated at the right hand of God.

> **"So then after the Lord had spoken unto them, he was received up into heaven, and sat on the right hand of God" (Mk.16:19; see Lu.22:69; Ep.1:20).**
> **"Wherefore God also hath highly exalted him, and given him a name which is above every name" (Ph.2:9; see Re.5:12).**

V. There Was the Gold Medallion Worn on the Turban (a Headdress Cloth or Cap) (vv.36-38).

The gold medallion was the most significant piece of the turban. Note the special instructions for the gold medallion:
1. The gold medallion was to be engraved with these words: HOLY TO THE LORD (v.36). What a great proclamation to wear! It is important to note where this medallion was to be worn: on the forehead, right where it would attract attention. It was probably the first item to attract people.

Thought
What a great difference in the behavior of believers if "HOLY TO THE LORD" were strapped to their foreheads. Pressed next to the mind, the gold medallion would be a constant reminder for the believer to live a holy life. Yet this is the very thing we must do, do mentally, do diligently. We must live holy lives.
a) We must put no worthless thing before our eyes.

> **"I will set no wicked thing before mine eyes: I hate the work of them that turn aside; it shall not cleave to me" (Ps.101:3).**

b) We must guard and restrain our tongues.

> **"Keep thy tongue from evil, and thy lips from speaking guile [deceit]" (Ps.34:13).**

c) We must think only upon things that are pure and holy.

> **"Finally, brethren, whatsoever things are true, whatsoever things are honest, whatsoever things are just, whatsoever things are pure, whatsoever things are lovely, whatsoever things are of good report; if there be any virtue, and if there be any praise, think on these things" (Ph.4:8).**

d) We must live lives that are HOLY TO THE LORD.

> **"For I am the LORD that bringeth you up out of the land of Egypt, to be your God: ye shall therefore be holy, for I am holy" (Le.11:45).**
> **"Having therefore these promises, dearly beloved, let us cleanse ourselves from all filthiness of the flesh and spirit, perfecting holiness in the fear of God" (2 Co.7:1; see Ep.4:24; He.12:14; 1 Pe.1:16; 2 Pe.3:11).**

2. The gold medallion was to be attached to the front of the turban by a blue cord (v.37).
3. The purpose of the medallion was twofold (v.38):
   a. To symbolize that the High Priest bore the guilt for the shortcomings and errors of the people as they presented their offerings to God (v.38). The people came short—ever so short—of the glory and holiness of God.
   b. To symbolize that the people must seek the acceptance of a holy God (v.38).

   Thought
   Two strong lessons are seen in the medallion and its purposes.
   a) Jesus Christ bore the guilt for the shortcomings and errors of us all. Man needs a perfect, sinless sacrifice, and Jesus Christ is that sacrifice.

   > **"[Christ] who gave himself for our sins, that he might deliver us from this present evil world, according to the will of God and our Father" (Ga.1:4; see Is.53:5; Ro.5:8; Ga.3:13; Ep.5:2; Tit.2:14; 1 Pe.2:24).**
   > **"For Christ also hath once suffered for sins, the just for the unjust, that he might bring us to God, being put to death in the flesh, but quickened by the Spirit" (1 Pe.3:18).**

   b) We must seek the acceptance of God by approaching God through Christ and through Christ alone.

   > **"For God so loved the world, that he gave his only begotten Son, that whosoever believeth in him should not perish, but have everlasting life" (Jn.3:16; see Jn.6:38; 8:24; 14:6).**
   > **"Neither is there salvation in any other: for there is none other name under heaven given among men, whereby we must be saved" (Ac.4:12; see 1 Co.3:11).**

VI. There Were the Final Instructions Governing Clothing (vv.39-43).

Note the exact instructions that God gave to Moses:
1. The turban and tunic (a long coat-like garment) were to be made of fine linen (v.39).
2. The sash (worn around the waist) was to be embroidered (v.39).
3. The clothing for the other priests was not as ornate as the High Priest's clothes, but the clothes still had to meet the same criteria: they had to be made according to God's pattern. The other priests were to have tunics, sashes, and headdresses (v.40). The purpose of their clothing was to set their call and office apart for dignity and respect (v.41).
4. The priests were to be clothed in the special garments, then ordained (v.41). (See outline and notes—Chapter Eight, Ex.29:1-46 for discussion on the ordination of the priests.)
5. The linen underclothing was the final garment to be made.
   a. It was to be worn next to the body, covering the priest from the waist to the thigh (v.42).
   b. It was always to be worn when serving God (v.43).

c. The purpose of the linen underclothing was modesty and purity: to cover their nakedness as they climbed the steps of the altar. God's anger and judgment are aroused against immodesty and immorality (v.43).

Thought
It has become quite fashionable for people to do good works in the name of God. And yet so many things are done in God's name that are worldly, carnal, and selfish. We who serve the LORD must not bring shame and embarrassment to the cause of Christ by living immoral and immodest lives. In the service of Christ, there is no room for the flesh, for man's sinful nature, not for the believer who wants to be a faithful follower of Christ.

a) The faithful believer must forsake all and follow Christ.

> **"Then said Jesus unto his disciples, If any man will come after me, let him deny himself, and take up his cross, and follow me" (Mt.16:24; see Lu.14:26; 14:33).**

b) The faithful believer must abide in God's Word.

> **"Then said Jesus to those Jews which believed on him, If ye continue in my word, then are ye my disciples indeed" (Jn.8:31).**
>
> **"Study to show thyself approved unto God, a workman that needeth not to be ashamed, rightly dividing the word of truth" (2 Ti.2:15).**

c) The faithful believer must bear fruit, much fruit.

> **"Herein is my Father glorified, that ye bear much fruit; so shall ye be my disciples" (Jn.15:8).**
>
> **"But the fruit of the Spirit is love, joy, peace, longsuffering, gentleness, goodness, faith, Meekness, temperance: against such there is no law" (Ga.5:22-23).**

d) The faithful believer must live a life that is godly and above reproach.

> **"For this is the will of God, even your sanctification, that ye should abstain from fornication" (1 Th.4:3).**
>
> **"Teaching us that, denying ungodliness and worldly lusts, we should live soberly, righteously, and godly, in this present world; Looking for that blessed hope, and the glorious appearing of the great God and our Saviour Jesus Christ" (Tit.2:12-13).**

TYPES, SYMBOLS, AND PICTURES
(Exodus 28:1-43)

Historical Term	Type or Picture (Scriptural Basis)	Life Application for Today's Believer	Biblical Application for Today's Believer
The Sash (Ex.28:4; 39:29) See also Ex.28:39	*The multi-colored sash of fine linen was symbolic of truth, the truth of God's Word. It is comparable to the belt of truth in the armor of God that the believer is to put on (Ep.6:14). The Word of God*	What the Sash taught: ⇒ Jesus Christ is the Truth, the Living Word of God. It is the Word of God that holds everything together. ⇒ A person needs help and support in	*"Jesus saith unto him, I am the way, the truth, and the life: no man cometh unto the Father, but by me" (Jn.14:6). "Stand therefore, having your loins girt about with truth, and*

Historical Term	Type or Picture (Scriptural Basis)	Life Application for Today's Believer	Biblical Application for Today's Believer
	enlightens and wraps together everything in the believer's spiritual wardrobe. **"And these are the garments which they shall make; a breast-plate, and an ephod, and a robe, and a broi-dered coat, a mitre, and a girdle [sash]: and they shall make holy garments for Aaron thy brother, and his sons, that he may minister unto me in the priest's of-fice" (Ex. 28:4).** **"And a girdle [sash]** *of* **fine twined linen, and blue, and purple, and scarlet,** *of* **needlework; as the** LORD **commanded Moses" (Ex.39:29).**	life because he does not have the strength to conquer the terrible trials and temptations of life, the trials and temptations that drag him ever downward toward the grave and eter-nal separation from God. Only the liv-ing Word of God can strengthen and hold us together as we walk through life.	*having on the breast-plate of righteous-ness" (Ep.6:14).* *"Sanctify them through thy truth: thy word is truth" (Jn. 17:17).* *"All scripture is given by inspiration of God, and is profitable for doctrine, for re-proof, for correction, for instruction in righ-teousness" (2 Ti.3:16).* *"For the word of God is quick, and powerful, and sharper than any twoedged sword, piercing even to the dividing asun-der of soul and spirit, and of the joints and marrow, and is a dis-cerner of the thoughts and intents of the heart" (He.4:12).*
Purple (Ex.28:5-6)	*Purple is the color of royalty; therefore, purple is a symbol of Christ as the King of kings and* LORD *of lords* **"And they shall take gold, and blue, and purple, and scar-let, and fine linen. And they shall make the ephod** *of* **gold,** *of* **blue, and** *of* **purple,** *of* **scarlet, and fine twined linen, with cunning work" (Ex. 28:5-6).**	⇒ Jesus Christ is the King of kings and LORD of lords, the Sovereign Ruler and Majesty of the universe. A person needs to give Christ the honor and praise He deserves, the respect and thanksgiving that is due Him as Savior and Deliverer. Nothing less is ac-ceptable.	*"And they clothed him with purple, and platted a crown of thorns, and put it about his head, And began to salute him, Hail, King of the Jews!" (Mk.15:17-18; see Re.19:16).* *"Jesus Christ, who is the faithful witness, and the first begotten of the dead, and the prince of the kings of the earth. Unto him that loved us, and washed us from our sins in his own blood" (Re.1:5; see Re.17:14).*
The Ephod (Ex.28:4, 6-14; 39:6-7) See also Ex.39:2-7	*The Ephod symbolized that the priest repre-sented and carried the names of God's people before the* LORD. **"And they shall make the ephod of gold, of blue, and of purple, of scarlet,**	What the Ephod taught: ⇒ A person cannot represent himself before God because he is a sinner. A person needs an Advocate, an Inter-cessor, a Mediator, a Savior who can	*"Come unto me, all ye that labour and are heavy laden, and I will give you rest. Take my yoke upon you, and learn of me; for I am meek and lowly in heart: and ye shall find rest unto your souls. For my*

Historical Term	Type or Picture (Scriptural Basis)	Life Application for Today's Believer	Biblical Application for Today's Believer
	and fine twined linen, with cunning work" (Ex.28:6). "And they wrought onyx stones inclosed in ouches of gold, graven, as signets are graven, with the names of the children of Israel. And he put them on the shoulders of the ephod, *that they should be* stones for a memorial to the children of Israel; as the LORD commanded Moses" (Ex.39:6-7).	approach God legally and perfectly. A person cannot do any of this; therefore, a person needs Someone who can. That person is the Lord Jesus Christ. ⇒ No matter what our burden, no matter how heavy or terrifying our trial, God knows us, knows us personally. He knows all about our burdens and trials—all because Christ represents us and carries our names before the Father.	*yoke is easy, and my burden is light" (Mt.11:28-30; see Ro. 8:34).* *"For we have not an high priest which cannot be touched with the feeling of our infirmities; but was in all points tempted like as we are, yet without sin. Let us therefore come boldly unto the throne of grace, that we may obtain mercy, and find grace to help in time of need" (He. 4:14-15; see 1 Pe. 5:7).*
Scarlet (Ex.28:15)	*Scarlet, a bright shade of red, symbolizes sacrifice. Therefore, scarlet pictures the entire scene of sacrifice and redemption through Jesus Christ* "And thou shalt make the breastplate of judgment with cunning work; after the work of the ephod thou shalt make it; *of* gold, *of* blue, and *of* purple, and *of* scarlet, and *of* fine twined linen, shalt thou make it" (Ex.28:15).	⇒ Jesus Christ is the Lamb of God, the One who was sacrificed to take away the sins of the world and to redeem mankind. It is only through the shed blood of Jesus Christ that we are saved and delivered.	*"So Christ was once offered to bear the sins of many; and unto them that look for him shall he appear the second time without sin unto salvation" (He.9:28).* *"How much more shall the blood of Christ, who through the eternal Spirit offered himself without spot to God, purge your conscience from dead works to serve the living God?" (He.9:14; see He. 9:11-13, 19-20, 23).*
The Breastpiece or Chestpiece (Ex.28:4, 15-20; 28:29) See also Ex.39:8-21	*The Breastpiece was a garment that was worn close to the heart of the High Priest. The purpose for the Chestpiece was twofold:* *a. First, to symbolize that the High Priest represented and carried the names of God's people upon his heart, that he represented them before the LORD continually (28:29).*	What the Breastpiece or Chestpiece taught: a. This is a strong picture of the love of God: how much God loves His people. He loves us so much that He keeps us ever so close to His heart, keeps us continually before His face.	*"Before I formed thee in the belly I knew thee; and before thou camest forth out of the womb I sanctified thee, and I ordained thee a prophet unto the nations" (Je.1:5).*

Historical Term	Type or Picture (Scriptural Basis)	Life Application for Today's Believer	Biblical Application for Today's Believer
		God is not a God who is... • removed from the feelings of His people • calloused in His heart when His people are suffering • too busy to listen to the desperate cries of those who need His help God is never caught off guard by the circumstances that come our way. God knows and God cares.	*"Behold, God is mine helper: the Lord is with them that uphold my soul" (Ps.54:4).* *"The LORD is nigh unto them that are of a broken heart; and saveth such as be of a contrite spirit" (Ps. 34:18; see Re.3:8).* *"But even the very hairs of your head are all numbered. Fear not therefore: ye are of more value than many sparrows" (Lu.12:7).*
	b. The second purpose of the Chestpiece was to hold the urim and thummim (probably two stones or lots) next to the High Priest's heart (Ex.28:30). This symbolized the High Priest's seeking God's will for the people. Imagine the scene as the High Priest entered into the Holy Place. He was there on behalf of the people of God and would not leave until God had made His will clear. **"And thou shalt make the breastplate of judgment with cunning work; after the work of the ephod thou shalt make it; of gold, of blue, and of purple, and of scarlet, and of fine twined linen, shalt thou make it" (Ex.28:15).** **"And Aaron shall bear the names of the children of Israel in the breastplate of**	b. Jesus Christ is our great High Priest who represents and carries our names upon His heart and before the LORD God continually. Jesus Christ wants the very best for us. He prays for us, seeking nothing less than God's perfect will for us.	*"I pray for them [believers]: I pray not for the world, but for them which thou hast given me; for they are thine" (Jn. 17:9).* *"Wherefore he is able also to save them to the uttermost that come unto God by him, seeing he ever liveth to make intercession for them [believers]" (He. 7:25).*

Historical Term	Type or Picture (Scriptural Basis)	Life Application for Today's Believer	Biblical Application for Today's Believer
	judgment upon his heart, when he goeth in unto the holy *place*, for a memorial before the LORD continually" (Ex.28:29).		
The Robe of the Ephod (Ex.28:4, 31-35) See also Ex.39:22-26	*The Robe of the Ephod was worn by the High Priest as he entered through the Veil and ministered to the LORD in the Sanctuary. The Robe of the Ephod was symbolic of two things:*	What the Robe of the Ephod taught:	
	a. *The Robe of the Ephod symbolized the sounding forth of the intercessory ministry of the High Priest.*	a. Jesus Christ is our great High Priest who sounds forth the intercessory ministry of the High Priest. His intercession never ends, never stops. This is a strong lesson for us: we too must pray without ceasing. We must become intercessors—great intercessors—for our loved ones and for the lost of the world.	*"But this man, because he continueth ever, hath an unchangeable priesthood. Wherefore he is able also to save them to the uttermost that come unto God by him, seeing he ever liveth to make intercession for them" (He.7:24-25).* *"Praying always with all prayer and supplication in the Spirit, and watching thereunto with all perseverance and supplication for all saints" (Ep.6:18; see 1 Chr. 16:11; Ps. 55:17).*
	b. *The Robe of the Ephod symbolized the sounding forth of a wonderful fact: that God accepted the offering of the High Priest, that he had not been stricken dead.* "And it shall be upon Aaron to minister: and his sound shall be heard when he goeth in unto the holy place before the LORD, and when he cometh out, that he die not" (Ex.28:35).	b. We should rejoice in the fact that the sacrifice made by Jesus Christ was perfectly acceptable to God the Father. Once we have been saved, we no longer have to worry about being judged guilty or condemned to die.	*"Who shall lay any thing to the charge of God's elect? It is God that justifieth. Who is he that condemneth? It is Christ that died, yea rather, that is risen again, who is even at the right hand of God, who also maketh intercession for us" (Ro.8:33-34; see Jn.1:29; Ph.2:9).* *"Wherefore in all things it behoved him to be made like unto his brethren, that he might be a merciful and faithful high priest in things*

Historical Term	Type or Picture (Scriptural Basis)	Life Application for Today's Believer	Biblical Application for Today's Believer
			pertaining to God, to make reconciliation for the sins of the people" (He.2:17).
The Gold Medallion or Diadem (Ex.28:36-38; 39:30-31)	*The Gold Medallion was attached with a blue ribbon to the head of the High Priest and was the crowning piece of the High Priest's wardrobe. The words "HOLINESS TO THE LORD" were written upon the Medallion.*	What the Gold Medallion taught:	
	a. *The Gold Medallion symbolized that the High Priest bore the guilt for the shortcomings of the people.*	a. We are ever so short of the glory and holiness of God. We desperately need Someone to bear the guilt for our shortcoming. That person is Jesus Christ. It is Jesus Christ who bore the guilt for the shortcomings and errors of the people. A person needs a perfect sacrifice, and that Sacrifice is Jesus Christ, who died upon the cross for our sins.	*"Who gave himself for us, that he might redeem us from all iniquity, and purify unto himself a peculiar people, zealous of good works" (Tit.2:14).* *"For Christ also hath once suffered for sins, the just for the unjust, that he might bring us to God, being put to death in the flesh, but quickened by the Spirit" (1 Pe. 3:18).*
	b. *The Gold Medallion symbolized that the people must seek the acceptance of a holy God.* **"And thou shalt make a plate of pure gold, and grave upon it, like the engravings of a signet, HOLINESS TO THE LORD" (Ex.28:36)** **"And they made the plate of the holy crown** *of* **pure gold, and wrote upon it a writing,** *like to* **the engravings of a signet, HOLINESS TO THE**	b. We are guilty of sin. Our sin indicts us and places us at the mercy of a holy and righteous Judge. God beckons each person to come to Him on the basis of the merit of Christ and His righteousness. We must seek the approval of God by approaching God through Christ and Christ alone.	*"Jesus saith unto him, I am the way, the truth, and the life: no man cometh unto the Father, but by me" (Jn.14:6).* *"Neither is there salvation in any other: for there is none other name under heaven given among men, whereby we must be saved" (Ac.4:12).*

Historical Term	Type or Picture (Scriptural Basis)	Life Application for Today's Believer	Biblical Application for Today's Believer
	LORD. And they tied unto it a lace of blue, to fasten *it* on high upon the mitre; as the LORD commanded Moses" (Ex. 39:30-31).		
The Linen Turbans and Tunics (Ex.28:4, 39; 39:27-28)	*Linen is symbolic of righteousness. The Linen Turban and Tunic (a long coat-like garment that essentially covered the whole body) were symbolic of putting on God's righteousness.* "And thou shalt embroider the coat of fine linen, and thou shalt make the mitre of fine linen, and thou shalt make the girdle of needlework" (Ex.28:39). "And they made coats *of* fine linen *of* woven work for Aaron, and for his sons, And a mitre *of* fine linen, and goodly bonnets *of* fine linen, and linen breeches *of* fine twined linen" (Ex. 39:27-28).	What the Linen Turbans and Tunics taught: ⇒ If a person wishes to live in God's presence, he must put on the righteousness of Christ. A person is depraved and totally inadequate, having no righteousness of his own. Therefore, a person cannot walk before God or serve God unless he puts on the righteousness of Christ.	*"For he hath made him to be sin for us, who knew no sin; that we might be made the righteousness of God in him" (2 Co.5:21).* *"I put on righteousness, and it clothed me: my judgment was as a robe and a diadem" (Jb. 29:14; see Is.61:10).* *"But of him are ye in Christ Jesus, who of God is made unto us wisdom, and righteousness, and sanctification, and redemption" (1 Co.1:30; see Is.64:6).*
The Linen Headband (Ex.28:40) See also Ex.39:28	*The Linen Headband symbolized the need for a person to subject his mind and his thoughts to God and His righteousness. (Remember, the linen pictures the righteousness of God.)* "And for Aaron's sons thou shalt make coats, and thou shalt make for them girdles, and bonnets shalt thou make for them, for glory and for beauty" (Ex. 28:40).	What the Linen Headband taught: ⇒ It is Jesus Christ who has established His Lordship over every thought, every idea, every agenda of a person. The believer must willingly submit his mind and will, his thoughts and agenda to God.	*"Teach me to do thy will; for thou art my God: thy spirit is good; lead me into the land of uprightness" (Ps.143:10).* *"I beseech you therefore, brethren, by the mercies of God, that ye present your bodies a living sacrifice, holy, acceptable unto God, which is your reasonable service. And be not conformed to this world: but be ye transformed by the renewing of your mind, that ye may prove what is that good, and acceptable, and perfect, will of God" (Ro.12:1-2; see Ep.6:6; 2 Co.10:5).*

Historical Term	Type or Picture (Scriptural Basis)	Life Application for Today's Believer	Biblical Application for Today's Believer
The Linen Underclothing (Ex.28:42-43) See also Ex.39:28	*The Linen Underclothing was worn next to the body, covering the priests from the waist to the thigh. It was always to be worn when serving God. The purpose of the Linen Underclothing was modesty, to cover the nakedness of the priest as he climbed the steps of the altar. Thus, the Linen Underclothing symbolized the covering of the believer's spiritual nakedness before God.* **"And thou shalt make them linen breeches to cover their nakedness; from the loins even unto the thighs they shall reach: And they shall be upon Aaron, and upon his sons, when they come in unto the tabernacle of the congregation, or when they come near unto the altar to minister in the holy** *place;* **that they bear not iniquity, and die:** *it shall be* **a statute for ever unto him and his seed after him" (Ex.28:42-43).**	What the Linen Underclothing taught: ⇒ The person who is without Christ is spiritually naked; he is exposed and shamed. We must all put on the Lord Jesus Christ and His righteousness, making no provision for the flesh. ⇒ It is Jesus Christ who covers a person with His righteousness, protecting a person from exposure and shame before God and people.	*"Knowing this, that our old man is crucified with him, that the body of sin might be destroyed, that henceforth we should not serve sin" (Ro.6:6).* *"But put ye on the Lord Jesus Christ, and make not provision for the flesh, to fulfil the lusts thereof" (Ro.13:14).* *"And have put on the new man, which is renewed in knowledge after the image of him that created him" (Col.3:10).* *"Teaching us that, denying ungodliness and worldly lusts, we should live soberly, righteously, and godly, in this present world" (Tit.2:12).*

HIGH PRIEST

CHAPTER EIGHT

The Dedication, Consecration, and Ordination of the Priests: God's Qualifications for Leadership (Exodus 29:1-46)

Contents

The Dedication, Consecration, and Ordination of the Priests: God's Qualifications for Leadership (Exodus 29:1-46)

1. **The call for a dedication service**
   a. To consecrate the priests
   b. To secure the items needed
      1) A young bull & two rams with no defect
      2) Unleavened bread, cakes, & wafers: Made with wheat flour & oil
   c. To present the items to the LORD

2. **The moral cleansing, to wash the priests with water: A ceremonial washing—symbolized spiritual cleansing**

3. **The putting on of the holy clothes: Symbolized the clothing of righteousness**
   a. The tunic
   b. The robe of the ephod
   c. The ephod itself
   d. The chestpiece
   e. The sash
   f. The turban & the sacred diadem

And this is the thing that thou shalt do unto them to hallow them, to minister unto me in the priest's office: Take one young bullock, and two rams without blemish,

2 And unleavened bread, and cakes unleavened tempered with oil, and wafers unleavened anointed with oil: of wheaten flour shalt thou make them.

3 And thou shalt put them into one basket, and bring them in the basket, with the bullock and the two rams.

4 And Aaron and his sons thou shalt bring unto the door of the tabernacle of the congregation, and shalt wash them with water.

5 And thou shalt take the garments, and put upon Aaron the coat, and the robe of the ephod, and the ephod, and the breastplate, and gird him with the curious girdle of the ephod:

6 And thou shalt put the mitre upon his head, and put the holy crown upon the mitre.

7 Then shalt thou take the anointing oil, and pour it upon his head, and anoint him.

8 And thou shalt bring his sons, and put coats upon them.

9 And thou shalt gird them with girdles, Aaron and his sons, and put the bonnets on them: and the priest's office shall be theirs for a perpetual statute: and thou shalt consecrate Aaron and his sons.

10 And thou shalt cause a bullock to be brought before the tabernacle of the congregation: and Aaron and his sons shall put their hands upon the head of the bullock.

11 And thou shalt kill the bullock before the LORD, by the door of the tabernacle of the congregation.

12 And thou shalt take of the blood of the bullock, and put it upon the horns of the altar with thy finger, and pour all the blood beside

4. **The anointing: Symbolized being anointed with the Spirit & power of God**

5. **The permanence & security of the Priesthood**
   a. To dress Aaron's sons: Symbolic of righteousness
   b. The emphatic truth: The priest's ordination was permanent, forever

6. **The sacrifice of a bull as the sin offering: Sym. the judicial cleansing**
   a. To have the priests lay their hands on the bull's head: Symbolized identification, transferring their sins to the animal
   b. To slaughter it before the LORD: Symbolized appeasement, substitution (substituting the animal to bear God's judgment)
   c. To apply blood to the horns & base of the altar: Symbolized the sanctification of the place (worship center) as well as

119

the worshipper

d. To burn the fat & choice parts on the altar; but to take the bad—the flesh, hide, & waste—outside the camp & burn
   1) Symbolized that sin (the bad) had to be taken out of the camp, away from the worshipper
   2) Symbolized the sin offering: The taking away of sin by the sacrifice of one (Jesus Christ) for another

7. **The sacrifice of a ram as the burnt offering: Sym. the total dedication of life**
   a. To lay their hands on its head
   b. To slaughter it & sprinkle blood on all sides of the altar
   c. To cut the ram into pieces & wash the inner parts & legs
   d. To burn all the parts on the altar so the pleasing aroma would ascend up toward heaven: Symbolized that God accepted the person's sacrifice & dedication

8. **The sacrifice of a second ram: Sym. the consecration to service**
   a. To lay their hands on its head
   b. To slaughter it & put some blood...
      1) On the tip of the right ear: Setting it apart to listen

the bottom of the altar.
13 And thou shalt take all the fat that covereth the inwards, and the caul that is above the liver, and the two kidneys, and the fat that is upon them, and burn them upon the altar.
14 But the flesh of the bullock, and his skin, and his dung, shalt thou burn with fire without the camp: it is a sin offering.
15 Thou shalt also take one ram; and Aaron and his sons shall put their hands upon the head of the ram.
16 And thou shalt slay the ram, and thou shalt take his blood, and sprinkle it round about upon the altar.
17 And thou shalt cut the ram in pieces, and wash the inwards of him, and his legs, and put them unto his pieces, and unto his head.
18 And thou shalt burn the whole ram upon the altar: it is a burnt offering unto the LORD: it is a sweet savour, an offering made by fire unto the LORD.
19 And thou shalt take the other ram; and Aaron and his sons shall put their hands upon the head of the ram.
20 Then shalt thou kill the ram, and take of his blood, and put it upon the tip of the right ear of

Aaron, and upon the tip of the right ear of his sons, and upon the thumb of their right hand, and upon the great toe of their right foot, and sprinkle the blood upon the altar round about.
21 And thou shalt take of the blood that is upon the altar, and of the anointing oil, and sprinkle it upon Aaron, and upon his garments, and upon his sons, and upon the garments of his sons with him: and he shall be hallowed, and his garments, and his sons, and his sons' garments with him.
22 Also thou shalt take of the ram the fat and the rump, and the fat that covereth the inwards, and the caul above the liver, and the two kidneys, and the fat that is upon them, and the right shoulder; for it is a ram of consecration:
23 And one loaf of bread, and one cake of oiled bread, and one wafer out of the basket of the unleavened bread that is before the LORD:
24 And thou shalt put all in the hands of Aaron, and in the hands of his sons; and shalt wave them for a wave offering before the LORD.
25 And thou shalt receive them of their hands, and burn them upon the altar for a burnt offering,

2) On the thumb of the right hand: Setting it apart to do good
3) On the big toe of the right foot: Setting it apart to walk in the ways of God
4) On all sides of the altar

c. To mix some blood & anointing oil & sprinkle it on the priests & their clothes

d. The purpose: Symbolized full consecration to the service of God

9. **The ceremony of two wave offerings: Sym. the commitment to give God the best**
   a. The first wave offering
      1) To cut away the fat & *choice parts* from the ram of ordination
      2) To take one loaf of unleavened bread, one cake, & one wafer from the basket
      3) To put all these into the hands of the priests: To lift them up & wave them before the LORD as a wave offering
      4) To burn the items upon the altar as a pleasing aroma to the LORD:

Symbolized the pleasure & acceptance of the LORD

b. The second wave offering: To take the breast & shoulder of the ram, lift & wave it before the LORD

1) To sanctify—set apart as holy—the parts of the ram that belong to the priests

2) To always give these parts to the priests when making fellowship offerings (thanksgiving or peace offerings)

10. The passing down of the ordination clothes of the High Priest
a. To be worn in the ordination service by the succeeding descendant
b. To be worn seven days

11. The communion or fellowship meal
a. To boil the ram's meat

for a sweet savour before the LORD: it is an offering made by fire unto the LORD.

26 And thou shalt take the breast of the ram of Aaron's consecration, and wave it for a wave offering before the LORD: and it shall be thy part.

27 And thou shalt sanctify the breast of the wave offering, and the shoulder of the heave offering, which is waved, and which is heaved up, of the ram of the consecration, even of that which is for Aaron, and of that which is for his sons:

28 And it shall be Aaron's and his sons' by a statute for ever from the children of Israel: for it is an heave offering: and it shall be an heave offering from the children of Israel of the sacrifice of their peace offerings, even their heave offering unto the LORD.

29 And the holy garments of Aaron shall be his sons' after him, to be anointed therein, and to be consecrated in them.

30 And that son that is priest in his stead shall put them on seven days, when he cometh into the tabernacle of the congregation to minister in the holy place.

31 And thou shalt take the ram of the consecration, and seethe his flesh in the holy place.

26 And Aaron and his sons shall eat the flesh of the ram, and the bread that is in the basket, by the door of the tabernacle of the congregation.

27 And they shall eat those things wherewith the atonement was made, to consecrate and to sanctify them: but a stranger shall not eat thereof, because they are holy.

28 And if ought of the flesh of the consecrations, or of the bread, remain unto the morning, then thou shalt burn the remainder with fire: it shall not be eaten, because it is holy.

29 And thus shalt thou do unto Aaron, and to his sons, according to all things which I have commanded thee: seven days shalt thou consecrate them.

30 And thou shalt offer every day a bullock for a sin offering for atonement: and thou shalt cleanse the altar, when thou hast made an atonement for it, and thou shalt anoint it, to sanctify it.

31 Seven days thou shalt make an atonement for the altar, and sanctify it; and it shall be an altar most holy: whatsoever toucheth the altar shall be holy.

32 Now this is that which thou shalt offer upon the altar; two lambs of the first year day by day continually.

b. To hold a type of communion meal among the priests at the door of the tabernacle
1) To eat the ram's meat along with the bread in the basket
2) To eat the meat & bread sacrificed for their atonement: No one else was allowed to eat

3) To burn any sacrificial meat or bread left over: Not to be eaten, because it was holy (set apart to God)

12. The repetition of the ordination ceremony: To be repeated seven days
a. The stress: Obedience

b. To sacrifice a bull every day: As a sin offering
c. To purify & anoint the altar for seven days

1) Would make it holy (set apart to God)

2) Would make whatever touched it holy

13. The morning & evening sacrifices
a. To offer two one-year old lambs each day

1) One in the morning
2) One in the evening
 	
b. To offer the first lamb with two quarts of flour mixed with one quart of olive oil & wine: As a drink offering
 	
c. To offer the second lamb with the same items
d. The effect upon the LORD
  1) Is a pleasing aroma & sacrifice to the LORD
  2) Satisfies the fire (holiness) of the LORD
 	
e. The importance of the morning & evening sacrifice: To be observed daily
f. The results of the daily sacrifice:
	32 The one lamb thou shalt offer in the morning; and the other lamb thou shalt offer at even: 33 And with the one lamb a tenth deal of flour mingled with the fourth part of an hin of beaten oil; and the fourth part of an hin of wine for a drink offering. 34 And the other lamb thou shalt offer at even, and shalt do thereto according to the meat offering of the morning, and according to the drink offering thereof, for a sweet savour, an offering made by fire unto the LORD. 35 This shall be a continual burnt offering throughout your generations at the door of the tabernacle of the con-	gregation before the LORD: where I will meet you, to speak there unto thee. 43 And there I will meet with the children of Israel, and the tabernacle shall be sanctified by my glory. 44 And I will sanctify the tabernacle of the congregation, and the altar: I will sanctify also both Aaron and his sons, to minister to me in the priest's office. 45 And I will dwell among the children of Israel, and will be their God. 46 And they shall know that I am the LORD their God, that brought them forth out of the land of Egypt, that I may dwell among them: I am the LORD their God.	1) The LORD would meet & speak to His messenger (Moses)
			2) The LORD would meet & speak to the people
			3) The LORD would sanctify the Tabernacle with His glory
			4) The LORD would sanctify (set apart as holy) the Tabernacle, altar, & the priests—all to His service
			5) The LORD would dwell among His people & be their God
			6) The people would know that the LORD is the God who delivers & sets them free

People need good leaders. A terrible shortage of qualified leaders is confronting the world today. Serious cracks have arisen in the major institutions of society, cracks caused by a lack of qualified leaders.

⇒ There is a scarcity of good, diligent political leaders.
⇒ There is a scarcity of good, committed business leaders.
⇒ There is a scarcity of good, diligent employers and employees.
⇒ There is a scarcity of good, diligent managers.
⇒ There is a scarcity of good, diligent church leaders.
⇒ There is a scarcity of good, diligent teachers and students.
⇒ There is a scarcity of good, diligent parents, husbands, wives, and children.

Tragically, the qualifications for leadership have become so diluted that almost anyone can become a leader. Today, a person can become a leader because he has...

- some money
- some popularity
- some heightened self-image
- some professional image
- some social standing
- some personal charisma
- some political position
- some claim to fame

Good leadership is a critical need for God's people. This is the reason God has established a lofty standard for leadership. To become one of God's leaders, a person has to be...

- forgiven by God
- consecrated by God
- called by God
- prepared by God
- dedicated to God

This is the purpose of this section of Scripture, showing how God places a person into service for Him. It is: *The Dedication, Consecration, and Ordination of the Priest: God's Qualifications for Leadership*, Ex.29:1-46.

I. The call for a dedication service (vv.1-3).

II. The moral cleansing, to wash the priests with water: a ceremonial washing— symbolized spiritual cleansing (v.4).

III. The putting on of the holy clothes: symbolized the clothing of righteousness (vv.5-6).

IV. The anointing: symbolized being anointed with the Spirit and power of God (v.7).

V. The permanence and security of the Priesthood (vv.8-9).

VI. The sacrifice of a bull as the sin offering: symbolized the judicial cleansing (vv.10-14).

VII. The sacrifice of a ram as the burnt offering: symbolized the total dedication of life (vv.15-18).

VIII. The sacrifice of a second ram: symbolized the consecration to service (vv.19-21).

IX. The ceremony of two wave offerings: symbolized the commitment to give God the best (vv.22-28).

X. The passing down of the ordination clothes of the High Priest (vv.29-30).

XI. The communion or fellowship meal (vv.31-34).

XII. The repetition of the ordination ceremony: to be repeated seven days (vv.35-37).

XIII. The morning and evening sacrifices (vv.38-46).

I. There Was the Call for a Dedication Service (vv.1-3).

It was now time for Aaron and his sons to be publicly ordained and installed as the official priests for Israel. Note the word *dedicate* or *consecrate* (qadash): it means to sanctify, to set apart to God. The point is to publicly take Aaron and his sons and set them apart to God, set them apart before the people in a public service, focusing the attention of the people upon the fact that these men are to serve as their priests, the ministers of God among them. In preparation for the service, God told Moses two things.

1. Moses was to secure the items needed for the various offerings (v.1).

a. He was to secure a young bull and two rams with no defect (v.1). Note the requirement that the animals have *no defect*. The sacrifice had to be *perfect*. This type was fulfilled in Jesus Christ, the perfect, sinless Lamb of God (Jn.1:29).

b. He was to secure unleavened bread, cakes, and wafers that were made with wheat, flour, and oil (v.1). Remember, leavened bread is a symbol of evil and unleavened bread a symbol of righteousness. The picture is striking: the priests were to partake of or to take in righteousness.

2. Moses was to present the items to the LORD (v.3).

Thought

A person called by God to serve His people should be publicly set apart, ordained to God's service. The people's attention should be focused upon the fact...

• that this person has been called by God to serve God's people

• that this person is to serve and minister to them as God's appointed servant

> "Ye have not chosen me, but I have chosen you, and ordained you, that ye should go and bring forth fruit, and [that] your fruit should remain: that whatsoever ye shall ask of the Father in my name, he may give it you" (Jn.15:16; see Jn.21:17; Ac.9:15; 20:28; 1 Pe.5:2).
>
> "And I will give you pastors according to mine heart, which shall feed you with knowledge and understanding" (Je.3:15).
>
> "And I will set up shepherds over them which shall feed them: and they shall fear no more, nor be dismayed, neither shall they be lacking, saith the LORD" (Je.23:4).

II. There Was Moral Cleansing (v.4).

Note that this was a special cleansing that took place after the call to consecration. This was an *immediate, initial cleansing*. When God calls a person to consecration, the person is immediately to seek to be *morally cleansed* by the LORD. Note how God symbolized this moral cleansing for Aaron and his sons: they were to be publicly washed with water before the Tabernacle, washed in the presence of God's people.

Thought
The person who serves God must be clean, morally pure, cleansed from all filthiness of the flesh and spirit.

> "Having therefore these promises, dearly beloved, let us cleanse ourselves from all filthiness of the flesh and spirit, perfecting holiness in the fear of God" (2 Co.7:1; see 2 Ti.2:21; Js.4:8; Ps.79:9).
> "Wash you, make you clean; put away the evil of your doings from before mine eyes; cease to do evil" (Is.1:16).

III. There Was the Putting On of the Holy Clothes (vv.5-6).

Aaron was to be dressed in the priestly clothing:
⇒ the tunic
⇒ the robe of the ephod
⇒ the ephod itself
⇒ the chestpiece
⇒ the sash
⇒ the turban and the sacred diadem

Thought
Scripture says that believers are to be clothed with the righteousness of Jesus Christ, to put on—clothe themselves with—the new man. This is the picture seen in Aaron's putting on the holy clothes. The minister of God must put on Christ, put on the new man, the new nature of God. He must be clothed with righteousness.

> "But put ye on the Lord Jesus Christ, and make not provision for the flesh, to fulfil the lusts thereof" (Ro.13:14).
> "And that ye put on the new man, which after God is created in righteousness and true holiness" (Ep.4:24; see Col.3:10).
> "Put on therefore, as the elect of God, holy and beloved, bowels of mercies, kindness, humbleness of mind, meekness, longsuffering" (Col.3:12; see Ps.132:9; Is.61:10).

IV. There Was the Anointing with Oil (v.7).

The oil is a symbol of the Holy Spirit, and of God's appointment and power. The priest, the servant of God, was appointed by God; therefore, he was to be anointed with the Spirit and power of God.

Thought
This is a point that must be acknowledged. No minister can truly serve God apart from God's anointing, the anointing of God's Spirit and power.

> "But ye shall receive power, after that the Holy Ghost is come upon you: and ye shall be witnesses unto me both in Jerusalem, and in all Judaea, and in Samaria, and unto the uttermost part of the earth" (Ac.1:8; see Ac.10:38).
> "But the fruit of the Spirit is love, joy, peace, longsuffering, gentleness, goodness, faith, Meekness, temperance: against such there is no law" (Ga.5:22-23).
> "Be filled with the Spirit" (Ep.5:18; see Mi.3:8).

V. There Was the Permanence and Security of the Priesthood (vv.8-9).

Both Aaron and his sons were to be dressed in their priestly clothing. This, too, was symbolic of righteousness. Note the emphatic truth declared: the priest's call and ordination were permanent, forever.

Thought

Two strong lessons are seen in the permanence of God's call and ordination.

a) The minister and servant of God is called and ordained forever. He is forever responsible to serve God faithfully.

> "Moreover it is required in stewards, that a man be found faithful" (1 Co.4:2; see Lu.19:13).
> "Therefore, my beloved brethren, be ye stedfast, unmoveable, always abounding in the work of the Lord, forasmuch as ye know that your labour is not in vain in the Lord." (1 Co.15:58).

b) The office of priesthood was established forever by God. All believers are made priests of God; all believers are called to be representatives of God upon earth.

> "And ye shall be unto me a kingdom of priests, and an holy nation. These are the words which thou shalt speak unto the children of Israel" (Ex.19:6; see Is.61:6).
> "Ye also, as lively stones, are built up a spiritual house, an holy priesthood, to offer up spiritual sacrifices, acceptable to God by Jesus Christ" (1 Pe.2:5).
> "And [Christ] hath made us kings and priests unto God and his Father; to him be glory and dominion for ever and ever. Amen" (Re.1:6).

VI. There Was the Judicial Cleansing (vv.10-14).

A bull was to be sacrificed as the sin offering for Aaron and his sons. No person could serve God until he was cleansed and forgiven by God. Cleansing was based upon the atonement, upon being reconciled to God through the shed blood of the sacrifice. The sacrifice of the *sin offering* is rich with symbolic meaning. Note the clear instructions of God.

1. Moses was to have the priests lay their hands on the bull's head. This act symbolized *identification*, transferring their sins to the animal (v.10). The animal became the sin-bearer: the animal was to bear the judgment of God against sin, bear the judgment for the believer. This act of identification pointed to Jesus Christ as the sin-bearer of the world.

> "All we like sheep have gone astray; we have turned every one to his own way; and the LORD hath laid on him the iniquity of us all" (Is.53:6).
> "So Christ was once offered to bear the sins of many; and unto them that look for him shall he appear the second time without sin unto salvation" (He.9:28).
> "Who his own self bare our sins in his own body on the tree, that we, being dead to sins, should live unto righteousness: by whose stripes ye were healed" (1 Pe.2:24; see 1 Jn.3:5).

2. Moses was to slaughter the bull before the LORD. This act symbolized appeasement, substitution, substituting the animal to bear God's judgment (v.11). God's wrath toward sin can only be appeased by a sacrifice. During Old Testament history, God used animal sacrifice to point to Christ. But the only sacrifice that has ever satisfied God's eternal wrath was the Lamb of God Himself, the Lord Jesus Christ who was slaughtered on the cross. He and He alone was the *perfect sacrifice* who could atone for sin and pay the penalty demanded by God's holy righteousness.

"For when we were yet without strength, in due time Christ died for the ungodly" (Ro.5:6).

"But God commendeth his love toward us, in that, while we were yet sinners, Christ died for us. Much more then, being now justified by his blood, we shall be saved from wrath through him" (Ro.5:8-9; see Ro.5:10-11).

"Who gave himself for our sins, that he might deliver us from this present evil world, according to the will of God and our Father" (Ga.1:4; see Tit.2:14).

3. Moses was to apply blood to the horns and base of the altar. This symbolized the sanctification of the place (worship center) as well as the worshipper (v.12).

Thought
The shed blood of Christ is a constant reminder of His great love for His people. The cross without His blood is powerless, empty, and worthless. It is the blood of Christ that sanctified or set apart the altar of the cross as holy. And it is the blood of Christ that sanctifies or sets apart the believer as holy.

"How much more shall the blood of Christ, who through the eternal Spirit offered himself without spot to God, purge your conscience from dead works to serve the living God?" (He.9:14; see Mt.26:28).

"But if we walk in the light, as he is in the light, we have fellowship one with another, and the blood of Jesus Christ his Son cleanseth us from all sin" (1 Jn.1:7; see Re.1:5; 5:9).

4. Moses was to burn the fat and choice parts on the altar, but he was to take the bad—the flesh, skin, and waste—outside the camp and burn it (vv.13-14). This symbolized that sin (the bad) had to be taken out of the camp, away from the worshipper. It also symbolized the sin offering: the taking away of sin by the sacrifice of one (Jesus Christ) for another.

Thought
It was Jesus Christ who fulfilled this symbol by His own death on the cross: He was crucified outside the walls of Jerusalem on Calvary.

"Wherefore Jesus also, that he might sanctify [cleanse, purify, set apart] the people with his own blood, suffered without [outside the city] the gate" (He.13:12; see 2 Co.5:21; Ga.1:4).

"Who gave himself for us, that he might redeem us from all iniquity, and purify unto himself a peculiar people, zealous of good works" (Tit.2:14).

VII. There Was the Total Dedication of Life (vv.15-18).

Note that Aaron and his sons were to take a *whole ram* and sacrifice it to the LORD. This symbolized total dedication, the dedication of the priest's whole life to the LORD. Note the instructions that God gave Moses for this burnt offering of the ram:
1. The priests were to lay their hands on its head (v.15).
2. The priests were to slaughter it and sprinkle blood on all sides of the altar (v.16).
3. The priests were to cut the ram in pieces and wash the inner parts and legs (v.17).
4. The priests were to burn all the parts—the entire ram—on the altar so the pleasing aroma would ascend toward heaven (v.18). This symbolized that God accepted the person's sacrifice and dedication. God seeks and longs for people to give all they are and have to Him.

Thought

Believers are priests before the LORD, His representatives upon earth (1 Pe.2:5, 9). God's priests, God's people, must be willing to climb upon the altar and become a living sacrifice to God. God has no use for those...

- who want to go their own way
- who have their own agenda
- who have their own plans and programs

We must dedicate our entire beings to the LORD; we must make a total dedication to Christ. Nothing less than the dedication of our total being, of all our faculties, constitutes the *"entire ram" being laid upon the altar* (v.18).

> **"I beseech you therefore, brethren, by the mercies of God, that ye present your bodies a living sacrifice, holy, acceptable unto God, which is your reasonable service" (Ro.12:1).**
> **"And he said to [them] all, If any [man] will come after me, let him deny himself, and take up his cross daily, and follow me" (Lu.9:23).**
> **"So likewise, whosoever he be of you that forsaketh not all that he hath, he cannot be my disciple" (Lu.14:33; see 1 Pe.2:5; 2:9; Pr. 23:26).**

VIII. There Was the Consecration to Service (vv.19-21).

The instructions given by God are full of lessons for the believer.

1. The priests were to lay their hands on its head (v.19).
2. The priests were to slaughter the ram and put some blood...
   - on the tip of the right ear: setting it apart to listen (v.20)
   - on the thumb of the right hand: setting it apart to touch and do only righteous things (v.20)
   - on the big toe of the right foot: setting it apart to walk in the ways of God (v.20)
   - on all sides of the altar (v.20)

Thought

The priests of God (believers) are to be totally consecrated to the service of God. *Consecration* means that we are to be sanctified, purified, set apart totally to serving God.

a) Our ears are to be sanctified, purified, set apart to God. We are to guard what we listen to and hear, guard the...

- music
- films
- conversations
- jokes

Our ears are to be totally consecrated to God. We must be constantly listening to God and to the cries and needs of people.

> **"Blessed is the man that heareth me, watching daily at my gates, waiting at the posts of my doors" (Pr.8:34).**
> **"Wherefore, my beloved brethren, let every man be swift to hear, slow to speak, slow to wrath" (Js.1:19; see 2 Ti.4:4).**

b) Our fingers must be used to do good, to do only righteous deeds.

> **"As we have therefore opportunity, let us do good unto all men, especially unto them who are of the household of faith" (Ga.6:10; see Ga.6:2; Ps.2:11).**

    c)   Our feet are to be consecrated to walk in the ways of God.

> **"This I say then, Walk in the Spirit, and ye shall not fulfil the lust of the flesh" (Ga.5:16; see Ep.4:1; 1 Jn.1:7).**
> **"And now, Israel, what doth the LORD thy God require of thee, but to fear the LORD thy God, to walk in all his ways, and to love him, and to serve the LORD thy God with all thy heart and with all thy soul" (De.10:12).**

3. Some blood and anointing oil were to be sprinkled on the priests and their clothes (v.21). This command seems a bit strange. Why would God have His priests adorned in such splendid clothing only to *ruin* them with spots of blood and oil? Remember what this ram symbolized—a consecration to service. God's priests were not called to an easy task, never to get dirty, never to become involved in the sufferings and problems of people. The blood and the oil addressed the very purpose for the priests: to serve God and to serve His people, no matter how terrible the suffering or difficult the problem.

Thought
Far too many believers refuse to become soiled by the broken lives of people. Seeking some title or lofty position has become the norm for many believers. Getting dirty hands while ministering to the desperate needs of fallen people is offensive, repugnant, and vile to the person who does not want to get involved. God has a far different idea in mind for those who truly want to serve Him.

> **"And whosoever shall give to drink unto one of these little ones a cup of cold water only in the name of a disciple, verily I say unto you, he shall in no wise lose his reward" (Mt.10:42; see Ps.126:5).**
> **"Even as the Son of man came not to be ministered unto, but to minister, and to give his life a ransom for many" (Mt.20:28; see Lu.22:27; Ph.2:6-7).**

4. The purpose for slaughtering the second ram was to symbolize full consecration to the service of God.

> **"And now, Israel, what doth the LORD thy God require of thee, but to fear the LORD thy God, to walk in all his ways, and to love him, and to serve the LORD thy God with all thy heart and with all thy soul" (De.10:12; see Ps.2:11; Ep.6:7).**
> **"Wherefore we receiving a kingdom which cannot be moved, let us have grace, whereby we may serve God acceptably with reverence and godly fear" (He.12:28).**

IX. There Was the Commitment to Give God the Best (vv.22-28).

This was symbolized in the observance of two wave offerings.
1. There was the first wave offering (vv.22-25). The order of this first ceremony was unique.
    a. Moses was to cut away the fat and choice parts from the ram of ordination (v.22).
    b. Moses was to take one loaf of unleavened bread, one cake, and one wafer from the basket (v.23).
    c. Moses was to put all these into the hands of the priests. Then they were to lift them up and wave them before the LORD as a wave offering (v.24). The meaning of the original language comes from the original root (nuph) that translates wave as "to shake, agitate, move to and fro, or up and down."[1] This was a ceremony that required a physical act on the part of the priests. It required a personal

---

[1]   George Bush. *Commentary on Exodus.* (Grand Rapids, MI: Kregel Publications, 1993), p. 482.

involvement, an open show of thanksgiving to God. The Expositor's Bible Commentary adds more clarity to the form of this wave offering:

> *The waving was not from side to side but toward the altar and back, showing that the sacrifice was given to God and then received back by the priest for his use (cf. Le.7:30; 23:20). Everything that had been waved except the 'breast of the ram' was then to be burned on the altar.*[2]

d. Moses was to burn the items upon the altar as a burnt offering of pleasing aroma to the LORD, which symbolized the pleasure and acceptance of the LORD (v.25).

2. There was the second wave offering (vv.26-28). Moses was to take the breast and shoulder of the ram, lift and wave it before the LORD (v.26). God gave him two specific reasons for this:
   a. To sanctify—set apart as holy—the parts of the rams that belong to the priests (v.27).
   b. To always give these parts to the priests when making fellowship offerings (thanksgiving or peace offerings) (v.28).

Thought
Note that only the choice parts were offered to God. Only the very best should ever be offered to God. Only the very best pleases Him. What is the best that we can give to God? What are the things that please God the most?

⇒   God is pleased when we give Him our bodies.

> **"I beseech you therefore, brethren, by the mercies of God, that ye present your bodies a living sacrifice, holy, acceptable unto God, which is your reasonable service. And be not conformed to this world: but be ye transformed by the renewing of your mind, that ye may prove what is that good, and acceptable, and perfect, will of God" (Ro.12:1-2).**
> **"What? know ye not that your body is the temple of the Holy Ghost which is in you, which ye have of God, and ye are not your own? For ye are bought with a price: therefore glorify God in your body, and in your spirit, which are God's" (1 Co.6:19-20).**

⇒   God is pleased when we obey Him.

> **"And Samuel said, Hath the LORD as great delight in burnt offerings and sacrifices, as in obeying the voice of the LORD? Behold, to obey is better than sacrifice, and to hearken than the fat of rams" (1 S.15:22).**

⇒   God is pleased when we are faithful to Him.

> **"His lord said unto him, Well done, thou good and faithful servant: thou hast been faithful over a few things, I will make thee ruler over many things: enter thou into the joy of thy lord" (Mt.25:21).**

⇒   God is pleased when His people introduce a sinner to the *good news* of the gospel.

> **"Go, stand and speak in the temple to the people all the words of this life" (Ac.5:20; see Ac.1:8).**

---

[2]   Frank E. Gaebelein. *The Expositor's Bible Commentary*, Vol.2, p.470.

> "For I am not ashamed of the gospel of Christ: for it is the power of God unto salvation to every one that believeth; to the Jew first, and also to the Greek" (Ro.1:16).

⇒ God is pleased when His people do good and share with those in need.

> "But to do good and to communicate forget not: for with such sacrifices God is well pleased" (He.13:16).

X. There Was the Passing Down of the Ordination Clothes of the High Priest (vv.29-30).

These treasured garments would not be the sole possession of only one owner.
1. The ordination clothes were to be worn by the succeeding son in the ordination service (v.29).
2. The ordination clothes were to be worn for seven days (v.30). Often the number seven is seen in Scripture as perfection or completeness. The command for the clothes to be worn for seven days could be symbolic of the priest's perfection, that he was consecrating himself totally and completely to the LORD'S service.

Thought
The sons were to be as chosen by God in the priesthood as the fathers had been. Therefore, the clothes were to symbolize that they were to be as dedicated, consecrated, and set apart to God as their fathers who had served as priests before them.

The ministers of all succeeding generations must be as dedicated and consecrated to God—yea, even more so—than the previous generations. This is an absolute essential in order to complete the task of our Lord and Savior, Jesus Christ—the task of reaching every man, woman, and child of every generation yet to come.

> "I beseech you therefore, brethren, by the mercies of God, that ye present your bodies a living sacrifice, holy, acceptable unto God, which is your reasonable service. And be not conformed to this world: but be ye transformed by the renewing of your mind, that ye may prove what is that good, and acceptable, and perfect, will of God" (Ro.12:1-2).
> "And thou shalt love the LORD thy God with all thine heart, and with all thy soul, and with all thy might" (De.6:5).
> "'Ye have not chosen me, but I have chosen you, and ordained you, that he should go and bring forth fruit, and that your fruit should remain: that whatsoever ye shall ask of the Father in my name, he may give it you" (Jn.15:16; see 1 Ti.1:12).
> "And that ye put on [clothe yourself with] the new man, which after God is created in righteousness and true holiness" (Ep.4:24; see Ro.13:14).

XI. There Was the Communion or Fellowship Meal (vv.31-34).

Rooted deeply in the sacrificial system was the idea of feasts. The Hebrew calendar is filled with various sacrifices and feasts. Note the details of this particular meal:
1. Moses was to boil the ram's meat in the holy place (v.31). This was most probably done in the courtyard of the Tabernacle.
2. Moses was to hold a type of communion meal among the priests at the door of the Tabernacle (v.32).
   a. The priests were to eat the ram's meat along with the bread in the basket (v.32).
   b. The priests were to eat the meat and bread sacrificed for their atonement. This was a meal that no one else was allowed to eat because the food had been sanctified, set apart as holy to the LORD (v.33).

c. The priests were to burn any sacrificial meat or bread left over. It was not to be eaten because it was holy (set apart to God) (v.34).

Thought
Jesus Christ invites His people to come, eat, and commune with Him.

> **"Wherefore do ye spend money for that which is not bread? and your labour for that which satisfieth not? hearken diligently unto me, and eat ye that which is good, and let your soul delight itself in fatness" (Is.55:2).**
> **"And Jesus said unto them, I am the bread of life: he that cometh to me shall never hunger; and he that believeth on me shall never thirst" (Jn.6:35; see Jn.6:51).**
> **"Behold, I stand at the door, and knock: if any man hear my voice, and open the door, I will come in to him, and will sup with him, and he with me" (Re.3:20).**

XII. There Was the Repetition of the Ordination Ceremony That Was to Be Repeated for Seven Days (vv.35-37).

1. The stress was obedience—to do everything God commanded (v.35).
2. Moses was to sacrifice a bull every day as a sin offering to God (v.36).
3. Moses was to purify and anoint the altar for seven days for the following great purposes (v.36):
   a. It would make the altar holy (set apart to God) (v.37).
   b. It would make whatever touched the altar holy (v.37).

Thought
It is Jesus Christ who is holy, set apart to God. It is Jesus Christ who makes every sinful heart He touches holy. Jesus Christ takes every genuine believer and sets him apart to God.

> **"Wherefore come out from among them, and be ye separate, saith the Lord, and touch not the unclean thing; and I will receive you, And will be a Father unto you, and ye shall be my sons and daughters, saith the Lord Almighty. Having therefore these promises, dearly beloved, let us cleanse ourselves from all filthiness of the flesh and spirit, perfecting holiness in the fear of God" (2 Co.6:17-7:1; see Lu.1:74-75).**
> **"But as he which hath called you is holy, so be ye holy in all manner of conversation; Because it is written, Be ye holy; for I am holy" (1 Pe.1:15-16; see 1 Pe.2:9).**

XIII. There Were the Morning and Evening Sacrifices (vv.38-46).

The final charge in this portion of Scripture contains the *daily* offerings, the morning and evening sacrifices.
1. The priests were to offer two one-year old lambs each day, one in the morning and one in the evening (vv.38-39). These offerings were not to replace the other sacrifices; they were in addition to the others. The morning and evening sacrifices set the tone for the worship of God's people: they were to worship morning until night—all day, every day.

Thought
We need to be renewed in the morning before we begin our day and at night before we retire to sleep. This is the clear message from Scripture.

> "My voice shalt thou hear in the morning, O *LORD*; in the morn-
> ing will I direct my prayer unto thee, and will look up" (Ps.5:3; see
> 1 S.1:19; Jb.1:5).
> "Evening, and morning, and at noon, will I pray, and cry aloud:
> and he shall hear my voice" (Ps.55:17; see Ps.113:3).
> "Seven times a day do I praise thee because of thy righteous
> judgments" (Ps.119:164).
> "And in the morning, rising up a great while before day, he went
> out, and departed into a solitary place, and there prayed" (Mk.1:35;
> see 1 Th.3:10; 1 Ti.5:5).

2. The priests were to offer the first lamb with two quarts of flour mixed with one quart
of olive oil and wine. It was a drink offering (v.40).
3. The priests were to offer the second lamb with the same items (v.41).
4. The effect upon the LORD would be twofold:
    a. It would be a pleasing aroma and sacrifice to the LORD (v.41).
    b. It would satisfy the fire (holiness) of the LORD (v.41).
5. The critical importance of the morning and evening sacrifice was the heartbeat of the
believer's daily relationship with God. It was to be observed forever, throughout all generations (v.42).
6. If God's people were faithful in keeping the daily sacrifice—keeping it with a genuine, trusting heart—the results would be phenomenal (vv.42-46).
    a. The LORD would meet and speak to His messenger (Moses), guiding and giving
        him direction (v.42).

> "Thou shalt guide me with thy counsel, and afterward receive me
> to glory" (Ps.73:24).
> "And thine ears shall hear a word behind thee, saying, This is the
> way, walk ye in it, when ye turn to the right hand, and when ye turn
> to the left" (Is.30:21; see Jn.14:21).

    b. The LORD would meet and speak to the people (v.43).

Thought
God has promised to speak to His people in a voice they know, in a way that they
can understand.

> "My sheep hear my voice, and I know them, and they follow
> me" (Jn.10:27).
> "God, who at sundry times and in divers manners spake in
> time past unto the fathers by the prophets, Hath in these last
> days spoken unto us by his Son, whom he hath appointed heir of
> all things, by whom also he made the worlds" (He.1:1-2).
> "All scripture is given by inspiration of God, and is profitable
> for doctrine, for reproof, for correction, for instruction in right-
> eousness" (2 Ti.3:16).

    c. The LORD would sanctify the Tabernacle (place of worship) with His glory (v.44).

Thought
The Christian believer (his body and life) is the Tabernacle that God has sanctified with His glory.

> "And I will put my spirit within you, and cause you to walk in
> my statutes, and ye shall keep my judgments, and do them"
> (Eze.36:27).

> "What? know ye not that your body is the temple of the Holy Ghost which is in you, which ye have of God, and ye are not your own?" (1 Co.6:19; see 1 Co.3:16; Ga.2:20; Col.1:27; 2 Ti.1:14; 1 Jn.3:24).

d. The LORD would sanctify (set apart as holy) the Tabernacle, altar, and the priests—all to His service (v.44).

Thought

The goal of every believer should be to serve God, to be useful to God. God only uses those whom He sanctifies (makes holy), and He only sanctifies those whom He can use.

> "Sanctify them through thy truth: thy word is truth" (Jn.17:17).
>
> "But of him are ye in Christ Jesus, who of God is made unto us wisdom, and righteousness, and sanctification, and redemption" (1 Co.1:30; see Ep.5:26).
>
> "If a man therefore purge himself from these, he shall be a vessel unto honour, sanctified, and meet for the master's use, and prepared unto every good work" (2 Ti.2:21; see He.10:10; 13:12).

e. The LORD would dwell among His people and be their God (v.45).

Thought

There is a twofold blessing in this promise:

a) God will dwell among His people. God will live with them, care for them, love them.

> "And, behold, I am with thee, and will keep thee in all places whither thou goest, and will bring thee again into this land; for I will not leave thee, until I have done that which I have spoken to thee of" (Ge.28:15).
>
> "When thou passest through the waters, I will be with thee; and through the rivers, they shall not overflow thee: when thou walkest through the fire, thou shalt not be burned; neither shall the flame kindle upon thee" (Is.43:2).

b) God will be *their* God. God will be their Father, their LORD, their Savior.

> "I have redeemed thee, I have called thee by thy name; thou art mine" (Is.43:1).

f. The people would know that the LORD is the God who delivers and sets them free (v.46).

Thought

Jesus Christ is the only One who can deliver us from the bondage of sin and set us free.

> "And ye shall know the truth, and the truth shall make you free" (Jn.8:32; see Is.61:1; Ro.6:23).
>
> "There is therefore now no condemnation to them which are in Christ Jesus, who walk not after the flesh, but after the Spirit. For the law of the Spirit of life in Christ Jesus hath made me free from the law of sin and death" (Ro.8:1-2).

CHAPTER NINE

The Altar of Incense: The Symbol of the Prayers and Communion of God's People Ascending to God (Exodus 30:1-10)

Contents

The Altar of Incense: The Symbol of the Prayers and Communion of God's People Ascending to God (Exodus 30:1-10)

1. The design & materials

a. To be made of acacia wood (symbolized the perfection of Christ's intercession)

b. To be square: 18" x 18" x 3' high

c. To have horns on each corner, carved from the same piece of wood (symbolized the power of God in answer to prayer)

d. To be overlaid with gold & to have a gold molding (a symbol of deity, of the most valuable, prized possession)

e. To attach two gold rings on each side: To hold the two poles used to carry the Altar (a symbol that prayer is not limited to one geographical location: People are to pray everywhere)

f. To make the poles of acacia wood overlaid with gold

g. To place the Altar just outside the in-

And thou shalt make an altar to burn incense upon: of shittim wood shalt thou make it.

2 A cubit shall be the length thereof, and a cubit the breadth thereof; foursquare shall it be: and two cubits shall be the height thereof: the horns thereof shall be of the same.

3 And thou shalt overlay it with pure gold, the top thereof, and the sides thereof round about, and the horns thereof; and thou shalt make unto it a crown of gold round about.

4 And two golden rings shalt thou make to it under the crown of it, by the two corners thereof, upon the two sides of it shalt thou make it; and they shall be for places for the staves to bear it withal.

5 And thou shalt make the staves of shittim wood, and overlay them with gold.

6 And thou shalt put it before the

vail that is by the ark of the testimony, before the mercy seat that is over the testimony, where I will meet with thee.

7 And Aaron shall burn thereon sweet incense every morning: when he dresseth the lamps, he shall burn incense upon it.

8 And when Aaron lighteth the lamps at even, he shall burn incense upon it, a perpetual incense before the LORD throughout your generations.

9 Ye shall offer no strange incense thereon, nor burnt sacrifice, nor meat offering; neither shall ye pour drink offering thereon.

10 And Aaron shall make an atonement upon the horns of it once in a year with the blood of the sin offering of atonements: once in the year shall he make atonement upon it throughout your generations: it is most holy unto the LORD.

ner curtain opposite the Ark of the Covenant & its cover, the Mercy Seat (symbolized how prayer brings people near God)

2. The purpose of the Altar

a. To have the High Priest burn incense every morning when he tended the lamps & every evening when he lit them

b. To be a permanent incense ascending to the LORD (symbolized the permanent intercession of Christ & that we should pray always, morning & evening)

3. The holiness of the Altar

a. Never to allow the Altar to be desecrated nor misused

b. To purify the Altar once a year: By placing on its horns blood from the atoning sacrifice (a symbol that we can only approach God through the intercessory ministry, the atoning sacrifice of Christ)

c. The reason: Because the Altar was holy to the LORD

God answers prayer. When we face severe problems, trouble, or crises, God answers prayer. When we face terrible trial or temptation, God answers prayer. When we face sickness, disease, or accident, God answers prayer. When we face pain, suffering, terminal illness, or death, God answers prayer. When we face the difficult times of life—if we pray, cry out to God from the depths of our heart—God hears and answers our prayers. When we need comfort, guidance, assurance, security, companionship, friendship—God hears and answers our prayers. He meets our need always. This is the significance and purpose of the Altar of Incense. The Altar was used to offer up the most pleasing and acceptable aroma that can be imagined. This symbolized the pleasure and acceptance of God, that He was pleased with the aroma and accepted the offering being made. What was the offering? Prayer, the prayers of His dear people. The Altar of Incense symbolized the prayers of God's dear people ascending up to God. This is the subject of this important portion of Scripture: *The Altar of Incense: The Symbol of the Prayers and Communion of God's People Ascending to God,* Ex.30:1-10.

    I.   The design and materials of the Altar (vv.1-6).
   II. The purpose of the Altar (vv.7-8).
  III. The holiness of the Altar (vv.9-10).

I. There Was the Design and the Materials of the Altar of Incense (vv.1-6).

The incense on the Altar was to burn continuously, symbolizing two significant things:
    ⇒   the unbroken intercession of Jesus Christ for us
    ⇒   the prayers and communion of God's people ascending to God

Note again: God Himself is the One who designed this Altar. The Altar was to be made like every other piece of furniture in the Tabernacle, made according to God's perfect plan and design. These are the details for its construction:

1.   The Altar of Incense was to be made of acacia wood (v.1). We have already noted the quality of acacia wood and how it speaks of incorruptibility, the incorruption and perfection of Jesus Christ (see note—Chapter One, Ex.25:5). Jesus Christ is the One who intercedes for us, who stands between God and us and makes us acceptable to God. The intercession of Christ is not corrupt in any way; His intercession is perfect. He makes us acceptable to God.

> **"Wherefore he is able also to save them to the uttermost that come unto God by him, seeing he ever liveth to make intercession for them. For such an high priest became us, who is holy, harmless, undefiled, separate from sinners, and made higher than the heavens; Who needeth not daily, as those high priests, to offer up sacrifice, first for his own sins, and then for the people's: for this he did once, when he offered up himself" (He.7:25-27).**

2.   The Altar of Incense was to be square: 18 inches by 18 inches by 3 feet high (v.2).
3.   The Altar of Incense was to have horns on each corner, carved from the same piece of wood (v.2). Horns are symbolic of God's power and strength, God's salvation, protection, security, sanctuary, and help.

Thought
Note the strong lesson seen in the symbol of the horns. The horns are symbolic of God's power and strength. God's power and strength are available to help us in times of desperate need, times of...

• pain and anguish	• bankruptcy and loss
• loneliness and emptiness	• hunger and poverty
• accident and disease	• suffering and death
• temptation and sin	• broken trust and desertion

The Altar of Incense reminds us that God has the power and strength to deliver us through all trials, no matter how terrible.

> **"And the Lord shall deliver me from every evil work, and will preserve me unto his heavenly kingdom: to whom be glory for ever and ever. Amen" (2 Ti.4:18; see 2 Co.12:9; He.13:6; Ps.23:1-6; 28:7).**
> **"But I am poor and needy; yet the Lord thinketh upon me: thou art my help and my deliverer; make no tarrying, O my God" (Ps.40:17).**
> **"Fear thou not; for I am with thee: be not dismayed; for I am thy God: I will strengthen thee; yea, I will help thee; yea, I will uphold thee with the right hand of my righteousness" (Is.41:10; see Is.46:4).**

4. The Altar of Incense was to be overlaid with gold and have a gold molding (v.3). Just like the other holy pieces of furniture in the sanctuary, the Altar was covered with pure gold. The most precious of metals was God's choice for building this Altar of intercession. Remember, gold is a symbol of deity, a symbol of the most precious possession, God Himself. The golden Altar of Incense points to the Lord Jesus Christ...
- who is the most precious possession a person can have
- who is the *Perfect Intercessor*, the One who *lives* forever to make intercession, to passionately pray for the people of God

> **"Wherefore he is able also to save them to the uttermost that come unto God by him, seeing he ever liveth to make intercession for them" (He.7:25).**

The purpose for the gold molding was to keep the burning coals from falling off the Altar and burning out on the desert floor. What was the origin of the fire that was kept in the Altar? The live coals came from the Altar of burnt offerings, the Altar which symbolized the need for atonement with God. No effectual prayers can be offered to God unless a sacrifice has been offered to satisfy the righteous and just nature of a holy God. As the priests ministered at the Altar of Incense, the gold molding and hot coals reminded them of several things:
⇒ They were reminded of God's righteous and just nature and of His blazing judgment against sin.
⇒ This was clearly seen in the hot coals that burned red with heat.
⇒ They were reminded of God's wonderful mercy and grace that invited them to approach His holy throne.
⇒ They were reminded of their reason for being at the Altar: to intercede for the desperate needs of a sinful people who needed the help of God.

Thought
Our prayers should always be fervent, hot as the coals on the Altar. Prayer is not an occasion for complacency and lethargy but for the deep cry of the human spirit to touch the living God!

> **"The righteous cry, and the LORD heareth, and delivereth them out of all their troubles. The LORD is nigh unto them that are of a broken heart; and saveth such as be of a contrite spirit" (Ps.34:17-18; see Ps.40:1; 42:1-2).**
> **"O God, thou art my God; early will I seek thee: my soul thirsteth for thee, my flesh longeth for thee in a dry and thirsty land, where no water is" (Ps.63:1; see Ps.63:8).**

5. The Altar of Incense was to have two gold rings attached to each side. The rings were to hold the two poles used in carrying the Altar (v.4).
6. The Altar of Incense was to have two poles made of acacia wood overlaid with gold (v.5). The Altar, like the rest of the Tabernacle, was designed to be moved. The Altar of

Incense, of prayer, was to go with God's people whenever and wherever they traveled. This points to a beautiful, meaningful fact about prayer. Prayer is not limited to a single geographical location on the earth. God's people are to pray wherever they go, anyplace, anywhere, all the time.

> **"Pray without ceasing" (1 Th.5:17).**
> **"I will therefore that men pray every where, lifting up holy hands, without wrath and doubting" (1 Ti.2:8).**

7. God told Moses to place the Altar just outside the inner curtain. It was to be opposite the Ark of the Covenant and its cover, the Mercy Seat (v.6). The location of the Altar is significant. How close to the inner curtain was the Altar placed? No one knows, but what is known is that the Altar was *just outside* the curtain. It was very, very close to the presence of God. This is the great blessing of intercessory prayer: intercessory prayer...

- is close to the veil
- is close to the very throne of God
- is close to the glory of God
- is close to the place where God's eternal mercy and grace reside
- is close to the door of answered prayer
- is close to the most intimate fellowship and communion with God imaginable

Thought 1.
The one thing we are to seek above all else is to be near God, to fellowship and commune with Him in an unbroken sense of His presence.

> **"I have set the LORD always before me: because he is at my right hand, I shall not be moved" (Ps.16:8).**
> **"The LORD is nigh unto them that are of a broken heart; and saveth such as be of a contrite spirit" (Ps.34:18; see Ps.73:28).**
> **"The LORD is nigh unto all them that call upon him, to all that call upon him in truth" (Ps.145:18; see He.10:22; Js.4:8).**

Thought 2.
The inner curtain that had once separated the Altar of Incense from the Ark of God's presence was torn down, torn from top to bottom by God Himself. God ripped it open through the death of His Son, the Lord Jesus Christ. The way into God's presence is now open. We are now invited to come boldly and worship God at the Throne of Grace.

> **"Let us therefore come boldly unto the throne of grace, that we may obtain mercy, and find grace to help in time of need" (He.4:16).**

II. The Purpose for the Altar Was Twofold (vv.7-8).

1. The Altar was to be the place where sweet incense was offered up to the LORD every morning and evening. The High Priest burned incense every morning when he tended the lamps and every evening when he lit them (v.7). This symbolized the critical importance of praying every morning and evening.

2. The Altar of Incense was to be the place where a permanent incense ascended up to the LORD (v.8). This symbolized two things.

   a. There is the symbol of the permanent intercession of Jesus Christ. Jesus Christ is living forever—in the very presence of God—to make intercession for us. He died and arose from the dead for this very purpose: to stand before God as the great

Intercessor for us. (The following is taken from the Thompson Chain Reference Bible, the General Index # 1783.)[1]

⇒ Jesus Christ intercedes for sinners

"Therefore will I divide him a portion with the great, and he shall divide the spoil with the strong; because he hath poured out his soul unto death: and he was numbered with the transgressors; and he bare the sin of many, and made intercession for the transgressors" (Is.53:12).

⇒ Jesus Christ intercedes for weak believers

"But I have prayed for thee, that thy faith fail not: and when thou art converted, strengthen thy brethren" (Lu.22:32).

⇒ Jesus Christ intercedes for His enemies

"Then said Jesus, Father, forgive them; for they know not what they do. And they parted his raiment, and cast lots" (Lu.23:34).

⇒ Jesus Christ intercedes for the church

"I pray for them: I pray not for the world, but for them which thou hast given me; for they are thine" (Jn.17:9).

⇒ Jesus Christ intercedes for God to accept us

"Who is he that condemneth? It is Christ that died, yea rather, that is risen again, who is even at the right hand of God, who also maketh intercession for us" (Ro.8:34).

⇒ Jesus Christ intercedes for our salvation

"Wherefore he is able also to save them to the uttermost that come unto God by him, seeing he ever liveth to make intercession for them" (He.7:25).

⇒ Jesus Christ intercedes for the Holy Spirit to abide with us

"And I will pray the Father, and he shall give you another Comforter, that he may abide with you for ever" (Jn.14:16).

b. There is the symbol that believers are to pray morning and evening, to pray always, to develop an unbroken communion with God, to never cease being in a spirit of prayer.

"Seek the LORD and his strength, seek his face continually" (1 Chr.16:11).
"Ask, and it shall be given you; seek, and ye shall find; knock, and it shall be opened unto you" (Mt.7:7; see Lu.18:1).
"Praying always with all prayer and supplication in the Spirit, and watching thereunto with all perseverance and supplication for all saints" (Ep.6:18; see 1 Th.5:17).

---

[1] *The New Thompson Chain Reference Bible.* (Indianapolis, IN: B.B. Kirkbride Bible Co., Inc., 1964.)

III. The Holiness of the Altar of Incense Set It Apart as a Very Special Piece of Furniture (vv.9-10).

Note how forcefully God stressed the holiness of the Altar.

1. The priests were never to allow the Altar to be desecrated nor misused (v.9). Any foreign thing that was placed on the Altar was a direct affront to God. Prayer is holy to God. It is more intimate than any physical relationship experienced by people. Adding anything to His ordained plan for intercession and prayer was sin.

2. Once a year Aaron was to purify the Altar by placing on its horns some blood from the atoning sacrifice (the blood of the sin offering) (v.10). For the Altar of Incense to have any lasting significance, it had to be directly connected to the blood that was shed on the Altar of Burnt Offerings. Why? Because the prayers of believers have to be directly connected to the shed blood of Christ.

⇒ It is at the Altar of prayer where we plead the power of Christ's blood to cleanse and accept us.

⇒ It is at the Altar of prayer where we stand in Christ's atonement, where we are reconciled to God.

⇒ It is at the Altar of prayer where we go behind the inner curtain, in Christ's name, and experience the wonderful presence and glory of God Himself.

3. Why was this Altar to be purified? Because the Altar was most holy to the LORD (v.10). Prayer is a very serious thing to God. How He longs for people to stand before the holy Altar, offering an incense that is pleasing to Him. How He longs for people to live holy lives and pray, seeking His face continually.

The Altar of Incense is *most holy* to the LORD because it represents the *Intercessory Ministry*, the *atoning sacrifice,* of Christ. Nothing is as dear to the heart of God as His Son, the Lord Jesus Christ. God wanted Christ to die for us, to die as the atoning sacrifice for our sins. This Jesus Christ did. He died for us, died in obedience to God's will. Because He obeyed God—did what God the Father wanted—nothing touches the heart of God like the *Intercessory Ministry*, the atoning sacrifice, of His Son.

Thus God has taken the *Intercessory Ministry*, the *atoning sacrifice,* of His dear Son and made it holy: sanctified it, set it apart as very special in the eternal plan of redemption.

⇒ By the *Intercessory Ministry* of Christ, He stands forth as our eternal Mediator, making us acceptable to God.

"For there is one God, and one mediator between God and men, the man Christ Jesus; Who gave himself a ransom for all, to be testified in due time" (1 Ti.2:5-6; see Jn.14:6; He.9:15).

"For Christ is not entered into the holy places made with hands, which are the figures of the true; but into heaven itself, now to appear in the presence of God for us" (He.9:24).

"My little children, these things write I unto you, that ye sin not. And if any man sin, we have an advocate [mediator] with the Father, Jesus Christ the righteous: And he is the propitiation for our sins: and not for ours only, but also for the sins of the whole world" (1 Jn.2:1-2).

⇒ By the *Intercessory Ministry* of Christ, the door into God's presence is opened. We now have access into God's presence—anytime, anyplace—through prayer.

"I am the door: by me if any man enter in, he shall be saved, and shall go in and out, and find pasture" (Jn.10:9).

"Hitherto have ye asked nothing in my name: ask, and ye shall receive, that your joy may be full" (Jn.16:24).

"By whom also we have access by faith into this grace wherein we stand, and rejoice in hope of the glory of God" (Ro.5:2; see Ep.2:18; 3:12; He.10:22).

TYPES, SYMBOLS, AND PICTURES
(Exodus 30:1-10)

Historical Term	Type or Picture (Scriptural Basis)	Life Application for Today's Believer	Biblical Application for Today's Believer
The Altar of Incense (Ex.30:1-10; 40:26-27) See also Ex.35:15; 37:25-29; 39:38; 40:5	*The Altar of Incense filled the Sanctuary with a sweet-smelling incense. Twice a day, in the morning and evening, the High Priest burned incense on the Altar. The message of the Altar is at least two things:* a. *The intercession of the High Priest symbolized a permanent intercession, an intercession that never quits.*	What the Altar of Incense taught: a. Christ as our great High Priest is always praying and living in an unbroken communion with God the Father, interceding for God's people.	*"Seeing then that we have a great high priest [Intercessor], that is passed into the heavens, Jesus the Son of God, let us hold fast our profession. For we have not an high priest which cannot be touched with the feeling of our infirmities; but was in all points tempted like as we are, yet without sin" (He. 4:14-15; see Jn.17:9; Ro.8:34; He.7:25).* *"Wherefore he is able also to save them to the uttermost that come unto God by him, seeing he ever liveth to make intercession for them" (He.7:25).*
	b. *The Altar of Incense symbolized the prayers and unbroken communion of God's people ascending up to God and pleasing Him.* **"And thou shalt make an altar to burn incense upon: of shittim wood shalt thou make it" (Ex.30:1).** **"And he put the golden altar in the tent of the congregation before the vail: And he burnt sweet incense thereon; as the LORD commanded Moses" (Ex.40:26-27).**	b. Believers are to pray morning and evening, to pray always, to develop an unbroken communion with God, to never cease being in a spirit of prayer.	*"Seek the LORD and his strength, seek his face continually" (1 Chr.16:11).* *"Ask, and it shall be given you; seek, and ye shall find; knock, and it shall be opened unto you" (Mt.7:7; see Mt.26:41).* *"Hitherto have ye asked nothing in my name: ask, and ye shall receive, that your joy may be full" (Jn.16:24).* *"Praying always with all prayer and supplication in the Spirit, and watching thereunto with all perseverance and supplication for all saints" (Ep.6:18; see 1 Th.5:17).*

THE ALTAR OF INCENSE

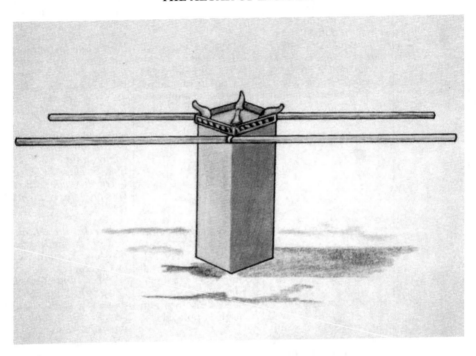

Other Instructions for the Tabernacle: Symbolizing Spiritual Health and Maturity (Exodus 30:11-38)

Contents

Other Instructions for the Tabernacle: Symbolizing Spiritual Health and Maturity (Exodus 30:11-38)

1. The raising of money for the Tabernacle offering: Symbolized the ransom paid for one's life

a. To pay a ransom tax every time a census was taken
   1) Would be a reminder of God's redemption
   2) Would assure God's protection: Erase any chance of God's judgment or plague

b. To pay one fifth of an ounce of silver

c. To include every person 20 years old & above

d. To be the same amount for both rich & poor: Because it is an offering to make atonement for the soul

e. The purpose of the offering (tax)
   1) A material purpose: To take care of the Tabernacle
   2) A spiritual purpose: To be a memorial pointing to the atonement or ransom being paid for one's life

2. The Bronze Wash Basin: Symbolized the washing, cleansing, & forgiveness of sin

a. To make the bronze basin with a bronze pedestal

b. To place it between the Tabernacle & Altar: Fill it with water

c. The purpose: For the priests to wash their hands & feet
   1) When they entered the Tabernacle
   2) When they approached the Altar to make sacrifice

---

11 And the LORD spake unto Moses, saying,

12 When thou takest the sum of the children of Israel after their number, then shall they give every man a ransom for his soul unto the LORD, when thou numberest them; that there be no plague among them, when thou numberest them.

13 This they shall give, every one that passeth among them that are numbered, half a shekel after the shekel of the sanctuary: (a shekel is twenty gerahs:) an half shekel shall be the offering of the LORD.

14 Every one that passeth among them that are numbered, from twenty years old and above, shall give an offering unto the LORD.

15 The rich shall not give more, and the poor shall not give less than half a shekel, when they give an offering unto the LORD, to make an atonement for your souls.

16 And thou shalt take the atonement money of the children of Israel, and shalt appoint it for the service of the tabernacle of the congregation; that it may be a memorial unto the children of Israel before the LORD, to make an atonement for your souls.

17 And the LORD spake unto Moses, saying,

18 Thou shalt also make a laver of brass, and his foot also of brass, to wash withal: and thou shalt put it between the tabernacle of the congregation and the altar, and thou shalt put water therein.

19 For Aaron and his sons shall wash their hands and their feet thereat:

20 When they go into the tabernacle of the congregation, they shall wash with water, that they die not; or when they come near to the altar to minister, to burn offering made

d. The warning: Must wash or die

e. The importance of the washing & cleansing: Was a permanent law for all generations

3. The anointing oil: Symbolized the Holy Spirit & God's appointment to service

a. To blend these choice spices
1) 12½ pounds of pure myrrh
2) 6¼ pounds of cinnamon
3) 6¼ pounds of sweet cane

4) 12½ pounds of cassia
5) 1 gallon of olive oil

b. To mix & blend into a holy anointing oil

c. To use the oil to anoint
• The Tabernacle & its furnishings
• The Ark of the Covenant
• The table & its utensils
• The Lampstand & its accessories
• The Altar of Incense
• The Altar of Burnt Offering & its utensils
• The Wash Basin

---

by fire unto the LORD:

21 So they shall wash their hands and their feet, that they die not: and it shall be a statute for ever to them, even to him and to his seed throughout their generations.

22 Moreover the LORD spake unto Moses, saying,

23 Take thou also unto thee principal spices, of pure myrrh five hundred shekels, and of sweet cinnamon half so much, even two hundred and fifty shekels, and of sweet calamus two hundred and fifty shekels,

24 And of cassia five hundred shekels, after the shekel of the sanctuary, and of oil olive an hin:

25 And thou shalt make it an oil of holy ointment, an ointment compound after the art of the apothecary: it shall be an holy anointing oil.

26 And thou shalt anoint the tabernacle of the congregation therewith, and the ark of the testimony,

27 And the table and all his vessels, and the candlestick and his vessels, and the altar of incense,

28 And the altar of burnt offering with all his vessels, and the laver and his foot.

29 And thou shalt sanctify them, that they may be most

---

holy: whatsoever toucheth them shall be holy.

30 And thou shalt anoint Aaron and his sons, and consecrate them, that they may minister unto me in the priest's office.

31 And thou shalt speak unto the children of Israel, saying, This shall be an holy anointing oil unto me throughout your generations.

32 Upon man's flesh shall it not be poured, neither shall ye make any other like it, after the composition of it: it is holy, and it shall be holy unto you.

33 Whosoever compoundeth any like it, or whosoever putteth any of it upon a stranger, shall even be cut off from his people.

34 And the LORD said unto Moses, Take unto thee sweet spices, stacte, and onycha, and galbanum; these sweet spices with pure frankincense: of each shall there be a like weight:

35 And thou shalt make it a perfume, a confection after the art of the apothecary, tempered together, pure and holy:

36 And thou shalt beat some of it very small, and put of it before the testimony in the tabernacle of the congregation, where I will meet with thee: it shall

---

with its stand

d. The purpose:
1) To sanctify the Tabernacle & its furnishings: That all be holy
2) To anoint the priests: That they be sanctified for the ministry

e. The importance of the anointing oil
1) Always to be God's holy anointing oil

2) Never to be misused...
• By pouring it on the ordinary person, someone not chosen by God
• By making it for one's own use

f. The warning: If ever misused, that person will be cut off from the community

4. The sweet incense: Symbolized the pleasing & acceptable aroma of prayer to God

a. The instructions
1) To gather sweet spices, the same amount of each
2) To blend & refine the spices using the techniques of a perfumer

b. The importance of the incense
1) To be made a pure & holy incense
2) To be put in front of the Ark of the Covenant, the very place where God meets people
3) To be counted

most holy	be unto you most holy.	of: it shall be unto thee holy for the LORD.	treated as holy
4) To be distinctive, the only incense made this way: Made exclusively for the Lord,	37 And as for the perfume which thou shalt make, ye shall not make to yourselves according to the composition there-	38 Whosoever shall make like unto that, to smell thereto, shall even be cut off from his people.	c. The warning: To judge any person who makes an incense like it: To be cut off

What makes a person spiritually healthy and mature? Four strong pictures are seen in this passage. To be spiritually healthy and mature, a believer...

- must be a giving person
- must be a morally pure person
- must be an anointed person, a person anointed by God for service
- must be a prayer warrior, an intercessor

These four pictures were also given to Israel in the wilderness. Note that these pictures center around the Tabernacle. If the Israelites were going to have spiritual health, these same four pictures had to become a part of their daily walk with the Lord. This is the subject of this section of Scripture. This is: *Other Instructions for the Tabernacle: Symbolizing Spiritual Health and Maturity,* Ex.30:11-38.

I. The raising of money for the Tabernacle offering: symbolized the ransom paid for one's life (vv.11-16).

II. The Bronze Wash Basin: symbolized the washing, cleansing, and forgiveness of sin (vv.17-21).

III. The anointing oil: symbolized the Holy Spirit and God's appointment to service (vv.22-33).

IV. The sweet incense: symbolized the pleasing and acceptable aroma of prayer to God (vv.34-38).

I. There Was the Raising of Money for the Tabernacle Offering (vv.11-16).

Note that the raising of money is inserted by Moses between the discussion of the Altar of Incense and the Bronze Wash Basin. This seems like an odd place to insert such information. What place does money have in the ministry of the Tabernacle? Why would God tell Moses to insert the raising of money in this portion of Scripture? There was a practical reason in relation to the Altar of Incense. We can pray and pray for God to meet the needs of His people, but God usually does not hear our prayers unless we have committed all we are and have to Him. God usually does not meet our needs if we are hoarding and not giving to meet the needs of others.

This passage declares a much needed lesson to us: prayer (the Altar of Incense) is available to us, and God will answer our prayer. But we must be giving to the cause and work of God if we expect God to hear our prayers.

> **"Bring ye all the tithes into the storehouse, that there may be meat in mine house, and prove me now herewith, saith the LORD of hosts, if I will not open you the windows of heaven, and pour you out a blessing, that there shall not be room enough to receive it" (Mal.3:10; see Pr.11:25; 22:9; Is.58:10; Lu.6:38).**
>
> **"But this I say, He which soweth sparingly shall reap also sparingly; and he which soweth bountifully shall reap also bountifully" (2 Co.9:6).**

Following are the facts concerning the raising of money for the Tabernacle:

1. The people were to pay a ransom tax (as an offering) every time a census was taken. This would be a constant reminder of God's redemption, the redemption of His precious

people. Obedience in paying this tax would assure God's protection and erase any chance of God's judgment or plague (v.12). Taking this census was no small thing, for hundreds of thousands of people needed to be counted. Why would Israel periodically need to take a census? For military and other public services. The leaders, just as in any other nation, needed to know how many men were available for their armed forces, how many men were old enough to fight in the event of a national crisis. Note what God says about the census: if the people believed God and were faithful in their worship, they would pay the tax willingly. If they were not faithful in their worship, they of course would become negligent in their duties, one of which would be paying the tax to keep up the Tabernacle. God promised the people this: if they were faithful, He would not judge (plague) them. But God also warned the people: if they were unfaithful, He would send a plague upon them.

2. Each person counted under the census was to pay one fifth of an ounce of silver as the tax or offering to the LORD (v.13).

3. The census was to include every person twenty years old and above (v.14).

4. The offering was to be the same amount for both the rich and the poor (v.15). Why was this? Because it was an offering to make atonement for one's life. An abundance of wealth will not secure a person's reconciliation with God, his place in the promised land (symbolic of heaven). Neither will a life of austere poverty. Everyone is equal in God's eyes: everyone is a sinner; everyone needs to be saved in the same way. Everyone needs to be redeemed by the blood of Jesus Christ.

⇒ Rich or poor, no one is righteous enough to save himself.

"As it is written, There is none righteous, no, not one" (Ro.3:10).

⇒ Rich or poor, no one is justified enough to save himself.

"Therefore by the deeds of the law there shall no flesh be justified in his sight: for by the law is the knowledge of sin" (Ro.3:20).

⇒ Rich or poor, no one can afford the cost of eternal life. Only Jesus Christ can pay the debt of sin.

"For the wages of sin is death; but the gift of God is eternal life through Jesus Christ our Lord" (Ro.6:23).

5. The purpose for the offering (tax) was twofold.

   a. The offering had a material purpose: to take care of the needs of the Tabernacle (v.16).

   Thought
   It is the responsibility of God's people to take care of the needs of the church and of believers. It is not the responsibility of the political leaders in government, nor is it the task of unbelievers.

   "Honour the LORD with thy substance, and with the firstfruits of all thine increase" (Pr.3:9; see Mal.3:10).
   "Every man shall give as he is able, according to the blessing of the LORD thy God which he hath given thee" (De.16:17; see Mt.10:8; 19:21).
   "For it hath pleased them of Macedonia and Achaia to make a certain contribution for the poor saints which are at Jerusalem. It hath pleased them verily; and their debtors they are. For if the Gentiles have been made partakers of their spiritual things, their duty is also to minister unto them in carnal things" (Ro.15:26-27).

> **"Upon the first day of the week let every one of you lay by him in store, as God hath prospered him, that there be no gatherings when I come" (1 Co.16:2; see 2 Co.9:7).**

b. The offering had a spiritual purpose: to be a memorial pointing to the atonement being made for the believer (v.16). The offering was to remind God's people of the rewards for obeying God. God had blessed them abundantly in so many ways:
- ⇒ He had delivered them from slavery in Egypt (the world).
- ⇒ He was going to lead them to Canaan (the Promised Land, a symbol of heaven).
- ⇒ He had bought them—ransomed, redeemed them—and now they were His people, God's very own possession. The silver tax was a reminder to Israel: they had been redeemed (bought) by God. Therefore, they owed *everything* to God. They were no longer their own.

Thought
When we say "yes" to Jesus Christ, we are redeemed, bought by His blood. Therefore, we are to give all we are and have to Him.

- ⇒ We are to give our material possessions to Christ.

> **"Jesus said unto him, If thou wilt be perfect [saved], go and sell that thou hast, and give to the poor, and thou shalt have treasure in heaven: and come and follow me" (Mt.19:21).**

- ⇒ We are to give our hopes and dreams to Christ.

> **"Then Jesus beholding him loved him, and said unto him, One thing thou lackest: go thy way, sell whatsoever thou hast, and give to the poor, and thou shalt have treasure in heaven: and come, take up the cross, and follow me" (Mk.10:21).**

- ⇒ We are to give our very lives to Christ.

> **"For to me to live is Christ, and to die is gain" (Ph.1:21).**
> **"That I may know him, and the power of his resurrection, and the fellowship of his sufferings, being made conformable unto his death" (Ph.3:10).**

II. There Was the Bronze Wash Basin (vv.17-21).

The second major piece of furniture in the courtyard of the Tabernacle was the Bronze Wash Basin. The materials for the bronze basin came from the freewill offerings of the women (see Ex.38:8). Made from polished bronze mirrors, the Bronze Wash Basin played a very significant role in the priest's service to God. These are the facts:
1. The builder was to make the bronze basin with a bronze pedestal (v.18).
2. The bronze basin was to be placed between the Tabernacle and the Altar of Burnt Offering (v.18). This was the logical place for the basin. Before a priest could go into the Holy Place and Most Holy Place, his first order of business was at the Altar of Burnt Offering. Blood had to be shed. A sacrifice had to be offered to appease the righteousness and justice of God. A portion of the blood was sprinkled on the Bronze Wash Basin, symbolizing that it was where the priest was cleansed. No one could approach God...
- unless a sacrifice had been offered
- unless blood had been shed
- unless he had been sanctified and set apart by the blood of the sacrifice

The Bronze Wash Basin was the next step in following the path of holiness, of entering into the presence of God.

3. The sole purpose of the Bronze Wash Basin was for the priests to wash their hands and feet (v.19). They were to wash when they entered the Tabernacle and when they approached the Altar to make a sacrifice. A man of God cannot minister with hands that have not been washed and cleansed, nor can he walk about ministering for the Lord until his feet have been cleansed (v.20).

Thought

There are many sins that entangle a believer. We must constantly be on guard, washing regularly and faithfully by coming to Christ, the Perfect Sacrifice, who alone can wash and cleanse us from sin.

> **"Wash you, make you clean; put away the evil of your doings from before mine eyes; cease to do evil" (Is.1:16; see Ps.26:6; Is.52:11; Acts 22:16).**
>
> **"In whom we have redemption through his blood, the forgiveness of sins, according to the riches of his grace" (Ep.1:7; see 2 Co.7:1).**
>
> **"If a man therefore purge himself from these, he shall be a vessel unto honour, sanctified, and meet for the master's use, and prepared unto every good work" (2 Ti.2:21; see Js.4:8).**
>
> **"If we confess our sins, he is faithful and just to forgive us our sins, and to cleanse us from all unrighteousness" (1 Jn.1:9).**

4. The warning was stark and blunt: the priests must wash or die (v.21). God is holy and He will not allow any person to bring sin into His presence. Their very lives depended upon obedience. The priests could not afford to skip this station and go into the Tabernacle. They could not afford to forget and wash later. God was serious, very serious: a person had to be washed and cleansed before approaching Him and before serving Him.

Thought

God is always serious about holiness. There are no exceptions.

> **"Having therefore these promises, dearly beloved, let us cleanse ourselves from all filthiness of the flesh and spirit, perfecting holiness in the fear of God" (2 Co.7:1).**
>
> **"Seeing then that all these things shall be dissolved, what manner of persons ought ye to be in all holy conversation and godliness" (2 Pe.3:11; see Re.15:4; Ex.15:11; Le.11:45; Ps.99:9; Is.6:3).**

5. The importance of the washing and cleansing cannot be overstressed: it was made a permanent law for all generations (v.21). The need to be cleansed from defilement was not a problem just for Aaron and his sons. Every believer—in every generation, in every culture—must be washed and cleansed from the defilement of sin.

Thought

God will cleanse us; this is His promise if we will only cry out for cleansing.

> **"Wash me throughly from mine iniquity, and cleanse me from my sin" (Ps.51:2; see Ps.19:12; 51:7; 79:9).**
>
> **"Come now, and let us reason together, saith the LORD: though your sins be as scarlet, they shall be as white as snow; though they be red like crimson, they shall be as wool" (Is.1:18).**
>
> **"How much more shall the blood of Christ, who through the eternal Spirit offered himself without spot to God, purge your conscience from dead works to serve the living God?" (He.9:14; see Jn.13:9; Ep.5:25-26).**

"But if we walk in the light, as he is in the light, we have fellowship one with another, and the blood of Jesus Christ his Son cleanseth us from all sin" (1 Jn.1:7).

III. There Was the Anointing Oil (vv.22-33).

The anointing oil symbolized the special call and appointment of God and the Holy Spirit, His equipping of a person for the service of God. Note these carefully worded instructions:

1. Moses was to collect and blend these choice spices.
   a. Myrrh: 12½ pounds of pure myrrh (v.23).
   b. Cinnamon: 6¼ pounds of cinnamon (v.23).
   c. Sweet cane: 6¼ pounds of sweet cane (v.23).
   d. Cassia: 12½ pounds of cassia (v.24).
   e. Olive oil: one gallon of olive oil (v.24).
2. The ingredients were to be mixed and blended into a holy anointing oil (v.25).
3. The end result would be a unique, special oil that would be used to anoint the Tabernacle and its priests (vv.26-28). The oil was to be used to anoint...
   - the Tabernacle and its furnishings
   - the Table and its utensils
   - the Altar of Incense
   - the Wash Basin with its stand
   - the Ark of the Covenant
   - the Lampstand and its accessories
   - the Altar of Burnt Offering and its utensils

4. The purpose of the anointing oil was twofold:
   a. To sanctify the Tabernacle and its furnishings: that all be holy (v.29).
   b. To anoint the priests: that they be sanctified for the ministry (v.30).
5. The importance of the anointing oil was stressed (vv.31-32). It was to be used as God's holy anointing oil and God's alone. It was never to be misused by pouring it on an ordinary person, someone not chosen and appointed by God. It was never to be misused by making it for one's own use. The anointing oil belonged to God and it was to be used for His purpose alone.
6. The stern warning was given: if the oil was ever misused, that person was to be cut off from the community (v.34).

Thought
The anointing is not man's to give. The anointing is God's. It is God who chooses, who calls, who appoints, and who gives His Holy Spirit. It is God who chooses to anoint and set apart both objects and people.
a) God does anoint things; He does set things apart for His service, set them apart as being needed for some very special purpose.

"And thou shalt anoint the tabernacle of the congregation therewith, and the ark of the testimony" (Ex.30:26; see Ex.29:36).
"And thou shalt anoint the altar of the burnt offering, and all his vessels, and sanctify the altar: and it shall be an altar most holy" (Ex.40:10; see Le.8:11; Nu.7:1).

b) God does anoint people; He does call and appoint people, setting people apart to serve Him. God gives His Spirit to people, equipping them in a very special way for His service.

"And Moses took of the anointing oil, and of the blood which was upon the altar, and sprinkled it upon Aaron, and upon his garments, and upon his sons, and upon his sons' garments with him; and sanctified Aaron, and his garments, and his sons, and his sons' garments with him" (Le.8:30; see 1 S.10:1).

"Then Samuel took the horn of oil, and anointed him in the midst of his brethren: and the Spirit of the Lord came upon David from that day forward. So Samuel rose up, and went to Ramah" (1 S.16:13; see 1 K.1:39).

IV. There Was the Sweet Incense (vv.34-38).

The sweet incense was prepared for worshipping God and for no other purpose. The incense was to be burned on the Gold Altar of Incense and was to fill the Tabernacle with the most pleasing aroma that can be imagined. This symbolized the pleasure of God, that He was pleased to see the prayers of His people and that He accepted their prayers.

1. Note the instructions for making the incense.
   a. To gather sweet spices, the same amount of each (v.34). There were resin droplets, mollusk scent, galbanum, and pure frankincense.
   b. To blend and refine the spices using the techniques of a perfumer (v.35).
2. Note the importance of the incense.
   a. The incense was to be made a pure and holy incense (v.35).
   b. The incense was to be put in front of the Ark of the Covenant, the very place where God meets people (v.36). This symbolized the prayers of God's people. Prayer is very special and precious to God, for prayer is communion and fellowship with God. Therefore, the sweet aroma of the incense was to ascend right next to the presence of God, the Ark of God.
   c. The incense was to be counted most holy (v.36).
   d. The incense was to be distinctive, the only incense made this way. It was to be made exclusively for the Lord and to be treated as holy (v.37).
3. Note the warning given by God: any person who made an incense like this incense was to be judged, cut off, excommunicated from the group, exiled from the nation (v.38).

Thought
Picture the pleasing aroma of the incense rising up and filling the Tabernacle of worship. The incense with its pleasing aroma is a picture...
   • of the believer's prayers ascending to God
   • of God's being pleased with the prayers of His people, receiving them, accepting them, and answering them

a) Remember God's hearing the prayer of Gideon.

"And Gideon said unto God, Let not thine anger be hot against me, and I will speak but this once: let me prove, I pray thee, but this once with the fleece; let it now be dry only upon the fleece, and upon all the ground let there be dew. And God did so that night: for it was dry upon the fleece only, and there was dew on all the ground" (Jud.6:39-40).

b) Remember God's hearing the prayer of Hannah.

"For this child I prayed; and the LORD hath given me my petition which I asked of him" (1 S.1:27).

c) Remember God's hearing the prayer of Samuel.

"And Samuel took a sucking lamb, and offered it for a burnt offering wholly unto the LORD: and Samuel cried unto the LORD for Israel; and the LORD heard him. And as Samuel was offering up the burnt offering, the Philistines drew near to battle against Israel: but the LORD thundered with a great thunder on that day upon the

Philistines, and discomfited them; and they were smitten before Israel" (1 S.7:9-10).

d) Remember God's hearing the prayer of Solomon.

"And the LORD said unto him, I have heard thy prayer and thy supplication, that thou hast made before me: I have hallowed this house, which thou hast built, to put my name there for ever; and mine eyes and mine heart shall be there perpetually" (1 K.9:3).

e) Remember God's hearing the prayer of Elijah.

"Hear me, O LORD, hear me, that this people may know that thou art the LORD God, and that thou hast turned their heart back again. Then the fire of the LORD fell, and consumed the burnt sacrifice, and the wood, and the stones, and the dust, and licked up the water that was in the trench" (1 K.18:37-38).

f) Remember God's hearing the prayer of Hezekiah.

"Now therefore, O LORD our God, I beseech thee, save thou us out of his hand, that all the kingdoms of the earth may know that thou art the LORD God, even thou only" (2 K.19:19).

g) Remember God's hearing the prayer of Jehoshaphat.

"And it came to pass, when the captains of the chariots saw Jehoshaphat, that they said, It is the king of Israel. Therefore they compassed about him to fight: but Jehoshaphat cried out, and the LORD helped him; and God moved them to depart from him" (2 Chr.18:31).

h) Remember God's hearing the prayer of Ezra.

"So we fasted and besought our God for this: and he was intreated of us" (Ezr.8:23).

i) Remember God's hearing the prayer of Zacharias, John the Baptist's father.

"But the angel said unto him, Fear not, Zacharias: for thy prayer is heard; and thy wife Elisabeth shall bear thee a son, and thou shalt call his name John" (Lu.1:13).

j) Remember God's hearing the prayers of the disciples and early believers.

"And when they had prayed, the place was shaken where they were assembled together; and they were all filled with the Holy Ghost, and they spake the word of God with boldness" (Ac.4:31).

k) Remember God's promise to us all.

"He shall call upon me, and I will answer him: I will be with him in trouble; I will deliver him, and honour him" (Ps.91:15).
"And it shall come to pass, that before they call, I will answer; and while they are yet speaking, I will hear" (Is.65:24).

l) Remember God's promise to those who ask in the name of Christ.

"Hitherto have ye asked nothing in my name: ask, and ye shall receive, that your joy may be full" (Jn.16:24).

m) Remember God's promise to those who abide in Him.

"If ye abide in me, and my words abide in you, ye shall ask what ye will, and it shall be done unto you" (Jn.15:7).

n) Remember God's promise to those who persevere in prayer.

"And I say unto you, Ask, and it shall be given you; seek, and ye shall find; knock, and it shall be opened unto you" (Lu.11:9).

TYPES, SYMBOLS, AND PICTURES
(Exodus 30:11-38)

Historical Term	Type or Picture (Scriptural Basis)	Life Application for Today's Believer	Biblical Application for Today's Believer
Silver (Ex.30:16)	*Silver is a symbol of redemption. The LORD literally required His people to pay "atonement money" (one fifth of an ounce of silver) to maintain the temple. This "atonement money" symbolized the ransom paid for one's life.* **"And thou shalt take the atonement money of the children of Israel, and shalt appoint it for the service of the tabernacle of the congregation; that it may be a memorial unto the children of Israel before the LORD, to make an atonement for your souls" (Ex.30:16; see 30:12-15).**	⇒ God has bought us, ransomed us, redeemed us through His Son, the Lord Jesus Christ. Now we are His people, God's very own possession. The silver tax is a reminder to the believer: we owe *everything* to God. We are no longer our own. He has redeemed us through Christ; therefore, we belong to Him.	*"For ye are bought with a price: therefore glorify God in your body, and in your spirit, which are God's" (1 Co.6:20).* *"In whom we have redemption through his blood, the forgiveness of sins, according to the riches of his grace" (Ep.1:7).* *"[God] who hath delivered us from the power of darkness, and hath translated us into the kingdom of his dear Son: In whom we have redemption through his blood, even the forgiveness of sins" (Col.1:13-14; see Tit.2:12-14; 1 Pe. 1:18-19).*
The Bronze Wash Basin (Ex.30:17-21; 38:8) See also Ex.35:16; 39:39; 40:7, 30-32	*The Bronze Wash Basin was placed just outside the Sanctuary for the purpose of cleansing. The priests used the Wash Basin to wash the blood, soot, and dirt from their hands and feet before they entered the Sanctuary and when*	What the Wash Basin taught:	

Historical Term	Type or Picture (Scriptural Basis)	Life Application for Today's Believer	Biblical Application for Today's Believer
	they approached the Altar to make a sacrifice.		
	a. The Bronze Wash Basin symbolized that a person must be cleansed before he can enter God's presence and before he can be saved.	a. The Wash Basin is a picture of our great need to be cleansed. A person *cannot enter God's presence* before he is cleansed and made pure. God cleanses us and forgives our sins through the blood of His Son, the Lord Jesus Christ, through His death and His death alone.	*"Then Peter said unto them, Repent, and be baptized every one of you in the name of Jesus Christ for the remission of sins, and ye shall receive the gift of the Holy Ghost" (Ac.2:38; see Ro.3:23-25).* *"Not by works of righteousness which we have done, but according to his mercy he saved us, by the washing of regeneration, and renewing of the Holy Ghost" (Tit.3:5; see Tit.2:14).*
	b. The Bronze Wash Basin symbolized a person's need to be cleansed before he could serve God.	b. The shed blood of Christ allows the believer to effectively serve God. A person cannot serve God until he is cleansed and made pure, made a clean vessel.	*"How much more shall the blood of Christ, who through the eternal Spirit offered himself without spot to God, purge your conscience from dead works to serve the living God?" (He.9:14; see Js.4:8; 1 Jn.1:9; 1 Jn.3:2-3).*
	c. The Bronze Wash Basin symbolized a person's need to be cleansed as he continually served God. **"And the LORD spake unto Moses, saying, Thou shalt also make a laver of brass, and his foot also of brass, to wash withal: and thou shalt put it between the tabernacle of the congregation and the altar, and thou shalt put water therein" (Ex.30:17).** **"And he made the**	c. The blood of Jesus Christ continues to wash the believer from the corruption of daily sin. We need to be washed, cleansed, and purified with His cleansing blood in order to *continually serve God.*	*"I beseech you therefore, brethren, by the mercies of God, that ye present your bodies a living sacrifice, holy, acceptable unto God, which is your reasonable service" (Ro. 12:1).* *"I am crucified with Christ: nevertheless I live; yet not I, but Christ liveth in me: and the life which I now live in the flesh I live by the faith of the Son of God, who loved me, and gave himself for me" (Ga.2:20).*

Historical Term	Type or Picture (Scriptural Basis)	Life Application for Today's Believer	Biblical Application for Today's Believer
	laver *of* brass, and the foot of it *of* brass, of *the* lookingglasses of *the women* assembling, which assembled *at* the door of the tabernacle of the congregation" (Ex.38:8).		
Anointing oil (Ex.30:23-33)	*Oil is a type of the Holy Spirit throughout Scripture. In this particular case, the anointing oil symbolized the special call and appointment of God, the anointing of the Holy Spirit, and His equipping of a person for the service of God.* **"Take thou also unto thee principal spices, of pure myrrh five hundred *shekels*, and of sweet cinnamon half so much, *even* two hundred and fifty *shekels*, and of sweet calamus two hundred and fifty *shekels*"** (Ex.30:23).	⇒ The anointing of the Holy Spirit for service comes from God. The anointing is not man's to give. It is God who chooses, who calls, who appoints, and who gives His Holy Spirit.	*"Now he which stablisheth us with you in Christ, and hath anointed us, is God" (2 Co.1:21).* *"But ye have an unction [an anointing] from the Holy One, and ye know all things" (1 Jn.2:20; see 1 Jn.2:27; Jn.6:63).* *"Howbeit when he, the Spirit of truth, is come, he will guide you into all truth: for he shall not speak of himself; but whatsoever he shall hear, that shall he speak: and he will show you things to come" (Jn.16:13; see Acts 1:8; Ro.8:14).*
Incense for the Golden Altar of Incense (Ex.30:35-36)	*Incense possesses a unique quality that dissolves away all other odors. As the incense burned on the Golden Altar, the Tabernacle was filled with the most pleasing aroma that can be imagined. The incense symbolized the sweet fragrance of Christ before God and the pleasure and acceptance of God concerning the prayers of His people.* **"And thou shalt make it a perfume [incense], a confection after the art of**	⇒ The most pleasing aroma a believer can offer up to God is that of praying, that of placing his trust and hope in the saving grace of God, in the sacrifice of Jesus Christ. Like the incense that drifted continually up to God, our prayers should be constantly ascending up and pleasing God.	*"He shall call upon me, and I will answer him: I will be with him in trouble; I will deliver him, and honour him" (Ps. 91:15).* *"And I say unto you, Ask, and it shall be given you; seek, and ye shall find; knock, and it shall be opened unto you" (Lu.11:9).* *"If ye abide in me, and my words abide in you, ye shall ask what ye will, and it shall be done unto you" (Jn.15:7).* *"Hitherto have ye asked nothing in my name: ask, and ye*

Historical Term	Type or Picture (Scriptural Basis)	Life Application for Today's Believer	Biblical Application for Today's Believer
	the apothecary, tempered together, pure *and* holy: And thou shalt beat *some* of it very small, and put of it before the testimony in the tabernacle of the congregation, where I will meet with thee: it shall be unto you most holy" (Ex. 30:35-36).		*shall receive, that your joy may be full"* (Jn.16:24). *"Praying always with all prayer and supplication in the Spirit, and watching thereunto with all perseverance and supplication for all saints"* (Ep.6:18). *"Pray without ceasing"* (1 Th.5:17).

THE BRONZE WASH BASIN

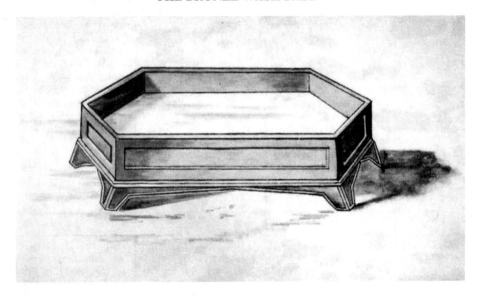

Other Instructions for the Tabernacle: Three Great Charges Given to Man (Exodus 31:1-18)

Contents

Other Instructions for the Tabernacle: Three Great Charges Given to Man (Exodus 31:1-18)

1. The charge to build the Tabernacle: The appointment of craftsmen a. The superintendent: Bezalel 　1) His call: Chosen by God 　2) His heritage 　3) His equipping by God 　　• Filled with God's Spirit 　　• Given skill & ability 　　• Given knowledge in crafts 　4) His skill & ability 　　• To work in metal 　　• To work in setting stone 　　• To work in woodwork 　　• To work in many crafts b. The assistant superintendent: Oholiab: 　1) His heritage 　2) His equipping by God c. The equipping of other craftsmen by God: Given skill to make everything 　1) The Tabernacle 　2) The Ark of the Covenant & the Mercy Seat 　3) The other	And the LORD spake unto Moses, saying, 2 See, I have called by name Bezaleel the son of Uri, the son of Hur, of the tribe of Judah: 3 And I have filled him with the spirit of God, in wisdom, and in understanding, and in knowledge, and in all manner of workmanship, 4 To devise cunning works, to work in gold, and in silver, and in brass, 5 And in cutting of stones, to set them, and in carving of timber, to work in all manner of workmanship. 6 And I, behold, I have given with him Aholiab, the son of Ahisamach, of the tribe of Dan: and in the hearts of all that are wise hearted I have put wisdom, that they may make all that I have commanded thee; 7 The tabernacle of the congregation, and the ark of the testimony, and the mercy seat that is thereupon, and all	the furniture of the tabernacle, 8 And the table and his furniture, and the pure candlestick with all his furniture, and the altar of incense, 9 And the altar of burnt offering with all his furniture, and the laver and his foot, 10 And the cloths of service, and the holy garments for Aaron the priest, and the garments of his sons, to minister in the priest's office, 11 And the anointing oil, and sweet incense for the holy place: according to all that I have commanded thee shall they do. 12 And the LORD spake unto Moses, saying, 13 Speak thou also unto the children of Israel, saying, Verily my sabbaths ye shall keep: for it is a sign between me and you throughout your generations; that ye may know that I am the LORD that doth sanctify you. 14 Ye shall keep the	furnishings 　4) The table & its utensils 　5) The Gold Lampstand 　6) The Altar of Incense 　7) The Altar of Burnt Offering & its utensils 　8) The basin & stand 　9) The beautifully stitched, holy garments for the priest 　10) The anointing oil 　11) The special incense d. The purpose & warning of God: To make everything just as God commanded **2. The charge to keep the Sabbath day** a. The commandment: Must keep while working on the Tabernacle 　1) Because it is a sign of the covenant between God & man forever 　2) Because it reminds man that God is the LORD: The One who makes us holy, sets us apart b. The warning

1) To be observed, kept holy 2) To be judged if violate Sabbath • To be executed if desecrate the Sabbath • To be cut off if work on the Sabbath c. The importance to God 1) Man has been given six days to work & one day to rest 2) The Sabbath is counted holy by God 3) If defile Sabbath, to be executed d. The commandment to be a perpetual covenant	sabbath therefore; for it is holy unto you: every one that defileth it shall surely be put to death: for whosoever doeth any work therein, that soul shall be cut off from among his people. 15 Six days may work be done; but in the seventh is the sabbath of rest, holy to the LORD: whosoever doeth any work in the sabbath day, he shall surely be put to death. 16 Wherefore the children of Israel shall keep the sab-	bath, to observe the sabbath throughout their generations, for a perpetual covenant. 17 It is a sign between me and the children of Israel for ever: for in six days the LORD made heaven and earth, and on the seventh day he rested, and was refreshed. 18 And he gave unto Moses, when he had made an end of communing with him upon mount Sinai, two tables of testimony, tables of stone, written with the finger of God.	1) A sign between God & His people (Israel) forever 2) The reason: Because God worked—He created heaven & earth in six days, but He rested on the Sabbath day **3. The charge to keep the Ten Commandments** a. The great gift of God to man: The two tablets of God's testimony, the 10 Com. b. Their extreme value: Written by the finger of God Himself

The heart-cry of every human being is for purpose, meaning, and significance in life. All over the world people are asking questions such as:

⇒ "What am I living for?"
⇒ "What is the sense of all this?"
⇒ "Am I making a difference?"

Far too often, the questions are quickly answered by feelings of emptiness and loneliness, a sense of helplessness, disappointment, depression, even despair and hopelessness. People find themselves trapped in an endless cycle of futility and emptiness. They live a life where nothing lasts, not for long. And tragically, in far too many lives, when the winds of time blow across their graves, nothing lasting will be found.

This is not so for the Christian believer who follows God, who takes the great charges of God and obeys them. It is the charges of God and obedience to them that brings purpose, meaning, and significance...

- to the rich and the poor
- to the weak and the strong
- to the sick and the healthy
- to the profound and the simple
- to the educated and the uneducated

God's great charges stir us to serve God; and when we serve God, we experience a deep, rich fulfillment. When we serve God, God gives us...

- a deep sense of satisfaction and completion
- a deep sense of purpose, meaning, and significance
- a deep sense of assurance and security, the assurance and security of being His, of being loved by God and of living forever

This is the picture of this present Scripture: *Other Instructions for the Tabernacle: Three Great Charges Given to Man,* Ex.31:1-18.

I. The charge to build the Tabernacle: the appointment of craftsmen (vv.1-11).
II. The charge to keep the Sabbath day (vv.12-17).
III. The charge to keep the Ten Commandments (v.18).

I. There Was the Appointment of Craftsmen, the People Who Were Charged to Build the Tabernacle and All of Its Furnishings (vv.1-11).

Remember, God had just finished giving Moses the blueprint, the pattern for the Tabernacle's design. The Tabernacle's blueprints were waiting for the construction superintendent to be appointed, waiting for God to appoint the man He wanted to build the Tabernacle. This is the story of what happens when God calls a man to serve Him.

1. The man appointed superintendent was Bezalel (vv.1-2). Who was Bezalel, the man appointed to oversee the construction of the Tabernacle of God, the very place where God Himself was to dwell among His people? Who was given such a privilege as this?

Bezalel had been born in slavery, raised in Egypt as a slave. He had obviously grown up toiling and laboring long, hard days, even to the point of utter exhaustion. He had known the hardness, the cruelty, and the savagery of slavery. But through it all, he had apparently learned trade after trade and skill after skill. He had obviously been a slave to several Egyptian craftsmen and businessmen and learned the crafts well. Note what Scripture says about Bezalel.

    a. God Himself appointed Bezalel to be superintendent of the construction. The name Bezalel means *under the shadow of God*, under God's protection and guidance. The picture is graphic: God had been protecting and guiding Bezalel throughout his life as an Egyptian slave...

- protecting him from serious harm
- guiding and preparing him, making sure he learned the skills necessary to serve God in the future—the skills necessary to build the Tabernacle of God

The point to see is that God Himself actually chose and appointed the man who was to serve Him as superintendent of the Tabernacle. The Hebrew actually says that God called "him by name." God knew Bezalel, knew Him personally, knew His name.

Thought
When God calls a person to service, He always calls the person by *name*. God's appointment is a *personal* call, an appointment that is always framed in God's love for His dear people. God knew that Bezalel was His man for the job before the foundation of the earth. God knew Bezalel even when he was still in his mother's womb. The God of the universe, the Creator of all things, knew Bezalel *personally*. The call of God is not an impersonal, bureaucratic, faceless procedure. The call of God goes right to the heart of the man, setting him apart to serve God's dear people.

> **"O Lord, thou hast searched me, and known me. Thou knowest my downsitting and mine uprising, thou understandest my thought afar off. Thou compassest my path and my lying down, and art acquainted with all my ways. For there is not a word in my tongue, but, lo, O Lord, thou knowest it altogether. Thou hast beset me behind and before, and laid thine hand upon me" (Ps.139:1-5; see Is.43:1).**
>
> **"Then the word of the Lord came unto me, saying, Before I formed thee in the belly I knew thee; and before thou camest forth out of the womb I sanctified thee, and I ordained thee a prophet unto the nations" (Je.1:4-5; see Ps.91:1-2).**
>
> **"Ye have not chosen me, but I have chosen you, and ordained you, that ye should go and bring forth fruit, and [that] your fruit should remain: that whatsoever ye shall ask of the Father in my name, he may give it you" (Jn.15:16).**

    b. Note the godly heritage, the godly upbringing of Bezalel (v.2). His godly heritage is suggested by three facts.

⇒ His father's name was Uri which means *light*. The word *light* always refers to positive facts: the light of knowledge, understanding, wisdom, sight, or the light of God. Being descendants of Abraham, his family knew about the great promises of God, the promise of the promised land and the promise of the promised seed, the Savior and Messiah of the world. Therefore, Uri was probably given his name because of the hope for the light and promises of God.

⇒ His grandfather's name was Hur which means *free*. This obviously refers to the hope of being freed from Egyptian slavery, being freed to journey to the promised land of God.

⇒ His tribe was the tribe of Judah which means *praise*. This refers to the praise due God. Judah led the way when the Tabernacle was moved from campsite to campsite.

Thought

A godly heritage can never be overstressed. Children and adults alike need godly parents and grandparents. We all need a godly heritage. And we need to be godly parents if we have children. We all need to build a godly heritage for our families and for the earth.

"For thou, O God, hast heard my vows: thou hast given me the heritage of those that fear thy name" (Ps.61:5).

"And he did that which was right in the sight of the LORD, according to all that his father Amaziah did" (2 Chr.26:4).

"When I call to remembrance the unfeigned faith that is in thee, which dwelt first in thy grandmother Lois, and thy mother Eunice; and I am persuaded that in thee also" (2 Ti.1:5).

c. Note the equipping of Bezalel: he was filled with God's Spirit (v.3). He was...
- given special skill and ability
- given special knowledge in all kinds of crafts

d. His skill and ability were to work in several areas (vv.4-5). He was equipped...
- to design and work in metals: gold, silver, and bronze
- to design and work in cutting and setting stones
- to design and work in woodwork
- to design and work in many crafts

Thought

When God calls a person, He equips the person to serve Him. The person is not left to himself, not left to do the work of God in his own strength. God fills him with the Holy Spirit, giving the person whatever skill and abilities he needs to do the work.

"And unto one he gave five talents, to another two, and to another one; to every man according to his several ability; and straightway took his journey" (Mt.25:15).

"Having then gifts differing according to the grace that is given to us, whether prophecy, let us prophesy according to the proportion of faith; Or ministry, let us wait on our ministering: or he that teacheth, on teaching; Or he that exhorteth, on exhortation: he that giveth, let him do it with simplicity; he that ruleth, with diligence; he that showeth mercy, with cheerfulness" (Ro.12:6-8; see 1 Co.12:4-6; Ep.4:11-12).

2. The man appointed to be the assistant superintendent was Oholiab (v.6). His name means either "tent of the father" or "the (divine) father is my tent."[1] Note the suggestion:

---

[1] Frank E. Gaebelein. *The Expositor's Bible Commentary*, Vol.2, p.475.

God had been covering, protecting, and looking after Oholiab just as He had Bezalel. God had been preparing him for future service.

a. Oholiab was from the tribe of Dan (v.6). Throughout Scripture, the citizens of Dan are seen to be a rough, rude, war-like people. Some generations later, Hiram, the chief craftsman for the ornamental work on Solomon's temple, was to be from the tribe of Dan (2 Chr.2:14). The nature of both men seems to be anything other than artistic. Oholiab definitely goes against the grain of his heritage and stands out as an artist who can be used mightily by God. The point is just this: both men show how a person can go against the grain of his heritage and stand out as a strong, gifted servant of God and society.

b. Note that God called Oholiab, equipping him for his work. He equipped him to be the helper, the assistant superintendent, in building the Tabernacle of God, the very place where God was to dwell among His people.

3. The other craftsmen were also equipped by God, given the skill to make everything (vv.6-11). They were appointed to work under the direct supervision of Bezalel and Oholiab. The building of the Tabernacle was to be Israel's most important construction project; therefore, it would take workmen who were willing to follow the leadership of Bezalel and Oholiab. When God's people come together and work, it must be done according to the design of God and in complete unity. As a result of their commitment to the LORD and to His blueprint, the Tabernacle would soon be built. This great task included...

- the Tabernacle
- the Ark of the Covenant and the Mercy Seat
- the Table and its utensils
- the other furnishings
- the Gold Lampstand

- the Altar of Incense
- the Altar of Burnt Offering and its utensils
- the basin and stand
- the beautifully stitched, holy garments for the priests
- the anointing oil and the special incense

4. There was the purpose and warning of God: to make everything just as God had commanded (v.11). God had left nothing to chance, nothing that could be misunderstood. God had called together a group of craftsmen who had to place their own pride aside and do things God's way. The blueprint was now complete: any changes—any additions or deletions from God's Master Plan—were forbidden. God did not call these men into service for their own wisdom and worldly ingenuity. He called these men to do exactly what He had called and prepared them to do: build the Tabernacle of God according to the design that He had shown to Moses.

Thought

The warning of God is clear: we are to do just what He says, obey His commandments, His Word. We must not try to add to nor take away from His commandments. Yet so many of us do. We add our reasoning to what God says by rationalizing and asking questions such as:

⇒ Does God really want me to forgive someone who has hurt me so deeply and caused so much pain and suffering?

> **"And when ye stand praying, forgive, if ye have ought against any: that your Father also which is in heaven may forgive you your trespasses. But if ye do not forgive, neither will your Father which is in heaven forgive your trespasses" (Mk.11:24-26).**

⇒ Is Jesus Christ really the true way to heaven? The only way?

> **"Jesus saith unto him, I am the way, the truth, and the life: no man cometh unto the Father, but by me" (Jn.14:6).**

⇒ Does God really want me to deny myself, my rights, my own ideas and personal agenda?

"But seek ye first the kingdom of God, and his righteousness; and all these things shall be added unto you" (Mt.6:33).

"And he said to them all, If any man will come after me, let him deny himself, and take up his cross daily, and follow me. For whosoever will save his life shall lose it: but whosoever will lose his life for my sake, the same shall save it. For what is a man advantaged, if he gain the whole world, and lose himself, or be cast away?" (Lu.9:23-25).

⇒ Does God really want my money? When I am so far in debt, does God really expect me to tithe?

"Bring ye all the tithes into the storehouse, that there may be meat in mine house, and prove me now herewith, saith the Lord of hosts, if I will not open you the windows of heaven, and pour you out a blessing, that there shall not be room enough to receive it" (Mal.3:10).

⇒ Does God really mean what He says? Are His commandments, His Word, really that important?

"For I testify unto every man that heareth the words of the prophecy of this book, If any man shall add unto these things, God shall add unto him the plagues that are written in this book: And if any man shall take away from the words of the book of this prophecy, God shall take away his part out of the book of life, and out of the holy city, and from the things which are written in this book" (Re.22:18-19).

II. There Were the Charges to Keep the Sabbath Day (vv.12-17).

In the beginning stages of this ambitious construction project, the people were excited, very excited. They were so excited that they were obviously ready to work around the clock, seven days a week. But note carefully God's instructions to Moses.

1. The commandment to keep the Sabbath had to be kept while everyone was working on the Tabernacle (v.13). Why did God require His people to *slow down* the production schedule in order to keep the Sabbath?

a. They were to keep the Sabbath because the Sabbath is a sign of the covenant between God and man, a perpetual sign of the covenant. This is important to note: God is here establishing the Sabbath as a sign of the covenant between Himself and man. Keeping the Sabbath is one of the Ten Commandments; therefore, if a person keeps the Sabbath—actually sets a whole day aside for God and for rest—he will most likely be seeking to obey God in all the other commandments. The importance of the Sabbath is seen in these facts:

⇒ The Sabbath day had been set aside as a day for rest and worship since creation (Ge.2:1-3).

⇒ The Sabbath day was given as a law to the nation of Israel before any other law (Ex.16:23).

⇒ The Sabbath day was given as one of the Ten Commandments, a part of the moral law of God (Ex.20:8-11).

⇒ The Sabbath day was even given as one of the civil and judicial laws of Israel (Ex.23:10-12).

⇒ The Sabbath day is here made a part of the religious and ceremonial law of Israel. Moreover, it is set up as the very sign of the covenant between God and His people, the sign that declares the very special relationship between God and those who follow and obey Him.

It is easy for people to forget the special relationship between God and His people. The Sabbath is to be a constant reminder that man and God have a very unique relationship, a relationship that must not be taken for granted, a relationship that must be cultivated and treasured. The Sabbath day has been given by God to help keep the relationship (covenant) between Himself and man alive.

b. They were to keep the Sabbath because it reminds man that God is the LORD, the only living and true God, the One who makes us holy, who sets us apart to be His people and to live pure and righteous lives. By keeping the Sabbath, it would be a keen reminder that the One who revealed the blueprints for the Tabernacle was the One who was to be worshipped and loved. A day was to be set aside that would be devoted to focusing upon the LORD and His great call to us, the call to be His holy people, set apart to live pure and righteous lives and to inherit the promised land of God.

2. Note that God gave a warning, a warning to keep this commandment (v.14).

a. It was to be observed and kept holy. "Holy" means set apart, sanctified, consecrated, kept pure and righteous. The Sabbath day is to be set apart as a very special day, as the day belonging to God and man, a day for the worship of God and for the rest and relaxation of man.

b. The person who violated this commandment was to be judged harshly.

⇒ He was to be executed if the Sabbath was desecrated, that is, if he did any evil thing on the Sabbath or refused to honor and keep the Sabbath.

⇒ If he worked on the Sabbath, he was to be cut off from his people, cut off from fellowshipping and living among the people of God.

3. The Sabbath is important to God (v.15). He has given man six days to work and one day to rest. The Sabbath is counted holy by God. If any man defiled the Sabbath, he was to be executed. This seems a bit harsh when viewed through the eyes of modern man. Why is God so serious about the Sabbath? As just stated, God is serious about the Sabbath because it is holy to God. The God who lives above space and time knows several facts:

⇒ God knows that man needs both work and rest, that man needs to work six days a week, but that he also needs—absolutely needs—to rest on the Sabbath day.

⇒ God knows that man needs both work and worship, that man needs to sense purpose and meaning in his life and work, that purpose and meaning are found in God and in God alone, in knowing that one is working and living for a higher cause than just for what this world offers. Man needs to know that he serves the LORD God Himself and that he is going to be rewarded with the promised land of God.

⇒ God knows that man will most likely keep the other laws if he keeps the Sabbath day. Why? If man obeys God by setting aside a whole day for true worship and rest, committing to God one full day out of every seven, he will most likely seek to obey God in all things.

The converse is also true and the point is most graphic: if the Sabbath day is not kept, people will most likely break any of the other laws of God. Thereby society crumbles. And no society can survive, not for long, not apart from God. This is the reason for the strict penalty against the violators of the Sabbath day.

4. Note that the commandment is a perpetual covenant (vv.16-17). The Sabbath was to be a sign between God and His people forever. Why was this a perpetual covenant? Because God worked and created heaven and earth in six days, but He rested on the Sabbath day. The commandment to keep the Sabbath day stretches from the creation to the end of the world, covering all people of all generations.

Thought 1.

The Sabbath day was not to be a temporary commandment made for Israel alone. It was to be a continuous, perpetual commandment. The Sabbath day was made for all generations of men, made for every man, woman, and child upon earth.

"And he said unto them, The Sabbath was made for man, and not man for the Sabbath" (Mk.2:27).

"For in six days the Lord made heaven and earth, the sea, and all that in them is, and rested the seventh day: wherefore the Lord blessed the Sabbath day, and hallowed it [for all people]" (Ex.20:11).

Thought 2.

When businesses have to operate seven days a week, what are the employees of these businesses to do about worship and rest? Two very practical things must be done throughout the remaining generations of history:

⇒ The church must provide other services throughout the week for worship and rest, provide them for people who have to work Saturday or Sunday (people such as medical, police, and other service workers).

⇒ People who work on the regular day of worship and rest must still worship God and rest at the alternate services and days scheduled by the church.

"Not forsaking the assembling of ourselves together, as the manner of some is; but exhorting one another: and so much the more, as ye see the day approaching" (He.10:25).

"And he came to Nazareth, where he had been brought up: and, as his custom was, he went into the synagogue on the sabbath day, and stood up for to read" (Lu.4:16).

"But when they departed from Perga, they came to Antioch in Pisidia, and went into the synagogue on the sabbath day, and sat down" (Ac.13:14).

III. There Was the Charge to Keep the Ten Commandments (v.18).

God gave a great gift to man: the two tablets of God's testimony, the Ten Commandments themselves. The very foundation of God's law was given to Moses, the great Lawgiver of Israel. The value of the Ten Commandments was *priceless*. They were conceived by God, written by the finger of God, crafted by God, and transmitted by God to His people. The mention of these tablets at this time of the Tabernacle's blueprints is a graphic reminder, a reminder that God cannot be worshipped if God's law and Word are not close at hand.

Thought

Man is to obey God's great gift, His commandments and His Word. We are to live righteous and pure lives, bearing witness that God does save and does lead people to the promised land of heaven.

"He that hath my commandments, and keepeth them, he it is that loveth me: and he that loveth me shall be loved of my Father, and I will love him, and will manifest myself to him" (Jn.14:21).

"If ye keep my commandments, ye shall abide in my love; even as I have kept my Father's commandments, and abide in his love" (Jn.15:10; see Jn.4:23-24; 17:17; 5:39; Ac.17:11).

"All scripture is given by inspiration of God, and is profitable for doctrine, for reproof, for correction, for instruction in righteousness" (2 Ti.3:16).

PART II

INTRODUCTION

THE TABERNACLE, ITS CONSTRUCTION AND DEDICATION: THE PEOPLE OBEY GOD
(Exodus 35:1–40:38)

The construction of the Tabernacle is the subject of these concluding chapters in Exodus. Reading through the chapters is often felt to be uninteresting and even unimportant. Why? Because most of the material covered here has already been covered earlier:

⇒ Exodus chapters 25-31 covered God's design and instructions for building the Tabernacle.

⇒ Exodus chapters 35-40 now cover the actual construction of the Tabernacle.

The two passages are almost identical except for switching from the future to the past tense. There are very few changes. Therefore the reader could feel there is no need to re-read the account, that he can pass over the account of the actual construction without missing anything. But this should not be. God has deliberately had the account included in His Holy Word, had the actual construction included for at least three very specific purposes.

1. Man must approach God correctly, exactly as God dictates. This is the great lesson of the Tabernacle, the great symbolic meaning of the Tabernacle. This is what God is doing by repeating the material, by stressing it, by re-emphasizing it, by declaring it time and again: there is one way and only one way to approach Him. The Tabernacle shows man...

- that he must approach God through the sacrifice of the lamb
- that God is holy and righteous and dwells in the Most Holy Place, dwells behind the inner veil of holiness, totally separated and cut off from man
- that God sits upon the Mercy Seat, that His very throne is a throne of mercy

On and on the lessons of the Tabernacle could be listed—all declaring that man must approach God exactly as God says. God cannot accept man apart from the blood of the sacrificial lamb. This truth must be emphasized time and time again. This is the first great purpose for repeating the material given in these chapters, the reason why Holy Scripture covers the actual construction of the Tabernacle. We must read the account time and again, noting how *exact* the design was and how *carefully* everything was constructed. All this points to the fact...

- that we must be *exact* in our approach and worship of God, approaching and worshipping Him exactly as He dictates
- that we must be *careful* in our approach and worship of God, again being careful to approach and worship Him exactly as He says

2. The actual construction of the Tabernacle emphasizes *obedience*, the obedience of God's dear servant (Moses) and God's dear people. Both Moses and the people built the

Tabernacle exactly as God designed. Their obedience is deliberately stressed. This is seen in two very clear passages: Exodus chapters 39 and 40. Note the sevenfold repetition in each of the passages, the forceful stress upon the fact that God's people did exactly "as the LORD [Yahweh] commanded Moses."

⇒ Note Exodus chapter 39.

> "And of the blue, and purple, and scarlet, they made cloths of service, to do service in the holy place, and made the holy garments for Aaron; as the LORD commanded Moses" (Ex.39:1).
> "And the curious girdle of his ephod, that was upon it, was of the same, according to the work thereof; of gold, blue, and purple, and scarlet, and fine twined linen; as the LORD commanded Moses" (Ex.39:5).
> "And he put them on the shoulders of the ephod, that they should be stones for a memorial to the children of Israel; as the LORD commanded Moses" (Ex.39:7).
> "And they did bind the breastplate by his rings unto the rings of the ephod with a lace of blue, that it might be above the curious girdle of the ephod, and that the breastplate might not be loosed from the ephod; as the LORD commanded Moses" (Ex.39:21).
> "A bell and a pomegranate, a bell and a pomegranate, round about the hem of the robe to minister in; as the LORD commanded Moses" (Ex.39:26).
> "And a girdle of fine twined linen, and blue, and purple, and scarlet, of needlework; as the LORD commanded Moses" (Ex.39:29).
> "And they tied unto it a lace of blue, to fasten it on high upon the mitre; as the LORD commanded Moses" (Ex.39:31).

⇒ Note Exodus chapter 40.

> "And he spread abroad the tent over the tabernacle, and put the covering of the tent above upon it; as the LORD commanded Moses" (Ex.40:19).
> "And he brought the ark into the tabernacle, and set up the vail of the covering, and covered the ark of the testimony; as the LORD commanded Moses" (Ex.40:21).
> "And he set the bread in order upon it before the LORD; as the LORD had commanded Moses" (Ex.40:23).
> "And he lighted the lamps before the LORD; as the LORD commanded Moses" (Ex.40:25).
> "And he burnt sweet incense thereon; as the LORD commanded Moses" (Ex.40:27).
> "And he put the altar of burnt offering by the door of the tabernacle of the tent of the congregation, and offered upon it the burnt offering and the meat offering; as the LORD commanded Moses" (Ex.40:29).
> "When they went into the tent of the congregation, and when they came near unto the altar, they washed; as the LORD commanded Moses" (Ex.40:32).

The lesson is clear: the people of God obeyed God exactly as He dictated. They built the Tabernacle according to God's design so they could approach and worship God precisely as He dictated.

3. The third purpose for recording the actual building of the Tabernacle is of vital importance: God wanted man to know that He is, above all else, *loving* and *faithful*, *merciful*, and *forgiving*. And God will dwell in the midst of His people if they will only obey Him, approach Him as He says. All this is symbolized in the Tabernacle.

Remember, the golden calf tragedy had just occurred (Exodus chapters 32-34). The people had just failed God, miserably failed Him. They had rejected God and chosen a man-made worship over the true worship of God. They had broken the Ten Commandments, broken the covenant, their commitment to God.

In recording the actual construction of the Tabernacle—after the terrible sin of the people—God is stressing this great lesson: He is loving and faithful, merciful and forgiving. Once man has repented and confessed his sin, God will actually come and dwell among His people. Despite man's terrible depravity, if man will truly approach God as God dictates, God will still prove faithful: He will...

- forgive man's sin
- restore man
- renew His covenant with man
- give man a new start, a new beginning
- dwell in the midst of man

Note that it takes six chapters in Exodus to cover the actual construction and dedication of the Tabernacle. The space given to the construction, six chapters out of forty, stresses the importance that God places upon the Tabernacle and the three purposes described above. This is the reason we must never pass over these chapters, feeling they are unimportant.

The details of the Tabernacle design have already been discussed in Exodus chapters 25-31. Now, our approach in discussing the construction will be to focus upon the outline and the practical application of the Tabernacle—the pictures, symbols, and types—the meaning that the Tabernacle holds for us in our day and time.

CHAPTER TWELVE

The Preparations for Building the Tabernacle: The Call to Give Sacrificially (Exodus 35:1-35)

Contents

The Preparations for Building the Tabernacle: The Call to Give Sacrificially (Exodus 35:1-35)

1. The call: Everyone is called to have a part in building the Tabernacle (worship center)

And Moses gathered all the congregation of the children of Israel together, and said unto them, These are the words which the LORD hath commanded, that ye should do them.

2. The most important instruction: Keep the Sabbath while building

a. To work six days but keep the Sabbath: As a holy day & day of rest

b. The importance stressed
  1) To execute violators
  2) To start no fires on the Sabbath

2 Six days shall work be done, but on the seventh day there shall be to you an holy day, a sabbath of rest to the LORD: whosoever doeth work therein shall be put to death. 3 Ye shall kindle no fire throughout your habitations upon the sabbath day.

3. The offerings to build the Tabernacle

a. The privilege of giving was presented to everyone

4 And Moses spake unto all the congregation of the children of Israel, saying, This is the thing which the LORD commanded, saying,

b. The offerings were to be given freely, only by willing hearts
  1) The metals

5 Take ye from among you an offering unto the LORD: whosoever is of a willing heart, let him bring it, an offering of the LORD; gold, and silver, and brass,

  2) The fabrics

6 And blue, and purple, and scarlet, and fine linen, and goats' hair,

7 And rams' skins dyed red, and badgers' skins, and shittim wood,

8 And oil for the light, and spices for anointing oil, and for the sweet incense,

9 And onyx stones, and stones to be set for the ephod, and for the breastplate.

10 And every wise hearted among you shall come, and make all that the LORD hath commanded;

11 The tabernacle, his tent, and his covering, his taches, and his boards, his bars, his pillars, and his sockets,

12 The ark, and the staves thereof, with the mercy seat, and the vail of the covering,

13 The table, and his staves, and all his vessels, and the showbread,

14 The candlestick also for the light, and his furniture, and his lamps, with the oil for the light,

15 And the incense altar, and his staves, and the anointing oil, and the

3) The (animal) skins
4) The wood

5) The oil, spices, & sweet incense

6) The stones & gems for the ephod & breastpiece

4. The challenge to the skilled workers: Come & make everything

a. The Tabernacle itself (symbolized God dwelling among His people & man's need to approach God as God dictates)

b. The Ark, Mercy Seat, & Veil (symbolized the presence, mercy, & holiness of God)

c. The Table of Showbread (pointed to Christ as the Bread of Life)

d. The Lampstand (pointed to Christ as the Light of the world)

e. The Altar of Incense (symbolized the prayers ascending up & pleasing God)

f. The outer veil or door (symbolized that God can be approached only through one door, Jesus Christ)

g. The Altar of Burnt Offering (symbolized the need for atonement, reconciliation)

h. The Wash Basin (sym. the need for cleansing)

i. The walls (curtains) of the courtyard (symbolized sacrifice)

j. The entrance veil (symbolized access to God & spiritual separation)

k. The tent pegs & ropes (symbolized Christ, the binding strength of believers)

l. The clothing for the priests (symbolized bringing dignity & honor to the name of God)

5. The response of the people to God's call & challenge

a. Every person who was willing & whose heart was stirred brought an offering to the LORD

b. Every person who was willing—both men & women—brought gold jewelry as an offering: Presented it as a thanksgiving offering to the LORD

sweet incense, and the hanging for the door at the entering in of the tabernacle, 16 The altar of burnt offering, with his brasen grate, his staves, and all his vessels, the laver and his foot, 17 The hangings of the court, his pillars, and their sockets, and the hanging for the door of the court, 18 The pins of the tabernacle, and the pins of the court, and their cords, 19 The cloths of service, to do service in the holy place, the holy garments for Aaron the priest, and the garments of his sons, to minister in the priest's office. 20 And all the congregation of the children of Israel departed from the presence of Moses. 21 And they came, every one whose heart stirred him up, and every one whom his spirit made willing, and they brought the LORD's offering to the work of the tabernacle of the congregation, and for all his service, and for the holy garments. 22 And they came, both men and women, as many as were willing hearted, and brought bracelets, and earrings, and rings, and tablets, all jewels of gold: and every man that offered offered an offering of gold unto the LORD. 23 And every man, with whom was found blue, and purple, and scarlet, and fine linen, and goats' hair, and red skins of rams, and badgers' skins, brought them. 24 Every one that did offer an offering of silver and brass brought the LORD's offering: and every man, with whom was found shittim wood for any work of the service, brought it. 25 And all the women that were wise hearted did spin with their hands, and brought that which they had spun, both of blue, and of purple, and of scarlet, and of fine linen. 26 And all the women whose heart stirred them up in wisdom spun goats' hair. 27 And the rulers brought onyx stones, and stones to be set, for the ephod, and for the breastplate; 28 And spice, and oil for the light, and for the anointing oil, and for the sweet incense. 29 The children of Israel brought a willing offering unto the LORD, every man and woman, whose heart made them willing to bring for all manner of work, which the

c. Everyone who had colored linen & animal skins brought them as an offering

d. Everyone who had silver or bronze brought it as an offering to the LORD

e. Every skilled woman who could sew & spin prepared the curtains
   1) Brought the linen curtains

   2) Brought the goat hair

f. Every leader made his contribution
   1) Brought the stones & gems for the ephod & breastpiece
   2) Brought spices & oil for the light & anointing oil for the incense

g. The glorious fact restated & stressed: All the men & women who were willing gave the LORD freewill offerings for the work

	LORD had commanded to be made by the hand of Moses.	them, and in carving of wood, to make any manner of cunning work.	• In wood-working • In all kinds of craftsmanship
6. The superintendent & his associate: Chosen by God a. The general superintendent: Bezalel	30 And Moses said unto the children of Israel, See, the LORD hath called by name Bezaleel the son of Uri, the son of Hur, of the tribe of Judah;	34 And he hath put in his heart that he may teach, both he, and Aholiab, the son of Ahisamach, of the tribe of Dan.	b. The associate superintendent: Oholiab 1) He & Bezalel were both equipped by God to teach others
1) God filled him with the Spirit 2) God filled him with intelligence, knowledge, & skill in construction	31 And he hath filled him with the spirit of God, in wisdom, in understanding, and in knowledge, and in all manner of workmanship;	35 Them hath he filled with wisdom of heart, to work all manner of work, of the engraver, and of the cunning workman, and of the embroiderer, in blue,	2) Both were filled by God, filled with skill to do all kinds of work • As craftsmen, designers, embroiderers, & weavers
• In designing metal objects • In cutting & setting stones	32 And to devise curious works, to work in gold, and in silver, and in brass, 33 And in the cutting of stones, to set	and in purple, in scarlet, and in fine linen, and of the weaver, even of them that do any work, and of those that devise cunning work.	• As master craftsmen & designers

What does it take to build a successful business? The person who wants to make his business successful has to do several things. He must be willing...

⇒ to invest significant sums of money.
⇒ to invest significant amounts of time.
⇒ to ask other talented and resourceful people to help him.
⇒ to make any sacrifice, to do whatever it takes to make his business a success.

These principles are true for anyone who wants to succeed in the business world. But they should be even more true in the believer's service for the LORD. How much sacrifice does God require of those who serve Him? What does God expect from His people? What kind of sacrifice does it take to make a successful church or ministry? God expects a full and total sacrifice from any person who follows Him. Note what Scripture says:

> **"And he said to [them] all, If any [man] will come after me, let him deny himself, and take up his cross daily, and follow me" (Lu.9:23).**

There are no short-cuts in serving God. There is no way to circumvent or go around the commitment God requires. This portion of Scripture speaks directly to the person whom God has called to serve Him. It is: *The Preparations for Building the Tabernacle: The Call to Give Sacrificially*, Ex.35:1-35.

I.   The call: everyone is called to have a part in building the Tabernacle (worship center) (v.1).
II. The most important instruction: keep the Sabbath (vv.2-3).
III. The offerings to build the Tabernacle (vv.4-9).
IV. The challenge to the skilled workers: come and make everything (vv.10-19).
V.   The response of the people to God's call and challenge (vv.20-29).
VI. The two supervisors or managers: chosen by God (vv.30-35).

I. There Was the Call: Everyone Was Called to Have a Part in Building the Tabernacle (Worship Center) (v.1).

Moses called a meeting of all the people; not a single person was left out nor considered unimportant. The call of God to build the worship center went to every person. And note: the call to build the Tabernacle was the command of God. The call was not to be altered or changed whatsoever. The call was to go out to every person, and every person was to *respond* and *obey* the call.

Thought
Every believer is called to build God's church here upon earth, is to become personally involved in the building of the LORD's house. This is not the sole responsibility of a select few nor the privileged right of the rich and powerful. Those who love God have been called to have a part in building God's church and Kingdom here upon earth.

> **"Ye have not chosen me, but I have chosen you, and ordained you, that ye should go and bring forth fruit, and [that] your fruit should remain: that whatsoever ye shall ask of the Father in my name, he may give it you" (Jn.15:16; see Lu.12:48; Jn.17:4).**
> **"For we are labourers together with God: ye are God's husbandry, ye are God's building" (1 Co.3:9).**
> **"Therefore, my beloved brethren, be ye stedfast, unmoveable, always abounding in the work of the Lord, forasmuch as ye know that your labour is not in vain in the Lord" (1 Co.15:58; see 2 Co.6:1; 1 Pe.4:11; Is.1:19).**

II. There Was the Most Important Instruction: Keep the Sabbath While Building the Tabernacle (vv.2-3).

Remember, the Sabbath was the sign of the covenant between God and man. If a person were committed to God—if he had made a covenant, an agreement to follow God—he kept the Sabbath. The Sabbath was the sign, the symbol, that he had made a covenant with God.

The Israelites faced a problem. They were very excited about building the Tabernacle. There was the danger that their excitement might cause them to keep right on working, forgetting the Sabbath. They might feel the Tabernacle was so important that they should just keep right on working seven days a week. But God says, "No." The Tabernacle is important: it is the work of God. But keeping the Sabbath, resting and worshipping God one day a week, is more important. Therefore keep the Sabbath. Above all else, rest and worship God one full day a week. Note the clear instructions of Scripture:

1. The believer is to work six days but keep the Sabbath as a holy day and a day of rest (v.2). There is nothing here about a three-day weekend set aside for personal indulgences. There is no mention here of over-working, nor any mention of working seven days a week. What is noted is this:
   ⇒ Man is to work six days, to work very hard.
   ⇒ Man is to set aside the seventh day of the week as a special day. The Sabbath is to be treated as a holy day and a day when man rests from his labor.

2. The importance of the Sabbath is stressed. Violators of the Sabbath were to be executed (v.2). Anyone who got so caught up in his work that he forgot the LORD was to be put to death. Even lighting a fire in the home on the Sabbath was emphatically prohibited (v.3). The lighting of a fire probably referred to a person's having to work by cooking and cleaning up after meals.

Thought 1.

Man would have a far healthier and more fruitful life if he learned how to work extremely hard six days a week and then rested and worshipped on the Sabbath day. Somehow in the extremes of life, periods of work and rest have both been warped and abused.

a)   God has commanded man to work and to work hard.

> "And the LORD God took the man, and put him into the garden of Eden to dress it and to keep it" (Ge.2:15; see Pr.14:23; Ec.9:10).
> "Let him that stole steal no more: but rather let him labour, working with his hands the thing which is good, that he may have to give to him that needeth" (Ep.4:28).
> "And whatsoever ye do in word or deed, do all in the name of the Lord Jesus, giving thanks to God and the Father by him" (Col.3:17; see Col.3:23).
> "Now them that are such [not working] we command and exhort by our Lord Jesus Christ, that with quietness they work, and eat their own bread" (2 Th.3:12).

b)   God has commanded man to keep the Sabbath, to rest and worship one day a week.

> "Six days shall work be done: but the seventh day is the sabbath of rest, an holy convocation; ye shall do no work therein: it is the sabbath of the LORD in all your dwellings" (Le.23:3; see Ex.23:12; 31:15; 34:21).
> "And he came to Nazareth, where he had been brought up: and, as his custom was, he went into the synagogue on the sabbath day, and stood up for to read" (Lu.4:16; see Mt.12:9; Mk.1:2).
> "Not forsaking the assembling of ourselves together, as the manner of some is; but exhorting one another: and so much the more, as ye see the day approaching" (He.10:25).

Thought 2.

Should a believer keep the Sabbath today? Rest and worship one day a week? What if he breaks it? Will God judge him and take his life? There is a principle in this portion of Scripture that every believer must face: we must never get so busy that we forget the LORD. God knows us better than we know ourselves; therefore, He knows how easily we slip into bad habits. God will not strike us down and kill us if we fail to keep the Sabbath, but we will be destroying ourselves. Those who break the Sabbath and forget about God will slip off into a life of sin, rebellion, and a loss of communion with God. Moreover, if a person works seven days a week, he weakens and eventually damages his body.

> "And it came to pass, that there went out some of the people on the seventh day for to gather, and they found none. And the LORD said unto Moses, How long refuse ye to keep my commandments and my laws?" (Ex.16:27-28; see Ex.31:14; Eze.20:13).
> "Thou hast despised mine holy things, and hast profaned my sabbaths" (Eze.22:8).

III. There Were the Offerings to Build the Tabernacle (vv.4-9).

There can be no building for God unless the people of God are willing to contribute their tithes and offerings, their talents and spiritual gifts to the LORD. Why does God, the Sovereign LORD and Majesty of the universe, want our resources? Because God wants us to be co-workers along with Him. Being a co-worker means that we labor and serve with God, that we bear witness with God, bear witness to a lost and dying world.

> "For we are labourers together with God: ye are God's husbandry, ye are God's building" (1 Co.3:9).
> "We then, as workers together with him, beseech you also that ye receive not the grace of God in vain" (2 Co.6:1).

Note two significant points.

1. The privilege of giving was presented to everyone (v.4). Everyone was given the opportunity to make an offering to God. Everyone was to have a part in building the Tabernacle, to feel they had a very special part in contributing to God's house of worship. The financial burden of the church is not to be placed upon the backs of the leadership and the *faithful few*. Everyone is to have a part in the support of the church.

2. The offerings were to be given freely, only by willing hearts (v.5). Note that God did not levy a tax to build the Tabernacle. When dealing with the financial support of the church and the mission to reach the world for Christ, God does not use a heavy hand with us. He does not lay a heavy financial yoke upon us; He does not burden us with a large financial obligation. God leaves the giving up to us; He wants us to judge what is right. God wants us to give freely, willingly, cheerfully. Note what the people offered in the building of the Tabernacle:

   a. They gave the right kind of metals (v.5).
   b. They gave the right kind of fabrics (v.6).
   c. They gave the right kind of animal skins (v.7).
   d. They gave the right kind of wood (v.7).
   e. They gave the right kind of oil, spices, and sweet incense (v.8).
   f. They gave the right kind of stones and gems for the ephod and breastpiece (v.9).

Thought 1.
God looks for people who are not stingy and greedy. God has no use for a person who gives with a clenched fist. God wants a cheerful giver, one who gives willingly and cheerfully. God wants people to consider every offering, every contribution, as an eternal investment with great dividends.

> "Every man shall give as he is able, according to the blessing of the LORD thy God which he hath given thee" (De.16:17; see 1 Chr.29:9; Ezr. 8:28).
> "Honour the LORD with thy substance, and with the firstfruits of all thine increase" (Pr.3:9).
> "Every man according as he purposeth in his heart, so let him give; not grudgingly, or of necessity: for God loveth a cheerful giver" (2 Co.9:7; see Mt.10:8).

Thought 2.
Too many believers are making generous contributions to things that have no eternal value. Contributions are being made...

- to multi-million dollar buildings that are used only one to three times a week, only two to six hours a week
- to programs that add to the already large indulgences of a materialistic people
- to ministries which exist solely for the financial benefit of the employed staff

The needs are too great and the funds are too precious for believers to misuse the offerings given to the LORD. The world reels under the weight of desperate need, and the needs must be met by the church.

> "The Spirit of the Lord is upon me, because he hath anointed me to preach the gospel to the poor; he hath sent me to heal the brokenhearted, to preach deliverance to the captives, and recovering of sight to the blind, to set at liberty them that are bruised" (Lu.4:18).

"For I was an hungred, and ye gave me meat: I was thirsty, and ye gave me drink: I was a stranger, and ye took me in" (Mt.25:35).

"For all the law is fulfilled in one word, even in this; Thou shalt love thy neighbour as thyself" (Ga.5:14).

"And he said unto them, Go ye into all the world, and preach the gospel to every creature" (Mk.16:15; see Mt.28:18-20; Lu.19:10; Jn.20:21).

Thought 3.
The people were obedient in their giving. Note: they did not bring anything that was not on God's list of materials. God's people gave exactly what God wanted from them.

IV. There Was the Challenge to the Skilled Workers: Come and Make Everything (vv.10-19).

The time had finally come to make the Tabernacle and all its furnishings. The time had come to show man exactly how God is to be approached and worshipped. It is easy to take for granted Israel's unique place in history. It is easy to assume...
- that they had been worshipping God in the right way for many years
- that they had always known how to approach God

But Israel had not always been faithful; Scripture is clear about this. Like the believers of today, they needed to be taught that there is only one living and true God and only one way to approach Him: through the blood of the sacrificial lamb. This was being symbolized in the Tabernacle. God was using the Tabernacle to teach this great truth; therefore the people needed to know the symbolism behind each piece of furniture. They needed to know how this eternal truth—that there is only one living and true God and only one way to approach Him—applied to their lives. In order to get the whole truth in the Tabernacle, it was critically important that the skilled workers make *everything* just as God designed, adding nothing, changing nothing, and leaving nothing out, not a single thing. Leaving even one thing out would have created a gap in God's truth for His people.

Note the carefully worded command to the skilled workers: to come and make everything the LORD commanded, make everything exactly as God designed (vv.10-19).
1. The workers were to make the *Tabernacle* itself. The Tabernacle symbolized God's dwelling among His people and man's need to approach God as God dictates (v.11). Man desperately needed to learn how to approach God. The Tabernacle was to teach man how to approach Him, that there is only one door, one way into God's holy presence. (See outline and notes—Chapter Five, Ex.26:1-37 for more discussion.)

"Jesus saith unto him, I am the way, the truth, and the life: no man cometh unto the Father, but by me" (Jn.14:6).

"For this is good and acceptable in the sight of God our Saviour; Who will have all men to be saved, and to come unto the knowledge of the truth. For there is one God, and one mediator between God and men, the man Christ Jesus; Who gave himself a ransom for all, to be testified in due time" (1 Ti.2:3-6).

2. The workers were to make the *Ark and the Mercy Seat and the Inner Veil* (v.12).
   ⇒ The Ark symbolized the presence of God. It symbolized the very throne of God, the place where the presence of God dwelt in a very special way. A very special manifestation of God's presence hovered right above the Ark. (See outline and notes—Chapter Two, Ex.25:10-22 for more discussion.)
   ⇒ The Mercy Seat sat upon the Ark and was the actual seat of the Ark. It symbolized the mercy of God, that God sat upon His throne to execute both justice and mercy. (See outline and note—Chapter Two, Ex.25:17-21 for more discussion.)

⇒ The Inner Veil symbolized the blazing holiness and righteousness of God, that He dwells in pure holiness and righteousness, so pure that He is totally separated from man, so pure that man cannot look upon God without being totally consumed. (See note—Chapter Five, Ex.26:31-35 for more discussion.)

The High Priest alone was allowed to enter the Holy of Holies, and he could enter only once a year. He appeared before God once a year to offer up the sacrificial blood of the lamb as the atonement—as the reconciliation and substitute—for the sins of the people. This, of course, pointed to Jesus Christ, the Lamb of God who takes away the sin of the world.

a. By taking away our sin, Jesus Christ makes us righteous in Himself, makes it possible for God to count us justified, righteous in Christ.

> **"Therefore being justified by faith, we have peace with God through our Lord Jesus Christ" (Ro.5:1).**
> **"And such were some of you: but ye are washed, but ye are sanctified, but ye are justified in the name of the Lord Jesus, and by the Spirit of our God" (1 Co.6:11).**
> **"For he hath made him to be sin for us, who knew no sin; that we might be made the righteousness of God in him" (2 Co.5:21).**

b. By taking away our sin, Jesus Christ reconciles us to God and brings us into the presence of God, making us acceptable to Him.

> **"The next day John seeth Jesus coming unto him, and saith, Behold the Lamb of God, which taketh away the sin of the world" (Jn.1:29).**
> **"Who his own self bare our sins in his own body on the tree, that we, being dead to sins, should live unto righteousness: by whose stripes ye were healed" (1 Pe.2:24).**
> **"For Christ also hath once suffered for sins, the just for the unjust, that he might bring us to God, being put to death in the flesh, but quickened by the Spirit" (1 Pe.3:18).**

3. The workers were to make the *Table of Showbread.* The Table pointed to Christ as the Bread of Life (v.13). Man will always have a deep hunger that only Jesus Christ can satisfy. Only Christ, the Bread of Life, can fill man's hungry soul. (See outline and notes—Chapter Three, Ex.25:23-30 for more discussion.)

> **"And Jesus said unto them, I am the bread of life: he that cometh to me shall never hunger; and he that believeth on me shall never thirst" (Jn.6:35; see Jn.6:33, 48, 50-51, 58).**

4. The workers were to make the *Lampstand.* The Lampstand pointed to Christ as the Light of the world (v.14). In a world darkened by sin and evil, Jesus Christ is the Light of the world. He points man to the light of life and righteousness, both now and eternally. (See outline and notes—Chapter Four, Ex.25:31-40 for more discussion.)

> **"Then spake Jesus again unto them, saying, I am the light of the world: he that followeth me shall not walk in darkness, but shall have the light of life" (Jn.8:12; see Jn.12:46; Ep.5:14; 2 Ti.1:10).**

5. The workers were to make the *Altar of Incense.* This Altar symbolized the prayers of God's people ascending up to God and pleasing Him (v.15). There was an incense always burning upon the Altar, always ascending up as a sweet aroma, filling the Tabernacle of God. This symbolized that God's people were to walk in unbroken prayer, always lifting up the sweet aroma of prayer to God. (See outline and note—Chapter Nine, Ex.30:1-10 for more discussion.)

"Seek the LORD and his strength, seek his face continually" (1 Chr.16:11; see Lu.18:1; Ep.6:18).
"Pray without ceasing" (1 Th.5:17).

6. The workers were to make the *Outer Veil or Door*. This symbolized that God can be approached—but only *one way*, only through *one door*. The way, the door into God's presence, is Jesus Christ (v.15). The world claims that there are many ways to God. But Scripture declares that there is only one approach to God, only one way, only one door: the LORD Jesus Christ Himself. (See outline and note—Chapter Five, Ex.26:36-37 for more discussion.)

"I am the door: by me if any man enter in, he shall be saved, and shall go in and out, and find pasture" (Jn.10:9).
"Jesus saith unto him, I am the way, the truth, and the life: no man cometh unto the Father, but by me" (Jn.14:6; see Acts 4:12; Ro.5:2; 1 Ti.2:5-6).

7. The workers were to make the *Altar of Burnt Offering*. This altar symbolized the need for atonement, for reconciliation with God (v.16). Every man needs to be reconciled to God. Jesus Christ is the Lamb of God who takes away the sin of the world and reconciles man to God. The atoning sacrifice of Jesus Christ has forevermore made man right with God. (See outline and note—Chapter Six, Ex.27:1-8 for more discussion.)

"The next day John seeth Jesus coming unto him, and saith, Behold the Lamb of God, which taketh away the sin of the world" (Jn.1:29; see Ep.2:16; Col.1:20).
"For if the blood of bulls and of goats, and the ashes of an heifer sprinkling the unclean, sanctifieth to the purifying of the flesh: How much more shall the blood of Christ, who through the eternal Spirit offered himself without spot to God, purge your conscience from dead works to serve the living God?" (He.9:13-14; see 1 Pe.1:18-19; 3:18).

8. The workers were to make the *Bronze Wash Basin* (v.16). This symbolized the washing away of sin, the cleansing and forgiveness of sin. (See notes—Chapter Ten, Ex.30:17-21; 38:3 for more discussion.) The wash basin symbolized Jesus Christ, His cleansing us from sin through His shed blood.

"In whom we have redemption through his blood, the forgiveness of sins, according to the riches of his grace" (Ep.1:7).
"But if we walk in the light, as he is in the light, we have fellowship one with another, and the blood of Jesus Christ his Son cleanseth us from all sin" (1 Jn.1:7; see 1 Jn.1:9; Re.1:5).

9. The workers were to make the *Walls or Curtains* of the Courtyard (v.17). The walls symbolized the need for sacrificial blood and separation from the world. Animals had to be slaughtered to provide the skins and hair for the tent coverings. The slaughtering of the animals was a natural picture of the need for sacrificial blood in approaching God. The coverings also provided a barrier, a wall of separation between God's presence and the world. In order to enter God's presence, man had to leave the world behind and enter the Tabernacle wall through the blood of the sacrificed lamb. All this, of course, pointed toward the blood of Jesus Christ that was to be sacrificed and shed for man. (See outline and note—Chapter Five, Ex.26:1-14 for more discussion.)

a. The walls symbolized the blood of the sacrifice that had to be made for man.

"Forasmuch as ye know that ye were not redeemed with corruptible things, as silver and gold, from your vain conversation received by tradition from your fathers; But with the precious blood of

Christ, as of a lamb without blemish and without spot" (1 Pe.1:18-19; see Ro.5:9; Gal.1:4; He.9:13-14; 1 Pe.2:24; 1 Jn.1:7; Re.1:5).

b. The walls symbolized the need for separation from the world.

"Wherefore come out from among them, and be ye separate, saith the Lord, and touch not the unclean thing; and I will receive you, And will be a Father unto you, and ye shall be my sons and daughters, saith the Lord Almighty" (2 Co.6:17-18; see 1 Jn.2:15-16).

10. The workers were to make the *Entrance Door or Outer Veil* (Curtain). The Outer Door symbolized that God can be approached (v.17). God's invitation is strong, and it is wide open. God's invitation is universal, open to every man, woman, and child upon earth: "whosoever will" may come. It is a door of welcome, of divine invitation, of calling repentant sinners to Himself. (See outline and notes—Chapter Five, Ex.26:36-37; Chapter Six, Ex.27:16 for more discussion.)

"For whosoever shall call upon the name of the Lord shall be saved" (Ro.10:13; see Is.45:22; 55:1; Jn.7:37).
"And the Spirit and the bride say, Come. And let him that heareth say, Come. And let him that is athirst come. And whosoever will, let him take the water of life freely" (Re.22:17).

11. The workers were to make the *Tent Stakes or Pegs* and their ropes. These pointed to Jesus Christ as the eternal, infinite love of God (v.18). The stakes and cords upheld the posts or pillars of the Tabernacle. It is Jesus Christ who upholds the pillars of the church. It is through the ministry of Jesus Christ that people are bound together in love. It is through His love that unity is realized.

"A new commandment I give unto you, That ye love one another; as I have loved you, that ye also love one another. By this shall all men know that ye are my disciples, if ye have love one to another" (Jn.13:34-35).
"And this is his commandment, That we should believe on the name of his Son Jesus Christ, and love one another, as he gave us commandment" (1 Jn.3:23).

12. The workers were to make the *Clothing* for the priests. The priests' clothing symbolized bringing dignity and honor to the name of God (v.19). By wearing the priestly garments, the priests were constantly reminded that they were serving God, the Sovereign LORD and Majesty of the universe. (See outline and note—Chapter Seven, Ex.28:1-43 for more discussion.)

"Let a man so account of us, as of the ministers of Christ, and stewards of the mysteries of God. Moreover it is required in stewards, that a man be found faithful" (1 Co.4:1-2).
"What? know ye not that your body is the temple of the Holy Ghost which is in you, which ye have of God, and ye are not your own? For ye are bought with a price: therefore glorify God in your body, and in your spirit, which are God's" (1 Co.6:19-20; see 1 Co.15:58; 1 Pe.4:10).

V. There Was the Response of the People to God's Call and Challenge (vv.20-29).

God offers an infinite number of opportunities for believers to serve Him. In fact, God brings a daily challenge to the believer who wants to serve Him. Note how the people responded to God's call and challenge:

1. Everyone who was willing and whose heart was stirred brought his offering to the LORD (vv.20-21). Millions of people heard the call and responded to the challenge. But note: not everyone responded to this great challenge. Some of the people held back. Not everyone had a heart willing to give. Not everyone brought his offering to the LORD.

Thought
We often miss an opportunity to be used by God. Why? Because we do not get involved. We refuse to serve in the church; we refuse to give and support God's work; we keep silent and do not bear witness to the saving grace of Christ.

> **"But this I say, He which soweth sparingly shall reap also sparingly; and he which soweth bountifully shall reap also bountifully" (2 Co.9:6; see 1 Co.3:8).**
> **"And, behold, I come quickly; and my reward is with me, to give every man according as his work shall be" (Re.22:12).**

2. Everyone who was willing—both men and women—brought their gold jewelry and presented it as an offering of thanksgiving to the LORD (v.22). The genuine believers were not selfish; they were not attached to the things of the world; they did not hoard their possessions or wealth. They gave *willingly* to the LORD. Their act of giving their gifts as a wave offering was a symbolic act saying, "LORD, here it is—all of it. We give it to You freely, confessing that You mean far more to us than gold."

Thought
The most liberated people on earth are those who are not owned by their possessions. The liberated person knows that nothing is as valuable as his relationship with God.

> **"Every man also to whom God hath given riches and wealth, and hath given him power to eat thereof, and to take his portion, and to rejoice in his labour; this is the gift of God" (Ec.5:19; see De.8:18; Pr.13:7).**
> **"Lay not up for yourselves treasures upon earth, where moth and rust doth corrupt, and where thieves break through and steal" (Mt.6:19).**
> **"[Moses] esteeming the reproach of Christ greater riches than the treasures in Egypt: for he had respect unto the recompence of the reward" (He.11:26).**

3. Everyone who had colored linen and animal skins brought them as an offering (v.23). The task of building the Tabernacle required precious materials like gold and gems. The Tabernacle also needed more common things like the skins of animals. No gift was too large or too small. Everything was needed in order to build what God wanted: a place where He could dwell with His people, a place that was set apart for the people to pray, worship, and seek His face.

Thought
God does not love a person because he can afford to give more to the work of God than someone else. Neither does God love the poor man just because he is poor. God loves us all. When it comes to giving, God is more interested in the heart behind the gift and in how much we keep than in how much we give.

> **"And Jesus sat over against the treasury, and beheld how the people cast money into the treasury: and many that were rich cast in much. And there came a certain poor widow, and she threw in two mites, which make a farthing. And he called unto him his disciples, and saith unto them, Verily I say unto you, That this poor widow hath cast more in, than all they which have cast into the treasury: For all**

> **they did cast in of their abundance; but she of her want did cast in all
> that she had, even all her living" (Mk.12:41-44).**

4. Everyone who had silver or bronze brought it as an offering to the LORD (v.24).
5. Every skilled woman who could sew and spin prepared the curtains (v.25). These talented women brought the linen curtains and the curtains of goat hair (v.26).
6. Every leader made his contribution as he brought stones and gems for the ephod and breastpiece (v.27). These leaders also brought spices and oil for the light and anointing oil for the incense (v.28).
7. The glorious fact is restated and stressed: all the men and women who were willing gave the LORD freewill offerings for the work (v.29).

Thought
We are to give and support the work of God, but we are to give willingly and cheerfully.

> **"Bring ye all the tithes into the storehouse, that there may be
> meat in mine house, and prove me now herewith, saith the LORD of
> hosts, if I will not open you the windows of heaven, and pour you out a
> blessing, that there shall not be room enough to receive it" (Mal.3:10;
> see Pr.3:9; 11:25; Lu.6:38; Acts 20:35).**
> **"But this I say, He which soweth sparingly shall reap also sparingly; and he which soweth bountifully shall reap also bountifully.
> Every man according as he purposeth in his heart, so let him give; not
> grudgingly, or of necessity: for God loveth a cheerful giver"**
> **(2 Co.9:6-7).**

VI. There Were the Two Supervisors or Managers Who Were Chosen by God (vv.30-35).

There is no higher calling and no greater responsibility given by God than to be a leader of His people. On this great construction project, God called two men to set the pace for the others to follow. God called two men who were able to communicate with others the master plan of God's design for the Tabernacle. God called two men who were willing to stick to the task at hand and not be swayed or corrupted by their own ideas. God called two men whom He could use.
1. There was the general superintendent named Bezalel (v.30). Note his special qualifications, the qualifications needed to build the Tabernacle:
   a. God filled him with the Holy Spirit (v.31).
   b. God filled him with intelligence, knowledge, and skill in construction (v.31). Bezalel was able to design metal objects (v.32) and able to cut and set precious stones (v.33). Bezalel was gifted by God in woodworking and in all kinds of craftsmanship (v.33). Bezalel was chosen and set apart by God for the most important building project in Israel's history. God chose a man and gave him the necessary skills to build the Tabernacle exactly as it was designed.
2. There was the associate superintendent named Oholiab (vv.34-35). He willingly served as a support to Bezalel. Oholiab had no desire to usurp Bezalel nor to buck his authority. Oholiab was committed to God, committed to using his gifts to the fullest of his ability, committed to the building of the Tabernacle. Note these facts:
   a. Oholiab and Bezalel were both equipped by God to teach others.
   b. Both were filled by the Holy Spirit of God, filled with skill to do all kinds of work.
   c. They were skilled to work as craftsmen, designers, embroiderers, and weavers.
   d. They were skilled as master craftsmen and designers.

God had everything and everyone in the right place. He had given Moses the blueprint, the pattern and design. He had called the people to give and they had responded. He had called the two supervisors to come and lead the way. The only thing that remained was the actual construction itself. The Tabernacle was soon to become a reality.

Thought

We should never fear nor shrink back from serving God. God will never call us to a task without first equipping us to do it. God equips us to serve Him, always equips us. He gives us exactly what we need to serve Him. Moreover, He runs ahead of us and strengthens us to follow Him.

> "For as we have many members in one body, and all members have not the same office: So we, being many, are one body in Christ, and every one members one of another. Having then gifts differing according to the grace that is given to us, whether prophecy, let us prophesy according to the proportion of faith; Or ministry, let us wait on our ministering: or he that teacheth, on teaching; Or he that exhorteth, on exhortation: he that giveth, let him do it with simplicity; he that ruleth, with diligence; he that showeth mercy, with cheerfulness" (Ro.12:4-8; see Mt.25:15; Jn.15:16; 1 Co.12:4-7).

> "For we are his workmanship, created in Christ Jesus unto good works, which God hath before ordained that we should walk in them" (Ep.2:10).

> "And he gave some, apostles; and some, prophets; and some, evangelists; and some, pastors and teachers; For the perfecting of the saints, for the work of the ministry, for the edifying of the body of Christ" (Ep.4:11-12; see Ph.4:13; 2 Ti.1:7).

CHAPTER THIRTEEN

The Construction of the Tabernacle: The Excitement of Building for God (Exodus 36:1-38)

Contents

The Construction of the Tabernacle: The Excitement of Building for God (Exodus 36:1-38)

1. The summons to skilled management & workers
a. To acknowledge one important fact: Their skills & abilities were from God
b. To build the Tabernacle exactly as God designed

c. To begin work: All were summoned, all who were gifted by the LORD & willing to serve Him

2. The overwhelming faithfulness of the people in giving
a. The offerings were passed out to the workmen
b. The offerings continued to be brought by the people morning after morning
c. The offerings overflowed so much they had to be stopped

1) The workmen told Moses they had enough materials

Then wrought Bezaleel and Aholiab, and every wise hearted man, in whom the LORD put wisdom and understanding to know how to work all manner of work for the service of the sanctuary, according to all that the LORD had commanded.
2 And Moses called Bezaleel and Aholiab, and every wise hearted man, in whose heart the LORD had put wisdom, even every one whose heart stirred him up to come unto the work to do it:
3 And they received of Moses all the offering, which the children of Israel had brought for the work of the service of the sanctuary, to make it withal. And they brought yet unto him free offerings every morning.
4 And all the wise men, that wrought all the work of the sanctuary, came every man from his work which they made;
5 And they spake unto Moses, saying, The people bring much more than enough for the ser-

vice of the work, which the LORD commanded to make.
6 And Moses gave commandment, and they caused it to be proclaimed throughout the camp, saying, Let neither man nor woman make any more work for the offering of the sanctuary. So the people were restrained from bringing.
7 For the stuff they had was sufficient for all the work to make it, and too much.
8 And every wise hearted man among them that wrought the work of the tabernacle made ten curtains of fine twined linen, and blue, and purple, and scarlet: with cherubims of cunning work made he them.
9 The length of one curtain was twenty and eight cubits, and the breadth of one curtain four cubits: the curtains were all of one size.
10 And he coupled the five curtains one unto another: and the other five curtains he coupled one unto another.
11 And he made

2) Moses had to stop the offerings
• Instructed the people not to bring any more offerings

• Had more than enough to do the work

3. The inside covering of fine linen: Pictured the purity & righteousness of God
a. The material: Ten curtains of fine linen

b. The size:
1) Each was to be 42' long x 6' wide

2) Two long sets were to be made by joining together five curtains in each set

c. The loops & clasps

1) Made the loops of blue material: Made them along the edge of the end curtains of the two sets

2) Made 50 loops on each set: Made them to match one another

3) Made 50 gold clasps: To join the two sets together

4) Joined the Tabernacle together as a unit

4. The three outer coverings of the Tabernacle: Symbolized sacrifice

a. The 11 curtains of goat hair: Pictured the need for a sin offering, for cleansing

1) The size:
- Each was 45' long x 6' wide
- Five were joined together to make one set & six into another set

2) The loops: Made 50 along the edge of the end curtains of each set

3) The clasps: Made 50 to join the two sets & tent together

---

loops of blue on the edge of one curtain from the selvedge in the coupling: likewise he made in the uttermost side of another curtain, in the coupling of the second.

12 Fifty loops made he in one curtain, and fifty loops made he in the edge of the curtain which was in the coupling of the second: the loops held one curtain to another.

13 And he made fifty taches of gold, and coupled the curtains one unto another with the taches: so it became one tabernacle.

14 And he made curtains of goats' hair for the tent over the tabernacle: eleven curtains he made them.

15 The length of one curtain was thirty cubits, and four cubits was the breadth of one curtain: the eleven curtains were of one size.

16 And he coupled five curtains by themselves, and six curtains by themselves.

17 And he made fifty loops upon the uttermost edge of the curtain in the coupling, and fifty loops made he upon the edge of the curtain which coupleth the second.

18 And he made fifty taches of brass to couple the tent together, that it might

be one.

19 And he made a covering for the tent of rams' skins dyed red, and a covering of badgers' skins above that.

20 And he made boards for the tabernacle of shittim wood, standing up.

21 The length of a board was ten cubits, and the breadth of a board one cubit and a half.

22 One board had two tenons, equally distant one from another: thus did he make for all the boards of the tabernacle.

23 And he made boards for the tabernacle; twenty boards for the south side southward:

24 And forty sockets of silver he made under the twenty boards; two sockets under one board for his two tenons, and two sockets under another board for his two tenons.

25 And for the other side of the tabernacle, which is toward the north corner, he made twenty boards,

26 And their forty sockets of silver; two sockets under one board, and two sockets under another board.

27 And for the sides of the tabernacle westward he made six boards.

28 And two boards made he for the corners of the tabernacle in the two sides.

29 And they were

---

b. The covering of ram skins dyed red: Pictured the blood

c. The covering of leather: Pictured a protective separation from the world

5. The frame: Symbolized stability, support, a strong foundation

a. The size of each framing board: 15' high x 2¼' wide

1) Made two pegs on each framing board (for hooking to the base)

2) Made all framing boards this way

b. The framing

1) Made a wall, a frame of 20 boards, for the south side
- A foundation of 40 silver sockets or bases
- Two under each board

2) Made a wall of 20 boards for the north side
- A foundation of 40 sockets
- Two under each board

3) Made a wall frame of six boards for the west side
- Made a framing post of two boards for each corner: Joined

together at the bottom & at the top, fitted into a single ring	coupled beneath, and coupled together at the head thereof, to one ring: thus he did to both of them in both the corners. 30 And there were eight boards; and their sockets were sixteen sockets of silver, under every board two sockets. 31 And he made bars of shittim wood; five for the boards of the one side of the tabernacle, 32 And five bars for the boards of the other side of the tabernacle, and five bars for the boards of the tabernacle for the sides westward. 33 And he made the middle bar to shoot through the boards from the one end to the other. 34 And he overlaid the boards with gold, and made their rings of gold to be	places for the bars, and overlaid the bars with gold. 35 And he made a vail of blue, and purple, and scarlet, and fine twined linen: with cherubims made he it of cunning work. 36 And he made thereunto four pillars of shittim wood, and overlaid them with gold: their hooks were of gold; and he cast for them four sockets of silver. 37 And he made an hanging for the tabernacle door of blue, and purple, and scarlet, and fine twined linen, of needlework; 38 And the five pillars of it with their hooks: and he overlaid their chapiters and their fillets with gold: but their five sockets were of brass.	rings to hold the crossbars
• Made for the west side: A total of 8 board frames & a foundation of 16 silver sockets, two under each board 4) Made strong, durable crossbars • 5 crossbars for the south • 5 crossbars for the north • 5 crossbars for the west			**6. The inner veil: Symbolized God's majestic holiness & man's separation from God** a. The materials b. The four posts: Made of acacia wood & overlaid with gold c. The hooks: Made of gold d. The bases or sockets: Made of silver
• The center crossbar was made to run from end to end in the middle of the frames • Covered the crossbars with gold & made gold			**7. The outer veil: Symbolized the door into God's presence** a. The materials b. The five posts: Made hooks for the curtains 1) Overlaid the tops & bands with gold 2) Made five bronze sockets or bases for them

How to spend one's time is one of the most important decisions a man makes, a decision he makes every day of his life. All kinds of things compete for his attention. There is the call of...

- family
- work
- business
- friendships

- entertainment
- hobbies and recreation
- church programs
- civic obligations and programs

Often it is the least important things that require the bulk of our time. Tragically, many people waste much of their time, pouring their lives into things that will not last, things that are more recreational than beneficial and productive, things that are wasteful and unprofitable, even sinful and evil.

God is concerned, very concerned, about how we use our time. God wants His people to use their time worshipping and serving Him by meeting the desperate needs of the world. God wants His people to invest their time in reaching people for Him and in building up His kingdom. There is nothing more exciting or more thrilling than to be involved in the work of building God's kingdom upon earth. God invites us to get involved, to be an active participant in His great design for the universe, in building His church and kingdom upon earth. This is the subject of this Scripture: *The Construction of the Tabernacle: The Excitement of Building for God*, Ex.36:1-38.

I. The summons to skilled management and workers (vv.1-2).
II. The unbelievable faithfulness of the people in giving (vv.3-7).
III. The inside covering of fine linen: pictured purity and righteousness (vv.8-13).
IV. The three outer coverings of the Tabernacle: symbolized sacrifice (vv.14-19).
V. The frame: symbolized stability, support, a strong foundation (vv.20-34).
VI. The inner veil: symbolized God's majestic holiness and man's separation from God (vv.35-36).
VII. The outer veil: symbolized the door into God's presence (vv.37-38).

I. There Was the Summons to Skilled Management and Workers (vv.1-2).

There comes a time—after all the preparation, the study, the search for workers, and the gathering of materials—to build. The time had come for God's people to put into action the plan of God. The design for the great worship center had been given to Moses and passed along to these skilled managers and workers. What a tragedy it would have been to have everything in place except the workers. No matter how much money had been collected, no matter how detailed the blueprints were, no matter how great the vision of the leaders was, if there were no one to do the work, all would have been lost.

Thought
This is the cry of the heart of God: for workers who are willing to use His resources. He has supplied almost everything that is needed for the harvest of souls. There is only one thing lacking: workers, laborers for the harvest.

> **"Then saith he unto his disciples, The harvest truly is plenteous, but the labourers are few; Pray ye therefore the Lord of the harvest, that he will send forth labourers into his harvest" (Mt.9:37-38).**

1. The skilled managers and workers were to acknowledge one important fact: their skills and abilities were from God (v.1). God was the source of their unique skills, and every worker was to know this: their abilities were directly traceable to God and God alone.

> **"Every good gift and every perfect gift is from above, and cometh down from the Father of lights, with whom is no variableness, neither shadow of turning" (Js.1:17).**
> **"Now there are diversities of gifts, but the same Spirit. And there are differences of administrations, but the same Lord. And there are diversities of operations, but it is the same God which worketh all in all" (1 Co.12:4-6).**

2. The skilled managers and workers were to build the Tabernacle exactly as God had designed (v.1). These people were given one of the greatest building projects in all of history: that of building the Tabernacle of God, the very place where God was going to dwell among His people. God trusted these workers with His dwelling place. God placed within their hands a hallowed trust, the trust that the workers would construct the Tabernacle exactly as He had designed.

Thought
God calls and chooses us because He counts us trustworthy. God trusts the believer to be faithful. It is up to us to be faithful, to be trustworthy.

> **"And he called his ten servants, and delivered them ten pounds, and said unto them, Occupy till I come" (Lu.19:13).**
> **"Moreover it is required in stewards, that a man be found faithful" (1 Co.4:2).**

> "Therefore, my beloved brethren, be ye stedfast, unmoveable, always abounding in the work of the Lord, forasmuch as ye know that your labour is not in vain in the Lord" (1 Co.15:58; see 1 Ti.1:12; 1 Ti.6:20).

3. The skilled managers and workers were to begin work: all were summoned, all who were gifted by the LORD and willing to serve Him (v.2). Imagine the scene: the cream of the community, the artists, the craftsmen, the skilled people of the nation of Israel were assembled for this great task. The workers came from different tribes to work on the Tabernacle.

⇒ Each person had a unique experience with God. God called each worker individually and personally.
⇒ Each person was given a special gift by God, a very special skill and ability.
⇒ God was able to take this wide representation of people and mold them into a single working unit with one goal in mind: to build the Tabernacle of God.

Everyone was willing to lay down his or her artistic talents, offering them at the feet of God. Personal pride was surrendered as these people yielded their wills to God and to God's plan.

> "I beseech you therefore, brethren, by the mercies of God, that ye present your bodies a living sacrifice, holy, acceptable unto God, which is your reasonable service" (Ro.12:1).
> "For we are labourers together with God: ye are God's husbandry, ye are God's building" (1 Co.3:9; see 1 Co.6:19-20; 2 Co.6:1).
> "Serve the LORD with fear, and rejoice with trembling" (Ps.2:11; see Is.1:19).

II. There Was the Unbelievable Faithfulness of the People in Giving (vv.3-7).

The hearts of the people were touched and touched deeply as they gave willingly. There was an enormous sense of excitement in being a part of something so very special. Note the experience of the people as they gave:
1. The offerings were passed out to the workmen (v.3). The people made sure that their offerings were going to the right place.

Thought
Sometimes monies are given to the LORD'S work but wind up in the wrong places. It does not take long for the cost of administration to soak up the gift of the giver. Instead of meeting the needs of the people for which the gifts were intended, the funds are generated to satisfy the never-ending appetite of the fund-raising machine. In addition to extravagant administrative costs, monies are sometimes...

- misused
- wasted
- stolen
- hoarded
- left unused

> "He that giveth unto the poor shall not lack: but he that hideth his eyes shall have many a curse" (Pr.28:27; see Pr.15:27; 21:13).
> "He that loveth silver shall not be satisfied with silver; nor he that loveth abundance with increase: this is also vanity" (Ec.5:10; see Ec.5:13).
> "Your gold and silver is cankered; and the rust of them shall be a witness against you, and shall eat your flesh as it were fire. Ye have heaped treasure together for the last days" (Js.5:3; see Ac.5:1-5).

2. The offerings continued to be brought by the people morning after morning (v.3).
3. The offerings overflowed so much they had to be stopped. Why? Because the generosity of the people was simply overwhelming (vv.4-7). The workmen told Moses they

had enough materials, so Moses had to restrain the people from bringing more offerings. He simply instructed the people not to bring any more offerings: they had more than enough to do all the work. Note: the workmen showed a great deal of integrity and accountability: it would have been very easy for them to line their own pockets with the excess offerings. They could have taken advantage of the generosity of the people and become wealthy. They could have become corrupted, but they did not. They refused to profit off their work for the LORD.

Thought 1.
The church is not a place for profiteering or greed, nor is it just a place to seek a profession, or job, or some financial security. The funds, the tithes and offerings of God's people, are to support the ministry of the church. The resources of the church are to be used...
- to meet the desperate needs of a suffering world
- to carry the gospel to a lost and dying world

"Lay not up for yourselves treasures upon earth, where moth and rust doth corrupt, and where thieves break through and steal: but lay up for yourselves treasures in heaven, where neither moth nor rust doth corrupt, and where thieves do not break through nor steal" (Mt.6:19-20; see Mt.6:24; Lu.9:25; 12:15-21).

Thought 2.
God's people are to give and give sacrificially in order to meet the desperate needs of the world. This is the clear declaration of Scripture.

"Jesus said unto him, If thou wilt be perfect, go [and] sell that thou hast, and give to the poor, and thou shalt have treasure in heaven: and come [and] follow me" (Mt.19:21; see Lu.12:33; Acts 4:34-35; 20:35).
"But this I say, He which soweth sparingly shall reap also sparingly; and he which soweth bountifully shall reap also bountifully" (2 Co.9:6; see Pr.11:25).

III. There Was the Inside Covering of Fine Linen That Pictured the Purity and Righteousness of God (vv.8-13).

This beautiful covering actually formed the inside walls and ceiling of the Tabernacle, and the inside covering was constantly before the face of the priests as they ministered to the LORD in the Tabernacle. It was a constant reminder that God is pure and righteous. These are the facts of the inside covering of fine linen:
1. The material consisted of ten curtains of fine linen (v.8).
2. The size of each curtain was to be 42 feet long by 6 feet wide (v.9). One group of five curtains was to be joined together to make one set and another five curtains joined together to make the second set (v.10).
3. The loops were made of blue material and were made along the edge of the end curtains of the two sets, 50 loops per set (v.11). The loops were made to match one another (v.12). Fifty gold clasps were made. These joined the two sets together, thereby joining the Tabernacle together as a unit (v.13). (See outline and notes—Chapter Five, Ex.26:1-6 for more discussion.)

Thought
No matter where the priests looked, they saw the inside covering of the Tabernacle. They were bound to soak in the great symbolism of the curtains, that God is pure and righteous. This is the great truth we all need to learn and remember: God is pure and righteous.

⇒   We need to remember that the very name of God is righteousness.

"In his days Judah shall be saved, and Israel shall dwell safely: and this is his name whereby he shall be called, THE LORD OUR RIGHTEOUSNESS" (Je.23:6).

⇒   We need to remember that God is righteous in *all* His ways.

"The LORD is righteous in all his ways, and holy in all his works" (Ps.145:17).

⇒   We need to remember that God's right hand is full of righteousness.

"According to thy name, O God, so is thy praise unto the ends of the earth: thy right hand is full of righteousness" (Ps.48:10).

⇒   We need to remember that we can only approach God with a pure (righteous) heart.

"Who shall ascend into the hill of the LORD? or who shall stand in his holy place? He that hath clean hands, and a pure heart; who hath not lifted up his soul unto vanity, nor sworn deceitfully" (Ps.24:3-4). "Blessed are the pure in heart: for they shall see God" (Mt.5:8).

⇒   We need to remember to keep ourselves pure.

"Lay hands suddenly on no man, neither be partaker of other men's sins: keep thyself pure" (1 Ti.5:22).

⇒   We need to remember to purify our souls by obeying the truth.

"Seeing ye have purified your souls in obeying the truth through the Spirit unto unfeigned love of the brethren, see that ye love one another with a pure heart fervently" (1 Pe.1:22).

⇒   We need to remember to seek God's righteousness before anything else.

"But seek ye first the kingdom of God, and his righteousness; and all these things shall be added unto you" (Mt.6:33).

IV. There Were the Three Outer Coverings of the Tabernacle (vv.14-19).

In general, the outer coverings symbolized sacrifice and separation from the world. However, each of the three coverings also had a specific symbolic meaning.
1. The first outer covering was the eleven curtains of goat hair (vv.14-18). Each curtain was 45 feet long and 6 feet wide. Five of the curtains were joined together to make one set, and six curtains were joined together to make another set. 50 loops were made along the edge of the end curtains of each set. In addition, 50 clasps were made to join the two sets and tent together—making one entire curtain.
The goat was sometimes offered as a *sin offering*. Therefore, the goat skins pictured the need for a *sin offering* and *cleansing*. The first inner curtain discussed in note 3 above symbolized God's purity and righteousness. God's perfect holiness cannot be mixed with man's sin. There has to be a sin offering if the righteous wrath of God is going to be satisfied.

Thought

Three great lessons can be learned from the covering of goat skins. Keep in mind that the goat skin covering symbolized the need for a sin offering and for cleansing. Therefore the covering of goat skins was placed on top of the inner curtain of linen, symbolizing that a sin offering was covering the worshipper as he approached the righteousness and purity of God.

a) If there is no sin offering, if there is no cleansing, the consequences are catastrophic!

    (1) Uncleansed sinners are miserable in their sin.

> **"Fools because of their transgression, and because of their iniquities, are afflicted" (Ps.107:17).**
> **"The way of transgressors is hard" (Pr.13:15; see Ro.2:9; 3:16; Js.5:1).**

    (2) Uncleansed sinners are never freed from sin's bondage.

> **"His own iniquities shall take the wicked himself, and he shall be holden with the cords of his sins" (Pr.5:22).**
> **"Jesus answered them, Verily, verily, I say unto you, Whosoever committeth sin is the servant of sin" (Jn.8:34; see Acts 8:23; Ro.6:16; 7:23-24).**

    (3) Uncleansed sinners are always hiding their secret sins, trying to protect their reputations from exposure.

> **"Thou hast set our iniquities before thee, our secret sins in the light of thy countenance" (Ps.90:8; see Ge.3:8; 2 K.17:9; Ps.19:12).**
> **"He that covereth his sins shall not prosper: but whoso confesseth and forsaketh them shall have mercy" (Pr.28:13).**
> **"Woe unto them that seek deep to hide their counsel from the LORD, and their works are in the dark, and they say, Who seeth us? and who knoweth us?" (Is.29:15; see Is.30:1; Eze.8:12).**
> **"For it is a shame even to speak of those things which are done of them in secret" (Ep.5:12).**

    (4) Uncleansed sinners are dead in their sins.

> **"The man that wandereth out of the way of understanding shall remain in the congregation of the dead" (Pr.21:16).**
> **"The soul that sinneth, it shall die" (Eze.18:20; see Jn.6:53).**
> **"And you hath he quickened, who were dead in trespasses and sins" (Ep.2:1; see Ep.5:14; Col.2:13; 1 Th.5:6).**

b) The perfect sin offering has now been made—once for all. That sin offering is Jesus Christ. Jesus Christ died for the sins of men.

> **"Who his own self bare our sins in his own body on the tree, that we, being dead to sins, should live unto righteousness: by whose stripes ye were healed" (1 Pe.2:24; see Mt.26:28; Ep.1:7; 1 Jn.1:7).**
> **"Unto him that loved us, and washed us from our sins in his own blood" (Re.1:5).**

c) Since Jesus Christ has made the perfect sin offering, a way has been made to cleanse the sin of man's darkened heart. Once a person's heart is cleansed and his sins forgiven, some wonderful things happen to him.

(1) The person who has been cleansed is forgiven all his sin, forgiven every sin he has ever committed.

> **"Thou hast forgiven the iniquity of thy people, thou hast covered all their sin" (Ps.85:2).**

(2) The person who has been cleansed experiences the mercy of God.

> **"Who is a God like unto thee, that pardoneth iniquity, and passeth by the transgression of the remnant of his heritage? he retaineth not his anger for ever, because he delighteth in mercy" (Mi.7:18).**

(3) The person who has been cleansed is cleansed from all unrighteousness.

> **"If we confess our sins, he is faithful and just to forgive us our sins, and to cleanse us from all unrighteousness" (1 Jn.1:9).**

(4) The person who has been cleansed is made alive.

> **"And you, being dead in your sins and the uncircumcision of your flesh, hath he quickened together with him, having forgiven you all trespasses" (Col.2:13).**

(5) The person who has been cleansed receives the gift of the Holy Spirit.

> **"Then Peter said unto them, Repent, and be baptized every one of you in the name of Jesus Christ for the remission of sins, and ye shall receive the gift of the Holy Ghost" (Ac.2:38).**

(6) The person who has been cleansed has his conscience purified for service to God.

> **"How much more shall the blood of Christ, who through the eternal Spirit offered himself without spot to God, purge your conscience from dead works to serve the living God?" (He.9:14).**

(7) The person who has been cleansed is given a close bond of fellowship with other believers.

> **"But if we walk in the light, as he is in the light, we have fellowship one with another, and the blood of Jesus Christ his Son cleanseth us from all sin" (1 Jn.1:7).**

(8) The person who has been cleansed lives with God forever: he never dies.

> **"For God so loved the world, that he gave his only begotten Son, that whosoever believeth in him should not perish, but have everlasting life" (Jn.3:16; see He.2:9).**
> **"Forasmuch then as the children are partakers of flesh and blood, he also himself likewise took part of the same; that through death he might destroy him that had the power of death, that is, the devil; And deliver them who through fear of death were all their lifetime subject to bondage" (He.2:14-15; see 1 Pe.2:24).**

2. The second outer covering was made of ram skins dyed red (v.19). The red covering, of course, pictured...
- the blood that had to be shed
- the sacrifice that had to be made in order to approach God
- the necessity to cover the Tabernacle with the sacrifice, the place where man and God met

The ram skins were symbolic of the shed blood of Jesus Christ. He is the Perfect Sacrifice, the Perfect Lamb of God who died for the sins of mankind. Jesus Christ is the sinless, perfect Man who died to redeem us from our sins. The point is this:

⇒ God's *Perfect Holiness and Righteousness* demand justice; demand that the penalty of sin be paid; demand that the people who curse, deny, reject, disobey, and rebel against God be judged. What is the judgment? Death, eternal separation from God.

⇒ The Son of God, Jesus Christ, is the *Perfect Sacrifice*, the *Perfect Lamb* of God who died for the sin of man. His death is the perfect, ideal death. As the perfect and ideal death, His death can cover and stand for every person's death. The person who trusts Jesus Christ, who trusts the shed blood of Jesus Christ to cover his sins, becomes acceptable to God. God forgives the person's sin—counts his sin as having already been paid in the death of Jesus Christ, the *Perfect Sacrifice*, the *Perfect Lamb of God*. As the *Perfect and Ideal Man*, He died for the sins of *the whole world, the entire universe*; therefore any person who approaches God through Jesus Christ becomes acceptable to God.

Thought 1.

This is what the ram skins dyed red pictured: the blood had to be shed, the sacrifice had to be made in order to cover the Tabernacle, the place where man and God met. Man becomes acceptable to God through the shed blood of Jesus Christ, through His death and only through His death. Note what Holy Scripture declares:

a) God sent His Son, the Lord Jesus Christ, to this lost and dying world to save us.

> **"For unto you is born this day in the city of David a Saviour, which is Christ the Lord" (Lu.2:11).**
> **"For the Son of man is come to seek and to save that which was lost" (Lu.19:10; see Jn.3:16-17).**
> **"This is a faithful saying, and worthy of all acceptation, that Christ Jesus came into the world to save sinners; of whom I am chief" (1 Ti.1:15).**

b) Jesus Christ died as our substitute.

> **"But he was wounded for our transgressions, he was bruised for our iniquities: the chastisement of our peace was upon him; and with his stripes we are healed" (Is.53:5).**
> **"For he hath made him to be sin for us, who knew no sin; that we might be made the righteousness of God in him" (2 Co.5:21).**
> **"Christ hath redeemed us from the curse of the law, being made a curse for us: for it is written, Cursed is every one that hangeth on a tree" (Ga.3:13).**
> **"But we see Jesus, who was made a little lower than the angels for the suffering of death, crowned with glory and honour; that he by the grace of God should taste death for every man" (He.2:9).**
> **"For Christ also hath once suffered for sins, the just for the unjust, that he might bring us to God, being put to death in the flesh, but quickened by the Spirit" (1 Pe.3:18; see 1 Co.5:7; Gal.1:4; Ep.5:2; Tit.2:14; 1 Jn.3:16).**

c) Jesus Christ took upon Himself the full weight of our sin.

> **"So Christ was once offered to bear the sins of many; and unto them that look for him shall he appear the second time without sin unto salvation" (He.9:28; see Is.53:12).**
> **"Who his own self bare our sins in his own body on the tree, that we, being dead to sins, should live unto righteousness: by whose stripes ye were healed" (1 Pe.2:24; see 1 Jn.3:5).**

d) Jesus Christ came as the Perfect Lamb of God, the Perfect Sacrifice for us.

> **"All we like sheep have gone astray; we have turned every one to his own way; and the LORD hath laid on him the iniquity of us all. He was oppressed, and he was afflicted, yet he opened not his mouth: he is brought as a lamb to the slaughter, and as a sheep before her shearers is dumb, so he openeth not his mouth" (Is.53:6-7).**
>
> **"The next day John seeth Jesus coming unto him, and saith, Behold the Lamb of God, which taketh away the sin of the world" (Jn.1:29; see 1 Co.5:7).**
>
> **"Forasmuch as ye know that ye were not redeemed with corruptible things, as silver and gold, from your vain conversation received by tradition from your fathers; But with the precious blood of Christ, as of a lamb without blemish and without spot" (1 Pe.1:18-19).**

e) Jesus Christ deliberately chose to die for us, willingly sacrificed Himself for us.

> **"I am the good shepherd: the good shepherd giveth his life for the sheep" (Jn.10:11; see 2 Co.5:15).**
>
> **"For ye know the grace of our Lord Jesus Christ, that, though he was rich, yet for your sakes he became poor, that ye through his poverty might be rich" (2 Co.8:9).**
>
> **"Who gave himself for our sins, that he might deliver us from this present evil world, according to the will of God and our Father" (Ga.1:4).**
>
> **"And walk in love, as Christ also hath loved us, and hath given himself for us an offering and a sacrifice to God for a sweetsmelling savour" (Ep.5:2; see Tit.2:14; 1 Jn.3:16).**

f) Jesus Christ both suffered for us and died for us—all to redeem us from our sins.

> **"But we see Jesus, who was made a little lower than the angels for the suffering of death, crowned with glory and honour; that he by the grace of God should taste death for every man" (He.2:9; see Is.53:5; Mk.15:34; Lu.22:42-44; He.12:3-4; Acts 8:33; Ro.5:6; 1 Co.15:3; Ph.2:6-8).**
>
> **"For it became him, for whom are all things, and by whom are all things, in bringing many sons unto glory, to make the captain of their salvation perfect through sufferings" (He.2:10; see He.2:14-15; 13:12).**
>
> **"For Christ also hath once suffered for sins, the just for the unjust, that he might bring us to God, being put to death in the flesh, but quickened by the Spirit" (1 Pe.3:18; Re.5:9).**

3. The third outer covering was made of leather, probably the skins of sea cows (v.19). This covering was the top covering, the covering that protected all the other coverings, that protected the Tabernacle and its furnishings from the weather and any other potential damage from the outside. This protective covering pictured a protective separation from the world.

Thought
As the believer walks throughout life day by day, he needs to be on guard lest he become spoiled by the world. The threat of worldliness is a very real danger to us all. The world can quickly stain the heart of even the most mature believer. We cannot go it alone and survive in the world. We need God's love and care, His protection and guidance. Only He can protect us and guide us as we walk through the world day by day. What dangers are there in the world? What is it in the world that threatens us?
a) There is the danger of being contaminated by the unclean things of the world, of touching things forbidden by the LORD.

"Depart ye, depart ye, go ye out from thence, touch no unclean thing; go ye out of the midst of her; be ye clean, that bear the vessels of the LORD" (Is.52:11).

"Wherefore come out from among them, and be ye separate, saith the Lord, and touch not the unclean thing; and I will receive you, And will be a Father unto you, and ye shall be my sons and daughters, saith the Lord Almighty" (2 Co.6:17-18).

b) There is the danger of loving the world and the things of the world too much.

"Set your affection on things above, not on things on the earth" (Col.3:2).

"Love not the world, neither the things that are in the world. If any man love the world, the love of the Father is not in him. For all that is in the world, the lust of the flesh, and the lust of the eyes, and the pride of life, is not of the Father, but is of the world" (1 Jn.2:15-16; see 2 Ti.2:4).

c) There is the danger of falling in love with the pleasures of sin.

"By faith Moses, when he was come to years, refused to be called the son of Pharaoh's daughter; Choosing rather to suffer affliction with the people of God, than to enjoy the pleasures of sin for a season" (He.11:24-25).

"And have no fellowship with the unfruitful works of darkness, but rather reprove them" (Ep.5:11).

d) There is the danger of being caught up in the friendship of the world, of giving in to its sexual and immoral ways.

"Ye adulterers and adulteresses, know ye not that the friendship of the world is enmity with God? whosoever therefore will be a friend of the world is the enemy of God" (Js.4:4).

e) There is the danger of being caught up and enslaved by worldly lusts.

"Teaching us that, denying ungodliness and worldly lusts, we should live soberly, righteously, and godly, in this present world; Looking for that blessed hope, and the glorious appearing of the great God and our Saviour Jesus Christ" (Tit.2:12-13).

f) There is the danger of being ensnared by the deceitfulness of the world.

"He also that received seed among the thorns is he that heareth the word; and the care of this world, and the deceitfulness of riches, choke the word, and he becometh unfruitful" (Mt.13:22).

g) There is the danger of being consumed with the ways of the world and cares of this life, of being caught off guard.

"And take heed to yourselves, lest at any time your hearts be overcharged with surfeiting, and drunkenness, and cares of this life, and [so] that day come upon you unawares" (Lu.21:34).

h) There is the danger of forgetting the godly, righteous things one has been taught and giving in to the influence of the world.

"And they rejected his statutes, and his covenant that he made with their fathers, and his testimonies which he testified against them; and they followed vanity, and became vain, and went after the heathen that were round about them, concerning whom the LORD had charged them, that they should not do like them" (2 K.17:15).

i) There is the danger of being led into sin by getting caught up with the wrong crowd.

"Thou shalt not follow a multitude to do evil; neither shalt thou speak in a cause to decline after many to wrest judgment" (Ex.23:2).
"Depart from me, ye evildoers: for I will keep the commandments of my God" (Ps.119:115; see 2 Th.3:6).

j) There is the danger of being conformed to the world, of allowing one's mind to be captivated by the things of the world instead of the things of God.

"And be not conformed to this world: but be ye transformed by the renewing of your mind, that ye may prove what is that good, and acceptable, and perfect, will of God" (Ro.12:2).

k) There is the danger of returning to the world because of ridicule and persecution.

"If ye were of the world, the world would love his own: but because ye are not of the world, but I have chosen you out of the world, therefore the world hateth you" (Jn.15:19).

l) There is the danger of following the false gods and worship of the world.

"Take heed to thyself that thou be not snared by following them, after that they be destroyed from before thee; and that thou inquire not after their gods, saying, How did these nations serve their gods? even so will I do likewise" (De.12:30).

m) There is the danger of losing one's soul.

"For what is a man profited, if he shall gain the whole world, and lose his own soul? or what shall a man give in exchange for his soul?" (Mt.16:26).

V. There Was the Frame of the Tabernacle (vv.20-34).

The frame symbolized stability, support, a strong foundation. The curtains and outer coverings would have been absolutely useless without the frame, and the beautiful and ornate furnishings of the Tabernacle would have been at the mercy of the desert's weather. Without the frame, the Tabernacle's message would have been impossible to see, the message...
- that God is holy and righteous but also merciful and loving
- that man must approach God in the exact and precise way He designed: through the sacrificial blood of the lamb
- that man is to live a life of separation from the world, a righteous life of prayer and fellowship with God

Without the frame, there would have been no tent, no sanctuary, no Most Holy Place in which God could dwell.

1. The size of each framing board was 15 feet high by 2¼ feet wide. It was made with two pegs on each framing board for hooking to the base. Each framing board was to be made the same way (vv.21-22).

2. Note the following facts about the framing of the Tabernacle.

⇒ The workers made a wall, a frame of 20 boards, for the south side. This wall was supported by a foundation of 40 silver sockets or bases—two under each board (vv.23-24).

⇒ The workers made an identical wall for the north side and then supported it in the same fashion as the south side (vv.25-26).

⇒ The workers then made the west side, a wall frame of six boards. This west wall also included a framing post of two boards for each corner that were joined together at the bottom and joined together at the top, fitted into a single ring (vv.27-29). For the west side, a total of eight board frames and a foundation of sixteen silver sockets were made, two under each board (v.30).

⇒ The builders also made strong, durable crossbars: five for the south, five for the north, and five for the west walls (vv.31-32). There was also a center crossbar that was made to run from end to end in the middle of the frames (v.33). Each one of the crossbars was covered with gold. Gold rings were made to hold the crossbars (v.34).

Thought

One of the strongest messages of the Tabernacle is the symbolism of the frame. The frame was the foundation, the support that held up and stabilized the tent or Tabernacle. Jesus Christ is the foundation of the believer's life, the support that holds up and stabilizes the believer as he journeys to the promised land of heaven. Jesus Christ gives the believer stability. He gives the believer support. The New Testament tells us that the passages in the Old Testament that refer to the Rock or Stone are prophecies pointing to the Messiah, the Lord Jesus Christ Himself (1 Pe.2:6).

a) Jesus Christ is the foundation of life, the very Rock upon which we must build our lives.

(1) Jesus Christ is the Rock, the Cornerstone, a sure foundation.

> **"Wherefore also it is contained in the scripture, Behold, I lay in Sion a chief corner stone, elect, precious: and he that believeth on him shall not be confounded" (1 Pe.2:6).**
> **"Therefore thus saith the LORD God, Behold, I lay in Zion for a foundation a stone, a tried stone, a precious corner stone, a sure foundation: he that believeth shall not make haste" (Is.28:16).**

(2) Jesus Christ is the Rock, the only foundation that will last.

> **"For other foundation can no man lay than that is laid, which is Jesus Christ. Now if any man build upon this foundation gold, silver, precious stones, wood, hay, stubble" (1 Co.3:10-12).**

(3) Jesus Christ is the Rock of our salvation.

> **"O come, let us sing unto the LORD: let us make a joyful noise to the rock of our salvation" (Ps.95:1).**

(4) Jesus Christ is the Rock that gives us a firm place to stand.

> **"He brought me up also out of an horrible pit, out of the miry clay, and set my feet upon a rock, and established my goings" (Ps.40:2).**

(5) Jesus Christ is the Rock that protects us from the storms of life.

> **"Therefore whosoever heareth these sayings of mine, and doeth them, I will liken him unto a wise man, which built his house upon a rock: And the rain descended, and the floods came, and the winds blew, and beat upon that house; and it fell not: for it was founded upon a rock" (Mt.7:24-25).**

(6) Jesus Christ is the Rock that protects us from all enemies.

> **"And he said, The LORD is my rock, and my fortress, and my deliverer; The God of my rock; in him will I trust: he is my shield, and the horn of my salvation, my high tower, and my refuge, my saviour; thou savest me from violence" (2 S.22:2-3).**

(7) Jesus Christ is the Rock who will never bring shame to us.

> **"As it is written, Behold, I lay in Sion a stumblingstone and rock of offence: and whosoever believeth on him shall not be ashamed" (Ro.9:33).**

(8) Jesus Christ is the Rock that stands firm and makes us eternally secure.

> **"Nevertheless the foundation of God standeth sure, having this seal, The Lord knoweth them that are his. And, Let every one that nameth the name of Christ depart from iniquity" (2 Ti.2:19).**

(9) Jesus Christ is the Rock upon which the church is built.

> **"And I say also unto thee, That thou art Peter, and upon this rock I will build my church; and the gates of hell shall not prevail against it" (Mt.16:18).**

(10) Jesus Christ is a Rock like no other.

> **"How should one chase a thousand, and two put ten thousand to flight, except their Rock had sold them, and the LORD had shut them up? For their rock is not as our Rock, even our enemies themselves being judges" (De.32:30-31).**

b) Jesus Christ is faithful, as strong as a rock: He gives us strong support and stabilizes us as we walk day by day throughout life.
   (1) Jesus Christ is faithful to forgive us our sins.

> **"If we confess our sins, he is faithful and just to forgive us our sins, and to cleanse us from all unrighteousness" (1 Jn.1:9).**
> **"Unto him that loved us, and washed us from our sins in his own blood" (Re.1:5).**

(2) Jesus Christ is faithful to reconcile us with God.

> **"Wherefore in all things it behooved him to be made like unto his brethren, that he might be a merciful and faithful high priest in things pertaining to God, to make reconciliation for the sins of the people" (He.2:17).**

(3) Jesus Christ is faithful to strengthen and protect us from evil.

> "But the Lord is faithful, who shall stablish you, and keep you from evil" (2 Th.3:3).

(4) Jesus Christ is faithful to deliver us from temptation.

> "There hath no temptation taken you but such as is common to man: but God is faithful, who will not suffer you to be tempted above that ye are able; but will with the temptation also make a way to escape, that ye may be able to bear it" (1 Co.10:13).

(5) Jesus Christ is faithful to keep us from wavering in our faith.

> "Let us hold fast the profession of our faith without wavering; (for he is faithful that promised)" (He.10:23).

(6) Jesus Christ is faithful to help us even if we fail to trust and believe.

> "If we believe not, yet he abideth faithful: he cannot deny himself" (2 Ti.2:13).

c) God Himself is faithful, as strong as a rock in helping us as we walk throughout life day by day.
(1) God is faithful to keep His promises to believers.

> "Know therefore that the LORD thy God, he is God, the faithful God, which keepeth covenant and mercy with them that love him and keep his commandments to a thousand generations" (De.7:9).
> "Blessed be the LORD, that hath given rest unto his people Israel, according to all that he promised: there hath not failed one word of all his good promise, which he promised by the hand of Moses his servant " (1 K.8:56).

(2) God is faithful to all generations of people.

> "I will sing of the mercies of the LORD for ever: with my mouth will I make known thy faithfulness to all generations" (Ps.89:1).

(3) God is faithful to grant the fellowship of His Son, Jesus Christ our Lord.

> "For this cause we also, since the day we heard it, do not cease to pray for you, and to desire that ye might be filled with the knowledge of his will in all wisdom and spiritual understanding" (Col.1:9).

(4) God is faithful to give refuge and fulfill the hope that He has set before us.

> "That by two immutable things, in which it was impossible for God to lie, we might have a strong consolation, who have fled for refuge to lay hold upon the hope set before us" (He.6:18).

(5) God is faithful in that He will keep and secure our souls until the end.

> "And the Lord shall deliver me from every evil work, and will preserve me unto his heavenly kingdom: to whom be glory for ever and ever. Amen" (2 Ti.4:18).

"Wherefore let them that suffer according to the will of God commit the keeping of their souls to him in well doing, as unto a faithful Creator" (1 Pe.4:19).

VI. There Was the Inner Veil That Separated the Most Holy Place from the Rest of the Tabernacle (vv.35-36).

Remember the Most Holy Place was where the Ark or throne of God sat. The veil shielded and separated the Ark of God—His presence, His holiness, and His mercy—from everything else. Therefore, the Inner Veil symbolized God's majestic holiness and man's separation from God. Note the facts about the construction of the veil:
1. The materials: the veil was made of beautiful colored yarn and elegant linen. Skilled workers embroidered cherubim in the veil (v.35).
2. The four posts: were made of acacia wood and overlaid with gold (v.36).
3. The hooks: were made of gold (v.36).
4. The bases or sockets: were made of silver (v.36).

Thought
There are at least three symbolic lessons gleaned from the Inner Veil.
a) God is holy.

> "Exalt the LORD our God, and worship at his holy hill; for the LORD our God is holy" (Ps.99:9; see Ex.15:11).
> "And one [angelic being] cried unto another, and said, Holy, holy, holy, is the LORD of hosts: the whole earth is full of his glory" (Is.6:3; see Eze.39:7; Hab.1:13; Re.4:8; Re.15:4).

b) Man is sinful and separated from God's holy presence. The blackness of sin has covered his heart, marring the image of God within him, destroying his perfect relationship with God. Sin is the opposite of God's holy presence: sin is on one end of the spectrum and God's holiness is on the other end. The two will never be compatible.

> "As it is written, There is none righteous, no, not one: There is none that understandeth, there is none that seeketh after God. They are all gone out of the way, they are together become unprofitable; there is none that doeth good, no, not one. Their throat is an open sepulchre; with their tongues they have used deceit; the poison of asps is under their lips: Whose mouth is full of cursing and bitterness: Their feet are swift to shed blood: Destruction and misery are in their ways: And the way of peace have they not known: There is no fear of God before their eyes" (Ro.3:10-18).
> "For all have sinned, and come short of the glory of God" (Ro.3:23; see 1 Jn.1:8; Ge.6:5; Pr.20:9).
> "But your iniquities have separated between you and your God, and your sins have hid his face from you, that he will not hear" (Is.59:2).
> "But we are all as an unclean thing, and all our righteousnesses are as filthy rags; and we all do fade as a leaf; and our iniquities, like the wind, have taken us away" (Is.64:6; see Is.64:7; Ho.5:6).

c) Jesus Christ has bridged the great gulf between God's holiness and man's sin. He is the Entrance, the Veil, that man must enter to approach God and become acceptable to God. We can now approach God through the veil of Jesus Christ.

"Jesus, when he had cried again with a loud voice, yielded up the ghost. And, behold, the veil of the temple [the Inner Veil] was rent in twain from the top to the bottom; and the earth did quake, and the rocks rent" (Mt.27:50-51).

"I am the door: by me if any man enter in, he shall be saved, and shall go in and out, and find pasture" (Jn.10:9).

"Jesus saith unto him, I am the way [door, veil], the truth, and the life: no man cometh unto the Father, but by me" (Jn.14:6).

"Which hope [the hope of heaven, of being accepted by God] we have as an anchor of the soul, both sure and stedfast, and which entereth into that within the veil; Whither the forerunner is for us entered, even Jesus, made an high priest for ever after the order of Melchisedec" (He.6:19-20).

"Having therefore, brethren, boldness to enter into the holiest by the blood of Jesus, By a new and living way, which he hath consecrated for us, through the veil, that is to say, his flesh; And having an high priest over the house of God; Let us draw near with a true heart in full assurance of faith, having our hearts sprinkled from an evil conscience, and our bodies washed with pure water" (He. 10:19-22).

VII. There Was the Outer Veil That Symbolized the Door into God's Presence (vv.37-38).

The pathway from the Courtyard to the Holy Place was marked off by the Outer Veil. The Outer Veil was the only passageway into the presence of God. There was no other way. It was made of the same material as the beautiful Inner Veil and lacked only the embroidered cherubim (v.37). Five posts with hooks were made to hold the Outer Veil. The tops of the posts and their bands were overlaid with gold. Five bronze sockets or bases were made for the posts (v.38).

Thought

The Outer Veil is symbolic of the door that leads into God's presence. In the most gracious act imaginable, God has provided a way for man to enter into His presence. Man no longer has to guess about God. Man no longer has to stumble and grope about in the dark, wondering if there is a God, and if there is, how to find Him. God is not way off in outer space, someplace unreachable and undiscoverable. God has revealed Himself to us in the person of His Son, the Lord Jesus Christ. The door into God's presence is none other than Jesus Christ Himself.

a) Jesus Christ came to earth to show us the way to God.

"Then said Jesus unto them again, Verily, verily, I say unto you, I am the door of the sheep" (Jn.10:7; see Jn.10:1-2).

"I am the door: by me if any man enter in, he shall be saved, and shall go in and out, and find pasture" (Jn.10:9).

"Jesus saith unto him, I am the way, the truth, and the life: no man cometh unto the Father, but by me" (Jn.14:6).

b) Jesus Christ came to earth to give us life, life abundant and life eternal, a life filled with love, joy, and peace.

"I am come that they might have life, and that they might have it more abundantly" (Jn.10:10; see Jn.16:24).

"Therefore being justified by faith, we have peace with God through our Lord Jesus Christ: By whom also we have access by faith into this grace wherein we stand, and rejoice in hope of the glory of God" (Ro.5:1-2).

"And God is able to make all grace abound toward you; that ye, always having all sufficiency in all things, may abound to every good work" (2 Co.9:8).

"But the fruit of the Spirit is love, joy, peace, longsuffering, gentleness, goodness, faith, Meekness, temperance: against such there is no law. And they that are Christ's have crucified the flesh with the affections and lusts. If we live in the Spirit, let us also walk in the Spirit" (Ga.5:22-25).

"Now unto him that is able to do exceeding abundantly above all that we ask or think, according to the power that worketh in us" (Ep.3:20).

"But my God shall supply all your need according to his riches in glory by Christ Jesus" (Ph.4:19).

"And the Lord shall deliver me from every evil work, and will preserve me unto his heavenly kingdom: to whom be glory for ever and ever. Amen" (2 Ti.4:18).

(Please note: The Types, Symbols, and Pictures for this Section can be found on pages 70-77, after their initial discussion.)

The Building of the Furnishings for the Tabernacle (Part 1): Learning the Only Way to Approach God (Exodus 37:1-29)

Contents

The Building of the Furnishings for the Tabernacle (Part 1): Learning the Only Way to Approach God (Exodus 37:1-29)

1. The Ark of God: Symbolized the throne & presence of God

a. The material: Acacia wood

b. The size: 3¾' long x 2¼' wide x 2¼' high

c. The covering: Overlaid with gold, both inside & out, with a gold molding

d. The four gold rings: Were fastened to its four corners

e. The carrying poles
   1) Made of acacia wood & overlaid with gold
   2) Were inserted into the rings for carrying the Ark

2. The Mercy Seat: Symbolized the atonement, reconciliation, & mercy of God

a. The material: Pure gold

b. The size: 3¾' wide x 2¼' high

c. The two cherubim: One at each end

And Bezaleel made the ark of shittim wood: two cubits and a half was the length of it, and a cubit and a half the breadth of it, and a cubit and a half the height of it: 2 And he overlaid it with pure gold within and without, and made a crown of gold to it round about. 3 And he cast for it four rings of gold, to be set by the four corners of it; even two rings upon the one side of it, and two rings upon the other side of it. 4 And he made staves of shittim wood, and overlaid them with gold. 5 And he put the staves into the rings by the sides of the ark, to bear the ark. 6 And he made the mercy seat of pure gold: two cubits and a half was the length thereof, and one cubit and a half the breadth thereof. 7 And he made two cherubims of gold, beaten out of one piece made he them,

on the two ends of the mercy seat; 8 One cherub on the end on this side, and another cherub on the other end on that side: out of the mercy seat made he the cherubims on the two ends thereof. 9 And the cherubims spread out their wings on high, and covered with their wings over the mercy seat, with their faces one to another; even to the mercy seatward were the faces of the cherubims. 10 And he made the table of shittim wood: two cubits was the length thereof, and a cubit the breadth thereof, and a cubit and a half the height thereof: 11 And he overlaid it with pure gold, and made thereunto a crown of gold round about. 12 Also he made thereunto a border of an handbreadth round about; and made a crown of gold for the border thereof round about.

1) Made them by hammering out the gold of the Mercy Seat

2) Made them at the two ends of the Mercy Seat

3) Made them one piece with the Mercy Seat

4) Made their wings upward overshadowing the Mercy Seat

5) Made them facing one another & looking down on the Mercy Seat

3. The Table of Showbread: Symbolized God as the Bread of Life

a. The material: Acacia wood

b. The size: 3' long x 1½' wide x 2¼' high

c. The covering: Overlaid with pure gold

d. The 3" rim or trim: Made of gold

e. The four rings
  1) Made of gold & fastened to the four corners

  2) Made for carrying the table

f. The two carrying poles: Made of acacia wood overlaid with gold

g. The utensils:
  1) Made the plates, dishes, bowls, & pitchers of gold
  2) Made for the pouring out of the drink offerings

4. The Lampstand: Symbolized God as the Light of the world
a. The material
  1) Used pure hammered gold
  2) Made of one piece: The base, shaft, lamp cups, buds, & blossoms

b. The six branches
  1) Made three branches on each side of the center shaft or stem

  2) Made three cups shaped like almond flowers with buds & blossoms for each branch

  3) Made four similar almond flower-like cups on the center shaft or stem
  4) Made one blossom under each pair of branches

  5) Hammered out all the decorations & branches as one piece with the Lampstand
c. The seven lamps & accessories
  1) Made of pure gold
  2) Made from 75 pounds of pure gold

5. The Altar of Incense: Symbolized the prayers & communion of God's people ascending up to God & pleasing Him
a. The material: Acacia wood
b. The size: 18" x 18" x 3' high
c. The covering: Overlaid with pure gold—the top, sides, horns, & molding

d. The gold rings: Two were placed on each side for carrying the Altar

---

13 And he cast for it four rings of gold, and put the rings upon the four corners that were in the four feet thereof.

14 Over against the border were the rings, the places for the staves to bear the table.

15 And he made the staves of shittim wood, and overlaid them with gold, to bear the table.

16 And he made the vessels which were upon the table, his dishes, and his spoons, and his bowls, and his covers to cover withal, of pure gold.

17 And he made the candlestick of pure gold: of beaten work made he the candlestick; his shaft, and his branch, his bowls, his knops, and his flowers, were of the same:

18 And six branches going out of the sides thereof; three branches of the candlestick out of the one side thereof, and three branches of the candlestick out of the other side thereof:

19 Three bowls made after the fashion of almonds in one branch, a knop and a flower; and three bowls made like almonds in another branch, a knop and a flower: so throughout the six branches going out of the candlestick.

20 And in the candlestick were four bowls made like almonds, his knops, and his flowers:

21 And a knop under two branches of the same, and a knop under two branches of the same, and a knop under two branches of the same, according to the six branches going out of it.

22 Their knops and their branches were of the same: all of it was one beaten work of pure gold.

23 And he made his seven lamps, and his snuffers, and his snuffdishes, of pure gold.

24 Of a talent of pure gold made he it, and all the vessels thereof.

25 And he made the incense altar of shittim wood: the length of it was a cubit, and the breadth of it a cubit; it was foursquare; and two cubits was the height of it; the horns thereof were of the same.

26 And he overlaid it with pure gold, both the top of it, and the sides thereof round about, and the horns of it: also he made unto it a crown of gold round about.

27 And he made two rings of gold for it under the crown thereof, by the two corners of it, upon the two sides there-

	of, to be places for the staves to bear it withal. 28 And he made the staves of shittim wood, and overlaid them with gold.	29 And he made the holy anointing oil, and the pure incense of sweet spices, according to the work of the apothecary.	
e. The carrying poles: Made of acacia wood & overlaid with gold			f. The anointing oil & fragrant incense: Made by skilled perfumers

There is a saying that declares "ignorance is bliss." While this may sometimes be true in trivial matters, ignorance is not bliss if it keeps a person from progressing, moving ahead, succeeding or embracing a much needed truth. This is certainly true when dealing with the LORD, the only living and true God, the great Creator and Sustainer of the universe. A person who is ignorant about God suffers a great handicap. A person who cannot relate to God...

- has no answer for the emptiness and loneliness he feels in his heart
- has no solution for the meaningless tasks of life
- has no direction or guide as he walks through the dark days of life
- has no power outside himself
- has no hope at the end of this life
- has no assurance—absolute certainty—of living eternally
- has no idea how *merciful and loving* God is
- has no concept about how *holy and awesome* God is

The greatest challenge faced by man is just this: to learn how to relate to God. But note: the task of learning about God is too great for man alone. Therefore, God has provided the way to learn about Him, the way to approach Him. This is the subject of this section of Scripture: *The Building of the Furnishings for the Tabernacle (Part 1): Learning the Only Way to Approach God, Ex.37:1-29.*

I. The Ark of God: symbolized the throne and presence of God (vv.1-5).
II. The Mercy Seat: symbolized the atonement, reconciliation, and mercy of God (vv.6-9).
III. The Table of Showbread: symbolized God as the Bread of Life (vv.10-16).
IV. The Lampstand: symbolized God as the Light of the world (vv.17-24).
V. The Altar of Incense: symbolized the prayers and communion of God's people ascending up to God and pleasing Him (vv.25-29).

I. There Was the Ark of God That Symbolized the Throne and Presence of God (vv.1-5).

It was Bezalel who was given the great privilege of making the Ark of God. Bezalel was God's choice to make the piece of furniture that would serve as a constant reminder of God's presence among His people. The Ark or throne of God was made of acacia wood and was 3¾ feet long by 2¼ feet wide by 2¼ feet high (v.1). It was overlaid with pure gold, both inside and out, with a gold molding (v.2). Bezalel made four gold rings that were fastened to the Ark's four corners (v.3). He then made two poles of acacia wood that were overlaid with gold (v.4). These poles were then inserted into the rings for carrying the Ark (v.5).

Thought
How important is the throne of God? The throne of God was the place where God promised to meet with His people and instruct them. The throne of God is the place where we all are to come, fall down and prostrate ourselves, casting our very lives upon the Sovereign King and Majesty of the universe. The Scriptures have much to say about the throne of God.

208 / CHAPTER FOURTEEN

a) The description of the throne of God.
   (1) God's throne is a great white throne.

> "And I saw a great white throne, and him that sat on it, from whose face the earth and the heaven fled away; and there was found no place for them" (Re.20:11).

   (2) God's throne is a high, glorious throne.

> "Thy throne, O God, is for ever and ever: the sceptre of thy kingdom is a right sceptre" (Ps.45:6).
> "The Lord hath prepared his throne in the heavens; and his kingdom ruleth over all" (Ps.103:19; see Is.66:1; Mt.5:34).

   (3) God's throne is like a fiery flame.

> "I beheld till the thrones were cast down, and the Ancient of days did sit, whose garment was white as snow, and the hair of his head like the pure wool: his throne was like the fiery flame, and his wheels as burning fire" (Da.7:9).

   (4) God's throne is surrounded by a rainbow.

> "And he that sat was to look upon like a jasper and a sardine stone: and there was a rainbow round about the throne, in sight like unto an emerald" (Re.4:3).

   (5) God's throne is a place of lightning, thunderclaps, voices, and fire.

> "And out of the throne proceeded lightnings and thunderings and voices: and there were seven lamps of fire burning before the throne, which are the seven Spirits of God" (Re.4:5).

   (6) God's throne has a sea of glass in front of it and is surrounded by twenty-four seats, with elders sitting upon the seats.

> "And before the throne there was a sea of glass like unto crystal: and in the midst of the throne, and round about the throne, were four beasts full of eyes before and behind" (Re.4:6).
> "And round about the throne were four and twenty seats: and upon the seats I saw four and twenty elders sitting, clothed in white raiment; and they had on their heads crowns of gold" (Re.4:4).

   (7) God's throne has a pure river, clear as crystal, that flows from it and from the Lamb. It is the water of life.

> "And he showed me a pure river of water of life, clear as crystal, proceeding out of the throne of God and of the Lamb" (Re.22:1).

b) The purpose of the throne of God.
   (1) God's throne is the place where God Himself sits as the Sovereign LORD and Majesty of the universe.

> "To him that overcometh will I grant to sit with me in my throne, even as I also overcame, and am set down with my Father in his throne" (Re.3:21; see Re.5:7; Je.3:17).

"God reigneth over the heathen: God sitteth upon the throne of his holiness" (Ps.47:8).

(2) God's throne is the place where God is worshipped and praised.

"After this I beheld, and, lo, a great multitude, which no man could number, of all nations, and kindreds, and people, and tongues, stood before the throne, and before the Lamb, clothed with white robes, and palms in their hands; And cried with a loud voice, saying, Salvation to our God which sitteth upon the throne, and unto the Lamb. And all the angels stood round about the throne, and about the elders and the four beasts, and fell before the throne on their faces, and worshipped God" (Re.7:9-11; see Re.4:6, 9, 10-11; 5:13; 14:3; 19:4-5).

(3) God's throne is the place where judgment and justice (the wrath of God) are executed.

"Justice and judgment are the habitation of thy throne: mercy and truth shall go before thy face" (Ps.89:14; see Ps.9:7; 97:2; Is.9:7).

"And said to the mountains and rocks, Fall on us, and hide us from the face of him that sitteth on the throne, and from the wrath of the Lamb" (Re.6:16).

(4) God's throne is the place where mercy and grace, provision and comfort flow out.

"And in mercy shall the throne be established: and he shall sit upon it in truth in the tabernacle of David, judging, and seeking judgment, and hasting righteousness" (Is.16:5).

"Let us therefore come boldly unto the throne of grace, that we may obtain mercy, and find grace to help in time of need" (He.4:16).

"For the Lamb which is in the midst of the throne shall feed them, and shall lead them unto living fountains of waters: and God shall wipe away all tears from their eyes" (Re.7:17).

(5) God's throne is the place where the prayers of saints are directed.

"Therefore are they before the throne of God, and serve him day and night in his temple: and he that sitteth on the throne shall dwell among them" (Re.7:15; see Re.8:3).

(6) God's throne is the place where believers are accepted by God, where no deceit or fault is found in them.

"And in their mouth was found no guile: for they are without fault before the throne of God" (Re.14:5).

(7) God's throne is the place where all things are made new.

"And he that sat upon the throne said, Behold, I make all things new. And he said unto me, Write: for these words are true and faithful" (Re.21:5).

c) The location of the throne of God.
   (1) God's throne is in Heaven.

> "The LORD is in his holy temple, the LORD's throne is in heaven: his eyes behold, his eyelids try, the children of men" (Ps.11:4; see Ps.103:19; Is.66:1; Mt.23:22).
>
> "Heaven is my throne, and earth is my footstool: what house will ye build me? saith the Lord: or what is the place of my rest?" (Ac.7:49; see Re.4:2).

(2) God's throne will be in the new Jerusalem, the capital of the new heavens and earth.

> "And I saw a new heaven and a new earth: for the first heaven and the first earth were passed away; and there was no more sea. And I John saw the holy city, new Jerusalem, coming down from God out of heaven, prepared as a bride adorned for her husband....And there shall be no more curse: but the throne of God and of the Lamb shall be in it; and his servants shall serve him" (Re.21:1-2; 22:3).

d) The security and permanence of the throne of God.

> "Thy throne, O God, is for ever and ever: the sceptre of thy kingdom is a right sceptre" (Ps.45:6).
>
> "But unto the Son he saith, Thy throne, O God, is for ever and ever: a sceptre of righteousness is the sceptre of thy kingdom" (He.1:8; see Ps.89:36; 93:2).

e) The relationship of Jesus Christ to the throne of God.
   (1) God's throne is where Jesus Christ sits next to His Father.

> "Looking unto Jesus the author and finisher of our faith; who for the joy that was set before him endured the cross, despising the shame, and is set down at the right hand of the throne of God" (He.12:2).

(2) God's throne is the place where Jesus Christ sits as the slain Lamb of God.

> "And I beheld, and, lo, in the midst of the throne and of the four beasts, and in the midst of the elders, stood a Lamb as it had been slain, having seven horns and seven eyes, which are the seven Spirits of God sent forth into all the earth" (Re.5:6).

(3) God's throne is the place where Jesus Christ sits as our great High Priest.

> "Now of the things which we have spoken this is the sum: We have such an high priest, who is set on the right hand of the throne of the Majesty in the heavens" (He.8:1).

(4) God's throne is the place where Jesus Christ, the Lion of Judah, sits with the seven seals of judgment.

> "And I saw in the right hand of him that sat on the throne a book written within and on the backside, sealed with seven seals" (Re.5:1).

II. There Was the Mercy Seat or Atonement Cover for the Ark (vv.6-9).

Note what it is that sets God's throne apart from the thrones of men: the covering. God's holy throne is covered with mercy, with the merciful heart of a God who grants forgiveness to sinners. Every aspect of the Mercy Seat symbolizes and speaks of mercy and forgiveness, atonement and reconciliation. The Mercy Seat was made of pure gold, symbolic of deity (v.6). Remember, only God has the authority to forgive a man's sin.

> **"When Jesus saw their faith, he said unto the sick of the palsy, Son, thy sins be forgiven thee. But there were certain of the scribes sitting there, and reasoning in their hearts, Why doth this man thus speak blasphemies? who can forgive sins but God only? And immediately when Jesus perceived in his spirit that they so reasoned within themselves, he said unto them, Why reason ye these things in your hearts? Whether is it easier to say to the sick of the palsy, Thy sins be forgiven thee; or to say, Arise, and take up thy bed, and walk? But that ye may know that the Son of man hath power on earth to forgive sins, (he saith to the sick of the palsy,) I say unto thee, Arise, and take up thy bed, and go thy way into thine house. And immediately he arose, took up the bed, and went forth before them all; insomuch that they were all amazed, and glorified God, saying, We never saw it on this fashion" (Mk.2:5-12).**

The size of the Mercy Seat was a perfect fit for the Ark. It was exactly 3¼ feet wide and 2¼ feet high (v.6). At each end of the Mercy Seat was a cherubim (v.7). These cherubim were made by hammering out the gold and being made of one piece with the Mercy Seat (v.8). Their wings were made upward, overshadowing the Mercy Seat (v.9). Bezalel made them facing one another and looking down on the Mercy Seat (v.9).

Thought
The Mercy Seat or Atonement Cover is symbolic of God's great mercy, of atonement and reconciliation with Him, of His willingness to forgive sinners. What impact does God's mercy have upon the believer?
a) God's mercy causes us to repent, to turn away from sin and toward God.

> **"And rend your heart, and not your garments, and turn unto the LORD your God: for he is gracious and merciful, slow to anger, and of great kindness, and repenteth him of the evil" (Joel 2:13).**

b) God's mercy forgives our sins.

> **"Who is a God like unto thee, that pardoneth iniquity, and passeth by the transgression of the remnant of his heritage? he retaineth not his anger for ever, because he delighteth in mercy" (Mi.7:18).**

c) God's mercy saves us.

> **"Not by works of righteousness which we have done, but according to his mercy he saved us, by the washing of regeneration, and renewing of the Holy Ghost" (Tit.3:5).**

d) God's mercy saves us from being consumed by God's fierce judgment.

> **"It is of the LORD's mercies that we are not consumed, because his compassions fail not. They are new every morning: great is thy faithfulness" (Lam.3:22-23).**

e) God's mercy cannot be measured.

> **"For thy mercy is great above the heavens: and thy truth reacheth unto the clouds" (Ps.108:4).**

f) God's mercy will last forever.

> **"But the mercy of the LORD is from everlasting to everlasting upon them that fear him, and his righteousness unto children's children" (Ps.103:17).**

III. There Was the Table of Showbread That Symbolized God as the Bread of Life (vv.10-16).

Only God can satisfy a man's constant craving to fill his empty heart. Located in the Holy Place behind the Outer Veil, the Table of Showbread pointed to one of man's most important needs: the need to feed his hunger for God. The Table was made of acacia wood and was 3 feet long by 1½ feet wide by 2¼ feet high (v.10).

After the Table was built, it was then covered with pure gold (v.11). On the top of the Table, a three inch gold rim or trim ran along all the edges (v.12). Four rings were made of gold and fastened to the four corners of the Table (v.13). This enabled the Table to be carried with two acacia poles that were covered with gold (vv.13-15). The utensils used with the Table were also made of gold. They included plates, dishes, bowls, and pitchers. These were used for the pouring out of drink offerings (v.16).

Thought
God feeds us spiritually, satisfies the gnawing hunger within our hearts. When we come to God for spiritual food, He feeds and satisfies us.

a) We are satisfied with good things.

> **"Who satisfieth thy mouth with good things; so that thy youth is renewed like the eagle's" (Ps.103:5).**
> **"For he satisfieth the longing soul, and filleth the hungry soul with goodness" (Ps.107:9).**

b) We are satisfied within our souls.

> **"My soul shall be satisfied as with marrow and fatness; and my mouth shall praise thee with joyful lips" (Ps.63:5).**

c) We are filled to the brim with joy.

> **"These things have I spoken unto you, that my joy might remain in you, and [that] your joy might be full" (Jn.15:11).**

d) We are filled with the fullness of God Himself.

> **"And to know the love of Christ, which passeth knowledge, that ye might be filled with all the fulness of God" (Ep.3:19).**

e) We are filled with the knowledge of God's will and with wisdom.

> **"For this cause we also, since the day we heard it, do not cease to pray for you, and to desire that ye might be filled with the knowledge of his will in all wisdom and spiritual understanding" (Col.1:9).**

f) We are nourished by the LORD even during the barren and unfruitful times of life.

> **"And the LORD shall guide thee continually, and satisfy thy soul in drought, and make fat thy bones: and thou shalt be like a watered garden, and like a spring of water, whose waters fail not" (Is.58:11).**

g) We are filled with an overflowing cup even when opposed by enemies.

> **"Thou preparest a table before me in the presence of mine enemies: thou anointest my head with oil; my cup runneth over" (Ps.23:5).**

h) We will be satisfied when we see God's face.

> **"As for me, I will behold thy face in righteousness: I shall be satisfied, when I awake, with thy likeness" (Ps.17:15).**

IV. There Was the Lampstand That Symbolized God as the Light of the World (vv.17-24).

One of the most significant attributes of God is light. Without God's light, the world would be lost in darkness. No one could see the way: the purpose, meaning, and significance of life. Light helps men see the way and the truth, what life is all about. Light shines on God's handiwork, showing everyone His power and might in the lives of men.
1. The actual Lampstand itself was made of one piece of pure hammered gold. This one piece of gold made the base, the shaft, the six branches, the lamp cups, the buds, and the blossoms (v.17).
2. The six branches were made with three branches on each side of the center shaft or stem (v.18). Three cups shaped like almond flowers with buds and blossoms for each branch were made (v.19). On the center staff or stem, four similar almond flower-like cups were made (v.20). One blossom under each pair of branches was made (v.21). The builders of the Lampstand hammered out all the decorations and branches—all as one piece forming the Lampstand (v.22).
3. The seven lamps and accessories were made of pure gold (v.23). The Lampstand, the lamps, and all the accessories were made from 75 pounds of pure gold (v.24).

Thought
The Lampstand illuminated anyone who entered into the Holy Place of the Tabernacle. Thus it is with the believer. When the believer enters the presence of God, the Light of God shines upon the believer. The believer becomes God's light to the world.
a) Note what Scripture says about God's light.
  (1) God's light demands that we believe and trust in the light.

> **"While ye have light, believe in the light, that ye may be the children of light. These things spake Jesus, and departed, and did hide himself from them" (Jn.12:36).**

  (2) God's light eliminates fear within us.

> **"The LORD is my light and my salvation; whom shall I fear? the LORD is the strength of my life; of whom shall I be afraid?" (Ps.27:1).**

  (3) God's light shows us the way even when darkness is all around.

> **"Rejoice not against me, O mine enemy: when I fall, I shall arise; when I sit in darkness, the LORD shall be a light unto me" (Mi.7:8).**

(4) God's light demands that we work for God while we can.

> **"I must work the works of him that sent me, while it is day: the night cometh, when no man can work" (Jn.9:4).**

(5) God's light will never burn out; it lasts forever.

> **"Thy sun shall no more go down; neither shall thy moon withdraw itself: for the LORD shall be thine everlasting light, and the days of thy mourning shall be ended" (Is.60:20).**

(6) God's light shines through us to the world.

> **"Ye are the light of the world. A city that is set on an hill cannot be hid" (Mt.5:14; see Is.60:3; Acts 13:47).**
> **"For ye were sometimes darkness, but now are ye light in the Lord: walk as children of light" (Ep.5:8; see Ph.2:15; 1 Th.5:5).**

b) Note what Scripture says about the light of Jesus Christ.
(1) The light of Jesus Christ is the True light.

> **"That was the true Light, which lighteth every man that cometh into the world" (Jn.1:9).**
> **"Again, a new commandment I write unto you, which thing is true in him and in you: because the darkness is past, and the true light now shineth" (1 Jn.2:8).**

(2) Jesus Christ is the Light of the world and His light eliminates all darkness.

> **"Then spake Jesus again unto them, saying, I am the light of the world: he that followeth me shall not walk in darkness, but shall have the light of life" (Jn.8:12).**

(3) The light of Jesus Christ gives life to men.

> **"In him was life; and the life was the light of men" (Jn.1:4).**

(4) The light of Jesus Christ shines in our hearts, giving us the knowledge of God.

> **"For God, who commanded the light to shine out of darkness, hath shined in our hearts, to give the light of the knowledge of the glory of God in the face of Jesus Christ" (2 Co.4:6).**

(5) The light of Jesus Christ gives light to those who live in darkness, to those who live in the shadow of death.

> **"To give light to them that sit in darkness and in the shadow of death, to guide our feet into the way of peace" (Lu.1:79).**

(6) The light of Jesus Christ is a great light.

> **"The people which sat in darkness saw great light; and to them which sat in the region and shadow of death light is sprung up" (Mt.4:16; see Is.9:2).**

(7) The light of Jesus Christ will illuminate the New Jerusalem.

> **"And the city had no need of the sun, neither of the moon, to shine in it: for the glory of God did lighten it, and the Lamb is the light thereof" (Re.21:23).**

V. There Was the Altar of Incense (vv.25-35).

The Altar of Incense was made of acacia wood that was 18 inches square and 3 feet high (v.25). The altar was covered with pure gold including the top, sides, horns, and molding (v.26). Two gold rings were made and placed on each side for carrying the Altar (v.27). The carrying poles were made of acacia wood and overlaid with gold (v.28). The anointing oil and fragrant incense were made by skilled perfumers (v.29).

The Altar of Incense symbolized the prayers and communion of God's people ascending up to God and pleasing Him. (See outline and notes—Chapter Nine, Ex.30:1-10 for more discussion.) Prayer is the most powerful tool God gives His people, but unfortunately it is the least used. There are believers who know the importance of prayer but seldom pray. Why? Why do more believers not pray as they should? Remember the subject of this portion of Scripture: *Learning the Only Way to Approach God*. Many people do not pray simply because they have never learned how to approach God.

Thought
The Altar was small in stature, but by no means was it small in importance. The job of the priest was incomplete and unfinished if he bypassed the Altar of Incense. His job included prayer as well as tending to the Lampstand and the Table of Showbread. Sometimes we become so busy that we forget to tend to the Altar of Incense; we get so caught up in life that we forget to pray. This Altar is too important to overlook, too important to ignore. This Altar symbolized the prayers and communion of God's people ascending up to God and pleasing Him. The lesson is forceful: we must pray; we must intercede at the Altar of Incense.

- We must call upon the name of the LORD.

> **"I will offer to thee the sacrifice of thanksgiving, and will call upon the name of the LORD" (Ps.116:17; see Zep.3:9).**
> **"For whosoever shall call upon the name of the Lord shall be saved" (Ro.10:13).**

- We must pray and pray, making an eternal deposit of prayer with God.

> **"And when he had taken the book, the four beasts and four and twenty elders fell down before the Lamb, having every one of them harps, and golden vials full of odours, which are the prayers of saints" (Re.5:8).**
> **"And another angel came and stood at the altar, having a golden censer; and there was given unto him much incense, that he should offer it with the prayers of all saints upon the golden altar which was before the throne" (Re.8:3).**

- We must seek God and His strength continually.

> **"Seek the LORD and his strength, seek his face continually" (1 Chr.16:11).**

- We must watch and pray, resisting temptation.

> **"Watch and pray, that ye enter not into temptation: the spirit indeed is willing, but the flesh is weak" (Mt.26:41).**

- We must not give up but continue to stand in prayer.

    "And he spake a parable unto them to this end, that men ought always to pray, and not to faint" (Lu.18:1).

- We must make our request in the name of Jesus Christ.

    "Hitherto have ye asked nothing in my name: ask, and ye shall receive, that your joy may be full" (Jn.16:24).

- We must pray, trusting God's Spirit to help us as we pray.

    "Likewise the Spirit also helpeth our infirmities: for we know not what we should pray for as we ought: but the Spirit itself maketh intercession for us with groanings which cannot be uttered. And he that searcheth the hearts knoweth what is the mind of the Spirit, because he maketh intercession for the saints according to the will of God" (Ro.8:26-27; see Ep.6:18).

- We must pray always.

    "Pray without ceasing" (1 Th.5:17).

- We must pray in humility.

    "If my people, which are called by my name, shall humble themselves, and pray, and seek my face, and turn from their wicked ways; then will I hear from heaven, and will forgive their sin, and will heal their land" (2 Chr.7:14).

- We must pray with our whole hearts.

    "And ye shall seek me, and find me, when ye shall search for me with all your heart" (Je.29:13).

- We must pray with unshakable faith.

    "Therefore I say unto you, What things soever ye desire, when ye pray, believe that ye receive them, and ye shall have them" (Mk.11:24).
    "And this is the confidence that we have in him, that, if we ask any thing according to his will, he heareth us" (1 Jn.5:14).

- We must pray with fervent energy.

    "Confess your faults one to another, and pray one for another, that ye may be healed. The effectual fervent prayer of a righteous man availeth much" (Js.5:16).

- We must do those things that are pleasing to God.

    "And whatsoever we ask, we receive of him, because we keep his commandments, and do those things that are pleasing in his sight" (1 Jn.3:22).

(Please note: The Types, Symbols, and Pictures for this Section can be found on pages 30-35, 42-43, 51-52, and 141, after their initial discussion.)

The Building of the Furnishings for the Tabernacle (Part 2): Learning the Only Way to Approach God (Exodus 38:1-31)

Contents

The Building of the Furnishings for the Tabernacle (Part 2): Learning the Only Way to Approach God (Exodus 38:1-31)

1. The Altar of Burnt Offering: Symbolized the need for atonement, reconciliation with God

a. The material: Acacia wood

b. The size: 7½' x 7½' x 4½' high

c. The horns
1) Made a horn at each of the four corners—all of one piece
2) Was overlaid with bronze

d. The utensils: Made of bronze

e. The grate: Made of bronze
1) Placed under the ledge halfway up the altar
2) Made 4 bronze rings for each corner: To hold the carrying poles

f. The carrying poles
1) Made of acacia wood & overlaid with bronze
2) Were inserted into the rings

And he made the altar of burnt offering of shittim wood: five cubits was the length thereof, and five cubits the breadth thereof; it was foursquare; and three cubits the height thereof.

2 And he made the horns thereof on the four corners of it; the horns thereof were of the same: and he overlaid it with brass.

3 And he made all the vessels of the altar, the pots, and the shovels, and the basons, and the fleshhooks, and the firepans: all the vessels thereof made he of brass.

4 And he made for the altar a brasen grate of network under the compass thereof beneath unto the midst of it.

5 And he cast four rings for the four ends of the grate of brass, to be places for the staves.

6 And he made the staves of shittim wood, and overlaid them with brass.

7 And he put the staves into the rings

on the sides of the altar, to bear it withal; he made the altar hollow with boards.

8 And he made the laver of brass, and the foot of it of brass, of the lookingglasses of the women assembling, which assembled at the door of the tabernacle of the congregation.

9 And he made the court: on the south side southward the hangings of the court were of fine twined linen, an hundred cubits:

10 Their pillars were twenty, and their brasen sockets twenty; the hooks of the pillars and their fillets were of silver.

11 And for the north side the hangings were an hundred cubits, their pillars were twenty, and their sockets of brass twenty; the hooks of the pillars and their fillets of silver.

12 And for the west side were hangings of fifty cubits, their pillars ten, and their sockets ten; the hooks of the pillars

for carrying the altar

g. The altar was made hollow

2. The Bronze Wash Basin: Symbolized the washing, cleansing, & forgiveness of sin

a. Made with a bronze stand

b. Made from mirrors given by the women who served the LORD

3. The Courtyard: Symbolized that God can be approached

a. The south side
1) Made 150' of linen curtains
2) Made 20 posts that set into 20 bronze bases
3) Made silver hooks & bands to hold the curtains

b. The north side
1) Made 150' long
2) Made 20 posts that were set into 20 bronze bases
3) Made silver hooks & bands

c. The west end
1) Made 75' of curtains
2) Made 10 posts & 10 bases
3) Made silver

hooks & bands

d. The east end: 75' wide

e. The curtained walls on each side of the entrance
1) Made one side 22½' long with 3 posts & 3 bases
2) Made the other side 22½' long with 3 posts & 3 bases

f. The curtains of the Courtyard: Made of fine linen

g. The posts & bases
1) The bases: Made of bronze
2) The hooks & bands on each post: Made of silver
3) The tops of the posts & the bands to hold up the curtains: Made of solid silver

h. The entrance (door) to the Courtyard
1) Made of linen & embroidered with blue, purple, & scarlet yarn
2) Made 30' long x 7½' high: Just like the Courtyard curtained walls
3) Made 4 posts & set into 4 bronze bases
4) Made hooks & bands of silver & overlaid the top of the posts with silver

and their fillets of silver. 13 And for the east side eastward fifty cubits. 14 The hangings of the one side of the gate were fifteen cubits; their pillars three, and their sockets three. 15 And for the other side of the court gate, on this hand and that hand, were hangings of fifteen cubits; their pillars three, and their sockets three. 16 All the hangings of the court round about were of fine twined linen. 17 And the sockets for the pillars were of brass; the hooks of the pillars and their fillets of silver; and the overlaying of their chapiters of silver; and all the pillars of the court were filleted with silver. 18 And the hanging for the gate of the court was needlework, of blue, and purple, and scarlet, and fine twined linen: and twenty cubits was the length, and the height in the breadth was five cubits, answerable to the hangings of the court. 19 And their pillars were four, and their sockets of brass four; their hooks of silver, and the overlaying of their chapiters and their fillets of silver.

20 And all the pins of the tabernacle, and of the court round about, were of brass. 21 This is the sum of the tabernacle, even of the tabernacle of testimony, as it was counted, according to the commandment of Moses, for the service of the Levites, by the hand of Ithamar, son to Aaron the priest. 22 And Bezaleel the son of Uri, the son of Hur, of the tribe of Judah, made all that the LORD commanded Moses. 23 And with him was Aholiab, son of Ahisamach, of the tribe of Dan, an engraver, and a cunning workman, and an embroiderer in blue, and in purple, and in scarlet, and fine linen. 24 All the gold that was occupied for the work in all the work of the holy place, even the gold of the offering, was twenty and nine talents, and seven hundred and thirty shekels, after the shekel of the sanctuary. 25 And the silver of them that were numbered of the congregation was an hundred talents, and a thousand seven hundred and threescore and fifteen shekels, after the shekel of the sanctuary: 26 A bekah for every

i. The tent pegs for the Tabernacle & Courtyard: Made of bronze

4. The inventory used in building the Tabernacle: Pictured the faithfulness of God's people
a. The compilers of the figures: The Levites
b. The recorder: Ithamar, son of Aaron
c. The superintendent of the construction: Bezalel
1) His heritage
2) His faithfulness: Made everything the LORD commanded
d. The assistant superintendent: Oholiab
1) His heritage
2) His skill

e. The gifts of gold
1) Taken up through a wave offering
2) Totaled 2200 pounds

f. The gifts of silver
1) Totaled about 7545 pounds
2) Was collected

through the census tax or ransom tax • Was 1/15 of an ounce of silver • Was collected from every man 20 years or older, a total of 603,550 men 3) About 7500 pounds of silver was used to make the 100 bases for the sanctuary walls & the posts supporting the inner curtain: About 75 pounds for each base 4) About 45 pounds of silver was used to make the bands & hooks & to	man, that is, half a shekel, after the shekel of the sanctuary, for every one that went to be numbered, from twenty years old and upward, for six hundred thousand and three thousand and five hundred and fifty men. 27 And of the hundred talents of silver were cast the sockets of the sanctuary, and the sockets of the vail; an hundred sockets of the hundred talents, a talent for a socket. 28 And of the thousand seven hundred seventy and five shekels he made hooks for the pillars,	and overlaid their chapiters, and filleted them. 29 And the brass of the offering was seventy talents, and two thousand and four hundred shekels. 30 And therewith he made the sockets to the door of the tabernacle of the congregation, and the brasen altar, and the brasen grate for it, and all the vessels of the altar, 31 And the sockets of the court round about, and the sockets of the court gate, and all the pins of the tabernacle, and all the pins of the court round about.	overlay the posts g. The gifts of bronze 1) Totaled about 5310 pounds 2) Used to make all the bases • For the posts at the entrance to the Tabernacle • For the Bronze Altar & its utensils • For the surrounding Courtyard • For the curtain at the entrance of the Courtyard 3) Used to make all the tent pegs

What is the greatest problem that confronts man? Is it possible to even designate one problem as being the greatest problem? Yes. The greatest problem facing man today is the same problem that has confronted man down through the centuries.

⇒ How does man approach God, approach Him so that God accepts him?

This is the greatest problem facing man. How can we say this? Because a person's eternal destiny is determined—entirely determined—by how he approaches God.

⇒ If a person denies, questions, or neglects God, just has little or nothing to do with God, or if a person approaches God in the wrong way, then he is doomed to what the Bible calls hell, a life of eternal separation from God.

⇒ If a person believes God and approaches God in the right way, then God pours out the greatest of blessings: love, joy, peace, reconciliation, forgiveness of sin, power, a sound mind, eternal life—the greatest virtues known to man.

Think of this: the greatest things known to man—the greatest virtues and gifts—are given to a person when that person approaches God in such a way that God accepts that person. But note: the key is to approach God in the right way. And Scripture makes an astounding declaration: there is only one way to approach God, and that way is narrow. Tragically, only a few walk in the narrow way. What is the right way? This is the subject of this passage: *The Building of the Furnishings for the Tabernacle (Part 2): Learning the Only Way to Approach God,* Ex.38:1-31.

I. The Altar of Burnt Offering: symbolized the need for atonement, reconciliation with God (vv.1-7).

II. The Bronze Wash Basin: symbolized the washing, cleansing, and forgiveness of sin (v.8).

III. The Courtyard: symbolized that God can be approached (vv.9-20).

IV. The inventory used in building the Tabernacle: pictured the faithfulness of God's people (vv.21-31).

I. There Was the Altar of Burnt Offering: Symbolized the Need for Atonement, Reconciliation with God (vv.1-7).

There it sat—the blazing Altar consuming every sacrifice placed upon it—just inside the entrance of the Courtyard. No one could ignore it. No one could walk by it without being stirred by its vicarious ministry, the ministry of substituting the life of an animal for one's sins, for one's own life. Thereby, one became reconciled and acceptable to God. No one could escape the strong pull of the Altar that was a symbol of the cross, the cross of our LORD and Savior, Jesus Christ. These are the facts about how this Altar was built:
1. The Altar was made of acacia wood (v.1).
2. The size of the Altar was 7½ feet square and 4½ feet high (v.1).
3. The horns of the Altar were made at each of the four corners—all of one piece (v.2). The entire Altar was overlaid with bronze (v.2).
4. The utensils were made of bronze (v.3).
5. The grate was made of bronze and placed under the ledge half-way up the Altar (v.4). Four bronze rings for carrying the Altar were made for the corners (v.5). These rings held the carrying poles.
6. The carrying poles were made of acacia wood, overlaid with bronze, and inserted into the rings for carrying the Altar (vv.6-7).
7. The Altar was made hollow (v.7).

Thought 1.
The Altar of Burnt Offering symbolized the great need of man for atonement, the great need for reconciliation with God.
    a) Scripture declares that we need the atonement, need to be reconciled with God.
        (1) Our sins have separated us from God.

> **"But your iniquities have separated between you and your God, and your sins have hid his face from you, that he will not hear" (Is.59:2).**
> **"And there is none that calleth upon thy name, that stirreth up himself to take hold of thee: for thou hast hid thy face from us, and hast consumed us, because of our iniquities" (Is.64:7).**
> **"If I regard iniquity in my heart, the LORD will not hear me" (Ps.66:18).**

        (2) Our forsaking God has separated us from God.

> **"The LORD is with you, while ye be with him; and if ye seek him, he will be found of you; but if ye forsake him, he will forsake you" (2 Chr.15:2).**
> **"The hand of our God is upon all them for good that seek him; but his power and his wrath is against all them that forsake him" (Ezr.8:22; see Je.1:16; Je.2:13).**

        (3) Our wicked works have separated us from God.

> **"And you, that were sometime alienated and enemies in your mind by wicked works" (Col.1:21).**

        (4) Our worldly walk and lives have separated us from God.

> **"Wherein in time past ye walked according to the course of this world, according to the prince of the power of the air, the spirit that now worketh in the children of disobedience: Among whom also we all had our conversation in times past in the lusts of**

our flesh, fulfilling the desires of the flesh and of the mind; and were by nature the children of wrath, even as others" (Ep.2:2-3).

(5) Our rejection of Christ has separated us from God.

"That at that time ye were without Christ, being aliens from the commonwealth of Israel, and strangers from the covenants of promise, having no hope, and without God in the world" (Ep.2:12).

(6) Our lusts have separated us from God.

"So I gave them up unto their own hearts' lust: and they walked in their own counsels" (Ps.81:12).
"Wherefore God also gave them up to uncleanness through the lusts of their own hearts, to dishonour their own bodies between themselves" (Ro.1:24).

(7) Our unfaithfulness has separated us from God.

"They shall go with their flocks and with their herds to seek the LORD; but they shall not find him; he hath withdrawn himself from them. They have dealt treacherously [been unfaithful] against the LORD: for they have begotten strange children: now shall a month devour them with their portions" (Ho.5:6-7).

b) Scripture declares that God reconciles us to Himself by Jesus Christ and only by Jesus Christ.

"But God commendeth his love toward us, in that, while we were yet sinners, Christ died for us. Much more then, being now justified by his blood, we shall be saved from wrath through him. For if, when we were enemies, we were reconciled to God by the death of his Son, much more, being reconciled, we shall be saved by his life. And not only so, but we also joy in God through our Lord Jesus Christ, by whom we have now received the atonement [reconciliation]" (Ro.5:8-11; see 2 Co.5:18).
"But now in Christ Jesus ye who sometimes were far off are made nigh by the blood of Christ" (Ep.2:13; see Ep.2:16; Col.1:20-22; He.2:17).

Thought 2.
Note where the Altar of Burnt Offering was *not* placed: it was not placed *outside* the Courtyard, outside the gate or entrance. The Altar of Burnt Offering was placed *inside* the walls of the Courtyard. It is only *inside* the Tabernacle (the presence of God) that atonement can be applied to man's sinful heart. It is only *inside* the Tabernacle that reconciliation can be made with God. It is only *inside* the walls of the Tabernacle that the power of sin can be annulled by the cross.

"And the Word was made flesh, and dwelt [or tabernacled] among us, (and we beheld his glory, the glory as of the only begotten of the Father,) full of grace and truth" (Jn.1:14).

Every part, every aspect, every detail of the Tabernacle pointed to the Person of Jesus Christ and His work of redemption. The Tabernacle is a clear picture of reconciliation: the Tabernacle pictures the only way a person can be reconciled to God. He must be *in Christ*. There is no benefit, there is no blessing, there is no salvation for the person who does not approach God *in Christ*. Note the great benefits of being *in Christ*:

a) If we are in Christ, we receive the greatest gifts and blessings imaginable.
> ⇒ In Christ, a person will never be separated from the love of God.

"Who shall separate us from the love of Christ? shall tribulation, or distress, or persecution, or famine, or nakedness, or peril, or sword?...Nay, in all these things we are more than conquerors through him that loved us. For I am persuaded, that neither death, nor life, nor angels, nor principalities, nor powers, nor things present, nor things to come, Nor height, nor depth, nor any other creature, shall be able to separate us from the love of God, which is in Christ Jesus our Lord" (Ro.8:35, 37-39).

> ⇒ In Christ, a person is sanctified.

"Unto the church of God which is at Corinth, to them that are sanctified in Christ Jesus, called to be saints, with all that in every place call upon the name of Jesus Christ our Lord, both theirs and ours" (1 Co.1:2).

> ⇒ In Christ, a person receives wisdom, righteousness, sanctification, and redemption.

"But of him are ye in Christ Jesus, who of God is made unto us wisdom, and righteousness, and sanctification, and redemption" (1 Co.1:30).

> ⇒ In Christ, a person becomes a child of God by faith.

"For ye are all the children of God by faith in Christ Jesus" (Ga.3:26).

> ⇒ In Christ, a person has access to all the blessings of God.

"Blessed be the God and Father of our Lord Jesus Christ, who hath blessed us with all spiritual blessings in heavenly places in Christ" (Ep.1:3).

> ⇒ In Christ, a person is raised up to sit with Christ in heavenly places.

"And hath raised us up together, and made us sit together in heavenly places in Christ Jesus" (Ep.2:6).

> ⇒ In Christ, a person is brought near God by the blood of Christ.

"But now in Christ Jesus ye who sometimes were far off are made nigh by the blood of Christ" (Ep.2:13).

> ⇒ In Christ, a person becomes a partaker of God's promise.

"That the Gentiles should be fellowheirs, and of the same body, and partakers of his promise in Christ by the gospel" (Ep.3:6).

> ⇒ In Christ, a person will be made perfect.

"Whom we preach, warning every man, and teaching every man in all wisdom; that we may present every man perfect in Christ Jesus" (Col.1:28).

⇒ In Christ, a person receives the promise of life.

"Paul, an apostle of Jesus Christ by the will of God, according to the promise of life which is in Christ Jesus" (2 Ti.1:1).

⇒ In Christ, a person will experience His peace.

"Peace I leave with you, my peace I give unto you: not as the world giveth, give I unto you. Let not your heart be troubled, neither let it be afraid" (Jn.14:27).
"These things I have spoken unto you, that in me ye might have peace. In the world ye shall have tribulation: but be of good cheer; I have overcome the world" (Jn.16:33).
"Greet ye one another with a kiss of charity. Peace be with you all that are in Christ Jesus. Amen" (1 Pe.5:14).

b) If we are in Christ, we are changed: we are saved, delivered, redeemed, and set free.
⇒ In Christ, a person is justified by His grace.

"Being justified freely by his grace through the redemption that is in Christ Jesus" (Ro.3:24).

⇒ In Christ, a person is free from condemnation.

"There is therefore now no condemnation to them which are in Christ Jesus, who walk not after the flesh, but after the Spirit. For the law of the Spirit of life in Christ Jesus hath made me free from the law of sin and death" (Ro.8:1-2).

⇒ In Christ, a person is made alive.

"For as in Adam all die, even so in Christ shall all be made alive" (1 Co.15:22).

⇒ In Christ, a person becomes a new creation.

"Therefore if any man be in Christ, he is a new creature: old things are passed away; behold, all things are become new" (2 Co.5:17).
"For in Christ Jesus neither circumcision availeth any thing, nor uncircumcision, but a new creature" (Ga.6:15).

⇒ In Christ, a person is reconciled to God.

"To wit, that God was in Christ, reconciling the world unto himself, not imputing their trespasses unto them; and hath committed unto us the word of reconciliation" (2 Co.5:19).

⇒ In Christ, a person is saved by Him.

"Who hath saved us, and called us with an holy calling, not according to our works, but according to his own purpose and grace, which was given us in Christ Jesus before the world began" (2 Ti.1:9).
"Therefore I endure all things for the elect's sakes, that they may also obtain the salvation which is in Christ Jesus with eternal glory" (2 Ti.2:10).

"And that from a child thou hast known the holy scriptures, which are able to make thee wise unto salvation through faith which is in Christ Jesus" (2 Ti.3:15).

c) If we are in Christ, we are to go forth conquering and triumphing for God.

⇒ In Christ, a person will triumph.

"Now thanks be unto God, which always causeth us to triumph in Christ, and maketh manifest the savour of his knowledge by us in every place" (2 Co.2:14).

⇒ In Christ, a person is created to do good works.

"For we are his workmanship, created in Christ Jesus unto good works, which God hath before ordained that we should walk in them" (Ep.2:10).

⇒ In Christ, a person presses on toward the high calling of God.

"I press toward the mark for the prize of the high calling of God in Christ Jesus" (Ph.3:14).

⇒ In Christ, a person is able to give thanks for all the experiences of life.

"In every thing give thanks: for this is the will of God in Christ Jesus concerning you" (1 Th.5:18).

II. There Was the Bronze Wash Basin: Symbolized the Washing Away of Sin, the Cleansing and Forgiveness of Sin (v.8).

This Bronze Wash Basin was made with a bronze stand and with mirrors given by the women who served the LORD. This important furnishing was placed between the Altar of Burnt Offering and the Outer Veil. A priest could not minister to the LORD without first being cleansed, without being washed, without being forgiven of his sin.

Thought
The Wash Basin was a symbol of Christ. God cleanses us and forgives our sins through the blood of His Son, the Lord Jesus Christ, through His death and His death alone.

"In whom we have redemption through his blood, the forgiveness of sins, according to the riches of his grace" (Ep.1:7; see Mt.26:28; Acts 2:38; 5:31; 13:38; Ro.3:23-25; He.9:12-14, 22, 28).
"But if we walk in the light, as he is in the light, we have fellowship one with another, and the blood of Jesus Christ his Son cleanseth us from all sin" (1 Jn.1:7).
"If we confess our sins, he is faithful and just to forgive us our sins, and to cleanse us from all unrighteousness" (1 Jn.1:9; see Re.1:5; Is.53:6).

III. There Was the Courtyard: Symbolized That God Can Be Approached (vv.9-20).

Who is like the LORD God? There is none like Him. God is the great Creator and Sustainer of the entire universe, the Eternal LORD and Majesty of the universe. God is Sovereign, ruling over all. God is Omnipresent, all seeing, present everywhere. God is omnipotent, all powerful. God is omniscient, all knowing and all wise. God is holy, perfect in right-eousness and purity. How can One who is so high and lifted up be approached by people, people who are...

- unholy and unrighteous?
- weak and feeble?
- limited in their understanding?

It is impossible for people to approach God on their own. God knows this. But in the most amazing and wonderful way possible, God has made a way for people to come to Him. The way is clearly demonstrated in the Tabernacle. In the middle of the wilderness, God had His people build a Courtyard that would be a visible symbol that God could be approached. Note the facts of its construction:

1. The south side was made of 150 feet of linen curtains (v.9). Twenty posts were made and set into 20 bronze bases (v.10). Silver hooks and bands were made to hold the curtains (v.10).

2. The north side was made of 150 feet of linen curtains. Like the south side, 20 posts were made and set into 20 bronze bases. Silver hooks and bands were made to hold the curtains (v.11).

3. The west end of the Courtyard was made of 75 feet of linen curtains. Ten posts and 10 bases were made along with silver hooks that held the curtains (v.12).

4. The east end was made of 75 feet of linen curtains (v.13).

5. The curtained walls on each side of the entrance were made with one side 22½ feet long and the other side also 22½ feet. Three posts and three bases were made for each side of the entrance (vv.14-15).

6. All the curtains of the Courtyard were made of fine linen (v.16).

7. All the posts and bases were made of bronze while all the hooks and bands were made of silver (v.17). The tops of the posts and bands that were to hold up the curtains were made of silver (v.17).

8. The entrance or door to the Courtyard was made of linen and embroidered with blue, purple, and scarlet yarn. It was made 30 feet long and 7½ feet high—just like the Court-yard curtained walls (v.18). The builders made four posts and set them into four bronze bases. Hooks and bands of silver were made, and the top of each post was overlaid with silver (v.19).

9. The tent pegs for the Tabernacle and Courtyard were made of bronze (v.20).

Thought
The Courtyard of the Tabernacle was a visible invitation for people to come and ap-proach God. God has invited man to come and approach Him. This great invitation of God to sinful man is found throughout Scripture:

a) There is the great invitation of God to *come* to Him. These verses might be titled *"The 'Come' Invitations of God."*

    (1) "Come and enter" the ark of salvation; "come" and escape the judgment of God. This is symbolized in the invitation of God given to Noah.

> **"And the LORD said unto Noah, Come thou and all thy house into the ark; for thee have I seen righteous before me in this generation" (Ge.7:1).**

    (2) "Come" for the cleansing from sin.

> **"Come now, and let us reason together, saith the LORD: though your sins be as scarlet, they shall be as white as snow; though they be red like crimson, they shall be as wool" (Is.1:18).**

    (3) "Come" and have your spiritual hunger and thirst satisfied.

> **"Ho, every one that thirsteth, come ye to the waters, and he that hath no money; come ye, buy, and eat; yea, come, buy wine and milk without money and without price" (Is.55:1).**

(4) "Come" for the rest of your soul.

> **"Come unto me, all [ye] that labour and are heavy laden, and I will give you rest" (Mt.11:28).**

(5) "Come" to the great marriage feast of the Lord.

> **"Again, he sent forth other servants, saying, Tell them which are bidden, Behold, I have prepared my dinner: my oxen and [my] fatlings [are] killed, and all things [are] ready: come unto the marriage" (Mt.22:4).**

(6) "Come" to the great supper of God in heaven.

> **"And sent his servant at supper time to say to them that were bidden, Come; for all things are now ready" (Lu.14:17).**

(7) "Come" to Christ and drink the water of life

> **"And the Spirit and the bride say, Come. And let him that heareth say, Come. And let him that is athirst come. And whosoever will, let him take the water of life freely" (Re.22:17).**

b) There are the results of accepting God's great invitation, the results of *coming* to God.

(1) The person who comes to God will live.

> **"Incline your ear, and come unto me: hear, and your soul shall live; and I will make an everlasting covenant with you, even the sure mercies of David" (Is.55:3).**

(2) The person who comes to God will be secure, never rejected, never cast out by Jesus Christ.

> **"All that the Father giveth me shall come to me; and him that cometh to me I will in no wise cast out" (Jn.6:37).**

(3) The person who comes to God will receive rest.

> **"Come unto me, all ye that labour and are heavy laden, and I will give you rest" (Mt.11:28).**

(4) The person who comes to God will have his thirst quenched by the Lord Jesus.

> **"In the last day, that great day of the feast, Jesus stood and cried, saying, If any man thirst, let him come unto me, and drink" (Jn.7:37).**

(5) The person who comes to God will be raised up on the last day to live eternally with God.

> **"No man can come to me, except the Father which hath sent me draw him: and I will raise him up at the last day" (Jn.6:44).**

IV. There Was the Inventory Used in Building the Tabernacle (vv.21-31).

A list of the inventory shows how faithful God's people were in their labor for God. Note that Moses, always the precise writer, summarized everything that went into building the Tabernacle. This master checklist itemized every important detail.

1. The compilers of the figures were the Levites (v.21).
2. The recorder of the figures was Ithamar, son of Aaron (v.21).
3. The superintendent of the construction was Bezalel, a man with a rich heritage: son of Uri and grandson of Hur. Bezalel was a member of the tribe of Judah (v.22). Bezalel was a faithful man. He made everything the LORD commanded (v.22).
4. Bezalel's assistant superintendent was Oholiab, the son of Ahisamach, of the tribe of Dan. Oholiab was a craftsman who was skilled at engraving, designing, and embroidering (v.23).
5. There were the offerings of gold that were taken up through a wave offering. The total amount of gold given to build the Tabernacle was 2,200 pounds (v.24).
6. There were the offerings of silver that totaled about 7,545 pounds. The silver was collected through the census tax or ransom tax. This tax was 1/15 of an ounce of silver and was collected from every man 20 years or older, a total of 603,550 men (vv.25-26). About 7,500 pounds of silver was used to make the 100 bases for the sanctuary walls and for the posts supporting the inner curtain (about 75 pounds for each base) (v.27). About 45 pounds of silver was used to make the bands and hooks as well as overlay the posts (v.28).
7. There were the gifts of bronze that totaled about 5,310 pounds (v.29). The bronze was used to make all the bases...
- for the posts at the entrance to the Tabernacle
- for the Bronze Altar and its utensils
- for the surrounding Courtyard
- for the curtain at the entrance of the Courtyard (vv.30-31)

The bronze was also used to make all the tent pegs for the Tabernacle and for the Courtyard (v.31).

Thought
Note two lessons.
a) We must be faithful in our labor for the LORD: work and work hard; be diligent and zealous. We must do our best to complete the work of God upon earth, to finish the task He has given us to do.

> **"Therefore, my beloved brethren, be ye stedfast, unmoveable, always abounding in the work of the Lord, forasmuch as ye know that your labour is not in vain in the Lord"** (1 Co.15:58; see Jn.4:34; 4:35; 17:4; Acts 20:24; 1 Co.3:9; 2 Co.6:1).
>
> **"Wherefore I put thee in remembrance that thou stir up the gift of God, which is in thee by the putting on of my hands"** (2 Ti.1:6; see 2 Ti.4:7).
>
> **"Whatsoever thy hand findeth to do, do it with thy might; for there is no work, nor device, nor knowledge, nor wisdom, in the grave, whither thou goest"** (Ec.9:10).

b) God will always supply what is needed to do His work.

> **"But ye shall receive power, after that the Holy Ghost is come upon you: and ye shall be witnesses unto me both in Jerusalem, and in all Judaea, and in Samaria, and unto the uttermost part of the earth"** (Ac.1:8; see Acts 4:33).
>
> **"And God is able to make all grace abound toward you; that ye, always having all sufficiency in all things, may abound to every good work"** (2 Co.9:8).

"Now unto him that is able to do exceeding abundantly above all that we ask or think, according to the power that worketh in us" (Ep.3:20).

(Please note: The Types, Symbols, and Pictures for this outline can be found on pages 89-93, 153-155, and 258-259, where they are initially discussed.)

CHAPTER SIXTEEN

The Making of the Garments for the Priests: Being Clothed in Righteousness (Exodus 39:1-43)

Contents

The Making of the Garments for the Priests: Being Clothed in Righteousness (Exodus 39:1-43)

1. The sacred garments, the garments of service: Symbolized the dignity & honor of God's call
a. Made from blue, purple, & scarlet yarn
b. Made for ministering
c. Made as God commanded
2. The ephod: Symbolized that the priest represented & carried the names of God's people before the Lord
a. The material: Yarn & linen
b. The method of securing
  1) Hammered out thin sheets of gold
  2) Cut thin strands & worked them into the yarn & linen
c. The shoulder pieces: Made & attached to two corners
 	
d. The waistband: Made one piece with the ephod
  1) Made of the yarn & linen
  2) Made exactly as God commanded
 	
e. The two onyx stones
	And of the blue, and purple, and scarlet, they made cloths of service, to do service in the holy place, and made the holy garments for Aaron; as the LORD commanded Moses. 2 And he made the ephod of gold, blue, and purple, and scarlet, and fine twined linen. 3 And they did beat the gold into thin plates, and cut it into wires, to work it in the blue, and in the purple, and in the scarlet, and in the fine linen, with cunning work. 4 They made shoulderpieces for it, to couple it together: by the two edges was it coupled together. 5 And the curious girdle of his ephod, that was upon it, was of the same, according to the work thereof; of gold, blue, and purple, and scarlet, and fine twined linen; as the LORD commanded Moses. 6 And they wrought onyx stones enclosed	in ouches of gold, graven, as signets are graven, with the names of the children of Israel. 7 And he put them on the shoulders of the ephod, that they should be stones for a memorial to the children of Israel; as the LORD commanded Moses. 8 And he made the breastplate of cunning work, like the work of the ephod; of gold, blue, and purple, and scarlet, and fine twined linen. 9 It was foursquare; they made the breastplate double: a span was the length thereof, and a span the breadth thereof, being doubled. 10 And they set in it four rows of stones: the first row was a sardius, a topaz, and a carbuncle: this was the first row. 11 And the second row, an emerald, a sapphire, and a diamond. 12 And the third row, a ligure, an agate, and an amethyst. 13 And the fourth	1) Mounted in gold filigree settings
			2) Engraved the names of Israel's tribes on them
			3) Fastened the stones on the shoulder pieces of the ephod
			
			3. The breastpiece or chestpiece, a pouch-like garment: Symbolized that the priest represented & carried the names of God's people upon his heart & before the Lord continually
			a. The materials: Gold, yarn, & linen
			b. The design
			  1) Made square, folded double
			  2) Attached four rows of precious stones to it
			  • The 1st row of stones
			
			  • The 2nd row of stones
			
			  • The 3rd row of stones
			
			  • The 4th row

of stones

3) The stones were mounted in gold

4) There were 12 stones, one for each of the 12 tribes

5) The name of a different tribe was engraved on each of the 12 stones

c. Attached the chestpiece to the ephod
1) Made braided chains of pure gold
2) Made two gold settings & rings: Fastened the rings to two corners of the chestpiece
3) Fastened the two gold chains to the rings of the chestpiece & the other ends of the chains to the two settings: Attached them to the shoulder pieces

4) Made two more gold rings: Attached them to the other two ends of the chestpiece—on the inside next to the ephod garment
5) Made two more gold rings: Attached them to the ephod garment next to the sash

row, a beryl, an onyx, and a jasper: they were inclosed in ouches of gold in their enclosings. 14 And the stones were according to the names of the children of Israel, twelve, according to their names, like the engravings of a signet, every one with his name, according to the twelve tribes. 15 And they made upon the breastplate chains at the ends, of wreathen work of pure gold. 16 And they made two ouches of gold, and two gold rings; and put the two rings in the two ends of the breastplate. 17 And they put the two wreathen chains of gold in the two rings on the ends of the breastplate. 18 And the two ends of the two wreathen chains they fastened in the two ouches, and put them on the shoulderpieces of the ephod, before it. 19 And they made two rings of gold, and put them on the two ends of the breastplate, upon the border of it, which was on the side of the ephod inward. 20 And they made two other golden rings, and put them on the two sides of the ephod underneath, toward the forepart of it, over against the other coupling thereof, above the curious girdle of the ephod. 21 And they did bind the breastplate by his rings unto the rings of the ephod with a lace of blue, that it might be above the curious girdle of the ephod, and that the breastplate might not be loosed from the ephod; as the LORD commanded Moses. 22 And he made the robe of the ephod of woven work, all of blue. 23 And there was an hole in the midst of the robe, as the hole of an habergeon, with a band round about the hole, that it should not rend. 24 And they made upon the hems of the robe pomegranates of blue, and purple, and scarlet, and twined linen. 25 And they made bells of pure gold, and put the bells between the pomegranates upon the hem of the robe, round about between the pomegranates; 26 A bell and a pomegranate, a bell and a pomegranate, round about the hem of the robe to minister in; as the LORD commanded Moses. 27 And they made coats of fine linen of woven work for Aaron, and for his sons, 28 And a mitre of fine linen, and goodly bonnets of fine linen, and linen

6) Tied the rings of the chestpiece to the rings of the ephod with blue cord: To hold the two together

4. The robe of the ephod: Symbolized the prayer ministry of the High Priest
a. The material
b. The opening for the head: Was reinforced with a woven collar so it would not tear

c. The pomegranates & bells for the hem
1) Made yarn & linen in the shape of pomegranates: Attached to the hem
2) Made gold bells: Attached around the hem between the pomegranates

d. The purpose: Was worn for ministering—as the LORD commanded
e. The symbolic purpose: To sound forth the intercessory ministry of the High Priest

5. The other garments for the priests: Symbolized the putting on of God's righteousness
a. Made tunics of fine linen
b. Made the turban of fine linen

c. Made linen headbands d. Made linen underwear e. Made the sash f. Made all exactly as the LORD had commanded **6. The gold medallion or diadem: Symbolized that the High Priest bore the guilt for the shortcomings of the people** a. Engraved with the words: HOLY TO THE LORD b. Attached to the front of the turban with a blue cord c. Made exactly as the LORD commanded **7. The work on the Tabernacle was completed** a. The construction: Was built exactly as the LORD commanded b. The presentation to Moses 1) The tent & its furnishings 2) The coverings 3) The inner curtain: Enclosed the Holy of Holies 4) The Ark of the Covenant & the Mercy Seat 5) The Table of Showbread with its utensils & the	breeches of fine twined linen, 29 And a girdle of fine twined linen, and blue, and purple, and scarlet, of needlework; as the LORD commanded Moses. 30 And they made the plate of the holy crown of pure gold, and wrote upon it a writing, like to the engravings of a signet, HOLINESS TO THE LORD. 31 And they tied unto it a lace of blue, to fasten it on high upon the mitre; as the LORD commanded Moses. 32 Thus was all the work of the tabernacle of the tent of the congregation finished: and the children of Israel did according to all that the LORD commanded Moses, so did they. 33 And they brought the tabernacle unto Moses, the tent, and all his furniture, his taches, his boards, his bars, and his pillars, and his sockets, 34 And the covering of rams' skins dyed red, and the covering of badgers' skins, and the vail of the covering, 35 The ark of the testimony, and the staves thereof, and the mercy seat, 36 The table, and all the vessels thereof, and the	showbread, 37 The pure candlestick, with the lamps thereof, even with the lamps to be set in order, and all the vessels thereof, and the oil for light, 38 And the golden altar, and the anointing oil, and the sweet incense, and the hanging for the tabernacle door, 39 The brasen altar, and his grate of brass, his staves, and all his vessels, the laver and his foot, 40 The hangings of the court, his pillars, and his sockets, and the hanging for the court gate, his cords, and his pins, and all the vessels of the service of the tabernacle, for the tent of the congregation, 41 The cloths of service to do service in the holy place, and the holy garments for Aaron the priest, and his sons' garments, to minister in the priest's office. 42 According to all that the LORD commanded Moses, so the children of Israel made all the work. 43 And Moses did look upon all the work, and, behold, they have done it as the LORD had commanded, even so had they done it: and Moses blessed them.	bread 6) The Gold Lampstand with its accessories & oil 7) The Gold Altar with its oil & incense 8) The entrance curtain 9) The Bronze Altar with its grating, poles, & utensils 10) The Wash Basin & pedestal 11) The Courtyard curtains with their support posts, bases, & all the accessories 12) The Courtyard curtain for the entrance & all the articles used in the Tabernacle 13) The priestly garments: The sacred garments worn by the High Priest & the other priests c. The final inspection 1) The builders had built the Tabernacle exactly as God had designed 2) Moses inspected the project & saw the excellent workmanship: The people had been faithful—had built exactly as God had designed 3) Moses blessed them

It has been said that *clothes make the man*. In other words, what a person wears says a lot about the image he presents to others—whether he intends to present the image or not. If a person is always sloppy, an impression of being unkempt or unclean is presented. If a person goes to the other extreme, openly flaunting his expensive clothes, he presents an image of pride. In the same sense, how a believer is dressed in his spiritual clothing makes the man. The believer who continues to wear the sinful nature, the flesh, projects an image of one who does not care about his testimony. The believer who "puts on" his religious rituals presents an image of self-righteousness or of being religious. The believer who "puts on" his knowledge projects an image of spiritual pride. God wants His people to wear the right spiritual clothing.

> **"Put on therefore, as the elect of God, holy and beloved, bowels of mercies, kindness, humbleness of mind, meekness, longsuffering" (Col.3:12).**

Note that each of these traits concern behavior, spiritual qualities of character. What does God have to say about what His people wear? This is the subject of this portion of Scripture. God made it clear: the person who is going to serve Him has to put on the right garments. He has to wear clothing that brings dignity to what he is doing: serving and working for the LORD. This is: *The Making of the Garments for the Priests: Being Clothed in Righteousness*, Ex.39:1-43.

I. The sacred garments, the garments of service: symbolized dignity and honor for God's call (v.1).

II. The ephod: symbolized that the priest represented and carried the names of God's people before the LORD (vv.2-7).

III. The breastpiece or chestpiece, a pouch-like garment: symbolized that the priest represented and carried the names of God's people upon his heart and before the LORD continually (vv.8-21).

IV. The robe of the ephod: symbolized the prayer ministry of the High Priest (vv.22-26).

V. The other garments for the priests: symbolized putting on God's righteousness (vv.27-29).

VI. The gold medallion or diadem: symbolized that the High Priest bore the guilt for the shortcomings of the people (vv.30-31).

VII. The work on the Tabernacle was completed (vv.32-43).

I. There Were the Sacred Garments of Service (v.1).

The sacred garments symbolized the dignity and honor of God's call. (See Chapter Seven, Ex.28:1-5 for more discussion.) Note the particular facts about these special clothes: the garments were made from blue, purple, and scarlet yarn. These were no ordinary garments: their sole purpose was for ministering in the Holy Place. The garments were made just as God commanded.

Thought
There is no greater call than the call of God. When God calls the believer into service, the believer has a unique opportunity, an opportunity...

- to minister in the sanctuary, the church of God Himself
- to give his life in service to the LORD God of the universe
- to receive some of the greatest blessings of God
- to experience a deep sense of purpose and fulfillment throughout life
- to minister to people in their deepest needs, when they need help the most
- to preach and teach the unsearchable riches of Christ
- to reach people for Christ, snatching them from an eternity of hell and saving them for heaven
- to lead people to life—life abundant and life eternal—all through Christ

"He saith unto him the third time, Simon, [son] of Jonas, lovest thou me? Peter was grieved because he said unto him the third time, Lovest thou me? And he said unto him, Lord, thou knowest all things; thou knowest that I love thee. Jesus saith unto him, Feed my sheep" (Jn.21:17; see Mt.20:27-28; 28:19-20; Mk.16:15; Lu.19:10; Jn.20:21).

"Take heed therefore unto yourselves, and to all the flock, over the which the Holy Ghost hath made you overseers, to feed the church of God, which he hath purchased with his own blood" (Ac.20:28).

"For we preach not ourselves, but Christ Jesus the Lord; and ourselves your servants for Jesus' sake" (2 Co.4:5; see 1 Pe.5:2).

II. There Was the Ephod (vv.2-7).

The ephod symbolized that the priest represented and carried the names of God's people before the LORD. (See outline and note—Chapter Seven, Ex.28:6-14 for more discussion.) Remember, God had created the nation of ancient Israel through the seed (descendants) of Abraham. God had created Israel to be His witnesses to a lost and dying world. In an act of His sovereign will, God had selected the Israelites to be His chosen people. This fact was symbolized with the ephod. Note the facts about how it was made:

1. The ephod was made of blue, purple and scarlet yarn and fine linen (v.2).
2. The ephod was made by hammering out thin sheets of gold that were cut into thin strands. The strands were then worked into the yarn and linen (v.3).
3. The shoulder pieces were made and attached to the two corners of the ephod (v.4).
4. The waistband was made as one piece with the ephod and was made of the multicolored yarn and linen. The waistband was made exactly as God commanded (v.5).
5. The two onyx stones were mounted in gold filigree settings. The names of Israel's twelve tribes were engraved on the stones (v.6). The stones were then fastened to the shoulder pieces of the ephod (v.7). Again, this was done just as the LORD had commanded Moses.

Thought
When the High Priest went before the LORD, the names of God's people were carried with him. Why is this significant for the believer?

a) God wants a personal relationship with His dear people. He wants, He desires, He longs for a personal relationship with each one of us. He wants us coming into His presence constantly, coming to worship, fellowship, and commune, seeking His guidance and help.

"Let us draw near with a true heart in full assurance of faith, having our hearts sprinkled from an evil conscience, and our bodies washed with pure water" (He.10:22; see Mt.18:20; 1 Co.1:9; Js.4:8; 1 Jn.1:3).

"Behold, I stand at the door, and knock: if any man hear my voice, and open the door, I will come in to him, and will sup [fellowship] with him, and he with me" (Re.3:20).

"The LORD is nigh unto them that are of a broken heart; and saveth such as be of a contrite spirit" (Ps.34:18; see Ps.73:28; 145:18; Is.43:2).

b) God knows every believer by name: He knows the name of every one of us. We are His sons and daughters, part of the adopted family of God.

"But when the fulness of the time was come, God sent forth his Son, made of a woman, made under the law, To redeem them that were under the law, that we might receive the adoption of sons. And because ye are sons, God hath sent forth the Spirit of his Son into your hearts, crying, Abba, Father" (Ga.4:4-6; see Lu.10:20; Jn.1:12; 10:3; 2 Co.6:17-18).

"He that overcometh, the same shall be clothed in white raiment; and I will not blot out his name out of the book of life, but I will confess his name before my Father, and before his angels" (Re.3:5).

"Fear not: for I have redeemed thee, I have called thee by thy name; thou art mine" (Is.43:1).

III. There Was the Breastpiece or Chestpiece, a Pouch-like Garment (vv.8-21).

The chestpiece symbolized that the priest represented and carried the names of God's people upon his heart and before the LORD continually. The fact that the chestpiece was worn upon the High Priest's heart was significant. He was to hold God's people ever so near and dear to his heart, constantly praying and upholding them before the LORD and ministering to them as needed. The breastpiece or chestpiece was fashioned in the following way:

1. The materials in the chestpiece were gold, blue, purple, and scarlet yarn and fine linen (v.8).
2. The design of the chestpiece was as follows:
   a. The chestpiece was made square and folded double (v.9).
   b. There were four rows of precious stones attached to it (vv.10-13).
      ⇒ The first row held a ruby, a topaz, and a beryl.
      ⇒ The second row held a turquoise, a sapphire, and an emerald.
      ⇒ The third row held a jacinth, an agate, and an amethyst.
      ⇒ The fourth row held a chrysolite, an onyx, and a jasper.

   c. The precious stones were mounted in gold filigree settings (v.13).
   d. The twelve stones symbolized each of the twelve tribes of Israel.
   e. The name of a different tribe was engraved on each of the twelve stones (v.14).
3. The chestpiece was then attached to the ephod. This was done by making braided chains of pure gold (v.15). Two gold settings were made along with two gold rings. The rings were fastened to the two corners of the chestpiece (v.16). Then the two gold chains were fastened to the rings of the chestpiece and the other ends of the chains to the two settings. This attached them to the shoulder pieces (vv.17-18). Two more gold rings were made and attached to the other two ends of the chestpiece—on the inside next to the ephod garment (v.19). An additional two rings were made and attached to the ephod garment next to the sash (v.21). The rings on the chestpiece were then tied together with the rings of the ephod, tied with blue cord. This final act held the two garments together (v.21).

Thought
The chestpiece symbolized that the priest represented and carried the names of God's people upon his heart and before the LORD continually. This is a strong picture of how much we mean to God, just how dear we are to Him. God loves us, keeping us ever so close to His heart.
a) God knows us personally and intimately.

"For thou hast possessed my reins: thou hast covered me in my mother's womb. I will praise thee; for I am fearfully and wonderfully made: marvelous are thy works; and that my soul knoweth right well. My substance was not hid from thee, when I was made in secret, and curiously wrought in the lowest parts of the earth. Thine eyes did see my substance, yet being unperfect; and in thy book all my members were written, which in continuance were fashioned, when as yet there was none of them" (Ps.139:13-16).

"Fear not: for I have redeemed thee, I have called thee by thy name; thou art mine" (Is.43:1).

"Before I formed thee in the belly I knew thee; and before thou camest forth out of the womb I sanctified thee, and I ordained thee a prophet unto the nations" (Je.1:5).

"I am the good shepherd, and know my sheep, and am known of mine" (Jn.10:14).

b) God knows our every need.

"Therefore take no thought, saying, What shall we eat? or, What shall we drink? or, Wherewithal shall we be clothed? (For after all these things do the Gentiles seek:) for your heavenly Father knoweth that ye have need of all these things" (Mt.6:31-32; see Mt.6:8; Ph.4:19; Ex.33:14; De.33:27; Ps.40:17; 54:4).

"For thou hast been a strength to the poor, a strength to the needy in his distress, a refuge from the storm, a shadow from the heat, when the blast of the terrible ones is as a storm against the wall" (Is.25:4; see Is.43:2).

c) God knows the pain of every lonely, hurting heart.

"The LORD is nigh unto them that are of a broken heart; and saveth such as be of a contrite spirit" (Ps.34:18; see Ge.28:15; Ps.37:28; Is.66:13).

"Fear thou not; for I am with thee: be not dismayed; for I am thy God: I will strengthen thee; yea, I will help thee; yea, I will uphold thee with the right hand of my righteousness" (Is.41:10; see Is.46:4; Jn.14:1; 2 Co.1:3).

d) God knows everything that we do for Him.

"I know thy works: behold, I have set before thee an open door, and no man can shut it: for thou hast a little strength, and hast kept my word, and hast not denied my name" (Re.3:8; see Dan.2:22).

e) God knows the most minute details of our lives, even our thoughts.

"Casting all your care upon him; for he careth for you" (1 Pe.5:7; see 1 Chr.28:9; Ps.115:12; Je.17:10; Je.23:24).

"But even the very hairs of your head are all numbered. Fear not therefore: ye are of more value than many sparrows" (Lu.12:7; see 1 Co.3:20).

IV. There Was the Robe of the Ephod (vv.22-26).

The ephod symbolized the prayer ministry of the High Priest. (See outline and note—Chapter Seven, Ex.28:31-35.) Just imagine someone who has a personal relationship with the Ruler of a nation (a President, a King, or a Premier). Suppose this person were *your* advocate, your personal representative who brought all your needs before the Ruler. Think what the Ruler could do for you, how much he could do to meet your needs and enrich your life.

This was the exact situation with Israel. God's people could not approach God on their own. Christ had not yet come. Therefore, they did not have the personal, intimate relationship with God that is now possible. The Israelites needed someone who could stand in their place, someone who could speak on their behalf. When the High Priest put on the robe of the ephod, the people knew what he was about to do. He was about to approach God to plead the concerns of every man, woman, and child. This is how the robe of the ephod was made:

1. The weaver used only blue cloth to make the robe (v.22).

2. The opening for the head was reinforced with a woven collar so it would not tear when the High Priest pulled the robe over his head (v.23).

3. The pomegranates and bells were made and attached to the hem of the robe. The pomegranates were made of blue, purple, and scarlet yarn and fine linen (v.24). The bells were made of gold and attached around the hem of the robe between the pomegranates (v.25).

4. The purpose of the robe was to wear for ministering—as the LORD commanded. Its symbolic purpose was to sound forth the intercessory ministry of the High Priest (v.26).

Thought

Jesus Christ is our advocate, our High Priest who lives to make intercession for us. He loves us. He cares for us. He prays for us. He carries our needs before the Sovereign Majesty of the universe, the LORD God Himself (Jehovah - Yahweh).

a) Jesus Christ prays for the sinner, that he will forsake his sin and be saved.

> **"Therefore will I divide him a portion with the great, and he shall divide the spoil with the strong; because he hath poured out his soul unto death: and he was numbered with the transgressors; and he bare the sin of many, and made intercession for the transgressors" (Is.53:12).**

b) Jesus Christ prays for those who hate and reject Him even as He prayed for those who crucified Him.

> **"But I say unto you, Love your enemies, bless them that curse you, do good to them that hate you, and pray for them which despitefully use you, and persecute you" (Mt.5:44).**
>
> **"Then said Jesus, Father, forgive them; for they know not what they do. And they parted his raiment, and cast lots" (Lu.23:34).**

c) Jesus Christ prays for all unbelievers, for all who are condemned.

> **"Who shall lay any thing to the charge of God's elect? It is God that justifieth. Who is he that condemneth? It is Christ that died, yea rather, that is risen again, who is even at the right hand of God, who also maketh intercession for us" (Ro.8:33-34).**

d) Jesus Christ prays for those whom He saves.

> **"Wherefore he is able also to save them to the uttermost that come unto God by him, seeing he ever liveth to make intercession for them" (He.7:25).**

e) Jesus Christ prays for those who belong to Him, for those who believe and follow Him.

> **"I pray for them: I pray not for the world, but for them which thou hast given me; for they are thine" (Jn.17:9).**

f) Jesus Christ prays for the believers of every generation.

> **"Neither pray I for these alone, but for them also which shall believe on me through their word" (Jn.17:20).**

g) Jesus Christ prays for those who need His comfort and care.

> **"And I will pray the Father, and he shall give you another Comforter, that he may abide with you for ever" (Jn.14:16).**

h) Jesus Christ prays for those who are weak and frail in their faith.

> **"But I have prayed for thee, that thy faith fail not: and when thou art converted, strengthen thy brethren" (Lu.22:32).**

i) Jesus Christ prays for those who are facing strong temptations.

> **"And when he was at the place, he said unto them, Pray that ye enter not into temptation. And he was withdrawn from them about a stone's cast, and kneeled down, and prayed" (Lu.22:40-41).**

j) Jesus Christ prays for our protection against the power of evil.

> **"I pray not that thou shouldest take them out of the world, but that thou shouldest keep them from the evil" (Jn.17:15).**

V. There Were the Other Garments for the Priests (vv.27-31).

The priestly garments were symbolic of putting on God's righteousness. (See outline and note—Chapter Seven, Ex.28:39-43 for more discussion.) Tunics of fine linen were made by a weaver (v.27). Turbans were made of fine linen, as well as the headbands (v.28). The undergarments were made of fine twisted linen (v.28). The sash for each priest was made of fine linen and multi-colored yarn (v.29). All of these garments were made exactly as the LORD commanded Moses (v.29).

Thought 1.
The turbans and tunics (long coat-like garments) essentially covered the whole body. They are therefore symbolic of putting on God's righteousness. Those who minister in God's name must bear His righteousness. Anything less than God's righteousness is totally insufficient.

> **"I will greatly rejoice in the LORD, my soul shall be joyful in my God; for he hath clothed me with the garments of salvation, he hath covered me with the robe of righteousness, as a bridegroom decketh himself with ornaments, and as a bride adorneth herself with her jewels" (Is.61:10; see Job 29:14; Ps.132:9; 132:16).**
> **"But put ye on the Lord Jesus Christ, and make not provision for the flesh, to fulfil the lusts thereof" (Ro.13:14; see 1 Co.1:30).**
> **"For he hath made him to be sin for us, who knew no sin; that we might be made the righteousness of God in him" (2 Co.5:21).**

Thought 2.
The linen headbands were of course worn on the head. They were symbolic of the believer's mind and will being subjected to God. The believer is to willingly submit his will, his thoughts, and his own personal agenda to God.

> **"I beseech you therefore, brethren, by the mercies of God, that ye present your bodies a living sacrifice, holy, acceptable unto God, which is your reasonable service. And be not conformed to this world: but be ye transformed by the renewing of your mind, that ye may prove what is that good, and acceptable, and perfect, will of God" (Ro.12:1-2; see Ps.40:8; 143:10; 2 Co.10:5).**
> **"Not with eyeservice, as menpleasers; but as the servants of Christ, doing the will of God from the heart" (Ep.6:6).**

Thought 3.
The linen underwear was symbolic of covering the believer's spiritual nakedness. The person who is without Christ in his life will be exposed and shamed. We must put on the Lord Jesus Christ and make no provision for the flesh.

> "He shall put on the holy linen coat, and he shall have the linen breeches upon his flesh, and shall be girded with a linen girdle, and with the linen mitre shall he be attired: these are holy garments; therefore shall he wash [symbolic of spiritual cleansing] his flesh in water, and so put them on" (Le.16:4; see Ro.6:6).
> "But put ye on the Lord Jesus Christ, and make not provision for the flesh, to fulfil the lusts thereof" (Ro.13:14).
> "And that ye put on the new man, which after God is created in righteousness and true holiness" (Ep.4:24).
> "And have put on the new man, which is renewed in knowledge after the image of him that created him" (Col.3:10).

Thought 4.
The multi-colored sash of fine linen was symbolic of truth, the truth of God's Word. It is comparable to the *belt of truth* in the armor of God that the believer is to put on (Ep.6:14). The Word of God enlightens and wraps everything in the believer's spiritual wardrobe together. It is the Word of God that holds everything together.

> "And ye shall know the truth, and the truth shall make you free" (Jn.8:32).
> "Sanctify them through thy truth: thy word is truth" (Jn.17:17; see Jn.20:31; Ro.15:4).
> "Wherefore take unto you the whole armour of God, that ye may be able to withstand in the evil day, and having done all, to stand. Stand therefore, having your loins girt about with truth, and having on the breastplate of righteousness" (Ep.6:13-14; see 2 Ti.3:16-17; He.4:12).

VI. There Was the Gold Medallion or Diadem (vv.30-31).

The medallion symbolized that the High Priest bore the guilt for the shortcomings of the people. The sacred diadem had these words engraved upon it: HOLY TO THE LORD (v.30). These powerful words summarized the High Priest's entire wardrobe. These words were the crowning glory of the High Priest, declaring that he was to be completely set apart for God's purpose. The High Priest was sanctified, consecrated, set apart for the sole purpose of declaring that he was bringing honor and glory to God. The High Priest was challenged...

- to the high standard of holiness
- to the high call of personal sacrifice
- to the high service of God and His dear people

This medallion was attached to the front of the linen turban with a blue cord (v.31). The gold medallion or diadem was made exactly as the LORD commanded Moses (v.31).

Thought
We need a High Priest who not only bears the guilt of our shortcomings, but a High Priest who can take away the guilt and condemnation of sin. Scripture declares that Jesus Christ is our great High Priest.
a) As our great High Priest, Jesus Christ took our sins upon Himself.

"So Christ was once offered to bear the sins of many; and unto them that look for him shall he appear the second time without sin unto salvation" (He.9:28; see Is.53:12; 1 Pe.2:24).

"And ye know that he was manifested to take away our sins; and in him is no sin" (1 Jn.3:5).

b) As our great High Priest, Jesus Christ became the sacrifice for our sins, once for all.

"And as it is appointed unto men once to die, but after this the judgment: So Christ was once offered to bear the sins of many; and unto them that look for him shall he appear the second time without sin unto salvation" (He.9:28; see Gal.1:4; Ep.5:2; Tit.2:14).

"By the which will [God's will] we are sanctified through the offering of the body of Jesus Christ once for all" (He.10:10; see 1 Jn.3:16; Re.1:5).

c) As our great High Priest, Jesus Christ makes reconciliation for our sins.

"Wherefore in all things it behooved him to be made like unto his brethren, that he might be a merciful and faithful high priest in things pertaining to God, to make reconciliation for the sins of the people" (He.2:17).

d) As our great High Priest, Jesus Christ is touched with the feelings of our weaknesses.

"Seeing then that we have a great high priest, that is passed into the heavens, Jesus the Son of God, let us hold fast our profession. For we have not an high priest which cannot be touched with the feeling of our infirmities; but was in all points tempted like as we are, yet without sin" (He.4:14-15).

e) As our great High Priest, Jesus Christ has brought us eternal salvation.

"So also Christ glorified not himself to be made an high priest; but he that said unto him, Thou art my Son, to day have I begotten thee....And being made perfect, he became the author of eternal salvation unto all them that obey him" (He.5:5, 9).

f) As our great High Priest, Jesus Christ has brought us the great hope of heaven, of living forever in God's presence.

"Which hope [of heaven] we have as an anchor of the soul, both sure and stedfast, and which entereth into that within the veil; Whither the forerunner is for us entered, even Jesus, made an high priest for ever after the order of Melchisedec" (He.6:19-20).

g) As our great High Priest, Jesus Christ brings us the forgiveness of sin.

"For such an high priest became us, who is holy, harmless, undefiled, separate from sinners, and made higher than the heavens; Who needeth not daily, as those high priests, to offer up sacrifice, first for his own sins, and then for the people's: for this he did once, when he offered up himself" (He.7:26-27).

h) As our great High Priest, Jesus Christ sits at the right hand of God for us.

"Now of the things which we have spoken this is the sum: We have such an high priest, who is set on the right hand of the throne of the Majesty in the heavens" (He.8:1).

i) As our great High Priest, Jesus Christ brings us an abundance of good things.

> **"But Christ being come an high priest of good things to come, by a greater and more perfect tabernacle, not made with hands, that is to say, not of this building" (He.9:11).**

j) As our great High Priest, Jesus Christ gives us access into God's presence.

> **"And having an high priest [Jesus Christ] over the house of God; Let us draw near with a true heart in full assurance of faith, having our hearts sprinkled from an evil conscience, and our bodies washed with pure water" (He.10:21-22).**

k) As our great High Priest, Jesus Christ saves us to the uttermost, completely, permanently, and forever.

> **"But this man, because he continueth ever, hath an unchangeable priesthood. Wherefore he is able also to save them to the uttermost that come unto God by him, seeing he ever liveth to make intercession for them" (He.7:24-25).**

VII. The Work on the Tabernacle Was Completed (vv.32-43).

Finally, the long-awaited time had come. The Tabernacle of God was built and completed by His people.

1. The construction of the Tabernacle was built exactly as the LORD commanded (v.32). Note several things:
    a. All of the work was done. Nothing was left incomplete.
    b. The Israelites (God's people) did the work. God did not entrust this important project to unbelievers.
    c. The Israelites did everything just as the LORD commanded Moses. There was no human input or changes to the plans for the Tabernacle. They followed the instructions exactly, completely, and entirely.

> **Thought 1.**
> God counts only those things that last as being successful. If we do things God's way, the work will always be completed. God wants us to have a lasting impact upon the lives of those whom we touch with the gospel.
>
> > **"Herein is my Father glorified, that ye bear much fruit; so shall ye be my disciples" (Jn.15:8).**
> > **"Ye have not chosen me, but I have chosen you, and ordained you, that ye should go and bring forth fruit, and that your fruit should remain: that whatsoever ye shall ask of the Father in my name, he may give it you" (Jn.15:16).**

> **Thought 2.**
> It should be the cry of every human heart to obey the LORD. We should all seek to know the ways of God, to learn what He wants us to do. And we should obey Him with perfect trust and confidence.
>
> > **"O that there were such an heart in them, that they would fear me, and keep all my commandments always, that it might be well with them, and with their children for ever!" (De.5:29).**

"Therefore whosoever heareth these sayings of mine, and doeth them, I will liken him unto a wise man, which built his house upon a rock" (Mt.7:24).

"Jesus answered and said unto him, If a man love me, he will keep my words: and my Father will love him, and we will come unto him, and make our abode with him" (Jn.14:23; see Js.1:25).

"Blessed are they that do his commandments, that they may have right to the tree of life, and may enter in through the gates into the city" (Re.22:14).

2. The workers who built the Tabernacle and made the priest's garments brought them all to Moses (vv.33-41).
   a. They brought the tent and its furnishings (v.33).
   b. They brought the coverings for the tent (v.34).
   c. They brought the inner curtains that enclosed the Holy of Holies (v.34).
   d. They brought the Ark of the Covenant and the Mercy Seat with its poles (v.35).
   e. They brought the Table of Showbread with its utensils and the bread (v.36).
   f. They brought the Gold Lampstand with its accessories and oil (v.37).
   g. They brought the Gold Altar with its oil and incense (v.38).
   h. They brought the entrance curtain (v.38).
   i. They brought the Bronze Altar with its grating, poles, and utensils (v.39).
   j. They brought the Wash Basin and pedestal (v.39).
   k. They brought the Courtyard curtains with their support posts, bases, and all the accessories (v.40).
   l. They brought the Courtyard curtain for the entrance and all the articles used in the Tabernacle (v.40).
   m. They brought the priestly garments: the sacred garments worn by the High Priest and the other priests (v.41).

3. The final inspection was now at hand. The builders had constructed the Tabernacle exactly as God had designed (v.42). Moses, the man who had been given the blueprints, inspected the project and saw the excellent workmanship done by the workers. He saw that they had been faithful as well as diligent. Everything was built exactly as God had designed (v.43). After his thorough inspection, Moses blessed the workers and offered up prayers to God on their behalf (v.43).

Thought
We are to be faithful to our work. No matter what our call or profession is, we are to work and work hard, being diligent and zealous, doing the very best job we can. We are to be faithful.

Note that Moses was given the responsibility to inspect the quality of the work. He did not just "rubber stamp" the whole undertaking. Moses carefully inspected the finished project. Whenever God places His people in places of great responsibility, He expects them to be diligent, to manage in His name. We are to be faithful, working ever so diligently and doing a good job.

"Therefore, my beloved brethren, be ye stedfast, unmoveable, always abounding in the work of the Lord, forasmuch as ye know that your labour is not in vain in the Lord" (1 Co.15:58).

"And whatsoever ye do in word or deed, do all in the name of the Lord Jesus, giving thanks to God and the Father by him" (Col.3:17; see Lu.19:17; Col.3:23; 2 Ti.1:6; 2 Pe.1:10; 3:14).

"Be thou faithful unto death, and I will give thee a crown of life" (Re.2:10; see Re.22:12; Ne.4:21).

"Whatsoever thy hand findeth to do, do it with thy might; for there is no work, nor device, nor knowledge, nor wisdom, in the grave, whither thou goest" (Ec.9:10).

TYPES, SYMBOLS, AND PICTURES
(Exodus 39:1-43)

Historical Term	Type or Picture (Scriptural Basis)	Life Application for Today's Believer	Biblical Application for Today's Believer
The precious stones for the breast-piece (Ex.39:10-14)	*Twelve precious stones were attached to the breastpiece that was worn close to the heart of the High Priest. These stones symbolized that the High Priest represented and carried the names of God's people (all of God's people, all twelve tribes) upon His heart, that He represented them before the* LORD *continually.* "And they set in it four rows of stones: *the first* row *was* a sardius, a topaz, and a carbuncle: this *was* the first row. And the second row, an emerald, a sapphire, and a diamond. And the third row, a ligure, an agate, and an amethyst. And the fourth row, a beryl, an onyx, and a jasper: *they were* inclosed in ouches of gold in their inclosings. And the stones *were* according to the names of the children of Israel, twelve, according to their names, *like* the engravings of a signet, every one with his name, according to the twelve tribes" (Ex.39:10-14).	⇒ Jesus Christ, as the great High Priest, keeps all His people close to His heart. He is always mindful of what His people are going through and what they need from Him. We are like precious gems to Him, gems that He lovingly and tenderly cares for.	*"Casting all your care upon him; for he careth for you" (1 Pe. 5:7).* *"But I am poor and needy; yet the Lord thinketh upon me: thou art my help and my deliverer; make no tarrying, O my God" (Ps.40:17).* *"Fear thou not; for I am with thee: be not dismayed; for I am thy God: I will strengthen thee; yea, I will help thee; yea, I will uphold thee with the right hand of my righteousness" (Is.41:10).* *"Fear not: for I have redeemed thee, I have called thee by thy name; thou art mine. When thou passest through the waters, I will be with thee; and through the rivers, they shall not overflow thee: when thou walkest through the fire, thou shalt not be burned; neither shall the flame kindle upon thee" (Is.43:1-2).*

(Please note: other Types, Symbols, and Pictures for this outline can be found at the end of Chapter Seven, Exodus 28, where they are initially discussed.)

CHAPTER SEVENTEEN

The Assembly and Dedication of the Tabernacle, the Center of Worship: Experiencing the Presence of the LORD (Exodus 40:1-38)

Contents

The Assembly and Dedication of the Tabernacle, the Center of Worship: Experiencing the Presence of the Lord (Exodus 40:1-38)

1. The instructions of the Lord

a. The Tabernacle: To be assembled on the 1st day of the first month

b. The furnishings to be set in place
1) The Ark of the Testimony
2) The curtain to shield the Ark
3) The Table of Showbread & its utensils
4) The Lampstand & its lamps
5) The Gold Altar of Incense: Put in front of the Ark of Testimony
6) The curtain for the entrance to the Tabernacle
7) The Altar of Burnt Offering: Put in front of the entrance
8) The Wash Basin: Put between the Tent of Meeting & the Altar & fill with water

And the LORD spake unto Moses, saying,

2 On the first day of the first month shalt thou set up the tabernacle of the tent of the congregation.

3 And thou shalt put therein the ark of the testimony, and cover the ark with the vail.

4 And thou shalt bring in the table, and set in order the things that are to be set in order upon it; and thou shalt bring in the candlestick, and light the lamps thereof.

5 And thou shalt set the altar of gold for the incense before the ark of the testimony, and put the hanging of the door to the tabernacle.

6 And thou shalt set the altar of the burnt offering before the door of the tabernacle of the tent of the congregation.

7 And thou shalt set the laver between the tent of the congregation and the altar, and shalt put water therein.

8 And thou shalt set up the court round about, and hang up the hanging at the court gate.

9 And thou shalt take the anointing oil, and anoint the tabernacle, and all that is therein, and shalt hallow it, and all the vessels thereof: and it shall be holy.

10 And thou shalt anoint the altar of the burnt offering, and all his vessels, and sanctify the altar: and it shall be an altar most holy.

11 And thou shalt anoint the laver and his foot, and sanctify it.

12 And thou shalt bring Aaron and his sons unto the door of the tabernacle of the congregation, and wash them with water.

13 And thou shalt put upon Aaron the holy garments, and anoint him, and sanctify him; that he may minister unto me in the priest's office.

9) The Courtyard
10) The curtain at the entrance to the Courtyard

c. The dedication of the Tabernacle & its furnishings
1) Anoint the Tabernacle & its furnishings: Make them holy (set apart to God)
2) Anoint the Altar of Burnt Offering & its utensils: Make them holy
3) Anoint the Wash Basin & pedestal: Consecrate them

d. The consecration of the priests
1) Bring the priests to the entrance of the Tabernacle and wash them
2) Dress the High Priest in sacred clothing: Anoint & consecrate him

3) Bring his sons & dress them in tunics 4) Anoint his sons 5) The purpose: To anoint the priesthood for all generations (set apart) **2. The obedience of Moses: He did everything God commanded** a. Set up the Tabernacle on the first day of the first month in the 2nd year 1) Constructed the bases, frames, crossbars, & posts 2) Spread the tent over the Tabernacle & put the covering over the tent 3) Did just as God commanded b. Placed the Testimony (Ten Commandments) in the Ark: Attached the poles & placed the Mercy Seat on the top of the Ark c. Placed the Ark in the Tabernacle 1) Hung the inner curtain 2) Shielded the Ark of Testimony	14 And thou shalt bring his sons, and clothe them with coats: 15 And thou shalt anoint them, as thou didst anoint their father, that they may minister unto me in the priest's office: for their anointing shall surely be an everlasting priesthood throughout their generations. 16 Thus did Moses: according to all that the LORD commanded him, so did he. 17 And it came to pass in the first month in the second year, on the first day of the month, that the tabernacle was reared up. 18 And Moses reared up the tabernacle, and fastened his sockets, and set up the boards thereof, and put in the bars thereof, and reared up his pillars. 19 And he spread abroad the tent over the tabernacle, and put the covering of the tent above upon it; as the LORD commanded Moses. 20 And he took and put the testimony into the ark, and set the staves on the ark, and put the mercy seat above upon the ark: 21 And he brought the ark into the tabernacle, and set up the vail of the covering, and covered the ark of the testimony;	as the LORD commanded Moses. 22 And he put the table in the tent of the congregation, upon the side of the tabernacle northward, without the vail. 23 And he set the bread in order upon it before the LORD; as the LORD had commanded Moses. 24 And he put the candlestick in the tent of the congregation, over against the table, on the side of the tabernacle southward. 25 And he lighted the lamps before the LORD; as the LORD commanded Moses. 26 And he put the golden altar in the tent of the congregation before the vail: 27 And he burnt sweet incense thereon; as the LORD commanded Moses. 28 And he set up the hanging at the door of the tabernacle. 29 And he put the altar of burnt offering by the door of the tabernacle of the tent of the congregation, and offered upon it the burnt offering and the meat offering; as the LORD commanded Moses. 30 And he set the laver between the tent of the congregation and the altar, and put water there, to wash withal. 31 And Moses and Aaron and his sons	3) Did just as God commanded d. Placed the Table in the Tent of Meeting 1) Set it on the north side outside the curtain 2) Set the bread before the LORD 3) Did just as God commanded e. Placed the Lampstand in the Tabernacle 1) Set it opposite the Table on the south side 2) Set up the lamps before the LORD 3) Did just as God commanded f. Placed the Altar of Incense in the Tent of Meeting in front of the curtain 1) Burned incense on it 2) Did just as God commanded g. Put up the curtain at the entrance h. Set the Altar of Burnt Offering near the entrance to the Tabernacle 1) Offered burnt offerings & grain offerings 2) Did just as God commanded i. Placed the Wash Basin between the Tent of Meeting & the Altar 1) Put water in it 2) Used it to symbolically wash

their hands & feet: Before entering the Tent of Meeting or approaching the Altar 3) Did just as God commanded j. Set up the Courtyard around the Tabernacle & the Altar & put up the entrance curtain to the Courtyard k. Finished the work **3. The response of the LORD** a. He covered & filled the Tabernacle with His glorious & awesome presence 1) Moses could not enter the	washed their hands and their feet thereat: 32 When they went into the tent of the congregation, and when they came near unto the altar, they washed; as the LORD commanded Moses. 33 And he reared up the court round about the tabernacle and the altar, and set up the hanging of the court gate. So Moses finished the work. 34 Then a cloud covered the tent of the congregation, and the glory of the LORD filled the tabernacle. 35 And Moses was not able to enter into	the tent of the congregation, because the cloud abode thereon, and the glory of the LORD filled the tabernacle. 36 And when the cloud was taken up from over the tabernacle, the children of Israel went onward in all their journeys: 37 But if the cloud were not taken up, then they journeyed not till the day that it was taken up. 38 For the cloud of the LORD was upon the tabernacle by day, and fire was on it by night, in the sight of all the house of Israel, throughout all their journeys.	Tabernacle 2) The fact re-emphasized: The awesome glory of the LORD filled the Tabernacle b. He guided the Israelites 1) If the cloud lifted from above the Tabernacle, the Israelites marched 2) If the cloud did not lift, the Israelites stayed put c. He gave the cloud to hang over the Tabernacle by day & a fire within the cloud by night 1) Gave it as a testimony: So all Israel could see it 2) Gave it during all the wilderness journey

Man is made to worship God. When man fails to worship God—fails to worship in the right way—his soul becomes empty, void of purpose. Man's soul begins to hunger and thirst after purpose, after meaning and significance. The only way a person's soul can be filled and fruitful is to worship God in the right way. If there is any one message man needs to heed, it is the truth just stated: The only way a person's soul can be filled and fruitful is to worship God and to worship Him in the right way. This is the reason God gave the Tabernacle to Israel, so they could worship Him and He could dwell among them...

- filling them with the fullness of life
- guiding and protecting them as they journeyed to the promised land

But there was another reason why God gave the Tabernacle to Israel: He wanted the Tabernacle to be a picture, a shadow of Christ. He wanted us to look at the Tabernacle and seek out its fulfillment in Christ. God intended that the Tabernacle of Moses benefit not only the people of Moses' day but us as well. Now, even today, the lessons and symbolism of the Tabernacle speak to the hearts of believers. The ministry of Jesus Christ leaps from the Tabernacle, its priesthood, and all of its furnishings—leaps and causes us to focus our worship upon God. This is the subject of this final portion of Scripture from the book of Exodus. It is the great climax to one of the most exciting stories in all of Scripture: *The Assembly and Dedication of the Tabernacle, the Center of Worship: Experiencing the Presence of the LORD,* Ex.40:1-38.

I.   The instructions of the LORD (vv.1-15).
II. The obedience of Moses: he did everything God commanded (vv.16-33).
III. The response of the LORD (vv.34-38).

I. There Were the Instructions of the LORD to Assemble the Tabernacle and Get Everything Ready for Worship (vv.1-15).

The history of Israel peaked during this *momentous occasion*. For about four hundred years the Israelites had lived as slaves in Egypt (a symbol of the world). But they had come a long, long way in just a brief period of time. It had been only two years earlier that they had been enslaved and were crying out to God for relief in their sufferings (see Ex.2:23). And imagine this: it had been just one year earlier when God had delivered His people from the bondage of slavery with a mighty display of His awesome power. And what a year it had been for Israel. In the course of the year, Israel had been journeying through the wilderness and had experienced...

- God's miraculous guidance through the pillar of cloud, His guidance by day and by night (Ex.13:17-22)
- God's pushing back the waters of the Red Sea (Ex.14:1-31)
- God's chastisement as they complained, grumbled, and murmured at the bitter waters of Marah (Ex.15:22-27)
- God's provision of food as they grumbled and did not believe the LORD (Ex.16:1-36)
- God's provision of water from the rock (Ex.17:1-7)
- God's victory during the war with the Amalekites (Ex.17:8-16)
- God's administration as He set their affairs in order (Ex.18:1-27)
- God's challenge as He gave the law to Moses (Ex.19:1-24:18)
- God's pattern as He showed Moses the plans for the Tabernacle (Ex.25:1-31:18)
- God's judgment as they rebelled against Him by making the golden calf (Ex.32:1-35)
- God's mercy as Moses interceded for them (Ex.33:1-23)
- God's renewal of His covenant with them (Ex.34:1-35)
- God's call to build the Tabernacle, the worship center (Ex.35:1-39:43)

1. Now, God told Moses to assemble the Tabernacle: on the first day of the first month of a brand new year (v.2; see v.17). All the experiences of the past year had taught Israel one great truth: God is the God of *new beginnings*. A person can start all over again, have a brand new life through the power of God. Establishing the Tabernacle was no different. This new beginning would be a symbolic reminder to God's people of *new beginnings*. The same God who created the heavens and the earth is also the One who gave His people a brand *new start*—from slavery to freedom, from lawlessness to law, from a land of idolatry to a Tabernacle where God was to dwell with His people and receive their worship.

2. Note that all the furnishings were now to be set in place. Note the order in which the various items were to be assembled and set in place:

   a. The Tabernacle itself, the Tent of Meeting (v.2).
   b. The Ark of God, the Ark that contained the Testimony of God (the Ten Commandments) (v.3).
   c. The curtain to shield the Ark (v.3).
   d. The Table of Showbread and its utensils (v.4).
   e. The Lampstand and its lamps (v.4).
   f. The Gold Altar of Incense was to be put in front of the Ark of Testimony (v.5).
   g. The curtain for the entrance to the Tabernacle (v.5).
   h. The Altar of Burnt Offering was to be put in front of the entrance to the Tabernacle (v.6).
   i. The Wash Basin was to be put between the Tent of Meeting and the Altar and then filled with water (v.7).
   j. The Courtyard (v.8).
   k. The curtain at the entrance to the Courtyard (v.8).

3. God then gave Moses instructions on the dedication of the Tabernacle and its furnishings. Moses was instructed to anoint the Tabernacle and its furnishings: to make them holy, to set them apart for God (v.9). Moses was also told to anoint the Altar of Burnt

Offering and its utensils for the purpose of making them holy (v.10). He was also instructed to anoint the Wash Basin and pedestal, consecrating them (v.11).

4. God then gave Moses instructions on the consecration of the priests. Moses was to bring the priests to the entrance of the Tabernacle and wash them with water (v.12). After washing the priest, Moses was to dress the High Priest in sacred clothing and anoint and consecrate him (v 13). God instructed Moses to bring in Aaron's sons and dress them in tunics, and then anoint them for service, just as he had anointed Aaron (v.14-15). The purpose for this instruction was to anoint the priesthood as an institution, as a permanent, lasting ministry down through all generations. Those who followed the original priests, Aaron and his sons, were to be set apart for service to God just as they were (v.15).

Thought

Note three lessons gleaned from the instructions of God to set up the Tabernacle.

a) God is the God of *new beginnings*. The assembly of the Tabernacle shows us that God gave His people a brand *new start*. God had delivered Israel from slavery in Egypt (a symbol of the world) to this point in their lives, the point of freedom. They now had the *freedom of self-government* and the *freedom of worship*. They were free to establish laws and free to set up the Tabernacle of God and free to worship God. Moreover, God had forgiven their terrible sin of the golden calf, the terrible sin of rejecting God and breaking His commandments. God had not rejected them but forgiven them. The proof of His forgiveness, proof that He had not rejected them, is seen in His instructions to build the Tabernacle. By instructing them to set up the Tabernacle, God was giving them a *new beginning*, a *new start*, a *new life* with Him.

God is the God of *new beginnings*. A person can start all over again, can have a brand new life through the power of God, through the Person who came to earth to dwell among us, the Son of God Himself, the Lord Jesus Christ. When we receive Christ, we experience the power and the presence of the LORD.

> **"A new heart also will I give you, and a new spirit will I put within you: and I will take away the stony heart out of your flesh, and I will give you an heart of flesh" (Eze.36:26; see Jn.1:12; Jn.3:3).**
>
> **"For whosoever shall call upon the name of the Lord shall be saved" (Ro.10:13).**
>
> **"Therefore if any man be in Christ, he is a new creature: old things are passed away; behold, all things are become new" (2 Co.5:17; see Ep.4:24; 1 Pe.1:23; 1 Jn.5:1).**

b) Every material thing we have should be dedicated to God, set apart for His purposes. Moses was told to anoint the Tabernacle and all its furnishings, to dedicate and consecrate everything to God. We too must dedicate and consecrate everything we have to God. If we cannot consecrate a material possession to God, then that item has become more important to us than God. What are the things that become so important to us, more important than God Himself? What are the things that cause such a struggle within our souls, that make us hesitate to set them apart for God? There is...

- money
- clothes
- cars, houses
- profession
- position
- property
- business
- recreation
- hobbies
- toys
- music, movies
- televisions, stereos

On and on the list could go, but God's Word is clear: we must never allow our material possessions to rob us of our relationship with God. We must offer everything to God with open hands of submission and not clenched fists of greed. When we obey, we experience the presence of the LORD.

> **"No man can serve two masters: for either he will hate the one, and love the other; or else he will hold to the one, and despise the other. Ye cannot serve God and mammon [money]" (Mt.6:24).**

> **"For what is a man advantaged, if he gain the whole world, and lose himself, or be cast away?" (Lu.9:25; see 1 Ti.6:9-10; 2 Ti.3:1-2).**

c) We must dedicate and consecrate ourselves to God as well as our material possessions. Moses was told to anoint and consecrate the priests, Aaron and his sons. God demands that we also be set apart to His service, that we dedicate and consecrate ourselves to Him and His great cause. When we obey, we experience the presence of the LORD.

> **"And he said to [them] all, If any [man] will come after me, let him deny himself, and take up his cross daily, and follow me" (Lu.9:23).**
> **"I beseech you therefore, brethren, by the mercies of God, that ye present your bodies a living sacrifice, holy, acceptable unto God, which is your reasonable service. And be not conformed to this world: but be ye transformed by the renewing of your mind, that ye may prove what is that good, and acceptable, and perfect, will of God" (Ro.12:1-2; see 1 Co.6:19-20; 1 Ti.1:12; Pr.23:26).**

II. There Was the Obedience of Moses: He Did Everything God Commanded (vv.16-33).

This is one of the major points and themes of this chapter: obedience to God. Moses did everything just as the LORD commanded. Note that his obedience is mentioned eight times, after each major step of setting up the Tabernacle (vv.16, 19, 21, 23, 25, 27, 29, 32). The wisdom behind God's choice of Moses is seen time and again in this portion of Scripture. God did not need...

- a man who wavered back and forth
- a man who might or might not follow instructions
- a man who might or might not finish the job

God needed a man just like Moses, a man who would be faithful to obey Him, a man who would follow instructions. God needed a man who would do exactly what God said. Moses was such a man.

1. Moses set up the Tabernacle exactly according to God's instructions: on the first day of the first month in the second year of their wilderness wanderings (vv.17-19). Moses constructed the bases, the frames, the crossbars, and the posts (v.18). He then spread the tent over the Tabernacle and put the covering over the tent. Note that he did all this just as God commanded (v.19).

Thought

It is very significant that the Tabernacle was the first thing God had Moses set up. Before God's glory could come, before His presence could dwell with men, before sacrifices could be made for sins, the Tabernacle had to be built. This was also true of Jesus Christ. Before He went to the cross and made an atonement for our sins, before He put His glory in us, Christ was born and came to *tabernacle* (dwell) with us. According to Strong's Concordance, Jesus Christ figuratively *encamped* with us. Jesus Christ resided with us "as God did in the Tabernacle of old, a symbol of protection and communion."[1] There had to be a Tabernacle in place before God could do anything else.

> **"And the Word was made flesh, and dwelt [tabernacled, encamped] among us, (and we beheld his glory, the glory as of the only begotten of the Father,) full of grace and truth" (Jn.1:14).**

---

[1] James Strong. *Strong's Exhaustive Concordance of the Bible,* # 4637.

"Therefore the LORD himself shall give you a sign; Behold, a virgin shall conceive, and bear a son, and shall call his name Immanuel [God with us]" (Is.7:14; see Is.9:6; Lu.1:31).

2. Moses then placed the Testimony [the Ten Commandments] in the Ark, attached the poles, and placed the Mercy Seat on the top (v.20). Note once again the great importance of these furnishings: the Ark and the Mercy Seat were the center for the worship of God. A special manifestation of God's presence and glory rested right above the Ark and Mercy Seat. The Ark symbolized God's presence: His rule and reign and His mercy. The fact that mercy flowed out from the presence of God is significant: this meant that man could find the mercy and help of God by coming into God's presence, by coming to the Tabernacle. The Mercy Seat pointed to the perfect demonstration of God's mercy and grace, the giving of His Son to die for the sins of the world.

"Let us therefore come boldly unto the throne of grace, that we may obtain mercy, and find grace to help in time of need" (He.4:16).

"For the grace of God that bringeth salvation hath appeared to all men" (Tit.2:11).

"Not by works of righteousness which we have done, but according to his mercy he saved us, by the washing of regeneration, and renewing of the Holy Ghost; Which he shed on us abundantly through Jesus Christ our Saviour" (Tit.3:5-6).

3. Moses placed the Ark in the Tabernacle (v.21). He then hung the inner curtain and shielded the Ark of Testimony just as God commanded (v.21). As everyone looked on, imagine the emotions that filled the hearts of the people. This would be the *last time* that Bezalel, the builder of the Ark, would ever see the Ark again. The crowning achievement of his life was being forever hidden from his sight. The other workers looked on, marveling at the beauty of the gold-covered chest. For them it would also be a final gaze as Moses hid the Ark from view. From now on, as long as the Ark remained in the Holy of Holies, only one man would be able to see the Ark and live: the High Priest. Note that Moses did all this just as God commanded (v.21).

Thought
It is through the ministry of Jesus Christ, our great High Priest, that we now have access to the very throne of God. In His name we come through the veil and gaze upon the glory of God.

"And, behold, the veil of the temple was rent in twain from the top to the bottom; and the earth did quake, and the rocks rent" (Mt.27:51).

"I am the door: by me if any man enter in, he shall be saved, and shall go in and out, and find pasture" (Jn.10:9; see Ro.5:1; He.6:19; Ep.2:18; Ep.3:12).

"Having therefore, brethren, boldness to enter into the holiest by the blood of Jesus, by a new and living way, which he hath consecrated for us, through the veil, that is to say, his flesh" (He.10:19-20).

4. Moses placed the Table of Showbread in the Tent of Meeting or Tabernacle (vv.22-23). He set it on the north side outside the inner curtain (v.22). Moses then set the bread before the LORD (v.23). All of this Moses did just as God commanded him (v.23).

"Then Jesus said unto them, Verily, verily, I say unto you, Moses gave you not that bread from heaven; but my Father giveth you the true bread from heaven. For the bread of God is he which cometh down from heaven, and giveth life unto the world. Then said they unto him, Lord, evermore give us this bread. And Jesus said unto them, I am the bread of life: he that cometh to me shall never hunger; and he that believeth on me shall never thirst" (Jn.6:32-35).

"I am the living bread which came down from heaven: if any man eat of this bread, he shall live for ever: and the bread that I will give is my flesh, which I will give for the life of the world" (Jn.6:51).

5. Moses placed the Lampstand in the Tabernacle, setting it opposite the Table on the south side (v.24). (See outline and notes—Chapter Four, Ex.25:31-40 for more discussion.) He set up the lamps before the LORD. Moses did all this just as God commanded (v.25). Remember, up to this point there was no light in the Tabernacle. The only light was coming through the entrance into the Holy Place. What had been set up so far could not be clearly seen, not the Tabernacle and its coverings, not the Ark and the Mercy Seat, not the inner curtain, and not the Table of Showbread. By this stage, the Holy Place was full of shadows. But after Moses lit the lamps before the LORD, the Holy Place was filled with light. This is the quality of light: it always melts the dark shadows and fills the void with rays of light. The Lampstand pointed to the coming of the Lord Jesus Christ, the Light of the world.

"Then spake Jesus again unto them, saying, I am the light of the world: he that followeth me shall not walk in darkness, but shall have the light of life" (Jn.8:12).

"I am come a light into the world, that whosoever believeth on me should not abide in darkness" (Jn.12:46).

"This then is the message which we have heard of him, and declare unto you, that God is light, and in him is no darkness at all" (1 Jn.1:5).

6. Moses placed the Altar of Incense in the Tent of Meeting in front of the curtain (v.26). He burned incense on it just as God commanded him to do (v.27). The Altar of Incense pointed to Jesus Christ as the great Intercessor and Mediator who represents us before God and makes our prayers acceptable to God.

"Hitherto have ye asked nothing in my name: ask, and ye shall receive, that your joy may be full" (Jn.16:24).

"Who is he that condemneth? It is Christ that died, yea rather, that is risen again, who is even at the right hand of God, who also maketh intercession for us" (Ro.8:34).

"Wherefore he is able also to save them to the uttermost that come unto God by him, seeing he ever liveth to make intercession for them" (He.7:25; see He.13:15).

7. Moses put up the curtain at the entrance (v.28). This curtain divided the Tent of Meeting from the Courtyard. This curtain shielded the Holy Place and prevented people from gazing into its holy sanctuary. The curtain pointed to Jesus Christ who made a new and living way into God's presence, who made it possible for us to approach and worship God in spirit and in truth.

"Having therefore, brethren, boldness to enter into the holiest by the blood of Jesus, By a new and living way, which he hath consecrated for us, through the veil, that is to say, his flesh" (He.10:19-20).

"God [is] a Spirit: and they that worship him must worship [him] in spirit and in truth" (Jn.4:24).

"Jesus saith unto him, I am the way, the truth, and the life: no man cometh unto the Father, but by me" (Jn.14:6).

8. Moses set the Altar of Burnt Offering near the entrance to the Tabernacle (v.29). Once he had set it up, Moses offered burnt offerings and grain offerings to the LORD (v.29); once again Moses was careful to set this up just as God commanded (v.29). The

Altar of Burnt Offering pointed to Jesus Christ as the Perfect Sacrifice for sin, as the Lamb of God who takes away the sins of the world.

> **"The next day John seeth Jesus coming unto him, and saith, Behold the Lamb of God, which taketh away the sin of the world" (Jn.1:29).**
> **"Forasmuch as ye know that ye were not redeemed with corruptible things, as silver and gold, from your vain conversation received by tradition from your fathers; But with the precious blood of Christ, as of a lamb without blemish and without spot" (1 Pe.1:18-19).**

9. Moses placed the Wash Basin between the Tent of Meeting and the Altar. He put water in it after he had set up the basin (v.30). The Wash Basin was used by Moses, Aaron, and his sons to wash their hands and feet before entering the Tent of Meeting or approaching the Altar (vv.30-32). Moses did this just as God commanded. Remember, the washing symbolized spiritual cleansing and forgiveness of sins. (See outline and note—Chapter Ten, Ex.30:17-21 for more discussion.) The Wash Basin pointed to Jesus Christ as the One who cleanses us from sin.

> **"In whom we have redemption through his blood, the forgiveness of sins, according to the riches of his grace" (Ep.1:7).**
> **"Who his own self bare our sins in his own body on the tree, that we, being dead to sins, should live unto righteousness: by whose stripes ye were healed" (1 Pe.2:24).**

10. Moses finished the work (v.33). Note Moses' final act: he hung the curtain that was the entrance into the Tabernacle, the one curtain or one door that stood for (symbolized) God's invitation for man to enter His presence.

Keep in mind that Moses could have quit and walked away, but he did not. Moses was faithful to God: he finished the work. Moreover, he did everything just as God commanded.

Thought 1.
Two strong lessons can be gleaned from the obedience of Moses.
a) We must obey God.

> **"This day the LORD thy God hath commanded thee to do these statutes and judgments: thou shalt therefore keep and do them with all thine heart, and with all thy soul" (De.26:16).**
> **"This book of the law shall not depart out of thy mouth; but thou shalt meditate therein day and night, that thou mayest observe to do according to all that is written therein: for then thou shalt make thy way prosperous, and then thou shalt have good success" (Jos.1:8; see 1 S.12:15; 15:22).**
> **"Not every one that saith unto me, Lord, Lord, shall enter into the kingdom of heaven; but he that doeth the will of my Father which is in heaven" (Mt.7:21; see Mt.7:24; 2 Th.1:7-9; He.2:3).**
> **"Blessed are they that do his commandments, that they may have right to the tree of life, and may enter in through the gates into the city [heaven]" (Re.22:14).**

b) We must finish and conclude what God gives us to do. We must never quit but endure and persevere to the end, completing the race and work set before us.

> **"Therefore, my beloved brethren, be ye stedfast, unmoveable, always abounding in the work of the Lord, forasmuch as ye know that your labour is not in vain in the Lord" (1 Co.15:58; see Ac.20:24).**

"And let us not be weary in well doing: for in due season we shall reap, if we faint not" (Ga.6:9).

"For I am now ready to be offered, and the time of my departure is at hand. I have fought a good fight, I have finished my course, I have kept the faith" (2 Ti.4:6-7; see He.12:1; 1 Pe.1:13; Re.3:11).

"The righteous also shall hold on his way, and he that hath clean hands shall be stronger and stronger" (Jb.17:9).

III. There Was the Response of the LORD (vv.34-38).

In one of the greatest manifestations of God's power in all of Scripture, God's glory came down upon the Tabernacle and filled it. Note how God responded to the completion of the Tabernacle.

1. God covered and filled the Tabernacle with His glorious and awesome presence, with the cloud of His glory (v.34). Remember the pillar of cloud that God had used to lead Israel through the wilderness wanderings: this was the cloud of God's glory, the Shekinah glory, the cloud that descended upon the Tabernacle. However, there was one difference in this event: a far greater display of God's glory descended upon the Tabernacle. How do we know this? Because Moses was not able to enter the Tabernacle. Remember Mt. Sinai, when the cloud of God's glory descended upon it (Ex.19:18-20); and remember Moses' tent that had been set up for worship, when God's glory covered it (Ex.33:7-11). Moses was able to stand before God's glory in both cases, but not now, not when God's glory filled the Tabernacle. Scripture declares...
   * that God is light

> **"This then is the message which we have heard of him, and declare unto you, that God is light, and in him is no darkness at all" (1 Jn.1:5).**

   * that God is a consuming fire

> **"For our God is a consuming fire" (He.12:29; see De.4:23-25).**

Just as the pillar of cloud descended upon the Tabernacle, there was obviously a burst of light that broke forth from the Holy of Holies, a burst of light...
   * that broke forth in all the splendor, radiance, brightness, and illumination of God's presence

The glory of God broke forth in the brightest light imaginable. The light of God's nature was shining so brightly that Moses could not enter without being blinded and consumed. God was giving His people a very special manifestation of His presence. His awesome presence was to remain in the Most Holy Place right above the throne of God, right between the two golden cherubim on the Mercy Seat. God's presence and glory were to give direction and lead His dear people to the promised land.

2. Note how God guided the Israelites with the cloud of His glory. If the cloud lifted from above the Tabernacle, the Israelites marched in the direction of the cloud (v.36). If the cloud did not lift, the Israelites stayed put (v.37).

3. Note this wonderful fact: God gave the cloud to hang over the Tabernacle by day and a fire within the cloud by night. God gave it as a testimony so that all of Israel could see it. By seeing the cloud, they would know that God was with them, guiding and protecting them as they journeyed to the promised land. Note that God was faithful to the very end: He led His dear people to the very end; He gave the cloud during all the wilderness journey (v.38). For the next thirty-eight years, this cloud would be a constant companion to God's people as they wandered in the wilderness. God led them until they reached their eternal destination, the promised land of God.

"And on the day that the tabernacle was reared up the cloud covered the tabernacle, namely, the tent of the testimony: and at even there was upon the tabernacle as it were the appearance of fire, until the morning. So it was alway: the cloud covered it by day, and the appearance of fire by night. And when the cloud was taken up from the tabernacle, then after that the children of Israel journeyed: and in the place where the cloud abode, there the children of Israel pitched their tents. At the commandment of the LORD the children of Israel journeyed, and at the commandment of the LORD they pitched: as long as the cloud abode upon the tabernacle they rested in their tents. And when the cloud tarried long upon the tabernacle many days, then the children of Israel kept the charge of the LORD and journeyed not. And so it was, when the cloud was a few days upon the tabernacle; according to the commandment of the LORD they abode in their tents, and according to the commandment of the LORD they journeyed. And so it was, when the cloud abode from even unto the morning, and that the cloud was taken up in the morning, then they journeyed: whether it was by day or by night that the cloud was taken up, they journeyed. Or whether it were two days, or a month, or a year, that the cloud tarried upon the tabernacle, remaining thereon, the children of Israel abode in their tents, and journeyed not: but when it was taken up, they journeyed. At the commandment of the LORD they rested in the tents, and at the commandment of the LORD they journeyed: they kept the charge of the LORD at the commandment of the LORD by the hand of Moses" (Nu.9:15-23).

God's promise to be with His dear people, to give His wonderful presence to His people, was now a reality. God's promise to guide and protect His dear people was now at hand. God's promise to live and dwell among His dear people was now beginning. Without question, they would reach the promised land of God. Nothing—no enemy, no force of nature, no form of evil—would be able to stand against them, not victoriously. God's people would be triumphant. All because God now dwelt among them and lived in their midst. God guided and protected them until their final destination was reached, the destination of the promised land of God.

Thought 1.
What caused the glory of God to fill the Tabernacle? What stirred God to give His people this special experience, this very special manifestation of His presence? Obedience. When we obey God—keep His commandments and do exactly what He says—God gives us a very special and very deep sense of His presence. Moreover, when we have a very special need, God gives us a most special manifestation of His glory. All because we obey Him.
a) When Moses obeyed the LORD and built a place for Him, God filled the Tabernacle with His presence and glory.

"Then a cloud covered the tent of the congregation, and the glory of the LORD filled the tabernacle. And Moses was not able to enter into the tent of the congregation, because the cloud abode thereon, and the glory of the LORD filled the tabernacle" (Ex.40:34-35).

b) When Solomon obeyed the LORD and built a place for Him, God filled the Temple with His presence and glory.

"And it came to pass, when the priests were come out of the holy place, that the cloud filled the house of the LORD, So that the priests could not stand to minister because of the cloud: for the glory of the LORD had filled the house of the LORD" (1 K.8:10-11).

c) When the Christian believer obeys the LORD and builds a place for Him, God fills the heart of the believer with His presence and glory.

"He that hath my commandments, and keepeth them, he it is that loveth me: and he that loveth me shall be loved of my Father, and I will love him, and will manifest myself to him [show myself, give special experiences to him]" (Jn.14:21).

"Jesus answered and said unto him, If a man love me, he will keep my words: and my Father will love him, and we will come unto him, and make our abode with him" (Jn.14:23; see Jn.15:10).

"And when the day of Pentecost was fully come, they were all with one accord in one place. And suddenly there came a sound from heaven as of a rushing mighty wind, and it filled all the house where they were sitting. And there appeared unto them cloven tongues like as of fire, and it sat upon each of them. And they were all filled with the Holy Ghost, and began to speak with other tongues, as the Spirit gave them utterance" (Ac.2:1-4; see 1 Co.3:16).

"What? know ye not that your body is the temple of the Holy Ghost which is in you, which ye have of God, and ye are not your own? For ye are bought with a price: therefore glorify God in your body, and in your spirit, which are God's" (1 Co.6:19-20; see 2 Co. 6:16; Ex.19:5).

Thought 2.
The glory of God was so brilliant and intense that Moses was unable to draw near God's presence. But what Moses could not do in that he was weak through the flesh, Jesus Christ did. Jesus Christ was obedient to God, obedient in the absolute sense. He never disobeyed God, not once. He was sinless, perfect before God. Therefore, He was able to enter God's presence, not only for Himself but for every man, woman, and child throughout all the ages. He is the Perfect, Ideal Man. Therefore He is able to stand before God as the Perfect, Ideal Man, able to stand before God in our behalf, as our High Priest, our Representative, our Intercessor, our Advocate (attorney). Jesus Christ opened up a new and living way into God's presence for us. Note this wonderful and glorious declaration of Scripture:

a) Through Christ, we can approach God in a new and living way.

"Having therefore, brethren, boldness to enter into the holiest by the blood of Jesus, By a new and living way, which he hath consecrated for us, through the veil, that is to say, his flesh [through His death upon the cross]" (He.10:19-20).

b) Through Christ we are acceptable to God and saved to the uttermost.

"Wherefore he is able also to save them to the uttermost that come unto God by him, seeing he ever liveth to make intercession for them" (He.7:25).

"For Christ is not entered into the holy places made with hands, which are the figures of the true; but into heaven itself, now to appear in the presence of God for us" (He.9:24).

c) Through Christ we will inherit the promised land of heaven, living with God forever and ever.

"For we know that if our earthly house of this tabernacle were dissolved [our flesh], we have a building of God, an house not made with hands, eternal in the heavens" (2 Co.5:1).

"For our conversation [citizenship] is in heaven; from whence also we look for the Saviour, the Lord Jesus Christ: Who shall

change our vile body, that it may be fashioned like unto his glorious body, according to the working whereby he is able even to subdue all things unto himself" (Ph.3:20-21).

"Blessed be the God and Father of our Lord Jesus Christ, which according to his abundant mercy hath begotten us again unto a lively hope by the resurrection of Jesus Christ from the dead, To an inheritance incorruptible, and undefiled, and that fadeth not away, reserved in heaven for you" (1 Pe.1:3-4).

TYPES, SYMBOLS, AND PICTURES
(Exodus 40:1-38)

Historical Term	Type or Picture (Scriptural Basis for Each)	Life Application for Today's Believer	Biblical Application for Today's Believer
The Altar of Burnt Offering [the brazen altar] (Ex.40:29) See also Ex.27:1-8; 35:16; 38:1-7; 39:39; 40:6	*The Altar of Burnt Offering was the most prominent furnishing in the Courtyard. The animal sacrifices offered to God were consumed on the Altar, consumed in a blazing, roaring fire. The picture of the Altar was graphic: unless there was a blood sacrifice for sins, there was no forgiveness.*	What the Altar taught:	*"For we have not an high priest which cannot be touched with the feeling of our infirmities; but was in all points tempted like as we are, yet without sin" (He.4:15).*
	a. The Altar of Burnt Offering symbolized the work of the Lord's cross, the death of a Perfect Sacrifice who was acceptable to God.	a. Substitutionary sacrifice is necessary for the forgiveness of sins. There is no forgiveness without the shedding of the blood of a sacrifice, the sacrifice of God's very own Son, the Lord Jesus Christ.	*"Forasmuch as ye know that ye were not redeemed with corruptible things, as silver and gold, from your vain conversation received by tradition from your fathers; But with the precious blood of Christ, as of a lamb without blemish and without spot" (1 Pe. 1:18-19).* *"Who did no sin, neither was guile found in his mouth.... Who his own self bare our sins in his own body on the tree, that we, being dead to sins, should live unto righteousness: by whose stripes ye were healed" (1 Pe.2:22, 24).*
	b. The Altar of Burnt Offering symbolized man's need for atonement, for reconciliation with God.	b. There is no way to approach God—to be saved and reconciled—other than through the death of a substitute. A person is hopelessly	*"But he was wounded for our transgressions, he was bruised for our iniquities: the chastisement of our peace was upon him; and with his*

Historical Term	Type or Picture (Scriptural Basis for Each)	Life Application for Today's Believer	Biblical Application for Today's Believer
	"And he put the altar of burnt offering *by* the door of the tabernacle of the tent of the congregation, and offered upon it the burnt offering and the meat offering; as the LORD commanded Moses" (Ex.40:29).	lost and cannot save himself from the bondage of sin. The only way a person can be saved is to be ransomed, to be bought with a price. Someone had to come forth and stand before God, offering Himself as the ransom, the price for our lives. That Someone was the Lord Jesus Christ Himself. God saved us by sacrificing His Son for us; and His Son, the Lord Jesus Christ, willingly laid down His life for us.	*stripes we are healed*" *(Is.53:5).* *"For God so loved the world, that he gave his only begotten Son, that whosoever believeth in him should not perish, but have everlasting life"* *(Jn.3:16).* *"Christ hath redeemed us from the curse of the law, being made a curse for us: for it is written, Cursed is every one that hangeth on a tree" (Ga.3:13).* *"For Christ also hath once suffered for sins, the just for the unjust, that he might bring us to God, being put to death in the flesh, but quickened by the Spirit"* *(1 Pe.3:18).*

(Please note: other Types, Symbols, and Pictures for this outline can be found at the end of Chapter Two, Ex.25:10-22; Chapter Three, Ex.25:23-30; and Chapter Nine, Ex.30:1-10, where they are initially discussed.)

PART III

THE TABERNACLE AND ARK
IN THE OLD TESTAMENT:
A DEVOTIONAL STUDY
(CHARTING THE ARK'S STORY
WITH PRACTICAL APPLICATION)

A careful survey of the Old Testament gives us a Scriptural record of the tabernacle and Ark, a record that is rich in personal application for the believer. At a certain point in history, the tabernacle and Ark disappeared from the eyes of men, but Scripture declares a wonderful fact: the fullness of God's presence dwells in the Tabernacle and Ark of heaven itself, and all believers will experience the fullness of God's presence throughout all eternity.

SCRIPTURE REFERENCE	HISTORICAL EVENT	PRACTICAL CONTEMPORARY APPLICATION
Le.8:10 In the wilderness or desert at Mount Sinai	*The Ark was to be anointed with oil when the Priests were set apart for ministry* *"And Moses took the anointing oil, and anointed the tabernacle and all that was therein, and sanctified them" (Le.8:10).*	Every believer has been set apart for ministry, just as the priests were. The call to minister is an awesome responsibility. God places the stewardship of the ministry into the hands of the person He calls. Just think for a moment: whatever the believer does with the ministry given him is all that will be done with his ministry—nothing more, nothing less. Only he can fulfill his own ministry. No one else can do it for him. What an awesome responsibility! **"Whereof I am made a minister, according to the dispensation of God which is given to me for you, to fulfil the word of God" (Col. 1:25).** **"But as we were allowed of God to be put in trust with the gospel, even so we speak; not as pleasing men, but God, which trieth our hearts" (1 Th.2:4).**
Nu.3:31 In the wilderness or desert at Mount Sinai	*The Kohathites were given the important responsibility of stewardship, of caring for the Ark and the other holy goods of the Tabernacle* *"And their [the Kohathites] charge shall be the ark, and the table, and the candlestick, and*	Every believer—no matter who he is—is to be a good steward of all that God has given him and entrusted into his care. Every believer is to do the best he can with what God has given him. **"Moreover it is required in stewards, that a man be found faithful" (1 Co.4:2).** **"And he called his ten servants, and delivered them ten pounds, and said unto them, Occupy till I come" (Lu.19:13).** "O Timothy, keep that which is

260

SCRIPTURE REFERENCE	HISTORICAL EVENT	PRACTICAL CONTEMPORARY APPLICATION
	the altars, and the vessels of the sanctuary wherewith they minister, and the hanging, and all the service thereof (Nu.3:31).	committed to thy trust, avoiding profane and vain babblings, and oppositions of science falsely so called" (1 Ti.6:20). "As every man hath received the gift, even so minister the same one to another, as good stewards of the manifold grace of God" (1 Pe.4:10).
Nu.4:4-15 In the wilderness or desert at Mount Sinai, moving from campsite to campsite	*The instructions for moving the Ark and Tabernacle from place to place are given. Note that a protective covering was to be placed over all the holy furnishings of the Tabernacle.* *"And when Aaron and his sons have made an end of covering the sanctuary, and all the vessels of the sanctuary, as the camp is to set forward; after that, the sons of Kohath shall come to bear it: but they shall not touch any holy thing, lest they die. These things are the burden of the sons of Kohath in the tabernacle of the congregation" (Nu.4:15).*	The Christian believer is on a godly journey just as the Israelites were. The Christian believer is marching through the wilderness of this world to the promised land of heaven. As he marches, he must protect, place a protective covering over, the holy things of God. "But put ye on the Lord Jesus Christ, and make not provision for the flesh, to fulfil the lusts thereof" (Ro.13:14). "And that ye put on the new man, which after God is created in righteousness and true holiness" (Ep.4:24). "Put on therefore, as the elect of God, holy and beloved, bowels of mercies, kindness, humbleness of mind, meekness, longsuffering" (Col.3:12). "And beside this, giving all diligence, add to your faith virtue; and to virtue knowledge" (2 Pe.1:5-7).
Nu.10:17,21,33 In the wilderness or desert at Mount Sinai	⇒ *The tabernacle was carried by the Gershonites and Meraites* ⇒ *The Ark, the presence of God, always led the way as Israel marched throughout the wilderness. The people always had the presence of God before their faces— out front—as they marched to the promised land of God* *"And they departed from the mount of the LORD three days' journey: and the ark of the covenant of the LORD went before them in the three days' journey, to search out a resting place for them" (Nu.10:33).*	Every believer should make it a regular habit to set God—His presence—before his face wherever he goes. When God leads the way... ⇒ the joy and fullness of life are experienced ⇒ the severe trials and temptations of life are conquered ⇒ the presence and care of God lead the believer day by day "Thou wilt show me the path of life: in thy presence *is* fulness of joy; at thy right hand *there are* pleasures for evermore" (Ps.16:11). "The LORD *is* nigh unto all them that call upon him, to all that call upon him in truth" (Ps.145:18). "When thou passest through the waters, I *will be* with thee; and through the rivers, they shall not overflow thee: when thou walkest through the fire, thou shalt not be burned; neither shall the flame kindle upon thee" (Is.43:2). "Draw nigh to God, and he will draw nigh to you. Cleanse *your* hands, ye sinners; and purify *your* hearts, ye double minded" (Js.4:8).

SCRIPTURE REFERENCE	HISTORICAL EVENT	PRACTICAL CONTEMPORARY APPLICATION
Nu.10:33-36 The Wilderness Wanderings	*The Israelites left Mount Sinai and traveled with the Ark out in front of them. With the Ark (the presence of God) leading hem, they marched to-ward Canaan, seeking the promised land of God.* *"And they departed from the mount of the LORD three days' jour-ney: and the ark of the covenant of the LORD went before them in the three days' journey, to search out a resting place for them" (Nu. 10:33).*	The believer is to stay focused upon God as he marches through the wilderness of this world. He is to actively seek the promised land of God. **"For he looked for a city which hath foundations, whose builder and maker is God" (He.11:10).** **"But now they desire a better country, that is, an heavenly: wherefore God is not ashamed to be called their God: for he hath prepared for them a city" (He.11:16; see Mt.6:20; 2 Co.5:1).** **"For our conversation is in heaven; from whence also we look for the Saviour, the Lord Jesus Christ: Who shall change our vile body, that it may be fashioned like unto his glorious body, according to the working whereby he is able even to subdue all things unto himself" (Ph.3:20-21).**
Nu.14:44 The Wilderness Wanderings: the battle at Hormah	*Israel chose to fight the Amalekites and Canaan-ites without the support of the Ark and Moses. They turned away from God, trusted their own ability, and fought in their own strength.* *"But they presumed to go up unto the hill top: nevertheless the ark of the covenant of the LORD, and Moses, de-parted not out of the camp" (Nu.14:44).*	How easy it is to trust in the ability and strength of man to conquer the trials and temptations of life. As soon as something bad happens, how often we go running to some person instead of God for help. People can sometimes help, but the ability and help of man can only help for a brief time. The abil-ity and strength of man are limited. The se-verest trials of life can be conquered only by God. And God alone can deliver us from the terrible evils and death of this world. **"When thou passest through the wa-ters, I will be with thee; and through the rivers, they shall not overflow thee: when thou walkest through the fire, thou shalt not be burned; neither shall the flame kin-dle upon thee" (Is.43:2).** **"There hath no temptation taken you but such as is common to man: but God is faithful, who will not suffer you to be tempted above that ye are able; but will with the temptation also make a way to es-cape, that ye may be able to bear it" (1 Co.10:13; see 2 Ti.4:18; He.2:14-15).**
Nu.17:10 The Wilderness Wanderings	*Aaron's staff was placed in front of the Ark as a sign to those who re-jected and rebelled against God. (Later his staff and a pot of Manna would be placed inside the Ark see He.9:4.)* *"And the LORD said unto Moses, Bring Aaron's rod again before the testimony, to be kept*	God's staff is a symbol of His authority and power. God's staff gives a constant warning to the rebellious heart of sinful man. No matter who we are, if we reject and rebel against God, He warns us: "My spirit shall not always strive with man" (Genesis 6:3; see Pr.29:1). This is a needful warning: when we feel pulled to make a decision to follow God and put the decision off for an hour or two, the pull fades, eventually dying completely. God's Spirit does not continue to strive with us. Most of us have experienced such move-ments and killed the Spirit's pull or striving.

SCRIPTURE REFERENCE	HISTORICAL EVENT	PRACTICAL CONTEMPORARY APPLICATION
	for a token against the rebels; and thou shalt quite take away their murmurings from me, that they die not" (Nu.17:10).	"And grieve not the holy Spirit of God, whereby ye are sealed unto the day of redemption" (Eph.4:30). "Quench not the Spirit" (1 Th.5:19).
Nu.31:6 (see 31:1-7)\n\nThe Wilderness Wanderings	*The Ark was apparently taken into battle against the Midianites*\n\n*"And Moses sent them to the war, a thousand of every tribe, them and Phinehas the son of Eleazar the priest, to the war, with the holy instruments [articles from the sanctuary], and the trumpets to blow in his hand" (Nu.31:6).*	A spiritual warfare is being fought for the minds and souls of people. The believer must take the presence of God right into the middle of the conflict. He is God's instrument to teach men—to teach them the way to God and righteousness. If God's people do not fight and struggle to lead lost people to God, then literally millions of souls will perish without ever knowing the way to God—without ever knowing that a person can actually live forever in the presence of God. This is the reason believers must arise and lead the charge into the battle for the minds and souls of men. So much depends upon the believer—so many souls, the hope and lives of so many—that he must be faithful and fight a good warfare.\n\n**"For we wrestle not against flesh and blood, but against principalities, against powers, against the rulers of the darkness of this world, against spiritual wickedness in high** *places***" (Ep.6:12; see 1 Ti.1:18).**\n**"But thou, O man of God, flee these things; and follow after righteousness, godliness, faith, love, patience, meekness. Fight the good fight of faith, lay hold on eternal life, whereunto thou art also called, and hast professed a good profession before many witnesses" (1 Ti.6:11-12; see 2 Ti.2:2-4).**
De.31:9-26\n\nThe Wilderness Wanderings	*Moses gave the order to place the Book of the Law, the inspired Word of God, beside the Ark. Note that the Word of God was placed in God's sanctuary as a witness against those who reject and rebel against God.*\n\n*"And it came to pass, when Moses had made an end of writing the words of this law in a book, until they were finished, That Moses commanded the Levites, which bare the ark of the covenant of the LORD, saying, Take this book of the law, and put it in the*	God's word is proclaimed from God's sanctuary: it is proclaimed as a witness against all who reject and rebel against God.\n\n**"For the word of God is quick, and powerful, and sharper than any twoedged sword, piercing even to the dividing asunder of soul and spirit, and of the joints and marrow, and is a discerner of the thoughts and intents of the heart. Neither is there any creature that is not manifest in his sight: but all things are naked and opened unto the eyes of him with whom we have to do" (He.4:12-13).**\n**"Is not my word like as a fire? saith the LORD; and like a hammer that breaketh the rock in pieces?" (Je.23:29).**\n**"By the word of the LORD were the heavens made; and all the host of them by the breath of his mouth" (Ps.33:6).**\n**"All scripture is given by inspiration of**

SCRIPTURE REFERENCE	HISTORICAL EVENT	PRACTICAL CONTEMPORARY APPLICATION
	side of the ark of the covenant of the LORD your God, that it may be there for a witness against thee" (De.31:24-26).	God, and is profitable for doctrine, for reproof, for correction, for instruction in righteousness" (2 Ti.3:16).
Jos.3-4 The Promised Land: The Jordan River	*The waters of the Jordan River were divided (pushed back) by God as the Ark was carried by the priests into the River* **"And the priests that bare the ark of the covenant of the LORD stood firm on dry ground in the midst of Jordan, and all the Israelites passed over on dry ground, until all the people were passed clean over Jordan" (Jos.3:17).**	God expects us to believe Him, to trust Him and His power, regardless of circumstances. No matter how impossible the circumstance, no matter how hopeless the situation, no matter how difficult the problem—the presence of God can deliver us through the terrible trial if we will only trust and follow Him. **"And the Lord shall deliver me from every evil work, and will preserve me unto his heavenly kingdom: to whom be glory for ever and ever. Amen" (2 Ti.4:18).** **"Surely he shall deliver thee from the snare of the fowler, and from the noisome pestilence" (Ps.91:3; see Is.43:2).** **"And even to your old age I am he; and even to hoar [gray] hairs will I carry you: I have made, and I will bear; even I will carry, and will deliver you" (Is.46:4).** **"Be not afraid of their faces: for I am with thee to deliver thee, saith the LORD" (Je.1:8; see Mt.19:26; Jb.42:2; Ps.115:3).**
Jos.6 The Promised Land: Jericho	*The mighty walls of Jericho collapsed before the Ark of God, giving a great victory to the people of God. God Himself—His presence and power—gave the victory to His people, gave them victory over their enemies of Jericho.* **"So the people shouted when the priests blew with the trumpets: and it came to pass, when the people heard the sound of the trumpet, and the people shouted with a great shout, that the wall fell down flat, so that the people went up into the city, every man straight before him, and they took the city" (Jos. 6:20).**	The one thing we need is victory over all that stands against us. Why? Because the world is full of enemies, enemies such as... <ul><li>suffering</li><li>corruption</li><li>murder</li><li>adultery</li><li>immorality</li><li>wickedness</li><li>homelessness</li><li>selfishness</li></ul><ul><li>disease</li><li>hate</li><li>war</li><li>pride</li><li>pain</li><li>drugs</li><li>hunger</li><li>hurt</li></ul><ul><li>accidents</li><li>bitterness</li><li>arguments</li><li>arrogance</li><li>greed</li><li>drunkenness</li><li>envy</li><li>backbiters</li></ul>Then there is the most fatal enemy of all: corruption and death. Without exception, we are all corrupt and we all die. As stated, the one thing we need above all else is victory over all the enemies of the world, the enemies that lead us to corruption and death. How then can we triumph and conquer the enemies of the world? By following God. By doing exactly what God says and following Him. **"Now thanks be unto God, which always causeth us to triumph in Christ, and maketh manifest the savour of his knowledge by us in every place" (2 Co.2:14).** **"Who shall separate us from the love of Christ? shall tribulation, or distress, or persecution, or famine, or nakedness, or**

SCRIPTURE REFERENCE	HISTORICAL EVENT	PRACTICAL CONTEMPORARY APPLICATION
		peril, or sword?...Nay, in all these things we are more than conquerors through him that loved us. For I am persuaded, that neither death, nor life, nor angels, nor principalities, nor powers, nor things present, nor things to come, nor height, nor depth, nor any other creature, shall be able to separate us from the love of God, which is in Christ Jesus our Lord" (Ro.8:35, 37-39; see 1 Jn.5:4-5; Ps.44:5).
Jos.8:30-35 (see De.27:11-26) The Promised Land: Mounts Ebal and Gerizim	⇒ *The Ark of God was placed between Mount Ebal and Mount Gerizim.* ⇒ *Two clear choices are set before God's people: blessings and cursings.* ⇒ *The striking symbolism is not lost concerning these two mountains, the mount of blessings (Gerizim) and the mount of cursings (Ebal).* *"And all Israel, and their elders, and officers, and their judges, stood on this side the ark and on that side before the priests the Levites, which bare the ark of the covenant of the LORD, as well the stranger, as he that was born among them; half of them over against mount Gerizim, and half of them over against mount Ebal; as Moses the servant of the LORD had commanded before, that they should bless the people of Israel. And afterward he read all the words of the law, the blessings and cursings, according to all that is written in the book of the law" (Jos.8:33-34; see De.27:12-13)*	The choice between a life that is blessed and a life that is cursed is just as striking today. The person who clings to the things of this world is really embracing a life that will be cursed. The person who wants God's blessings must be willing to forfeit this life. The person who abandons this life—who sacrifices and gives all that he is and has for Christ—will save his life. But the person who keeps his life and what he has and seeks more and more of this life, will lose his life completely and eternally. The person who "saves his life"... • by seeking to avoid the aging of the body and death and yet denies Christ will lose his life eternally. • by seeking to make his life more and more comfortable, easy, and secure (beyond what is necessary) and neglects Christ will lose his life eternally. • by seeking to gain wealth and power and fame by compromising Christ will lose his life eternally. • by seeking the thrills, excitement, and stimulation of this world by ignoring Christ will lose his life eternally. "And he that taketh not his cross, and followeth after me, is not worthy of me" (Mt.10:38). "Then Jesus beholding him loved him, and said unto him, One thing thou lackest: go thy way, sell whatsoever thou hast, and give to the poor, and thou shalt have treasure in heaven: and come, take up the cross, and follow me" (Mk.10:21). "No man that warreth entangleth himself with the affairs of *this* life; that he may please him who hath chosen him to be a soldier" (2 Ti.2:4).
Jos.18-19 The Promised Land: Shiloh	*The Tabernacle and Ark were officially set up in Shiloh, an important center for Israelite worship (from Joshua's time to Samuel's).* *The picture is striking:*	The worship of God, the only living and true God, is essential—an absolute essential—for every person and society upon earth. "But the hour cometh, and now is, when the true worshippers shall worship

SCRIPTURE REFERENCE	HISTORICAL EVENT	PRACTICAL CONTEMPORARY APPLICATION
	note that the presence and worship of God were placed at the very core of the Israelite life and society. *"And the whole congregation of the children of Israel assembled together at Shiloh, and set up the tabernacle of the congregation there. And the land was subdued before them" (Josh. 18:1).* *"These shall stand upon mount Gerizim to bless the people, when ye are come over Jordan; Simeon, and Levi, and Judah, and Issachar, and Joseph, and Benjamin: And these shall stand upon mount Ebal to curse; Reuben, Gad, and Asher, and Zebulun, Dan, and Naphtali" (De.27:12-13).*	the Father in spirit and in truth: for the Father seeketh such to worship him. God is a Spirit: and they that worship him must worship him in spirit and in truth" (Jn.4:23-24; see De.8:1; Ps.33:12; Pr.14:31). "Then saith Jesus unto him, Get thee hence, Satan: for it is written, Thou shalt worship the Lord thy God, and him only shalt thou serve" (Mt.4:10). "Not forsaking the assembling of ourselves together, as the manner of some is; but exhorting one another: and so much the more, as ye see the day approaching" (He.10:25; see Re. 14:7). "Give unto the LORD the glory due unto his name: bring an offering, and come before him: worship the LORD in the beauty of holiness" (1 Chr. 16:29; see Ps.95:6; 96:9).
Jos.24:1-26 The Promised Land: Shechem	*The Ark was moved by Joshua and the elders of Israel to Shechem. There—before the Ark, before the presence of God—Joshua challenged the people to serve God without reservation (see Jos.24:26)* *"And if it seem evil unto you to serve the LORD, choose you this day whom ye will serve; whether the gods which your fathers served that were on the other side of the flood, or the gods of the Amorites, in whose land ye dwell: but as for me and my house, we will serve the LORD" (Jos.24:15).*	The believer is to be devoted to God, without reservation. Everything he is and has is to be dedicated to the worship and service of God. Anything less than total devotion is short of God's glory: it is sin. Therefore, when discussing the believer's relationship to God, Scripture is strong in its exhortation. Without equivocation, Scripture urges total devotion. "And thou shalt love the LORD thy God with all thine heart, and with all thy soul, and with all thy might" (De.6:5). "Blessed *are* they that keep his testimonies, *and that* seek him with the whole heart" (Ps.119:2). "And ye shall seek me, and find *me,* when ye shall search for me with all your heart" (Je.29:13).
Jud.20:18, 26 The Promised Land: Bethel	*Before going into battle, the Israelites went up to the house of God, the Tabernacle, to pray, seeking the counsel and guidance of God.*	When trouble strikes or problems arise or enemies threaten us, the first thing needed is God. We need to enter the presence of God and seek His counsel and guidance. "Ask, and it shall be given you; seek, and ye shall find; knock, and it shall be

SCRIPTURE REFERENCE	HISTORICAL EVENT	PRACTICAL CONTEMPORARY APPLICATION
	"And the children of Israel arose, and went up to the house of God, and asked counsel of God, and said, Which of us shall go up first to the battle against the children of Benjamin? And the LORD said, Judah shall go up first" (Jud.20:18).	opened unto you" (Mt.7:7). "Watch and pray, that ye enter not into temptation: the spirit indeed is willing, but the flesh is weak" (Mt.26:41). "Is any among you afflicted? let him pray. Is any merry? let him sing psalms" (Js.5:13). "He shall call upon me, and I will answer him: I will be with him in trouble; I will deliver him, and honour him" (Ps.91:15). "And ye shall seek me, and find me, when ye shall search for me with all your heart" (Je.29:13).
1 S.3:3-14 The Promised Land: Shiloh	*The boy Samuel was lying down in the temple of the LORD (where the Ark was) when God called him. He had obviously entered the temple to pray.* *"And ere the lamp of God went out in the temple of the LORD, where the ark of God was, and Samuel was laid down to sleep; That the LORD called Samuel: and he answered, Here am I....And the LORD came, and stood, and called as at other times, Samuel, Samuel. Then Samuel answered, Speak; for thy servant heareth" (1 S.3:3-4, 10).*	The LORD reveals Himself and blesses those who pray and are bathed in prayer. Prayer—communion and fellowship with Him—is the primary channel through which He has chosen to bless His people. "If my people, which are called by my name, shall humble themselves, and pray, and seek my face, and turn from their wicked ways; then will I hear from heaven, and will forgive their sin, and will heal their land" (2 Chr.7:14). "The LORD is nigh unto all them that call upon him, to all that call upon him in truth" (Ps.145:18). "And ye shall seek me, and find me, when ye shall search for me with all your heart" (Je.29:13; see Js.5:16; 1 Jn.3:22).
1 S.4:5,7,10 The Promised Land: Ebenezer	*The Ark was captured during the battle between Israel and the Philistines and taken from Ebenezer to Ashdod (1 S.4:1-10). Why?* *a. Because the priests, the sons of Eli the High Priest, did not really know the LORD personally. They were counterfeit priests: they abused the ministry and seduced the women who came to worship.* *"Now the sons of Eli were sons of Belial; they knew not the LORD.... Now Eli was very old,*	God judges sin. God judges both the sins of a nation and the sins of individuals. God will judge any nation of people and any person who follows the path of unrighteousness. "As righteousness tendeth to life: so he that pursueth evil pursueth it to his own death" (Pr.11:19). "But your iniquities have separated between you and your God, and your sins have hid his face from you, that he will not hear" (Is.59:2). "Therefore thus saith the LORD, Behold, I will bring evil upon them, which they shall not be able to escape; and though they shall cry unto me, I will not hearken unto them" (Je.11:11). "The soul of the father, so also the soul of the son is mine: the soul that sinneth, it shall die" (Eze.18:4). "For the wages of sin is death; but the

SCRIPTURE REFERENCE	HISTORICAL EVENT	PRACTICAL CONTEMPORARY APPLICATION
	and heard all that his sons did unto all Israel; and how they lay with the women that assembled at the door of the tabernacle of the congregation" (1 S. 2:12, 22). *b. Because Eli did not discipline his sons.* **"For I have told him that I will judge his house for ever for the iniquity which he knoweth; because his sons made themselves vile, and he restrained them not" (1 S. 3:13).** **"And when the Philistines heard the noise of the shout, they said, What meaneth the noise of this great shout in the camp of the Hebrews? And they understood that the ark of the LORD was come into the camp" (1 S.4:6).**	**gift of God is eternal life through Jesus Christ our Lord" (Ro.6:23).** **"For when they shall say, Peace and safety; then sudden destruction cometh upon them, as travail upon a woman with child; and they shall not escape" (1 Th.5:3).**
1 S.5:1-8 The Promised Land: Ashdod	⇒ *The Ark was placed in the temple of Dagon, the Philistine's god.* ⇒ *Dagon repeatedly fell down and broke apart before the Ark* **"And when they of Ashdod arose early on the morrow, behold, Dagon was fallen upon his face to the earth before the ark of the LORD. And they took Dagon, and set him in his place again. And when they arose early on the morrow morning, behold, Dagon was fallen upon his face to the ground before the ark of the LORD; and the head of Dagon and both the palms of his hands were cut off upon the threshold; only the stump of Dagon was left to him" (1 S.5:3-4).**	No modern-day idol can stand before God. What is idolatry? Idolatry is putting something else before God. As Scripture says, covetousness is idolatry. An idolater is a person whose primary focus—his mind, his body, his thoughts, his time, his energy, his efforts, his loyalty—is upon something other than God. Idolatry is the sin of the mind and body against God; it is the failure to look up to God and acknowledge Him; the failure to give one's life to Him including one's thoughts, time, energy, effort, loyalty, and worship. Idolatry is putting other things before God: ⇒ money ⇒ profession ⇒ family ⇒ cars ⇒ power ⇒ recognition ⇒ possessions ⇒ food ⇒ recreation ⇒ popularity ⇒ fame ⇒ property ⇒ luxury ⇒ pleasure ⇒ position ⇒ esteem All idolaters will be destroyed, judged, and condemned—separated eternally from God. **"Wherefore, my dearly beloved, flee from idolatry" (1 Co.10:14).**

SCRIPTURE REFERENCE	HISTORICAL EVENT	PRACTICAL CONTEMPORARY APPLICATION
		"Now the works of the flesh are manifest, which are these; Adultery, fornication, uncleanness, lasciviousness, idolatry...they which do such things shall not inherit the kingdom of God" (Ga.5:19-21; see Ep.5:5; Col.3:5-6; Re.21:8; 22:15).
1 S.5:8-12; 6:1-2 The Promised Land: Ekron	*The Philistines had defeated Israel and taken the Ark of God. The battle had gone so well the Philistines thought...* • *that the God of Israel was either a false god or a weak god, that they had defeated the God of Israel* • *that they now controlled the God of Israel* • *that they were self-sufficient, strong and wise enough to take care of themselves.* *But note what happened: the Philistines, still in possession of the Ark, suffered the heavy hand of God's judgment. A deadly plague struck the Philistines.* **"So they sent and gathered together all the lords of the Philistines, and said, Send away the ark of the God of Israel, and let it go again to his own place, that it slay us not, and our people: for there was a deadly destruction throughout all the city; the hand of God was very heavy there" (1 S.5:11).**	How foolish people are who think they can control God; who think they are self-sufficient, strong, and wise enough to take care of themselves; who think they have no need for God. God will quickly bring the ax of judgment upon anyone who opposes Him. **"And now also the axe is laid unto the root of the trees: therefore every tree which bringeth not forth good fruit is hewn down, and cast into the fire" (Mt.3:10).** **"If a man abide not in me, he is cast forth as a branch, and is withered; and men gather them, and cast them into the fire, and they are burned" (Jn.15:6).** **"But that which beareth thorns and briers is rejected, and is nigh unto cursing: whose end is to be burned" (He.6:8).**
1 S.6:7-20 The Promised Land: Beth-Shemesh	⇒ *A new cart was made for the Ark* ⇒ *The Philistines rid themselves of the Ark* ⇒ *Thousands of men died because they looked into the Ark* **"And he smote the men of Beth-shemesh, because they had looked into the ark of the**	The instructions of God are clear and precise—very clear and precise—about how He is to be approached and worshipped. Failure to obey these instructions will always result in judgment. Why? Because God is holy, the very embodiment of perfect being and light. It is this that makes God different from man and from other false gods. His very nature, His very being, is different. God is both *pure being* and *pure light*, and He is *pure in being* and *in light*. God is holy in name and holy in being, set apart and different from all others.

SCRIPTURE REFERENCE	HISTORICAL EVENT	PRACTICAL CONTEMPORARY APPLICATION
	LORD, even he smote of the people fifty thousand and threescore and ten men: and the people lamented, because the LORD had smitten many of the people with a great slaughter. And the men of Beth-shemesh said, Who is able to stand before this holy LORD God? and to whom shall he go up from us?" (1 S.6:19-20).	"Who is like unto thee, O LORD, among the gods? Who is like thee, glorious in holiness, fearful in praises, doing wonders?" (Ex.15:11). "Exalt the LORD our God, and worship at his holy hill; for the LORD our God is holy" (Ps.99:9).
1 S.6:21; 7:1-2 The Promised Land: Kirjath-Jearim	⇒ The Ark was taken to Kirjath-Jearim and stayed there for twenty years ⇒ The Ark was taken to the house of Abinadab ⇒ Abinadab's son, Eleazar, was consecrated and given charge to guard the Ark of God, the Ark that symbolized the very presence of God Himself. "And the men of Kirjath-jearim came, and brought up the ark of the LORD, and brought it into the house of Abinadab in the hill, and sanctified Eleazar his son to keep the ark of the LORD" (1 S.7:1).	The Christian believer has been given the charge to guard the presence of God upon earth. Simply stated, the great trust committed to the Christian believer is... • the truth of God: that there is only one true and living God, only one Creator, only one Sovereign LORD and Majesty of the universe • the truth of life: that God has revealed the glorious truth of life to men in His Word and in the Lord Jesus Christ • the truth of salvation, of the gospel: that God has sent His Son to earth to die for man in order to save man The word trust is the picture of a deposit, of a faithful and diligent banker who looks after the money deposited into his care. The believer is to guard and keep, look after and care for, the truth of God, the truth of life, and the truth of salvation, of the gospel. The believer must never forget that God has deposited, actually laid, the truth of God into his hands. The believer is responsible to guard the presence and revelation of God upon earth. "Moreover it is required in stewards, that a man be found faithful" (1 Co.4:2). "And say to Archippus, Take heed to the ministry which thou hast received in the Lord, that thou fulfil it" (Col.4:17). "But as we were allowed of God to be put in trust with the gospel, even so we speak; not as pleasing men, but God, which trieth our hearts" (1 Th.2:4). "According to the glorious gospel of the blessed God, which was committed to my trust. And I thank Christ Jesus our Lord, who hath enabled me, for that he counted me faithful, putting me into the ministry" (1 Ti.1:11-12; see Tit.1:3).

SCRIPTURE REFERENCE	HISTORICAL EVENT	PRACTICAL CONTEMPORARY APPLICATION
1 S.14:16-18 The Promised Land: Gibeah	*King Saul consulted the Ark of God when facing battle and needing to make decisions. Note: the earthly king sought counsel from the God of heaven and earth, the God who is King of kings and LORD of lords.* **"And Saul said unto Ahiah, Bring hither the ark of God. For the ark of God was at that time with the children of Israel" (1 S.14:18).** **"And Saul asked counsel of God, Shall I go down after the Philistines? wilt thou deliver them into the hand of Israel? But he answered him not that day" (1 S.14:37).**	The victorious Christian life is the reward of those who pray to the One true and living God; however, there is more to prayer than just asking. A person asks, then he seeks and knocks at the door of heaven until God grants the request. **"Ask, and it shall be given you; seek, and ye shall find; knock, and it shall be opened unto you: for every one that asketh receiveth; and he that seeketh findeth; and to him that knocketh it shall be opened" (Mt.7:7-8).** Note that knocking contains two forceful ideas: the idea that we must knock and knock knock again. We must continue to knock and knock; we must wrestle with God, not giving Him rest until He opens. Such action shows dependence upon Him. And coming to Him in fellowship and communication is bound to please Him, just as such communication pleases an earthly father. **"Watch and pray, that ye enter not into temptation: the spirit indeed is willing, but the flesh is weak" (Mt.26:41).** **"And he spake a parable unto them to this end, that men ought always to pray, and not to faint" (Lu.18:1).** **"Seek the LORD and his strength, seek his face continually" (1 Chr. 16:11; see Is.55:6; Je.29:13; Ps.105:4; Pr.8:17).**
2 S.6:1-10 The Promised Land: Kirjath-Jearim (also called Balle of Judah)	*On the way to Jerusalem, God struck Uzzah down for touching the Ark. For a fatal, split second, Uzzah forgot to fear and reverence God. He was quickly judged for approaching God in the wrong way.* **"And when they came to Nachon's threshing-floor, Uzzah put forth his hand to the ark of God, and took hold of it; for the oxen shook it. And the anger of the LORD was kindled against Uzzah; and God smote him there for his error; and there he died by the ark of God" (2 S.6:6-7).**	Uzzah's error is a lesson to all concerning the fear of God. What does Scripture mean by the fear of God? It means two things. 1. To fear God means to hold Him in fear, dread, and terror. 2. To fear God means to hold Him in awe, to reverence the holiness, power, knowledge, wisdom, judgment and wrath of God. What Scripture teaches is this: man must reverence God and hold God in the highest esteem and honor. Only if man reverences God will he worship and serve God. Therefore, the fear that God wants man to have is a fear of reverence and awe, a fear that will stir man to love God with the deepest of emotions, with a true honor and esteem. But if man fails to reverence and love God, then he must fear the judgment and wrath of God. Why? Because man will have to bear the judgment of God. Therefore, fear is man's only hope; it is one of the forces that can drive him to cry out for the mercy of God.

SCRIPTURE REFERENCE	HISTORICAL EVENT	PRACTICAL CONTEMPORARY APPLICATION
		"Oh how great *is* thy goodness, which thou hast laid up for them that fear thee; *which* thou hast wrought for them that trust in thee before the sons of men!" (Ps.31:19; see Ps.33:8). "God is greatly to be feared in the assembly of the saints, and to be had in reverence of all *them that are* about him" (Ps.89:7; see Lu.1:50). "Honour all *men.* Love the brotherhood. Fear God. Honour the king" (1 Pe.2:17).
2 S.6:11 (see 1 Chr.13:14) The Promised Land: the House of Obed-Edom, the Gittite	*The house of Obed-Edom was blessed by the Ark's presence for three months* *"And the ark of the LORD continued in the house of Obed-edom the Gittite three months: and the LORD blessed Obed-edom, and all his household" (2 S.6:11).*	What benefit is there to being in God's presence, being brought into God's presence by Jesus Christ? When a person believes in Christ, truly believes, God takes the person's faith and counts it as righteousness. God counts the person to be in Christ, to be as righteous and acceptable as Christ. God sees the person identified with Christ, seated in heaven. And being seated in heaven, the person can experience all the fullness of life and all the blessings of heaven. Simply stated, to be in Christ means to believe in God's Son so much that God becomes elated—elated to the extent that God counts the person acceptable and worthy to be blessed with all the fullness of life and all the blessings of heaven. "Blessed *be* the God and Father of our Lord Jesus Christ, who hath blessed us with all spiritual blessings in heavenly *places* in Christ" (Ep.1:3). "For we are his workmanship, created in Christ Jesus unto good works, which God hath before ordained that we should walk in them" (Ep.2:10).
2 S.6:12-23 (see 1 Chr.15:1-29; 16:1-3) The Promised Land: the City of David (Jerusalem)	⇒ *David, in obedience to the LORD, brought the Ark to Jerusalem. He rejoiced and praised God with great energy and joy, for God's will was now able to be fulfilled.* ⇒ *David set the Ark in its place—in a tent that he had already pitched for the Ark* "And it was told king David, saying, The LORD hath blessed the house of Obed-edom, and all that *pertaineth* unto him, because of the ark of God. So David	Doing the will of God should always be a joy for the Christian believer. Doing God's will brings the most fulfilling sense of accomplishment that a person can experience. "I delight to do thy will, O my God: yea, thy law is within my heart" (Ps.40:8). "I beseech you therefore, brethren, by the mercies of God, that ye present your bodies a living sacrifice, holy, acceptable unto God, which is your reasonable service. And be not conformed to this world: but be ye transformed by the renewing of your mind, that ye may prove what is that good, and acceptable, and perfect, will of God" (Ro.12:1-2; see 1 Th. 4:3; 5:18; 1 Pe.2:15; 4:2).

SCRIPTURE REFERENCE	HISTORICAL EVENT	PRACTICAL CONTEMPORARY APPLICATION
	went and brought up the ark of God from the house of Obed-edom into the city of David with gladness" (2 S. 6:12).	
2 S.11:11 The Promised Land: the City of David (Jerusalem)	*Uriah, Bathsheba's husband, refused to sleep in his own house because the Ark and his fellow soldiers were covered by a tent.* **"And Uriah said unto David, The ark, and Israel, and Judah, abide in tents; and my lord Joab, and the servants of my lord, are encamped in the open fields; shall I then go into mine house, to eat and to drink, and to lie with my wife? as thou livest, and as thy soul liveth, I will not do this thing" (2 S.11:11).**	The character trait of humility is not formed all at once. God begins the process of forming humility within the person whose heart has been surrendered to God. Humility reaches its height when we lose our lives in the cause of Christ and the welfare of others. **"Whosoever therefore shall humble himself as this little child, the same is greatest in the kingdom of heaven" (Mt.18:4).** **"I tell you, this man went down to his house justified rather than the other: for every one that exalteth himself shall be abased; and he that humbleth himself shall be exalted" (Lu.18:14).**
2 S.15:24-25 The Promised Land: the City of David (Jerusalem)	*David had his men (Zadok and the Levites) return the Ark to Jerusalem after he had fled from Absolom's fury. In so doing, David placed his faith in the mercy of God. By faith, David resigned himself to the will of God and fully expected to see the Ark again in its rightful place, no matter what his current circumstances appeared to be.* **"And the king said unto Zadok, Carry back the ark of God into the city: if I shall find favour in the eyes of the LORD, he will bring me again, and show me both it, and his habitation" (2 S. 15:25).**	The lesson is clear. The very time for us to believe God is when the storms of life come. It is against the storms of life that our faith should rally and be aroused and exercised. **"Verily I say unto you, If ye have faith as a grain of mustard seed, ye shall say unto this mountain [trial], Remove hence to yonder place; and it shall remove; and nothing shall be impossible unto you" (Mt.17:20).** **"Jesus said unto him, If thou canst believe, all things are possible to him that believeth" (Mk.9:23).** **"Above all, taking the shield of faith, wherewith ye shall be able to quench all the fiery darts of the wicked" (Ep.6:16; see He.11:6).** **"If any of you lack wisdom, let him ask of God, that giveth to all men liberally, and upbraideth not; and it shall be given him. But let him ask in faith, nothing wavering. For he that wavereth is like a wave of the sea driven with the wind and tossed" (Js.1:5-6; see 2 Chr.2:20).**
1 K.6 The Promised Land: the City of David (Jerusalem)	*Solomon built the Temple on Mount Moriah (where the Ark would be placed), providing a habitation for the very special presence of God on earth.* **"And it came to pass in the four hundred and**	Every believer is called to build God's church here upon earth. Every believer is to become personally involved in the building of the LORD's church. This is not the sole responsibility of a select few nor the privileged right of the powerful and rich. Those who love God have all been called to have a part in building God's church and Kingdom here upon earth.

SCRIPTURE REFERENCE	HISTORICAL EVENT	PRACTICAL CONTEMPORARY APPLICATION
	eightieth year after the children of Israel were come out of the land of Egypt, in the fourth year of Solomon's reign over Israel, in the month Zif, which is the second month, that he began to build the house of the LORD*" (1 K.6:1).* *"So Solomon built the house, and finished it" (1 K.6:14).*	"For we are labourers together with God: ye are God's husbandry, ye are God's building" (1 Co.3:9; see Lu.12:48; Jn.15:16; 17:4). "Therefore, my beloved brethren, be ye stedfast, unmoveable, always abounding in the work of the Lord, forasmuch as ye know that your labour is not in vain in the Lord" (1 Co.15:58). "We then, as workers together with him, beseech you also that ye receive not the grace of God in vain" (2 Co.6:1; see 1 Pe.4:11; Is.1:19).
1 K.6:19, 23-28 The Promised Land: the City of David (Jerusalem)	*Solomon prepared an ornate room, sparing no expense, inside the Temple where the Ark was placed* *"And the oracle he prepared in the house within, to set there the ark of the covenant of the* LORD*. The inner sanctuary was twenty cubits long, twenty wide and twenty high. He overlaid the inside with pure gold, and he also overlaid the altar of cedar. Solomon covered the inside of the temple with pure gold, and he extended gold chains across the front of the inner sanctuary, which was overlaid with gold. So he overlaid the whole interior with gold. He also overlaid with gold the altar that belonged to the inner sanctuary" (1 K.6:19-22).*	We are commanded to give our best to God. No believer should ever settle for offering God a heart that is *cheap, half-filled,* or *worthless.* The heart should be filled with priceless and cherished spiritual treasures. There are things in heaven for which believers should seek and grasp. Christ calls these heavenly riches. Heavenly riches would be such things as... • a blameless life • becoming a true child of God • the forgiveness of sins • wisdom • understanding the will of God (purpose, meaning, and significance in life) • an marvelous inheritance that is eternal • a constant Comforter and Helper, the Holy Spirit of God Himself • life that is abundant and overflowing (Jn.10:10) "Lay not up for yourselves treasures upon earth, where moth and rust doth corrupt, and where thieves break through and steal: But lay up for yourselves treasures in heaven, where neither moth nor rust doth corrupt, and where thieves do not break through nor steal" (Mt.6:19-20). "I counsel thee to buy of me gold tried in the fire, that thou mayest be rich; and white raiment, that thou mayest be clothed, and *that* the shame of thy nakedness do not appear; and anoint thine eyes with eyesalve, that thou mayest see" (Re.3:18; see He.11:26; Ph.3:8).
1 K.7 (see 2 Chr.5) The Promised Land: the City of David (Jerusalem) on Mount Moriah	*After seven years of the Temple's construction, the Ark was carried from the city of Jerusalem and placed in the Temple on Mount Moriah.* *"So was ended all the work that king Solomon*	No matter how long it takes to do the will of God, we must stay the course and persevere until the end. There are many things, many of them good things, that are waiting to divert the believer from doing the will of God. We are often tempted to take unnecessary shortcuts in doing His will. God requires one thing from His people: obedience. We must be willing...

SCRIPTURE REFERENCE	HISTORICAL EVENT	PRACTICAL CONTEMPORARY APPLICATION
	made for the house of the LORD. And Solomon brought in the things which David his father had dedicated; even the silver, and the gold, and the vessels, did he put among the treasures of the house of the LORD" (1 K.7:51).	• to obey Him moment by moment • to obey Him day by day • to obey Him month by month • to obey Him year by year • to obey Him *always*! **"Not every one that saith unto me, Lord, Lord, shall enter into the kingdom of heaven; but he that doeth the will of my Father which is in heaven" (Mt.7:21; see Jos.1:8).** **"Blessed *are* they that do his commandments, that they may have right to the tree of life, and may enter in through the gates into the city" (Re.22:14).**
1 Chr.16:4-38 The Promised Land: the City of David (Jerusalem)	*David appointed some Levites to minister before the Ark* *"And he appointed certain of the Levites to minister before the ark of the LORD, and to record, and to thank and praise the LORD God of Israel" (1 Chr.16:4).*	What kind of person does Christ call to serve Him? Christ calls ordinary people, people who will simply make themselves available to Him. Note where Jesus called His first disciples: they were not in a religious nor a learning center. Neither were they in a position of authority or power, nor did they possess wealth or financial security. They were out in the work-a-day world. This is not to de-emphasize the importance of religion nor of learning, but it does teach a much needed lesson. God can use and call anyone who is really available, whether religious or nonreligious, learned or unlearned, ordinary or extraordinary. The main factor is to be available and willing to respond. **"For ye see your calling, brethren, how that not many wise men after the flesh, not many mighty, not many noble, are called: but God hath chosen the foolish things of the world to confound the wise; and God hath chosen the weak things of the world to confound the things which are mighty; and base things of the world, and things which are despised, hath God chosen, yea, and things which are not, to bring to nought things that are: that no flesh should glory in his presence" (1 Co.1:26-29).** **"For the which cause I also suffer these things: nevertheless I am not ashamed: for I know whom I have believed, and am persuaded that he is able to keep that which I have committed unto him against that day" (2 Ti.1:12; see Ep.4:1).**
1 Chr.17 (see 2 S.7:2)	⇒ *David compared his house of cedar with what had been given to house the Ark (a*	God has called believers to do great things for Him. In order to do great things for God, a person must be willing to become humble before God. King David was this kind of

SCRIPTURE REFERENCE	HISTORICAL EVENT	PRACTICAL CONTEMPORARY APPLICATION
The Promised Land: the City of David (Jerusalem)	*tent); consequently, David expressed the desire to build a house for God* ⇒ *Nathan, the prophet of God, spoke for the LORD and refused David's request* ⇒ *Later, Solomon would be given this task, to build a house for God* **"Now it came to pass, as David sat in his house, that David said to Nathan the prophet, Lo, I dwell in an house of cedars, but the ark of the covenant of the LORD remaineth under curtains" (1 Chr.17:1).**	man, a man marked by humility. What does Scripture teach concerning humility? Humility means lowliness of mind. It is a word that was coined by Christianity. Before Christ, a humble man was looked upon as a coward: a cringing, unappealing, effeminate type of person. However after Christ, humility was elevated to the most praiseworthy level. When men looked at Christ, they saw the strength of humility through the influence of One Who was perfect in meekness and lowliness of heart. Humility means five things. 1. To *walk* as a servant to others, always ready and willing to help (see Ph.2:8). 2. To *behave* in an unassuming manner, not being showy or pretentious, prideful or haughty, arrogant or assertive. 3. To *assume* a spirit of lowliness and submission, of oneness and identification with others, not showing conceit or superiority or being boastful. 4. To *possess* a sense of lowliness and unworthiness, to have a modest opinion of oneself, knowing that others are just as significant and valuable. 5. To *come* to God on a regular basis and confess one's spiritual need and unworthiness. **"Let nothing be done through strife or vainglory; but in lowliness of mind let each esteem other better than themselves. Look not every man on his own things, but every man also on the things of others" (Ph.2:3-4).** **"Likewise, ye younger, submit yourselves unto the elder. Yea, all of you be subject one to another, and be clothed with humility: for God resisteth the proud, and giveth grace to the humble. Humble yourselves therefore under the mighty hand of God, that he may exalt you in due time" (1 Pe.5:5-6; see Mt.18:4; 20:25-28; Lu. 22:25-26; Ac.20:19; Ro.12:3; 1 Pe.5:5-6).**

PART IV

THE TABERNACLE AND ARK IN THE NEW TESTAMENT: A DEVOTIONAL STUDY
THE FULFILLMENT OF THE TABERNACLE

A. God's Just Charge Against the Israelites: They Were Inexcusable—Because They Had Been So Greatly Blessed, Acts 7:44-47

1. The people had been given the tabernacle of God's presence	44 Our fathers had the tabernacle of witness in the wilderness, as he had appointed, speaking unto Moses, that he should make it according to the fashion that he had seen.	possession of the Gentiles, whom God drave out before the face of our fathers, unto the days of David. 46 Who found favour before God, and desired to find a tabernacle for the	
2. The people had been given the presence & favor of God in great leaders	45 Which also our fathers that came after brought in with Jesus into the	God of Jacob. 47 But Solomon built him an house.	**3. The people had been given the temple**

The story of the Tabernacle and Ark of God is woven into the history of Israel. Remember, God had chosen Abraham and his descendants, the Israelites, to be His witnesses to the unbelievers of the world. The very special presence of God had tabernacled or dwelled among the Israelites, the only nation upon earth that had been granted such a privilege. Every person in the nation of Israel should have been careful to live and appreciate such a great blessing. But the record of Scripture tells us the exact opposite. Many of the Israelites squandered the opportunity to have a personal relationship with the LORD, the very Architect of the Tabernacle. What went so horribly wrong?

The people (Israel) did what so many are doing today: they did not worship God but worshipped false gods (Ac.7:42). Just as the other unbelievers of the earth...

- many worshipped their own ideas of god, their own imaginations and creations of god
- still others were agnostic or atheistic, simply living for themselves, doing their own thing; doing what they wanted when they wanted, fulfilling the desires and lusts of their own hearts

- many others worshipped the "hosts of heaven," that is, the sun, moon, and stars (for example, the Zodiac, astrology, cosmic forces. See De. 17:3; 2 K.17:16; 2 K.21:3; 2 Chr.33:3; Jb.31:26-28; Je.8:2; 19:13.)

Note: the charge was dramatic. When Israel was making offerings and sacrifices to God, they were really worshipping false gods. That is, their hearts and thoughts were upon the world (Egypt) and the gods imagined and created in the mind of man.

The response of God was as it has always been toward the behavior of people: What they had sown, they were to reap.

⇒ Just as they had turned away from God, He had turned away from them.
⇒ Just as they had given themselves up to worship false gods, God had given them up to do as they pleased. God had given them up to their own lusts.

> **"Because that, when they knew God, they glorified him not as God, neither were thankful; but became vain in their imaginations, and their foolish heart was darkened. Professing themselves to be wise, they became fools....Wherefore God also gave them up to uncleanness through the lusts of their own hearts, to dishonour their own bodies between themselves" (Ro.1:21-22, 24; see Ro.1:26-28).**

God made a strong charge against the Israelites: publicly and outwardly the people were carrying the Tabernacle of God wherever they went, but their hearts and thoughts were not upon Him, not upon the only true and living God. Their hearts and thoughts were upon the false gods they themselves imagined and created in their own minds (Ac.7:43).

Consequently, God had no choice: He had to give them up to their lusts. Just as they had carried the Tabernacle with their hearts focused upon false gods, so God had carried them and given them up to the captivity of a heathen nation who worshipped false gods (see Acts 7:43; 2 K.17:6).

This is the context of the first mention of the Tabernacle and Ark in the New Testament. The people were inexcusable. Why? Because they had been greatly blessed (Ac.7:44-47). God had blessed them with three things in particular.

I. The people had been given the Tabernacle of God's presence (v.44).
II. The people had been given the presence and favor of God in great leaders (vv.45-46).
III. The people had been given the temple (v.47).

I. The People Had Been Given the Tabernacle of God's Presence (v.44).

God had blessed the people with the Tabernacle of His presence and testimony. Note that God had shown Moses a fashion, a design, that is, a figure, a pattern, a picture of the Tabernacle; and Moses had constructed it after the picture and design God had shown him.

II. The People Had Been Given the Presence and Favor of God in Great Leaders (vv.45-46).

God had blessed the people with great leaders, leaders who had been favored and appointed by God and who knew the Lord in a personal way. Israel's leaders knew the Lord, His daily presence and guidance. Note that Joshua, David, and Solomon are mentioned. All three had the favor and blessings of God upon their lives. Therefore, the people were greatly blessed through these leaders.

III. The People Had Been Given the Temple (v.47).

God had blessed the people with the temple. David had desired to build the temple, but it was Solomon whom God appointed to construct it. (See 1 K.6-8.) When the Jews returned from captivity to Jerusalem, Zerubbabel rebuilt the temple (516 B.C.). Herod the Great rebuilt the temple and made it one of the wonders of the world around 20 B.C. It was this temple in which the Jews gloried during the days of Christ.

The point is this: by being so blessed, the people (Israel) were inexcusable in their rejection of God. They had every opportunity, yet they still chose the world instead of God.

Thought

God is not limited to only one particular place (Ac.7:48-50; see Is.66:1-2). Solomon, the builder of the great temple, had proclaimed this truth.

> **"But will God indeed dwell on the earth? behold, the heaven and heaven of heavens cannot contain thee; how much less this house that I have builded" (1 K.8:27; see 2 Chr.6:18).**

God never intended for men to think that His presence was limited to the temple. Stephen's point struck home, for Jesus had taught that men must worship God in Spirit and in truth (Jn.4:24). Note also that Jesus had spoken these words to a Samaritan, a person of a different nationality. Anyone of any race or land could worship God just so they approached Him in Spirit and in truth. A particular land or temple had not been and is not necessary to approach and worship God. Only one thing is necessary to approach God: coming to Him in the name of the promised Messiah and Savior of the world, God's very own Son, the Lord Jesus Christ.

> **"God is a Spirit: and they that worship him must worship him in spirit and in truth" (Jn.4:24).**

B. Christ Is the Exalted High Priest: His Heavenly, Spiritual Ministry, Hebrews 8:1-5

1. The summary: Christ, the perfect High Priest	Now of the things which we have spoken this is the sum: We have such an High priest, who is set on the right hand of the throne of the Majesty in the heavens;	so to offer. 4 For if he were on earth, he should not be a priest, seeing that there are priests that offer gifts according to the law:
2. He is the exalted High Priest: At the right hand of God's throne		
3. He is the exalted Minister: Of the true tabernacle	2 A minister of the sanctuary, and of the true tabernacle, which the Lord pitched, and not man.	5 Who serve unto the example and shadow of heavenly things, as Moses was admonished of God when he was about to make the tabernacle: for, See, saith he, that thou make all things according to the pattern showed to thee in the mount.
4. He is the exalted Minister who offers the gifts & sacrifices of men to God	3 For every high priest is ordained to offer gifts and sacrifices: wherefore it is of necessity that this man have somewhat al-	

5. He is the exalted Minister of the real, heavenly world	
a. Not according to law	
b. Not just a shadow of heavenly things	

Note the words of verse one, "This is the sum." The word "sum" means chief point, major thrust, and principle thought. The writer is about to give the major thrust and principle thought of the High Priesthood of the Lord Jesus Christ. Jesus Christ is the great High Priest; He is the One who stands between God and man, the only Person who can make man acceptable to God. What is the major thrust and principle thought of His High Priesthood? It is *ministry*. Jesus Christ is the *great Minister* of God, the Supreme Minister who ministers *day and night* for man in both heaven and earth. Both places are significant.

Now, for the critical question: What is the great ministry of Jesus Christ? What is it that He does for us?

    I.   Jesus Christ is the Minister of a heavenly, spiritual priesthood, (v.1).
    II.   He is the exalted High Priest: at the right hand of God's throne (v.1).
   III.   He is the exalted Minister: of the true Tabernacle (v.2).
   IV.   He is the exalted Minister who offers the gifts and sacrifices of men to God (v.3).
    V.   He is the exalted Minister of the real, heavenly world (vv.4-5).

I. Jesus Christ Is the Minister of a Heavenly, Spiritual Priesthood (v.1).

There are qualifications for being a priest on earth; a man has to meet certain conditions in order to serve as an earthly priest. So it is in heaven and for God. If someone is going to stand before God for man, that someone has to meet certain conditions. The heavenly High Priest has to have certain qualifications. Note how the Lord Jesus Christ meets every one of these requirements.

    ⇒ He has to be perfect, completely faithful and true to God (He.2:17; 3:1-2; 5:8-9; 7:11; 7:19).
    ⇒ He has to be merciful and become the sacrifice for man's sins—become the sacrificial Lamb of God for man (He.2:17; 8:27).

⇒ He has to live as a man and undergo all the trials and temptations of men, conquering them all without ever sinning. He has to be sinless (He.2:18; 4:14-15; 7:26).

⇒ He has to succor, actually feel, man's infirmities and have compassion for man. He has to show mercy and help man when he needs help (He.2:18; 4:15-16).

⇒ He has to be appointed and ordained by God to be the High Priest in heaven (He.5:5-6; 7:28).

⇒ He has to become the perfect author of eternal salvation (He.5:9).

⇒ He has to be the priest who is after the order of Melchisedec and not after the order of earthly priests (He.5:6, 10; 6:20; 7:11; 7:21).

⇒ He has to be the forerunner into heaven (He.6:20).

⇒ He has to be eternal, that is, have an "endless life" (He.7:16; 7:17; see 7:3; 7:24; 7:28).

⇒ He has to live forever to make intercession for those who come to God by Him (He.7:25).

⇒ He has to be exalted to the right hand of God—exalted higher than the heavens (He.7:26; 8:1).

When someone meets all the above requirements, that someone is qualified to be the High Priest in heaven. *WITHOUT QUESTION...*

JESUS CHRIST MEETS ALL THE QUALIFICATIONS TO BE THE PERFECT HIGH PRIEST OF HEAVEN.

Jesus Christ is the Minister of the heavenly, spiritual priesthood. No one else is qualified—no one has ever been or ever will be qualified except Him. Now again, note the words, "this is the sum"—this is the chief point, the major emphasis of all that has been said.

II. He Is the Exalted High Priest at the Right Hand of God's Throne (v.1).

Jesus Christ is the exalted High Priest; He sits on the right hand of the Majesty in the heavens. There He sits with the Sovereign Majesty of the universe, with God Himself, ruling and reigning with all authority and power both in heaven and earth. There He sits in all the glory and honor, dominion and power of God Himself.

> **"So then, after the Lord had spoken unto them, he was received up into heaven, and sat on the right hand of God" (Mk.16:19).**
> **"Hereafter shall the Son of man sit on the right hand of the power of God" (Lu.22:69; see Ac.2:36; 5:31; Ep.1:20; Ph.2:9; 1 Ti.6:15; He.1:9; 1 Pe.3:22; Re.5:12).**

III. He Is the Exalted Minister of the True Tabernacle (v.2).

Jesus Christ is the exalted Minister of God, the Minister of the sanctuary of heaven. He is the exalted High Priest in heaven, but that is not all He is. He is also the exalted Minister of the sanctuary. He is not in heaven just to rule as Lord and to receive the honor and worship of subjects throughout the universe. He is not there ruling and reigning from a far distance, a Lord who can never be known or reached by His people. It is true that Jesus Christ is in heaven to reign in majesty and glory, but He is also in heaven to be the Minister of heaven, to be the Minister of the true sanctuary and Tabernacle or place of worship. He is there...

- to receive us as we come to God
- to hear our cries for mercy and grace to help in times of need
- to save us to the uttermost
- to represent us as the sacrificial offering for our sins
- to deliver us from all the trials and temptations of this corruptible and dying world
- to minister the Word of God to our hearts

Jesus Christ is not in heaven selfishly enjoying the wonder and glory of its sanctuary; He is not in heaven selfishly soaking up all its glory for Himself. Jesus Christ is in heaven ministering—looking after and reaching out to people.

⇒ He is listening and hearing the cries of people and ministering to their needs. In fact, He is ministering to every need that God's people have.

⇒ He is receiving the worship and praise of people and offering their names up to God.

Jesus Christ is actively ministering and looking after the true sanctuary and the true Tabernacle, the real place where men are to worship, that is, heaven itself. (Note: the true sanctuary and Tabernacle means that part of heaven where God sits upon His throne, where the very presence of God is. It is the very place where men are to offer their worship and praise to God. It is the place where Christ ministers as the High Priest before God.)

> "Wherefore in all things it behooved him to be made like unto his brethren, that he might be a merciful and faithful high priest in things pertaining to God, to make reconciliation for the sins of the people. For in that he himself hath suffered being tempted, he is able to succour them that are tempted" (He.2:17-18).
>
> "For we have not an High Priest which cannot be touched with the feeling of our infirmities; but was in all points tempted like as we are, yet without sin. Let us therefore come boldly unto the throne of grace, that we may obtain mercy, and find grace to help in time of need" (He.4:15-16; see Ps.40:17; Is.41:10).

IV. He Is the Exalted Minister Who Offers the Gifts and Sacrifices of Men to God (v.3).

Jesus Christ is the exalted Minister who offers the gifts and sacrifices of men to God. This is what is meant by this verse. The very purpose for High Priests was to offer gifts and sacrifices on behalf of men. High Priests were appointed; the very reason for their existence was to offer these gifts and sacrifices so that God would accept men. By making such offerings, it was felt that God would be pleased and would approve men for heaven.

The point is this: Jesus Christ is now the High Priest, the One who is to offer the gifts and sacrifices of men to God. But note: as seen in earlier passages, only perfect gifts and offerings are acceptable to God. And no man has a perfect gift and sacrifice to offer to God. What then can be done? If Jesus Christ is our great High Priest, He has to have something to offer for us. As this verse says, "It is of necessity that this man have something also to offer." But what could He offer? There was only one thing: He had to offer Himself, for He is the only gift and sacrifice in the world that is perfect. And He did it for us. What an unbelievable thing to do! But Jesus Christ did it.

⇒ He *actually offered* Himself, *becoming* our gift and sacrifice to God. Jesus Christ is the exalted Minister who offers the gifts and sacrifices of men to God.

> "Who gave himself for our sins, that he might deliver us from this present evil world, according to the will of God and our Father" (Ga.1:4).
>
> "And walk in love, as Christ also hath loved us, and hath given himself for us an offering and a sacrifice to God for a sweetsmelling savour" (Ep.5:2; see Tit.2:14; He.9:26-28; 1 Pe.1:18-19; 2:24; 3:18; 1 Jn.3:16; Re.1:5).

V. He Is the Exalted Minister of the Real, Heavenly World (vv.4-5).

Jesus Christ is the exalted Minister of the real, heavenly world. This is the meaning of these two verses. Verse four simply says that if Christ were a priest on earth, He would not be a priest at all. He simply was not born of the priestly tribe of men, the Levite tribe. And no man could serve as priest unless he was born into the priestly family.

This, of course, means something of critical importance: Jesus Christ is not the Minister of the *shadow* of heavenly things—of earthly gifts and sanctuaries and tabernacles. Jesus Christ is the Minister of heaven—of the real world, of the real sanctuary and Tabernacle of God. The word *example* (hupodeigmati) means copy, shadow, shadowy outline, a reflection. The things of religion and worship upon earth are only examples and shadows, copies and sketches, shadowy outlines and reflections of heavenly worship.

Note: there is a real world, a heavenly world; and there is a Tabernacle, a throne room in which the glorious presence of God dwells. It was the pattern from which Moses made the earthly Tabernacle (see Ex.25:40). God had shown Moses the real pattern of heavenly worship and told him to make a copy of it upon earth. That is what the Tabernacle was that was carried around by Israel in the wilderness wanderings.

The point is this: earthly priests can only give us the shadow and picture of heaven. But Jesus Christ is the Priest and Minister of the heavenly worship, of the real world. Therefore, He is the One who can lead men into heaven, into the world that is real and perfect and that has no end. He is the One who can lead us into the very presence of God.

> **"But lay up for yourselves treasures in heaven, where neither moth nor rust doth corrupt, and where thieves do not break through nor steal" (Mt.6:20).**
>
> **"Notwithstanding in this rejoice not, that the spirits are subject unto you; but rather rejoice, because your names are written in heaven" (Lu.10:20; see Jn.14:2; Ac.7:55-56; He.9:23; He.11:10; He.11:27; Re.7:9; Re.22:14).**

C. Christ is the Minister of the Greater and More Perfect Tabernacle or Sanctuary, Hebrews 9:1-14

(Please see Part 5, the Resource Chart Section, Chart 2, Page 312: "How Christ Fulfilled the Symbolism of the Tabernacle." A careful study of this important resource chart will help the reader more fully grasp the meaning of the Tabernacle).

1. The earthly sanctuary or tabernacle: Was for divine worship, but it was only an earthly sanctuary a. The outer sanctuary: The Holy Place 1) The Candlestick 2) The Table of the Showbread b. The inner sanctuary: The Holy of Holies 1) The Golden Censer 2) The Ark of the Covenant c. The priests entered the Holy Place daily & carried out their ministry & acts of worship d. The High Priest alone entered the Holy of Holies & that only once a year	Then verily the first covenant had also ordinances of divine service, and a worldly sanctuary. 2 For there was a tabernacle made; the first, wherein was the candlestick, and the table, and the showbread; which is called the sanctuary. 3 And after the second veil, the tabernacle which is called the Holiest of all; 4 Which had the golden censer, and the Ark of the covenant overlaid round about with gold, wherein was the golden pot that had manna, and Aaron's rod that budded, and the tables of the covenant; 5 And over it the cherubims of glory shadowing the mercyseat; of which we cannot now speak particularly. 6 Now when these things were thus ordained, the priests went always into the first tabernacle, accomplishing the service of God. 7 But into the second went the high priest alone once every year, not without blood, which he of-	fered for himself, and for the errors of the people: 8 The Holy Ghost this signifying, that the way into the holiest of all was not yet made manifest, while as the first tabernacle was yet standing: 9 Which was a figure for the time then present, in which were offered both gifts and sacrifices, that could not make him that did the service perfect, as pertaining to the conscience; 10 Which stood only in meats and drinks, and divers washings, and carnal ordinances, imposed on them until the time of reformation. 11 But Christ being come an high priest of good things to come, by a greater and more perfect tabernacle, not made with hands, that is to say, not of this building; 12 Neither by the blood of goats and calves, but by his own blood he entered in once into the holy place, having obtained eternal redemption for us. 13 For if the blood of bulls and of goats,	e. The inadequacies or lessons of the earthly sanctuary & worship 1) The way into God's presence was not yet open 2) The approach to God through gifts & sacrifices could not perfect worshippers 3) The great day of reformation—the day when imperfect worship would be transformed into perfect worship—could not be brought about by earthly worship **2. The heavenly sanctuary or tabernacle** a. The perfect High Priest: He ministers with better things b. A perfect sanctuary: Not made with hands c. A perfect sacrifice 1) Sacrificed His own blood 2) Sacrificed Himself once 3) Secured redemption for us d. A perfect salvation

1) The earthly sanctuary & worship purified only the flesh 2) The heavenly sanctuary &	and the ashes of an heifer sprinkling the unclean, sanctifieth to the purifying of the flesh: 14 How much more shall the blood of	Christ, who through the eternal Spirit offered himself without spot to God, purge your conscience from dead works to serve the living God?	worship purifies a person, even his conscience 3) The heavenly sanctuary & worship leads a person to serve God

How can a person become acceptable to God? How can a person gain access to God, fellowship and commune with Him? How can a person come to know God in a real and personal way—so personal that the individual can know that God is looking after and caring for him? How can a person gain and maintain a relationship with God? This is the concern of the writer of Hebrews. He has already shown how men try to approach God...

- through prophets (He.1:1-3)
- through angels (He.1:4-14)
- through leaders who are great men of God (He.3:1-6)
- through priests (He.4:14-8:5)
- through covenants or laws (by trying to be as good as they can) (He.8:1-13)

But as has been seen, every one of these approaches to God are inadequate. They are imperfect and incomplete. They may tell us some things about God; they may help us to understand God to some degree, but they do not give us the full story nor reveal the whole nature of God. They are only shadows and faint copies of the truth. They show us only a part of the truth about God. They do not reveal God to us, nor do they make us acceptable to God or give us fellowship with God.

The present passage deals with the same subject: How do men try to approach and worship God? Another way is through earthly sanctuaries or houses of worship. In the Old Testament—under the first covenant with God—the Jews or children of Israel built a Tabernacle, that is, a tent. The tent or Tabernacle was the place where they sought to worship and become acceptable to God. But as shall be seen, this approach to God was as inadequate as all the other approaches. Earthly sanctuaries and earthly worship cannot bring us near God—earthly sanctuaries and earthly worship cannot make us acceptable to God. Only Jesus Christ can bring us near and make us acceptable to God. This is the point of this passage: to show that Jesus Christ is the greater and more perfect Minister of the Tabernacle. He is the only Minister who brings us to God.

NOTE: Please see Part 5, the Resource Chart Section, Chart 2, Page 312: "How Christ Fulfilled the Symbolism of the Tabernacle." A careful study of this important resource chart will help the reader more fully grasp the meaning of the Tabernacle.

 I. The earthly sanctuary or Tabernacle: was for divine worship, but it was only an earthly sanctuary (vv.1-10).
 II. The heavenly sanctuary or Tabernacle (vv.11-14).

I. The Earthly Sanctuary or Tabernacle Was for Divine Worship, but It Was Only an Earthly Sanctuary (vv.1-10).

The earthly sanctuary was for the worship of God, but it was only an earthly sanctuary. It was totally inadequate in reaching God and in making a person acceptable to God. This is clear when one looks at the layout and worship of the earthly Tabernacle. (See drawing of the Tabernacle, p.18-19 for a better grasp of its layout and furnishings.)

1. First, there was the first or outer sanctuary which was the Holy Place (v.2). It was 30 feet long, 15 feet wide, and 15 feet high. Three pieces of furnishings were in the Holy Place; two are mentioned here.

a. There was the Candlestick or Lampstand which had seven lamps or flames. The Candlestick gave light to the room, for there were no windows in this outer sanctuary.

b. There was the Table of the Showbread. It was a small table, only 3 feet long, 1½ feet wide, and 2 feet 3 inches high. Twelve loaves of bread lay upon the table. They were neatly arranged in two rows of six.

2. Second, there was the second or inner sanctuary which was the holiest of all sanctuaries, the Holy of Holies or what is sometimes called the Most Holy Place (vv.3-5). Note that a veil or large curtain separated it from the sanctuary of the Holy Place. This was the sanctuary that could be entered only by the High Priest, and he could enter only once a year. Note: there was not a Lampstand in the Holy of Holies and there were no windows. The glory of God was to have given the room its light. Two furnishings are mentioned.

a. There was the Golden Censer or Altar of Incense which was a permanent piece of furniture in the Holy Place, but it was carried into the Holy of Holies on the Day of Atonement (v.4). It was a small table-like container 1½ feet square and 3 feet high. Incense was burned upon it every morning and evening symbolizing the prayers of the people reaching up to God.

b. There was the Ark of the Covenant which was a box or chest covered with gold on every side (vv.4-5). It contained three things.

⇒ The golden pot containing manna, which symbolized the manna used to feed the children of Israel in their wilderness wanderings (Ex.16:32-34).

⇒ The rod of Aaron (Nu.17:1-11).

⇒ The two slabs of the covenant or law upon which Moses had written the Ten Commandments (Ex.25:16f; De.9:9; 10:5).

Arising from both ends of the Ark were two angelic creatures called cherubim who reached over and shadowed the mercy seat. The very presence of God was to sit upon the lid or top of the Ark between the glory of the two cherubim (Ex.25:22).

Thought

The point to see is that the sanctuary was furnished with earthly furniture— furniture that has religious meaning, but the furniture is still earthly, still only a shadow and faint copy of real worship. The same is true with our sanctuaries today. We have our earthly sanctuaries and earthly furniture—furniture that has religious meaning for us. There is the pulpit, the table for the Lord's Supper, and the baptismal pool. But these are still earthly, only shadows and faint images of the real sanctuary and worship.

3. Third, the priests entered the outer sanctuary or Holy Place every day and carried out their ministry and acts of worship for the people (v.6). They did all they could to make the people acceptable to God, providing fellowship and communion with God. But again their service and ministry were *short of perfection*. No matter how much ministry they performed for the people, they could not make the people perfect. They could not make the people acceptable to God.

4. Fourth, the High Priest alone went into the inner sanctuary or the Holy of Holies (v.7). He went in to offer the blood of the sacrifice to God for the sins of the people. Man is sinful, guilty of sin and rebellion against God. Therefore, he must pay the penalty and judgment for his sins, or else a substitute has to bear the judgment for him. This was the idea behind the animal sacrifice. The life of the animal was sacrificed for the sins of the people. Therefore, people were released from the guilt of their sins and made acceptable to God.

But note: the High Priest could go into the Holy of Holies to make sacrifice for sins only once a year. This is what was known as the Day of Atonement. Does this mean that a person could be forgiven his sins only once a year? No. There were daily sacrifices and offerings for sin that a person could make. The Day of Atonement was a comprehensive sacrifice—a nationwide confession of sin. Israel was the chosen people of God with whom God had established His first covenant. Therefore, Israel or a body of people were to seek and worship God, and atonement or sacrifice was to be made for everything that concerned the nation:

> **"And he shall make an atonement for the holy sanctuary, and he shall make an atonement for the tabernacle of the congregation, and for the altar, and he shall make an atonement for the priests, and for all the people of the congregation" (Le.16:33).**

The point to note is this: sacrifice for sins had to be repeated year by year. There was no permanent sacrifice, no eternal Savior from sin.

5. Fifth, there were the inadequacies or lessons of the earthly Tabernacle and worship (v.8). Note that the Holy Spirit of God is the One who points out these inadequacies or lessons. He is the One who points out the following shortcomings of the Tabernacle and of earthly worship.

   a. First, the way into God's presence was not opened up by the earthly sanctuary or worship. Remember: the very presence of God dwelt in the Holy of Holies. And no one—not even a priest—could enter the Holy of Holies. Only the High Priest himself ever went into God's presence and that was only once a year. And when he entered, he went in with fear and trembling lest he displease God and be stricken dead. No one had access to God—not day by day—not in an unbroken communion and fellowship with God's Spirit.

Thought

No earthly sanctuary or worship can make a person acceptable to God. Everything on earth, including all worship and worship centers, are physical and material, short and imperfect. Nothing on this earth is perfect; therefore, nothing can bring perfection to man, not even sanctuaries and worship. Nothing that is earthly can make God accept man. Nothing on earth can give man access and fellowship and communion with God.

> **"For I say unto you, That except your righteousness shall exceed the righteousness of the scribes and Pharisees, ye shall in no case enter into the kingdom of heaven" (Mt.5:20).**
> **"Now this I say, brethren, that flesh and blood cannot inherit the kingdom of God; neither doth corruption inherit incorruption" (1 Co.15:50; see Re.21:27).**

   b. The approach to God through gifts and sacrifices could not perfect the worshippers. And note: the honest worshipper knew it; his conscience told him. Every thinking and honest person knows he cannot be made into a perfect person and cleanse his conscience...

- by offering gifts to God, even if those gifts are made sacrificially
- by offering animal sacrifices to God as a substitute for his sins

Such acts are earthly acts and deal with physical and material things (substances). They help us to see and understand God to some degree. They are shadows and faint copies of perfect worship, but they cannot remove guilt or sins nor can they make a man perfect.

> **"Envyings, murders, drunkenness, revellings, and such like: of the which I tell you before, as I have also told you in time past, that they which do such things shall not inherit the kingdom of God" (Ga.5:21).**
> **"For this ye know, that no whoremonger, nor unclean person, nor covetous man, who is an idolater, hath any inheritance in the kingdom of Christ and of God" (Ep.5:5; see Re.21:27).**

c. The great day of reformation—the day when the imperfect and material worship would be transformed into the perfect and eternal worship—could not be brought about by earthly worship. This is clearly seen: all the rituals and ceremonies of earthly sanctuaries and worship are only external and physical acts. This is true of all rituals and ceremonies, whether they involve...

- food
- drink
- water
- worship
- external rules and regulations

No matter what the ritual of worship is, it is external and physical—a mere act of man using some physical substance to help him worship God. And nothing that is earthly and external—physical and imperfect—can make us acceptable to God. Nothing on this earth can give us access, fellowship, and communion with God.

Earthly sanctuaries and worship are helpful as mere shadows, images, and faint copies of real worship—but they are all ever so inadequate. They leave the soul empty and unassured.

> **"He answered and said unto them, Well hath Esaias prophesied of you hypocrites, as it is written, This people honoureth me with their lips, but their heart is far from me" (Mk.7:6).**
>
> **"And ye are complete in him, which is the head of all principality and power" (Col.2:10; see 2 Ti.3:5; Tit.1:16; He.7:19; He.10:1; Is.29:13).**

II. The Heavenly Sanctuary or Tabernacle (vv.11-14).

The heavenly sanctuary is for the worship of God just as the earthly sanctuary is, but it is different from the earthly sanctuary and worship of men. How does it differ? There are at least four differences.

1. The heavenly sanctuary and worship has a *perfect priest*. The High Priest of heaven is not a man; He does not come from among mere men—men who are imperfect, frail, sinful, and ever so short just like all other men. The High Priest of heaven is the Son of God Himself, and as the Son of God, He is perfect and eternal. Therefore, He is able to bring better things to us. He is able to make intercession for us forever—He is able to save us to the uttermost when we come to God by Him.

2. The heavenly sanctuary and worship is *spiritual and perfect*. It is not made with human hands; it is not a part of this earthly, physical, and material world. It is not a part of this corruptible, decaying, aging, and dying world. It is not a part of this world that is only a shadow, picture, and faint copy of the real world. The spiritual and perfect sanctuary is the spiritual and perfect world—heaven itself—where the very presence of God is glorified and manifested for all to see and worship.

> **"For Christ is not entered into the holy places made with hands, which are the figures of the true; but into heaven itself, now to appear in the presence of God for us" (He.9:24).**
>
> **"No man can serve two masters: for either he will hate the one, and love the other; or else he will hold to the one, and despise the other. Ye cannot serve God and mammon" (Mt.6:24; see Jn.14:2-3; 2 Co.5:1; He.11:10; Re.7:9).**

3. The heavenly sanctuary and worship has a *perfect sacrifice* (v.12). Man is imperfect and sinful; he is guilty of disobeying, rejecting, and rebelling against God. Therefore, he must pay the penalty and judgment for his sins or else a substitute has to bear the judgment for him. This was the idea behind animal sacrifices. The animal's life was sacrificed for the sins of man. Note that three significant things are said in this verse.

a. Jesus Christ, the perfect High Priest, did not sacrifice the blood of animals for the sins of man; He sacrificed His own blood. He offered up His life as a sacrifice to God—as the sacrifice for the life of the people. Jesus Christ bore the guilt and judgment for the sins of man. Why would He do this? Because He is the Son of God and He loves man. He is the Son of God who came to earth as the God-Man; He is the ideal and perfect Man. As the ideal Man, whatever He does stands for and covers all men. Therefore, His blood covers the sins of all men who believe and trust Him. His sacrifice is the perfect and ideal sacrifice—the sacrifice that stands for and covers all men.

b. Jesus Christ, the perfect High Priest, entered into the Holy of Holies of heaven itself. But note: He had to enter only once. The earthly High Priest had to make continued sacrifices, but Jesus Christ had to make only one sacrifice. Why? Because His sacrifice was perfect and ideal. Being perfect and ideal, it could stand forever for every man of every generation.

c. Jesus Christ, the perfect High Priest, obtained eternal redemption for us. Sin, death, and condemnation have captured and kidnapped man. No man can escape from either one, no matter what he does. But Jesus Christ made it possible for man to be freed and delivered from all enemies. How? He paid the ransom price. He substituted Himself for man. He gave and sacrificed His life for man. He could do this because He is the perfect and ideal Man. He has redeemed and ransomed man from sin, death, and condemnation.

> **"For this is my blood of the new testament, which is shed for many for the remission of sins" (Mt.26:28).**
> **"Take heed therefore unto yourselves, and to all the flock, over the which the Holy Ghost hath made you overseers, to feed the church of God, which he hath purchased with his own blood" (Ac.20:28; see Ro.3:24; 5:9; 1 Co.1:30; Ga.3:13; Col.1:14; Tit.2:14; He.9:12; 9:14; 1 Pe.1:18-19; 1 Jn.1:7; Re.1:5; 5:9).**

4. The heavenly sanctuary and worship saves a *person perfectly* (vv.13-14). Note three points.

a. The earthly sanctuary and worship purifies and cleanses only the flesh. It takes an honest person to admit this. But as shown in previous points, the rituals and ceremonies of earthly and physical worship are external. They cannot cleanse man inwardly nor can they make him perfect and eternal.

b. The heavenly sanctuary and worship purifies and cleanses a person even down to his conscience—no matter how hardened and non-existent the conscience may be. When a person comes to God through Christ, God gives him a perfect assurance that he is accepted by God, that he has eternal life. How is this possible? When Jesus Christ was on earth, He lived a sinless life, obeying God perfectly in every act and thought. He therefore became the ideal (and perfect) Righteousness, the ideal Man who pleased God perfectly. This is especially true in the sacrifice of Christ. God loves man and wants to save man. Therefore, God willed and wanted His Son to show His perfect love to man, to show His love by sacrificing His life for the sins of man. No greater love could ever have been expressed, and it was God's love for us that led Him to sacrifice His Son for us. When Christ sacrificed Himself for our sins, the ultimate in obedience was reached. Jesus Christ obeyed God supremely; He died for our sins. Very simply stated, God will forgive and cleanse any man's sins because of His Son. Forgiveness and cleansing are guaranteed once-for-all to everyone who believes—all because of God's supreme love for His Son.

> **"For this is my blood of the new testament, which is shed for many for the remission of sins" (Mt.26:28).**
> **"Much more then, being now justified by his blood, we shall be saved from wrath through him" (Ro.5:9; see Ep.1:7; 5:25-26; Tit.3:4-5; He.9:14; 10:14; 10:21-22; 1 Pe.1:18-19; Re.1:5).**

c. The heavenly sanctuary and worship leads a person away from the dead works of this earth to serve the living God (v.14). Earthly religion in all its ritual and ceremony is *dead* to God. No matter how religious and good a person tries to be—no matter how many good works he does—it is not such earthly behavior that makes him acceptable to God. Jesus Christ alone makes a man acceptable. He and He alone gives man access to God and puts man into fellowship and communion with God. Jesus Christ has to live in the heart and life of a person—actually live in the body of a person through the Holy Spirit of God—for a person to be given the glorious privilege of walking in fellowship and communion with God.

> "Even the Spirit of truth; whom the world cannot receive, because it seeth him not, neither knoweth him: but ye know him; for he dwelleth with you, and shall be in you" (Jn.14:17).
>
> "Therefore being justified by faith, we have peace with God through our Lord Jesus Christ: by whom also we have access by faith into this grace wherein we stand, and rejoice in hope of the glory of God" (Ro.5:1-2; see Ro.8:9; 12:1-2; 1 Co.6:19-20; Ph.2:13; He.12:28; 1 Jn.2:27).

D. The Final Triumph Over Evil: An Overall Picture of Things to Come—God's Temple Is to Be Opened, Revelation 11:14-19

1. Scene 1: A period of terrible woe	14 The second woe is past; and, behold, the third woe cometh quickly.	thy great power, and hast reigned.	
2. Scene 2: This world becomes God's kingdom	15 And the seventh angel sounded; and there were great voices in heaven, saying, The kingdoms of this world are become the kingdoms of our Lord, and of his Christ; and he shall reign for ever and ever.	18 And the nations were angry, and thy wrath is come, and the time of the dead, that they should be judged, and that thou shouldest give reward unto thy servants the prophets, and to the saints, and them that fear thy name, small and great; and shouldest destroy them which destroy the earth.	**4. Scene 4: The nations make a final rebellion & are destroyed** a. The nations rebel b. The wrath of God falls c. The dead are judged d. The godly are rewarded e. The destroyers are destroyed
3. Scene 3: The Lord God Almighty is acclaimed a. By the elders b. As the eternal God c. For taking supreme authority	16 And the four and twenty elders, which sat before God on their seats, fell upon their faces, and worshipped God, 17 Saying, We give thee thanks, O Lord God Almighty, which art, and wast, and art to come; because thou hast taken to thee	19 And the temple of God was opened in heaven, and there was seen in his temple the Ark of his testament: and there were lightnings, and voices, and thunderings, and an earthquake, and great hail.	**5. Scene 5: God's temple is to be opened** a. God's covenant & promises are seen to be true b. God's majesty is experienced

In the great Book of Revelation, God is giving the apostle John a glimpse into the end time. God loves the world; therefore, God wants the world to turn to Him before the end time. God wants John to record the events as a warning and as an encouragement, showing that God is in control of human history and that the day is coming when He is going to triumph over all evil, even death itself.

God has been showing John that the end of world history will be a period of horror and tragedy. The world and its people will go through great tribulation, tribulation such as the world has never before seen. Scene after scene of catastrophe and horror have been painted throughout the Book of Revelation up to this point. Imagine what John was going through. He was having to look upon these scenes and be an eyewitness of these horrors. This is the reason here and there throughout Revelation Christ gives John a scene of hope and of the glory that is to come. This is what the present passage is all about. John once again needs to be lifted up and encouraged. Therefore, God gives him a broad overview of what is yet to come; John sees in sketch form the glory with the horror. And note point five in particular: part of the great glory that is to come is the opening of God's temple. The very presence of God will be eternally opened to all who believe and trust and follow God. This is the overall picture of things to come.

    I.   Scene 1: a period of terrible woe (vv.14-15).
    II.   Scene 2: this world becomes God's kingdom (v.15).
   III. Scene 3: the Lord God Almighty is acclaimed (vv.16-17).
   IV. Scene 4: the nations make a final rebellion and are destroyed (v.18).
    V.   Scene 5: God's temple is to be opened (v.19).

I. Scene 1: A Period of Terrible Woe (vv.14-15).

Revelation declares that there are to be three terrible woes in the end time. By woe is meant a period of extreme grief, distress, suffering, affliction, and calamity.

⇒ The first woe will be the demonic locust-like creatures that sweep the earth and torment people (Re.8:13-9:11).

⇒ The second woe will be demonic, military, horse-like creatures that sweep the earth, killing one third of the ungodly and evil population (Re.9:12-21).

⇒ The third woe is the seventh trumpet, the judgments that result from the blast of the seventh trumpet.

But note the Scripture above: when the seventh trumpet blasts there is no judgment, and there is no woe that comes forth. Why? Because there are some things that need to be seen and understood before the end of human history. And the first thing is most interesting: it is an overview of the events that are yet to take place in the Revelation. The present passage leaps ahead and shows us in a broad summary what is to happen over the next ten chapters of this great book. God prepared John's heart for the terrible events that were yet to be revealed to him, prepared him by showing that God would triumph over evil and establish His kingdom forever. God gave John and gives us five scenes of what is yet to come.

II. Scene 2: This World Becomes God's Kingdom (v.15).

Scene one—the kingdoms of this world have become the kingdoms of our Lord and of His Christ. The Greek tense is past tense, the kingdoms have become the Lord's kingdom. The scene jumps over all of history and shows our God and His Christ ruling over the whole world. All the kingdoms of this world are done away with, and all the people upon earth live and work as citizens of God's kingdom. Presently, in our day and time, human governments involve...

- authority and rule and reign: some earthly authorities and rulers are good and some are bad
- laws: earthly laws favor some people and treat others unjustly
- work: some have jobs and others do not have jobs
- economies: some earthly economies are healthy and others are bad
- protection: some earthly governments protect their citizens, others abuse and enslave them
- provision: some earthly governments provide for their citizens and help their citizens provide for themselves and others do not
- services: some earthly governments provide good services for their people such as roads, sewage, water, jobs, and health care or else they provide poor service

The point is this: earthly governments are imperfect and weak, unable to bring utopia to man. Earthly governments are flooded with the poor, hungry, homeless, sick, selfish, rich, proud, and all the other evils and imperfections that enslave the citizens of this world. Earthly governments focus upon this earth and all the pleasures and possessions of this earth, even upon war and conflict. This will be especially true in the end time under the antichrist. The world will be engulfed in sin and evil, selfishness and greed, war and conflict. But this is not the end: this is the glorious message of this point. The kingdoms of this world are going to become the kingdom of our God and His Christ. God is going to reign over the world, bringing heaven to this universe. When? During the millennium. The millennium simply means the period of time, a period of one thousand years, when Jesus Christ is to return to this earth and rule over the nations and people of the earth.

Thought
Just think! Utopia is coming to earth. Peace and prosperity are coming. There will no longer be hunger, thirst, homelessness, disease, war, murder, nor any of the other evils upon earth. But note: utopia will only come when Jesus Christ returns to rule the earth.

Man fails and fails miserably in his attempts to clean up the world and to establish peace. But God loves man and loves him dearly. Therefore, He is going to help man. God is going to send His dear Son back to earth to establish peace and prosperity for all. God is going to do for man what man has so miserably failed to do. This is the glorious promise of this passage.

> **"And I heard a loud voice saying in heaven, Now is come salvation, and strength, and the kingdom of our God, and the power of his Christ: for the accuser of our brethren is cast down, which accused them before our God day and night" (Re.12:10).**
>
> **"And I heard as it were the voice of a great multitude, and as the voice of many waters, and as the voice of mighty thunderings, saying, Alleluia: for the Lord God omnipotent reigneth" (Re.19:6; see Rev.19:16; 20:4-6; Lu.1:32-33; Dan.2:44; 4:3; 4:34; 6:26; 7:13-14).**

III. Scene 3: The Lord God Almighty Is Acclaimed (vv.16-17).

The angel gave a glimpse into the future showing the victory of God, showing the twenty four elders falling on their faces before God. They worshipped and praised Him for three things.

1. They praised God as the Lord God Almighty.
- ⇒ Lord: He deserved to be the Lord and Master, the Ruler over all lives.
- ⇒ God: He was the Creator and Maker of all, and He was the only one who deserved to be worshipped.
- ⇒ Almighty: He was omnipotent, that is, all powerful. He could do anything, and He would always be able to execute His will.

2. They praised Him as the Lord God who "is, and was, and is to come." That is, He is eternal. He is the One existing now, who always was existing, and always is to exist. The Lord God possesses life forever and ever. Therefore, He is able to give life to whom He wills.

3. They praised Him for taking His great power back from the world and beginning to reign in His rightful place. God has allowed Satan to have access to the world and to man. And, most unfortunately, man has chosen to follow Satan instead of God. But not all people. Some people have done exactly what God was after: freely chosen to believe and follow Him—freely chosen to love God supremely. The result has been a world inhabited by a mass of people who deny and ignore God and by only a few people who focus upon God. And the inevitable has happened: the selfishness, greed, and lust that grip people who focus only upon self has consumed the world. The world is wrecked with so much sin and evil that mammoth problems are now beyond solving.

But note: God is going to solve them. This is the declaration of the praise of the twenty four elders. They have just witnessed the scene of the future, the scene where God has just taken back His power over the world from Satan. They have witnessed the rule of God's love and righteousness upon earth.

> **"And, behold, thou shalt conceive in thy womb, and bring forth a son, and shalt call his name JESUS. He shall be great, and shall be called the Son of the Highest: and the Lord God shall give unto him the throne of his father David: and he shall reign over the house of Jacob for ever; and of his kingdom there shall be no end" (Lu.1:31-33).**
>
> **"Now unto the King eternal, immortal, invisible, the only wise God, be honour and glory for ever and ever" (1 Ti.1:17).**
>
> **"And they sing the song of Moses the servant of God, and the song of the Lamb, saying, Great and marvellous are thy works, Lord God Almighty; just and true are thy ways, thou King of saints" (Re.15:3; see Rev.19:6; Ex.15:18; 2 Chr.20:6; Ps.24:10).**

IV. Scene 4: The Nations Make a Final Rebellion and Are Destroyed (v.18).

Scene 3—the nations of the world will make a final rebellion against God and will be destroyed, facing the eternal judgment of God. Note five points.

1. There will be the final rebellion of the nations against the Lord Jesus Christ at the end of the millennium (the thousand-year rule of Christ upon earth). The devil and his followers are going to try to defeat Christ and His followers in a last ditch battle upon earth. Remember: Christ will be ruling upon earth for one thousand years, and that is a long, long time. Over the period of the thousand years, people will do what people so often do now: become dull and lethargic toward Christ and His power, toward His call and His will. Therefore when Satan is loosed to tempt and lead them, many will attempt to overthrow Christ and His followers.

The result will be quick and catastrophic for the ungodly nations and people of this earth.

> "And when the thousand years are expired, Satan shall be loosed out of his prison, and shall go out to deceive the nations which are in the four quarters of the earth, Gog and Magog, to gather them together to battle: the number of whom is as the sand of the sea. And they went up on the breadth of the earth, and compassed the camp of the saints about, and the beloved city [Jerusalem]: and fire came down from God out of heaven, and devoured them. And the devil that deceived them was cast into the lake of fire and brimstone, where the beast and the false prophet are, and shall be tormented day and night for ever and ever" (Re.20:7-10).

2. The wrath of God will fall.

> "He that believeth on the Son hath everlasting life: and he that believeth not the Son shall not see life; but the wrath of God abideth on him" (Jn.3:36).
>
> "For the wrath of God is revealed from heaven against all ungodliness and unrighteousness of men, who hold the truth in unrighteousness" (Ro.1:18; see Ro.2:8; Ep.5:6; Ps.2:12).

3. The dead will be judged.

> "When the Son of man shall come in his glory, and all the holy angels with him, then shall he sit upon the throne of his glory: and before him shall be gathered all nations: and he shall separate them one from another, as a shepherd divideth his sheep from the goats" (Mt.25:31-32).
>
> "And as it is appointed unto men once to die, but after this the judgment" (He.9:27; see 2 Pe.2:9; 3:7; 1 Jn.4:17; Jude 14-15).

4. The godly will be rewarded, that is, the believers, the prophets, and those who fear God's name.

> "Blessed are ye, when men shall revile you, and persecute you, and shall say all manner of evil against you falsely, for my sake. Rejoice, and be exceeding glad: for great is your reward in heaven: for so persecuted they the prophets which were before you" (Mt.5:11-12).
>
> "And whosoever shall give to drink unto one of these little ones a cup of cold water only in the name of a disciple, verily I say unto you, he shall in no wise lose his reward" (Mt.10:42; see Mt.25:23; Lu.6:35; Ep.6:8; Ps.2:12).

5. The destroyers of human life will have their own lives destroyed.

> **"And to you who are troubled rest with us, when the Lord Jesus shall be revealed from heaven with his mighty angels, in flaming fire taking vengeance on them that know not God, and that obey not the gospel of our Lord Jesus Christ: who shall be punished with everlasting destruction from the presence of the Lord, and from the glory of his power" (2 Th.1:7-9).**
>
> **"These are wells without water, clouds that are carried with tempest; to whom the mist of darkness is reserved for ever" (2 Pe.2:17; see Jude 14-15; Re.20:11-15).**

Thought

This is a strong warning to us all, a warning that must be heeded and heeded now or else we shall be eternally doomed.

a) A person must not join those who rebel against God. If he rebels against God, then he must face God as a rebel who stands opposed to God and who fights against the kingdom of God.

b) The wrath of God is going to fall against all who rebel against God.

c) The dead will face God. All the dead, every single person who has lived or ever will live—all shall stand face to face with God.

d) The godly will be rewarded. All who fear God's name will be greatly rewarded.

e) The ungodly and evil will be destroyed. All who destroy human life—their own lives or the lives of others—shall be destroyed.

V. Scene 5: God's Temple Is to Be Opened (v.19).

Scene four—God's temple will be opened. The presence and glory of God will be opened and fully experienced by all who trust and follow God—opened and fully experienced throughout all eternity. In fact, this is the picture of what eternity will be like. God will dwell with His own people in His temple—in all the universe. His promises will then be known to be true, and His majesty will be experienced.

1. There is a heavenly temple after which the earthly temple and Tabernacle were patterned or designed. Scripture clearly says this.

> **"And the cheurbims shall stretch forth their wings on high, covering the mercy seat with their wings, and their faces shall look one to another; toward the mercy seat shall the faces of the cherubims be" (Ex.25:20).**
>
> **"It was therefore necessary that the patterns of things in the heavens should be purified with these; but the heavenly things themselves with better sacrifices than these" (He.9:23).**

This is a wonderful thing, for it means that our earthly worship is patterned after the heavenly worship. However, we must never forget that the eternal, the new heavens and earth, will have no temple in them. Lehman Strauss states this well.

> *When the New Jerusalem comes down from Heaven, it is called 'the holy city' (Revelation 21:2), and John states expressly, 'I saw no temple there' (21:22). When the scenes in chapter 21 are fulfilled there will be no need for a temple as a place of worship. If all were holy on earth now, there would be no need for a place of worship. Jesus said, 'God is Spirit: and they that worship*

Him must worship Him in spirit and in truth' (John 4:24). True worship is a matter of the heart.[1]

2. There is another interpretation of this passage that needs to be noted. William Barclay states it well:

> The Temple is opened; but there is more than that. The Ark of the Covenant is seen. Now the Ark of the Covenant was in the Holy of Holies, the inside of which no ordinary person had ever seen, and into which even the High Priest went only on the Day of Atonement. This vision involves the opening up of the Temple and even the opening up of the Holy of Holies. This can have only one meaning; it must mean that now the glory of God is going to be fully displayed. That which was secret is going to be revealed; that which no man has seen is going to be opened to the sight of men. The full glory of God is going to burst upon men.
>
> Why the special reference to the Ark of the Covenant? This is to remind people of God's special covenant with His own people. Originally that covenant had been with the people Israel; but the new covenant is the covenant in Jesus Christ with all of every nation who love and who believe in Jesus. This means that in the full display of God's glory, in the destruction of God's enemies, God will remember His covenant and God will be true to His own. Whatever the terror and whatever the destruction to come, God will not break the covenant that He made with His people and will not be false to His promises.
>
> So this picture is a picture of the coming of the full glory of God, which is a terrifying threat to the enemies of God, but an uplifting promise to the people of God's covenant.[2]

---

[1]   Lehman Strauss. *The Book of the Revelation.* (Neptune, NJ: Loizeaux Brothers, 1964), p.225.

[2]   William Barclay. *The Revelation of John,* Vol.2. "The Daily Study Bible Series." (Philadelphia, PA, Westminster Press, 1960), p.89f.

E. The New Heaven and The New Earth: The Tabernacle of God—His Very Own Presence—Dwells With Men Eternally, Revelation 21:1-8

1. The new creation, the new heaven & the new earth	And I saw a new heaven and a new earth: for the first heaven and the first earth were passed away; and there was no more sea.	passed away. 5 And he that sat upon the throne said, Behold, I make all things new. And he said unto me, Write: for these words are true and faithful.
2. The new city of God	2 And I John saw the holy city, new Jerusalem, coming down from God out of heaven, prepared as a bride adorned for her husband.	6 And he said unto me, It is done. I am Alpha and Omega, the beginning and the end. I will give unto him that is athirst of the fountain of the water of life freely.
3. The immediate fellowship with God a. Declared by a loud voice b. The immediate presence & fellowship of God	3 And I heard a great voice out of heaven saying, Behold, the Tabernacle of God is with men, and he will dwell with them, and they shall be his people, and God himself shall be with them, and be their God.	7 He that overcometh shall inherit all things; and I will be his God, and he shall be my son.
4. The perfection of all things a. Life will be perfected	4 And God shall wipe away all tears from their eyes; and there shall be no more death, neither sorrow, nor crying, neither shall there be any more pain: for the former things are	8 But the fearful, and unbelieving, and the abominable, and murderers, and whoremongers, and sorcerers, and idolaters, and all liars, shall have their part in the lake which burneth with fire and brimstone: which is the second death.

b. The assurance that God is going to perfect all things 1) God assures it 2) God's Word assures it
3) God's sovereignty assures it
5. The citizens a. Those who thirst for life
b. Those who overcome 1) Will inherit all things 2) Will be sons of God
b. The rejected & their fate 1) Their identity
2) Their fate: The lake of fire—the second death

What will eternity be like? What will it be like to have an unbroken consciousness of the presence of God dwelling with us—to *tabernacle* among us and never leave our senses nor our thoughts? What will it be like to have all the truths and purposes of the Tabernacle fulfilled eternally? To have a perfect worship and consciousness of God's holy presence and guidance? To live forever and ever in the Shekinah glory of God? This chapter of Revelation gives us a glimpse into eternity. All the bad and negative things of this world are going to be conquered and destroyed. All the pollution and impurities, all the ungodliness and evil, all the suffering and pain, all the corruption and death—it is all going to be erased, eliminated, and done away with. The day is coming when there will be no more...

- corrupt government
- impure religion
- bad leaders

- pain and suffering
- sin and temptation

This is the glorious message of Revelation. God is going to take Satan and all the ungodly and evil of this world and destroy them. God is going to make a new heavens and a new earth. God is going to make all things new. And when He does, there will be...

- no more tears
- no more sorrow
- no more crying
- no more pain
- no more death

Believers will live in the presence of God eternally. God's presence will "tabernacle," set His tent, among us. God's presence will dwell among and fill all of the new heavens and earth, to the extent that men will have an unbroken consciousness of His presence and glory. The time will come when every believer will experience the ultimate consummation of the Tabernacle of God.

This is the great subject of this passage of Scripture: *The new heaven and the new earth.*

I.   The new creation, the new heaven and the new earth (v.1.).
II. The new city of God (v.2).
III. The immediate fellowship with God (v.3).
IV. The perfection of all things (vv.4-6).
V.   The citizens (vv.6-8).

I. The New Creation, the New Heaven and the New Earth (v.1).

The heaven (heavenly bodies in outer space) and earth that we know are going to pass away.

1. All the heavens above—the sun, moon, stars, and planets—are going to be destroyed and remade. God is going to make a new heaven. Think what this will mean. There will be...

- no more violent thunderstorms, typhoons, hurricanes, destructive rains, or other harmful weather
- no more stars or solar systems that are burned out

All of the heavens above will be remade, created anew and made alive. Think how glorious and beautiful the heavens look now when we look up on a starry night. But imagine what they will be like when God recreates them in all the glory and magnificence of a perfect universe. All things within the universe will be alive and reflect the glory and splendor of God Himself. The universe will be perfect, a place where nothing burns out, wears down, wastes away, or dies. Think about the light, the brilliance, the splendor, and the glory of all the heavenly bodies when God recreates the heavens. Think about what it will mean to have a universe full of *living planets and stars and solar systems*. We cannot imagine the glory and beauty. It is beyond our finite minds. But note the significant point: the Scripture declares emphatically that the heaven is to be remade and recreated into a new heaven.

2. The earth is going to pass away. There is going to be a new earth. The present earth is defective; it is cursed. The earth suffers under all kinds of natural disasters such as earthquakes, volcanic eruptions, destructive storms, floods, scorching heat, deserts, famines, diseases, and death. But the day is coming when God is going to remake the earth. God is going to create a new earth. Think what this will mean.

- ⇒ no more disasters or destruction
- ⇒ no more hunger or thirst
- ⇒ no more thorns or thistles
- ⇒ no more infertile or unproductive soil
- ⇒ no more disease, decay, erosion, or death

The new earth will flourish and be fruitful, bearing all the good that can be imagined. Think how beautiful, green, lush, productive, and fruitful it will be. Think how peaceful, serene, and comfortable it will be. Think of the security and provision, the abundance and overflowing of every good and perfect gift—the fullness of life that will be possible upon the earth. The earth will be new, perfected by God in every conceivable way.

Note the statement, "there was no more sea." This can mean one of two things. The sea will be eliminated, done away with, and the new earth will have no sea. Or it can mean the same thing that is meant with the heavens and the earth. The heavens and the earth and the sea are to pass away and be made anew and recreated. The sea that causes devastation and destruction will be destroyed right along with the earth and the heavens; but when they are recreated, the sea, being part of the earth, will be part of the new earth, part of the new creation.

A perfected earth is beyond our comprehension. But it is exactly what Scripture declares is going to happen. God is going to create a new earth as well as a new heaven.

> **"For verily I say unto you, Till heaven and earth pass, one jot or one tittle shall in no wise pass from the law, till all be fulfilled" (Mt.5:18).**
> **"Heaven and earth shall pass away, but my words shall not pass away" (Mt.24:35; see 2 Pe.3:10-13; Re.21:1; Ps.102:25-27; Is.34:4; 51:6; 65:17; 66:22).**

II. The New City of God (v.2).

There will be the new city of God, the holy city, the New Jerusalem. The idea is that the New Jerusalem will be the capital city in the new heaven and earth. It will be the place where the very presence of God is symbolized. God's presence, of course, will be manifested everywhere in the new heaven and earth, manifested in all of God's glory and majesty. But the holy city will give believers a place with which to identify as they serve God throughout the universe. The next verse shows this. The heavenly city is the Tabernacle, the very presence of God that comes down to dwell with man. The point in this verse is to show that God has prepared His own capital city to sit upon the earth. It will apparently be from the New Jerusalem that Jesus Christ will rule the universe and require His servants (believers) to occasionally visit and report on their work. The Lord's throne will sit in the New Jerusalem, and from there He will rule and reign throughout all eternity. Note that the city comes down out of heaven. It is not constructed here on earth; God has it built in heaven and then moves it to earth. Note also that it is said to be as beautifully prepared as a bride is for her husband. This points both to the beauty of the city and to our longing desire to have God's presence right here on earth with us.

Remember that Jesus Christ told His apostles that He was going away to prepare a place for them. There is the possibility that He was referring to His preparation of the New Jerusalem (Jn.14:2-3).

III. The Immediate Fellowship with God (v.3).

The very Tabernacle of God will be set up right here on earth. The Tabernacle is a picture of the Tabernacle of the Old Testament, the worship center of Israel, the place where the very presence and glory of God dwelt in a special way. The picture is this: when the New Jerusalem, the capital city of eternity, is moved to earth, then the very presence and glory of God will dwell and live right here upon earth. God's presence will never again be dulled or removed from the presence of people.

The one thing for which man longs is the presence of God, the glory and fulness of God in all the abundance of life. Man may not know it, but the longing of his heart is for God. Man tries to fill his longing with all sorts of worldly pleasures and possessions, but nothing satisfies—nothing but God, His presence and glory. Until man allows God to fill his heart, he goes through all kinds of negative experiences:

⇒ lack of purpose, meaning, and significance
⇒ emptiness, questioning, and wondering about life
⇒ routineness, dullness, and feeling drained
⇒ insecurity and fear and failure

But when man gives his life to God, he begins to fellowship with God and to experience all the fullness of life. The point is this: in the new heaven and earth the presence and glory of God will dwell with man all the time. Man will never be without the presence and glory of God. He will always experience the fellowship of God's presence and glory. Note how strong the fellowship will be:

> **"And I heard a great voice out of heaven saying, Behold, the tabernacle of God is with men, and he will dwell with them, and they shall be his people, and God himself shall be with them, and be their God" (v.3).**

Four things are said:
- ⇒ The Tabernacle of God, the very presence and glory of God, will be with men.
- ⇒ God will dwell with them.
- ⇒ They shall be His people.
- ⇒ God Himself shall be with them and be their God.

Think how wonderful it will be: we will never be without the presence and glory of God. We will have the immediate presence of God and be able to talk and share with God face to face: to fellowship and commune with Him; to laugh and rejoice with Him; to praise and worship Him; to serve and work for Him—all face to face. God says He is going to live and dwell with us; He is going to take over the management of our lives face to face, guiding and directing us day by day, face to face throughout all of eternity. We shall serve and work for God face to face, be under His immediate presence and fellowship. This is what eternity will be like, what the new heaven and earth will be like. The presence and glory of God will be living and dwelling with us right here on earth.

IV. The Perfection of All Things (vv.4-6).

Note two things.
1. Life will be perfected. This means that the body of man will be perfected; so will the environment and earth. Life will be totally different from what it is now. The very life and utopia for which man has longed will be a living reality. All the sufferings and evil of life and all the bad and negative experiences of life will be gone. Scripture explains the change in the most beautiful and striking way: it declares that "God shall wipe away all tears from their [believer's] eyes." Imagine a world so perfected that there would never again be a tear shed. Look at what Scripture says:

> **"And God shall wipe away all tears from their eyes; and there shall be no more death, neither sorrow, nor crying, neither shall there be any more pain: for the former things are passed away" (v.4).**

- ⇒ There will be no more death: no more aging, murder, killing or war. No more miscarriages or dying children, no more dying mothers or dying fathers, and no more parents who have passed on. No more funerals or cemeteries or burial grounds. Everyone will have a spiritual body, a body that will be perfected, made incorruptible and immortal, perfect in strength and honor. There will be no death in the new heaven and earth. God will wipe away the tears of death.
- ⇒ There will be no more sorrow: no more brokenness, disappointment, regret, guilt, failure, weakness, inferiority, inadequacy, or incapability. No more homelessness, starvation, hunger, or thirst. There will be nothing to make us sorrowful. We will be capable and able, successful and fruitful, confident and secure. There will never be a regret or failure to make us sorrowful. We will be perfected. We will be able to live and serve to the fullest degree without any shortcoming whatsoever. God will wipe away all the tears of sorrow in the new heaven and earth.
- ⇒ There will be no more crying: no more disappointment, arguing, fussing, cursing, divisiveness, drugs, evil, immorality, separation, bitterness, burdens, or

heartache—no more bad things that cut the heart and cause the heart and eyes to cry. Everyone will be perfected and live together in love, joy, and peace—never causing hurt to another person. God will wipe away the tears of crying.

⇒ There will be no more pain: no more diseases, accidents, distress, pressure, abuse, beatings, fights, afflictions, or agony. No more emotional or physical pain. No more of anything that causes pain of any kind. God will wipe away the tears of pain.

But note why. It is because God recreates the universe. It is because "the former things are passed away." God cannot state it any clearer: the earth as it is now is going to pass away. Note again how clear and exact Scripture describes what God is going to do:

> "For the Lamb which is in the midst of the throne shall feed them, and shall lead them unto living fountains of waters: and God shall wipe away all tears from their eyes" (Re.7:17).
> "And God shall wipe away all tears from their eyes; and there shall be no more death, neither sorrow, nor crying, neither shall there be any more pain: for the former things are passed away" (Re.21:4; see 1 Co.15:26; 15:54; 2 Co. 4:17; 1 Pe.4:12-13; Is.25:8; 35:10; 51:11; 60:20; 65:19).

How do we know for sure that God is going to recreate the universe? How do we know that God is going to perfect life for us? *The next point tells us.*

2. God assures us that He is going to perfect all things. He gives us three assurances.

a. God Himself assures us. Note that God Himself spoke from the throne of heaven and declared emphatically that He was going to make all things new:

> "And he that sat upon the throne said, Behold, I make all things new" (v.5).

b. God's Word assures it. God gave a double declaration. He declared that His Words are true and faithful. By true, He means true as opposed to false. He is not lying. He is God; therefore, what He says will happen. By faithful, He means that He will do exactly what He says. We can all count on it. And note: God instructed John to write down all that He said. God wanted us to know about His promise of a new heaven and earth, of a perfected body and life, and He wanted us to be assured of His promise.

c. God's sovereignty assures it. How? By the power and sovereignty of God. God declares, "I am the Alpha and Omega, the beginning and the end." Alpha is the first letter of the Greek alphabet and means *the beginning;* Omega is the last letter and means *the end.* God is declaring that He is the beginning and the ending, the Creator of all things. All things have their beginning in Him. And He is the end of all things, the consummation and goal and the end and objective of all things. All things find their meaning and being in Him. And He spans all things just as the beginning and end span all things. Therefore, He can do as He wills.

The point is this: God has willed a new heaven and earth. Therefore, He has already spoken it into being. He has already declared, "It is done." The clock is set and the event fixed. The minutes of time are ticking away, and the hour will come when the set time arrives.

> "Faithful is he that calleth you, who also will do it" (1 Th.5:24).
> "He abideth faithful: he cannot deny himself" (2 Ti.2:13; see Mt.5:18; Lu.21:33; 1 Co.1:9; 1 K.8:56; Ps.111:7; 146:6).

V. The Citizens (vv.6-8).

There will be the citizens of the new heaven and earth. Note that God Himself is still speaking. What He is saying is important, so important that He must make the declaration Himself. It is too important to have an angelic messenger declare the message. Note: God tells us who the citizens of His new heaven and earth will be; but note something else as well: He tells us who will not be citizens. He warns us that not everyone will live in the new heaven and earth, not everyone will be acceptable to Him. But He shows us how to make sure that we are acceptable, that we do receive the right to become citizens of the new heaven and earth. How?

1. The citizens of the new heaven and earth will be those who thirst for life. God says that He will give the water of life to all those who thirst after it. To thirst after life means that one thirsts...

- to know the life that God wants man to live
- to know the life that God gives
- to know the fulness of life that is in God Himself
- to know the hope of life that God has planned for man
- to know the perfection of life that God longs for man to live

Stated another way, to thirst after life means to thirst after the life that God gives, to thirst after God Himself. It means...

- to know God; to fellowship, commune, and share with God
- to know the salvation, forgiveness, and cleansing of God
- to know the hope, assurance, and security of God
- to live for God, to obey and follow God

2. The citizen of the new heaven and earth will be the overcomer. The overcomer is the person who overcomes this world and remains faithful and loyal to Christ. It means the person who remains pure and follows the Lord Jesus Christ. The overcomer is the person who conquers all the temptations and trials of life. Two great promises are made to the overcomer:

⇒ He will inherit all things, all that the new heaven and earth offer.
⇒ He will be a son of God.

> **"But as many as received him, to them gave he power to become the sons of God, even to them that believe on his name" (Jn.1:12).**
> **"For as many as are led by the Spirit of God, they are the sons of God. For ye have not received the spirit of bondage again to fear; but ye have received the Spirit of adoption, whereby we cry, Abba, Father. The Spirit itself beareth witness with our spirit, that we are the children of God: and if children, then heirs; heirs of God, and joint-heirs with Christ; if so be that we suffer with him, that we may be also glorified together" (Ro.8:14-17; see Ga.4:7; Ph.2:15; 1 Jn.1:3).**

3. The fate of the people who will be rejected is clearly spelled out. What a tragic list it is.

⇒ The *fearful or cowardly*: those who do not confess Christ because they fear what others might say; those who are afraid to give up the world and deny self; those who fear taking a stand for Christ; those who fear to fellowship or become identified with Christian people.

> **"Whosoever therefore shall confess me before men, him will I confess also before my Father which is in heaven. But whosoever shall deny me before men, him will I also deny before my Father which is in heaven" (Mt.10:32-33).**
> **"That if thou shalt confess with thy mouth the Lord Jesus, and shalt believe in thine heart that God hath raised him from the dead, thou shalt be saved" (Ro.10:9; see 2 Ti.2:12; Pr.29:25).**

⇒ The *unbelieving*: those who do not believe that Jesus Christ is the Son of God, the Savior of the world; those who reject Jesus Christ and His death upon the cross for their sins; those who profess Christ, but live hypocritical lives, who show by their sinful behavior that they do not really believe Him.

> "He that believeth on him is not condemned: but he that believeth not is condemned already, because he hath not believed in the name of the only begotten Son of God" (Jn.3:18).
> "I said therefore unto you, that ye shall die in your sins: for if ye believe not that I am he, ye shall die in your sins" (Jn.8:24; see Jn.12:48; 2 Co.4:4; 1 Jn.2:22-23).

⇒ The *abominable or polluted*: those who are worldly and who live worldly lives; those who reach out to touch and taste the impurities and lusts of the world; those who are stained and contaminated and polluted with worldliness; those who refuse to separate from the pleasures and possessions of this world and refuse to turn to God.

> "And take heed to yourselves, lest at any time your hearts be overcharged with surfeiting, and drunkenness, and cares of this life, and so that day come upon you unawares" (Lu.21:34).
> "And be not conformed to this world but be ye transformed by the renewing of your mind, that ye may prove what is that good, and acceptable, and perfect, will of God" (Ro.12:2; see 2 Co.6:17-18; Tit.2:12-13; Js.4:4; 1 Jn.2:15-16;).

⇒ The *murderers*: those who kill and take away the lives of others.

> "Thou shalt not kill" (Ex.20:13).
> "Jesus said, Thou shalt do no murder" (Mt.19:18; see Ro.13:9-10; 1 Pe.4:15; 1 Jn.3:15).

⇒ The *whoremongers or immoral*: those who are sexually impure; those who commit fornication or have sex before marriage; those who commit adultery and homosexuality and all other sexual acts that God forbids; those who look and lust, read and lust, think and lust.

> "Ye have heard that it was said by them of old time, Thou shalt not commit adultery: but I say unto you, That whosoever looketh on a woman to lust after her hath committed adultery with her already in his heart" (Mt.5:27-28).
> "And likewise also the men, leaving the natural use of the woman, burned in their lust one toward another; men with men working that which is unseemly, and receiving in themselves that recompence of their error which was meet" (Ro.1:27; see Ro.13:14; Ep.4:19; 1 Pe.2:11; 4:2-3).

⇒ The *sorcerers*: those who engage in astrology, witchcraft, devil-worship, spiritism, seances, palm-reading, fortune-telling, and all other forms of false beliefs that claim to reveal and control one's fate, life, and destiny.

> "So Saul died for his transgression which he committed against the LORD, even against the word of the LORD which he kept not, and also for asking counsel of one that had a familiar spirit, to inquire of it" (1 Chr.10:13).
> "And when they shall say unto you, Seek unto them that have familiar spirits, and unto wizards that peep, and that mutter: should not a people seek unto their God? for the living to the dead? To the law and

to the testimony: if they speak not according to this word, it is because there is no light in them" (Is.8:19-20; see Mi.5:12; Ga.5:19-20).

⇒ The *idolaters*: those who worship idols, whether idols made with one's hands or just conceived in one's mind; those who have an image of what God is like and worship and follow that image instead of following the God revealed by the Scriptures; those who put the things of this earth before God; those who give their primary attention and devotion to someone or something other than God.

"Wherefore, my dearly beloved, flee from idolatry" (1 Co.10:14).

"Now the works of the flesh are manifest, which are these; Adultery, fornication, uncleanness, lasciviousness, idolatry...they which do such things shall not inherit the kingdom of God" (Ga.5:19-21; see Ep.5:5; Col.3:5-6; Re.21:8; 22:15).

⇒ The *liars*: those who tell falsehoods and do not tell the truth; those who deceive and mislead others; those who are gossipers and talebearers and who pass rumors along.

"But the king shall rejoice in God; every one that sweareth by him shall glory: but the mouth of them that speak lies shall be stopped" (Ps.63:11).

"A false witness shall not be unpunished; and he that speaketh lies shall not escape" (Pr.19:5; Is.44:25; Re.21:8).

Any person who does not repent and turn away from these things—any person who does not turn to God for forgiveness of these things—any person who does not forsake these things—that person will not enter into the new heaven and earth. He will not be a citizen of the new heaven and earth. Where does he go? Scripture is clear:

"[They] shall have their part in the lake which burneth with fire and brimstone: which is the second death" (v.8).

PART V

RESOURCE
CHART
SECTION

Contents

CHART 1

THE PICTURE OF THE BELIEVER'S LIFE IN THE TABERNACLE

(The Seven Essential Steps of the Believer's Life or Walk)

The Tabernacle gives a descriptive picture of the believer's life. Seven *essential steps* are symbolized, picturing the believer's life as he walks day by day, marching toward the promised land of heaven. All seven steps are based upon the LORD God Himself, upon His Person, His holiness, and His mercy. His holiness demanded the life of the sinner, but His mercy accepted the sacrifice of a substitute. Through faith in this simple picture of the Tabernacle, a person can approach God and become acceptable to Him, can begin his walk or pilgrimage to the promised land of God, to heaven itself.

Note the facts about the seven essential steps:

⇒ A person must approach each step in proper sequence. It is important to note that God's design for the Tabernacle began from the inside and moved outward. God began with the Ark, the place where God's very presence dwelt, and ended with the Altar of Burnt Offering. This is the way of *grace*. This is looking at the Tabernacle from *God's perspective*. However, as man approached God he started from the outside of the Tabernacle. Man started by entering the only door into the Tabernacle and walking up to the Altar of Burnt Offering. He concluded his journey at the Ark and Mercy Seat where the High Priest approached the presence of God in his behalf. This is the way of *faith*. This is looking at the Tabernacle from *man's perspective*.

⇒ The believer must experience each step listed below as he follows God to the promised land of heaven. The gospel of Jesus Christ cannot be watered down with an easy *believism*. There are no shortcuts between the cross (the Altar of Burnt Offering) and the Throne of God (the Ark and Mercy Seat). Man must *experience* each symbol, each step on the march to the promised land. Anything less than this is not the true gospel.

⇒ The most important step is the first one. This is where a person's journey must begin: at the door.

Please note: This chart is useful in helping a seeker or a new believer understand the gospel of Jesus Christ. As you lead a person through the great foundational truths found in this chart, remember...

- to fully grasp the *purpose* of each furnishing. This will help you explain the furnishing and what it did.
- to fully grasp the practical *meaning* of each symbol. All Biblical truth must be joined with practical Biblical application.

306

STEP #1	THE PURPOSE OF THE FURNISHING OF THE TABERNACLE	THE PRACTICAL MEANING OF THE SYMBOL	SUPPORTING SCRIPTURE
God's Invitation to Man.	The Gate of the Outer Courtyard ⇒ There was only one gate into the Tabernacle. The purpose for this gate was to invite man to come into the presence of God. The only way for the person to approach God was to walk through the gate of the Outer Courtyard. **"And for the gate of the court *shall be* an hanging of twenty cubits, *of* blue, and purple, and scarlet, and fine twined linen, wrought with needlework: *and* their pillars *shall be* four, and their sockets four"** **(Ex.27:16).**	*God invites man to enter His presence: any person who will believe in and completely trust Jesus Christ will be welcomed into God's presence.* ⇒ The gate into the Tabernacle taught at least two things: • There is only one way to enter God's presence; there are not many ways as most men think and practice. • God has to be approached in a very specific way, in God's perfect way. No person will ever live with God unless he approaches God in the right way. Jesus Christ is the right way to God. **"For God so loved the world, that he gave his only begotten Son, that whosoever believeth in him should not perish, but have everlasting life" (Jn.3:16).**	*"Enter ye in at the strait gate: for wide is the gate, and broad is the way, that leadeth to destruction, and many there be which go in thereat: Because strait is the gate, and narrow is the way, which leadeth unto life, and few there be that find it" (Mt.7:13-14).*

STEP #2	THE PURPOSE OF THE FURNISHING OF THE TABERNACLE	THE PRACTICAL MEANING OF THE SYMBOL	SUPPORTING SCRIPTURE
God's Reconciliation with Man.	The Altar of Burnt Offering ⇒ The purpose of the Altar was to meet man's need for atonement or reconciliation with God through the sacrifice of the lamb. **"And thou shalt set the altar of the burnt**	*Jesus Christ is the Lamb of God who was sacrificed on the cross for the sins of mankind. Jesus Christ reconciles man to God by His death on the cross.* ⇒ The true Altar upon which the Lamb was slain for the sins of the believer was the cross of Jesus Christ.	*"Forasmuch as ye know that ye were not redeemed with corruptible things, as silver and gold, from your vain conversation received by tradition from your fathers; But with the precious blood of Christ, as of a lamb without blemish and without spot" (1 Pe. 1:18-19).*

	offering before the door of the tabernacle of the tent of the congregation" (Ex.40:6).	"The next day John seeth Jesus coming unto him, and saith, Behold the Lamb of God, which taketh away the sin of the world" (Jn.1:29). "Wherefore in all things it behooved him to be made like unto *his* brethren, that he might be a merciful and faithful high priest in things *pertaining* to God, to make reconciliation for the sins of the people" (He.2:17).	*"For he hath made him to be sin for us, who knew no sin; that we might be made the righteousness of God in him" (2 Co.5:21).*

STEP #3	THE PURPOSE OF THE FURNISHING OF THE TABERNACLE	THE PRACTICAL MEANING OF THE SYMBOL	SUPPORTING SCRIPTURE
The believer's sanctification: his washing & cleansing, the forgiveness of his sin.	The Bronze Wash Basin ⇒ The purpose of the Wash Basin was for the priests to wash off the blood, soot, and dirt from their hands and feet. "Thou shalt also make a laver *of* brass, and his foot *also of* brass, to wash *withal:* and thou shalt put it between the tabernacle of the congregation and the altar, and thou shalt put water therein. For Aaron and his sons shall wash their hands and their feet thereat: When they go into the tabernacle of the congregation, they shall wash with water, that they die not; or when they come near to the altar to minister, to burn offering made by fire unto the LORD: So they shall wash their hands and their feet, that they die not: and it shall be a statute for ever to them, *even* to him and to his seed throughout their generations" (Ex.30:18-21).	*God has sanctified the believer by washing and cleansing him, by forgiving his sin through the blood of Christ.* ⇒ The Word of God declares that we must be washed with the cleansing blood of Jesus Christ. It is the Word of God that reminds us of our need: that we must be... • sanctified • purified We must, therefore, study the Word of God in order to become more and more sanctified, more and more set apart to God. "Now ye are clean through the word which I have spoken unto you" (Jn.15:3).	*"Wherewithal shall a young man cleanse his way? by taking heed thereto according to thy word" (Ps.119:9). "Sanctify them through thy truth: thy word is truth" (Jn. 17:17). "That he might sanctify and cleanse it with the washing of water by the word" (Ep. 5:26; see Js.1:22-25). "Study to show thyself approved unto God, a workman that needeth not to be ashamed, rightly dividing the word of truth" (2 Ti. 2:15). "All scripture is given by inspiration of God, and is profitable for doctrine, for reproof, for correction, for instruction in righteousness" (2 Ti.3:16).*

STEP #4	THE PURPOSE OF THE FURNISHING OF THE TABERNACLE	THE PRACTICAL MEANING OF THE SYMBOL	SUPPORTING SCRIPTURE
The believer's walk with God.	The Lampstand ⇒ The purpose of the Lampstand was to illuminate the Holy Place, to show the High Priest he needed God's light in order to know... • how to know God • how to serve God • how to walk before God "And thou shalt make the seven lamps thereof: and they shall light the lamps thereof, that they may give light over against it" (Ex.25:37).	*The believer's heart is filled with God's guiding light. God as the Light of the world shows the believer how to walk with God:* ⇒ It is God who provides the light that burns perpetually, that dissolves all darkness from the life of the believer. "Then spake Jesus again unto them, saying, I am the light of the world: he that followeth me shall not walk in darkness, but shall have the light of life" (Jn.8:12). "That was the true Light, which lighteth every man that cometh into the world" (Jn.1:9; see 1 Jn.2:8).	"The LORD is my light and my salvation; whom shall I fear? the LORD is the strength of my life; of whom shall I be afraid?" (Ps.27:1). "The people that walked in darkness have seen a great light: they that dwell in the land of the shadow of death, upon them hath the light shined" (Is.9:2). "For God, who commanded the light to shine out of darkness, hath shined in our hearts, to give the light of the knowledge of the glory of God in the face of Jesus Christ" (2 Co. 4:6; see Re.21:23).

STEP #5	THE PURPOSE OF THE FURNISHING OF THE TABERNACLE	THE PRACTICAL MEANING OF THE SYMBOL	SUPPORTING SCRIPTURE
The believer's nourishment (food for the soul).	The Table of Showbread ⇒ The Table's purpose was to hold the showbread, to present the showbread before the face of God, to present it as an offering of thanksgiving and dependence upon God. "And thou shalt set upon the table showbread before me alway" (Ex.25:30).	*The believer's spiritual hunger is satisfied with God who is the bread of life* ⇒ Jesus Christ is the fulfillment of the Showbread. Jesus Christ is the Bread of Life who nourishes the believer's soul by giving the believer eternal joy, satisfaction, and fulfillment. "And Jesus said unto them, I am the bread of life: he that cometh to me shall never hunger; and he that believeth on me shall never thirst" (Jn.6:35; see Ps.107:9; Is.58:11).	"And he humbled thee, and suffered thee to hunger, and fed thee with manna, which thou knewest not, neither did thy fathers know; that he might make thee know that man doth not live by bread only, but by every word that proceedeth out of the mouth of the LORD doth man live" (De.8:3; see Jn.15:11; Ps.63:5). "For the bread of God is he which cometh down from heaven, and giveth life unto the world" (Jn.6:33; see Jn.10:10).

STEP #6	THE PURPOSE OF THE FURNISH-ING OF THE TABERNACLE	THE PRACTICAL MEANING OF THE SYMBOL	SUPPORTING SCRIPTURE
The believer's intercession, his prayer life.	The Altar of Incense ⇒ The purpose for the Altar was twofold: • The Altar was to be the place where sweet incense was offered up to the Lord every morning and evening. • The Altar of Incense was to be the place where a permanent incense ascended up to the LORD. "And Aaron shall burn thereon sweet incense every morning: when he dresseth the lamps, he shall burn incense upon it. And when Aaron lighteth the lamps at even, he shall burn incense upon it, a perpetual incense before the LORD throughout your generations" (Ex.30:7-8).	*The believer's prayers are to ascend up to God and be as consistent and common as breathing.* ⇒ The believer's prayer life is to be an unending communion and intercession with God "And whatsoever we ask, we receive of him, because we keep his commandments, and do those things that are pleasing in his sight" (1 Jn.3:22). "Pray without ceasing" (1 Th.5:17). "Praying always with all prayer and supplication in the Spirit, and watching thereunto with all perseverance and supplication for all saints" (Ep.6:18).	"And another angel came and stood at the altar, having a golden censer; and there was given unto him much incense, that he should offer it with the prayers of all saints upon the golden altar which was before the throne" (Re.8:3). "Seek the LORD and his strength, seek his face continually" (1 Chr. 16:11). "And he spake a parable unto them to this end, that men ought always to pray, and not to faint" (Lu. 18:1). "Hitherto have ye asked nothing in my name: ask, and ye shall receive, that your joy may be full" (Jn. 16:24). "And ye shall seek me, and find me, when ye shall search for me with all your heart" (Je.29:13).

STEP #7	THE PURPOSE OF THE FURNISH-ING OF THE TABERNACLE	THE PRACTICAL MEANING OF THE SYMBOL	SUPPORTING SCRIPTURE
The believer's communion & fellowship with God.	The Inner Veil, The Ark and The Mercy Seat ⇒ The purpose of the Inner Veil was to separate the Holy Place from the Most Holy Place. The Most Holy Place was where the presence of God was manifested in a very special way. "And thou shalt hang up the vail under the taches, that thou mayest bring in thither	*The ultimate goal for every believer should be to experience an intimate communion with the God of all mercy and grace* ⇒ The Ark and Mercy Seat is the place where the believer's most intimate moments of communion are spent with God, spent in His most Holy presence "Let us therefore come boldly unto the	"Now of the things which we have spoken this is the sum: We have such an high priest, who is set on the right hand of the throne of the Majesty in the heavens" (He.8:1). "Looking unto Jesus the author and finisher of our faith; who for the joy that was set before him endured the cross, despising the shame, and is set down at the right hand of the throne of God" (He.12:2).

within the vail the ark of the testimony: and the vail shall divide unto you between the holy *place* and the most holy" (Ex.26:33).

⇒ The Purpose of the Ark and Mercy Seat was...
- to be the place where God's testimony (the Ten Commandments) was kept, the place where God was to give very special instructions to His people
- to be the place where God met with His people
- to be the place of mercy, the place where God's mercy was symbolized
- to be the place where God would instruct and guide His people

"And there I will meet with thee, and I will commune with thee from above the mercy seat, from between the two cherubims which *are* upon the ark of the testimony, of all *things* which I will give thee in commandment unto the children of Israel" (Ex.25:22).

throne of grace, that we may obtain mercy, and find grace to help in time of need" (He.4:16).

"That which we have seen and heard declare we unto you, that ye also may have fellowship with us: and truly our fellowship *is* with the Father, and with his Son Jesus Christ" (1 Jn.1:3).

"Who *is* a God like unto thee, that pardoneth iniquity, and passeth by the transgression of the remnant of his heritage? he retaineth not his anger for ever, because he delighteth *in* mercy" (Mi.7:18).

"To him that overcometh will I grant to sit with me in my throne, even as I also overcame, and am set down with my Father in his throne" (Re.3:21).

"And the four and twenty elders and the four beasts fell down and worshipped God that sat on the throne, saying, Amen; Alleluia. And a voice came out of the throne, saying, Praise our God, all ye his servants, and ye that fear him, both small and great" (Re. 19:4-5).

CHART 2
HOW CHRIST FULFILLED
THE SYMBOLISM OF
THE TABERNACLE

I. THE SYMBOLIC LESSONS CONCERNING THE ARK OR CHEST, Ex.25:10-22; 35:12; 37:1-5; 39:35; 40:3, 20-21

II. THE SYMBOLIC LESSONS CONCERNING THE MERCY SEAT, Ex.25:17-21; 35:12; 37:6-9; 39:35; 40:3, 20

III. THE SYMBOLIC LESSONS CONCERNING THE TABLE OF SHOWBREAD, Ex.25:23-30; 35:13; 37:10-16; 39:36; 40:4, 22-23

IV. THE SYMBOLIC LESSONS CONCERNING THE LAMPSTAND, Ex.25:31-40; 27:20-21; 35:14; 37:17-24; 39:37; 40:4, 24-25

V. THE SYMBOLIC LESSONS CONCERNING THE SANCTUARY, Ex.26:1-30; 35:17-18, 23, 25-26; 36:8-34; 39:33-34; 40:17-19

VI. THE SYMBOLIC LESSONS CONCERNING THE INNER VEIL, Ex.26:31-35; 35:12; 36:35-36; 39:34; 40:3, 21

VII. THE SYMBOLIC LESSONS CONCERNING THE OUTER VEIL, Ex.26:36-37; 35:15; 36:37-38; 39:38; 40:5, 22

VIII. THE SYMBOLIC LESSONS CONCERNING THE BRAZEN ALTAR, Ex.27:1-8; 35:16; 38:1-7; 39:39; 40:6, 29

IX. THE SYMBOLIC LESSONS CONCERNING THE WALLS OF THE TABERNACLE, Ex.27:9-19; 35:17; 36:20-34; 38:9-20; 39:33, 40; 40:8, 33

X. THE SYMBOLIC LESSONS CONCERNING THE DOOR OR GATE, Ex.27:16; 35:17; 38:18-19; 39:40; 40:8, 33

XI. THE SYMBOLIC LESSONS CONCERNING THE ALTAR OF INCENSE, Ex.30:1-10; 35:15; 37:25-29; 39:38; 40:5, 26-27

XII. THE SYMBOLIC LESSONS CONCERNING THE BRONZE WASH BASIN, Ex.30:17-21; 35:16; 38:8; 39:39; 40:7, 30-32

I. THE SYMBOLIC LESSONS CONCERNING THE ARK OR CHEST, Ex.25:10-22; 35:12; 37:1-5; 39:35; 40:3, 20-21

THE FACTS CONCERNING THE ARK	WHAT IS TAUGHT BY THE ARK OR CHEST	HOW CHRIST FULFILLED THE SYMBOLISM
1. The facts: a. The Ark was made of acacia wood (v.10): a hard, durable wood, resistant to weather and insects. b. The Ark was a box-like or chest-like structure: 3¾' long x 2¼' wide x 2¼' high (1.1 meters by .07 meters by .07 meters) (v.10). c. The Ark was overlaid with pure gold both inside and out, and it had a gold molding around the rim (v.11). d. The Ark had four gold rings attached to its four lower corners, at the base of the ark (v.12). e. The Ark had two strong poles made of acacia wood overlaid with gold (v.13). f. The poles were slid into the gold rings on the Ark for the purpose of carrying it (v.14). And note: once inserted, the poles were never removed. They were a permanent part of the Ark of God. g. The *Testimony of God* (the stone tablets of God's covenant, the Ten Commandments) was put into the Ark. h. The Ark actually contained three items: the tables of the law or Ten Commandments (Ex. 25:16f; De.9:9; 10:5), the golden pot of manna (Ex.16:32-34), and Aaron's rod (Nu.17:1-11).	2. What the Ark of the Covenant taught: a. The Ark was the place—the very special place—where God met with His people (v.22). God's presence was manifested in a very special way above the Ark of the Covenant. The people knew this. Therefore, when they needed a special sense of God's presence—when they needed to feel a special closeness to God—they knew where to go. They went to the Tabernacle, the ground surrounding the Tabernacle, worshipping and seeking forgiveness by offering sacrifice to the LORD. b. The Ark was the place of mercy, the place where God's mercy was clearly pictured (v.22). God's mercy was pictured in the Mercy Seat that sat upon the Ark. (See The Mercy Seat—next chart.) The people were to learn all about the Mercy Seat and the blood sprinkled upon it. They were to learn that the blood made atonement for their sins, reconciled them to God. They were to learn that the mercy of God was to be showered upon them because of the blood, because they believed and trusted the blood of the sacrifice to cover their sins. c. The Ark was the place where God instructed and guided His people (v.22). The Ark was to be the symbol of the	3. How Christ fulfilled the symbolism of the Ark of the Covenant: a. Jesus Christ promised to be with His people always. **"For where two or three are gathered together in my name, there am I in the midst of them" (Mt.18:20).** **"Teaching them to observe all things whatsoever I have commanded you: and, lo, I am with you alway,** *even* **unto the end of the world. Amen" (Mt.28:20).** b. Jesus Christ shed His own blood and sprinkled it on the Mercy Seat, washing us from our sins. **"Who his own self bare our sins in his own body on the tree, that we, being dead to sins, should live unto righteousness: by whose stripes ye were healed" (1 Pe.2:24).** **"For Christ also hath once suffered for sins, the just for the unjust, that he might bring us to God, being put to death in the flesh, but quickened by the Spirit" (1 Pe.3:18).** **"Unto him that loved us, and washed us from our sins in his own blood" (Re.1:5).** c. Jesus Christ is the Good Shepherd, the One who leads, protects, and guides His people, the precious sheep of His pasture. **"I am the good shepherd: the good shepherd**

	throne of God. His divine presence was apparently manifested in a very special way right above the empty space of the Mercy Seat, right between the cherubim. From that position, God promised to speak to His people, to give them His commandments, instructions, and guidance; therefore, when God's people needed help or guidance, they were to come to the Tabernacle. d. The Ark of God held God's testimony, the two tablets of the covenant, that is, the Ten Commandments (v.21). Therefore, man is to keep the Ten Commandments.	**giveth his life for the sheep" (Jn.10:11).** d. Jesus Christ kept the Law of the covenant that was kept in the Ark, kept the Law perfectly, without sin. **"For we have not an high priest which cannot be touched with the feeling of our infirmities; but was in all points tempted like as *we are, yet* without sin" (He.4:15).**

II. THE SYMBOLIC LESSONS CONCERNING THE MERCY SEAT, Ex.25:17-21; 35:12; 37:6-9; 39:35; 40:3, 20

THE FACTS CONCERNING THE MERCY SEAT	WHAT IS TAUGHT BY THE MERCY SEAT	HOW CHRIST FULFILLED THE SYMBOLISM
1. The facts: Note the plan and design for the Mercy Seat or Atonement Cover. Keep in mind that it was placed on top of the Ark, that it served both as a *lid* to the Ark or Chest and as the Mercy Seat for God's Holy Presence. a. The Mercy Seat was made of pure gold (v.17). b. The Mercy Seat was oblong: the very same size as the Ark itself: 3¾' long x 2¼' wide (v.17). c. There was to be a cherubim at each end of the Mercy Seat (v.18-20). Note how the Mercy Seat was made: 1) It was made of pure gold 2) It was 3¾' long by 2¼' wide (1.1 meters by .07 meters)	2. What the Mercy Seat taught: a. There was the picture that points toward the *finished work* of Christ. The High Priest was never allowed to sit on the Mercy Seat, no matter how tired or weary he became. In fact, the priests were always working when in the Tabernacle. Their priestly work was never finished: they were continually offering sacrifice and ministering. b. There was the picture that pointed toward God covering the law with His mercy. No person can keep the law, not perfectly. And perfection is required in order to live in God's holy presence. How then can	3. How Christ fulfilled the symbolism of the Mercy Seat: a. When Jesus Christ offered Himself as the *Perfect Sacrifice* to God, His work was finished. His sacrifice for the sins of people was perfect: no other sacrifice was ever needed. Therefore, Christ was able to sit down on the right hand of God's throne. b. God's mercy has been given us through His Son, the Lord Jesus Christ. God gave His Son to be the *Perfect Sacrifice* for our sins. The mercy of God shown us in Jesus Christ covers the law, covers our sin, our failure to keep the law. When we trust Jesus Christ as our

3) It had a cherubim at each end of the Mercy Seat 4) It was made by hammering out the gold 5) One cherub was hammered out at one end of the Mercy Seat & the other cherub at the other end 6) The wings of the cherubim were spread upward overshadowing the Mercy Seat 7) The cherubim faced each other, looking toward the Mercy Seat d. The Mercy Seat was placed on top of the Ark (v.21).	we ever become acceptable to God, be allowed to live in heaven with Him? By His mercy. God's mercy has been given us through His Son, the Lord Jesus Christ. God gave His Son to be the *Perfect Sacrifice* for our sins. The mercy of God shown us in Jesus Christ covers the law, covers our sin, our failure to keep the law. When we trust Jesus Christ as our Savior, the mercy of God covers all the law—all the accusations of the law against us, all our failure to keep the law, all the guilt that gnaws at our hearts and convicts us.	Savior, the mercy of God covers all the law—all the accusations of the law against us, all our failure to keep the law, all the guilt that gnaws at our hearts and convicts us **"For all have sinned, and come short of the glory of God; Being justified freely by his grace through the redemption that is in Christ Jesus: Whom God hath set forth to be a propitiation through faith in his blood, to declare his righteousness for the remission of sins that are past, through the forbearance of God"** (Ro.3:23-25; see He.10:11-12; Ph.2:8-10).

III. THE SYMBOLIC LESSONS CONCERNING THE TABLE OF SHOWBREAD, Ex.25:23-30; 35:13; 37:10-16; 39:36; 40:4, 22-23

THE FACTS CONCERNING THE TABLE OF SHOWBREAD	WHAT IS TAUGHT BY THE TABLE OF SHOWBREAD	HOW CHRIST FULFILLED THE SYMBOLISM
1. The facts: a. The table was made of acacia wood: a hard and durable wood, resistant to insects, disease, and weather (v.23). b. The table was quite small: 3' long & 1½' wide & 2¼' high (.9 meters x .5 meters x .7 meters) (v.23). c. The table was overlaid with pure gold and had a gold molding that ran around it (v.24). d. The table had a rim three inches wide around the top with a gold molding around it (v.25). e. The table had four gold rings attached to the four corners where the legs were: to support the poles for carrying the table (vv.26-27). f. The poles to carry the table were made of	2. What the Table of Showbread taught: a. The twelve loaves of showbread represented an offering from each tribe of Israel, an offering of thanksgiving to God. Each tribe was represented as thanking God for the bread and food He provided, for meeting their physical needs. b. The twelve loaves also represented the people's dependence upon God. Note that the loaves sat in God's presence, before His very face. The people were to acknowledge their dependence upon God, acknowledge that they needed His provision. They needed His watchful eye upon the bread, upon them as His followers. They needed Him to continue to provide	3. How Christ fulfilled the symbolism of the table of showbread: • Jesus Christ is the Bread of Life, the nourishment upon which man must feed in order to know and worship God. **"I am that bread of life"** (Jn.6:48). **"For the bread of God is he which cometh down from heaven, and giveth life unto the world"** (Jn.6:33). **"And Jesus said unto them, I am the bread of life: he that cometh to me shall never hunger; and he that believeth on me shall never thirst"** (Jn.6:35). **"This is the bread which cometh down from heaven, that a man may eat thereof, and not die. I am the living bread which came down from heaven: if any man eat of this bread, he shall**

acacia wood and over-laid with gold (v.28).

g. The table's plates and dishes were made of gold as well as the pitchers and bowls that were used in pouring out drink offerings (v.29).

their bread and food, continue to look after and care for them. Their dependence upon God as the Provision of life was symbolized in the showbread as well as their offering of thanksgiving.

c. The twelve loaves also acknowledged their trust in God. By setting the bread before God, they were declaring their belief and trust that He would continue to meet their physical needs.

d. The showbread also pointed to Jesus Christ as the Bread of Life. Scripture declares that He is the Living Bread that came *out of* heaven to satisfy the hunger of a person's soul.

e. The showbread pointed to God Himself as the nourishment that man really needs. Far too often, man tries to live his life apart from God's provision and presence.

f. The showbread pointed to the great need of people for the bread of God's presence and worship. A constant diet of unhealthy things will cause a person to become sick and unhealthy.

g. The showbread pointed to the bread that we all desperately need, the bread...
  • that satisfies the hunger of our hearts
  • that supplies our needs
  • that provides for us
  • that nourishes fellowship among us (see 1 Jn.1:3; Re.3:20)

h. The showbread pointed to the spiritual needs of man. This is seen in that the showbread sat in the Tabernacle itself, the very place where spiritual needs were met. This truth was dictated by both God and His Son, the Lord Jesus Christ.

live for ever: and the bread that I will give is my flesh, which I will give for the life of the world" (Jn.6:50-51).

"This is that bread which came down from heaven: not as your fathers did eat manna, and are dead: he that eateth me, even he shall live by me" (Jn.6:58).

IV. THE SYMBOLIC LESSONS CONCERNING THE LAMPSTAND, Ex.25:31-40; 27:20-21; 35:14; 37:17-24; 39:37; 40:4, 24-25

THE FACTS CONCERNING THE LAMPSTAND	WHAT IS TAUGHT BY THE LAMPSTAND	HOW CHRIST FULFILLED THE SYMBOLISM
1. The facts: The design and materials of the Lampstand were exact and precise (25:31-39). Again, God Himself designed the Lampstand. Human creativity had no part in designing this item, no part in designing anything in the Tabernacle. No person knew the perfect way to approach God; no person knew perfectly how to please God in his worship. God and God alone knew how He was to be approached and worshipped. Therefore, God and God alone had to design the Lampstand and the other furnishings that were to be used in worshipping Him. a. The Lampstand was made of pure gold, hammered out as one piece (v.31). The entire Lampstand was of one piece of gold: the base and center stem, the flower-like lamp cups, buds, and blossoms. b. The Lampstand had six branches (vv.32-38). • Three branches were on each side (v.32). • Each branch had three cups shaped like almond flowers with buds and blossoms (v.33). c. The Lampstand had four similar flower-like cups, one flower bud under each pair of branches (v.34). d. The Lampstand had one blossom or bud under each pair of branches (v.35). All this means that the total number of ornaments was 69. Imagine 69 ornaments on one Lampstand. What beauty	2. What the Lampstand taught: a. The Lampstand taught that a person needs light and illumination in order to know God and serve God. b. The Lampstand pictures God's people (Israel) as the light of the world, as God's witness to the world. c. The Lampstand points to Jesus Christ as the Light of the world. d. The Lampstand points to God as the Light of the world, the Light that shows man how to approach and worship Him. It was God who planned and designed the Lampstand, who showed the Israelites exactly how to approach and worship Him. He does the same for us.	3. How Christ fulfilled the symbolism of the Lampstand: • Jesus Christ is the true Lampstand. Christ came into the world to give light and illumination so that we might know and serve God. As the Light of the world, Christ fulfills the symbolism of the Lampstand. Christ and Christ alone is able to bring people out of the darkness of sin and death and give them the light of salvation and eternal life. "The same [John the Baptist] came for a witness, to bear witness of the Light, that all *men* through him might believe. He was not that Light, but *was sent* to bear witness of that Light. *That* [Jesus Christ] was the true Light, which lighteth every man that cometh into the world" (Jn.1:7-9). "In him was life; and the life was the light of men. And the light shineth in darkness; and the darkness comprehended it not [can never extinguish it]" (Jn. 1:4-5). "Then spake Jesus again unto them, saying, I am the light of the world: he that followeth me shall not walk in darkness, but shall have the light of life" (Jn.8:12). "I am come a light into the world, that whosoever believeth on me should not abide in darkness" (Jn. 12:46). "Jesus saith unto him, I am the way, the truth, and the life: no man cometh unto the Father, but by me" (Jn.14:6).

		"For God, who commanded the light to shine out of darkness, hath shined in our hearts, to *give* the light of the knowledge of the glory of God in the face of Jesus Christ" (2 Co.4:6).
and splendor must have attracted the eye of the priest as he entered the Holy Place and saw the glowing, flickering flames arising from the seven light holders (six branches and the center stem).		
e. The decorations (flower buds) and branches were hammered out as one piece with the stem (v.36).		
f. The seven lamps were made for the Lampstand and set so they would reflect the light forward (v.37).		
g. The Lampstand and the accessories required 75 pounds of pure gold (v.39).		

V. THE SYMBOLIC LESSONS CONCERNING THE SANCTUARY, Ex.26:1-30; 35:17-18, 23, 25-26; 36:8-34; 39:33-34; 40:17-19

THE FACTS CONCERNING THE SANCTUARY	WHAT IS TAUGHT BY THE SANCTUARY	HOW CHRIST FULFILLED THE SYMBOLISM
1. The facts:	2. What the Sanctuary taught:	3. How Christ fulfilled the symbolism of the Sanctuary:
A. The Tabernacle was a tent constructed of four coverings that were to serve as the roof and sides of the Tabernacle.	A. The four coverings of the Tabernacle Tent	A. The symbol of the coverings of the Tabernacle Tent
a. The *first covering* was made of ten *linen curtains* that served as the inside ceiling and walls (vv.1-6). This inner covering was what the priests saw as they ministered in the Holy Place and in the Most Holy Place. To behold such a striking beauty was the greatest of privileges, a privilege that no one else had. Note the facts about these unique curtains:	a. There are different forms of worship, certain steps to take in approaching God. b. There are some initial steps to take in approaching God before one approaches Him in the most intimate worship. c. God is righteous and holy and completely separate from man, even from the religious who move about and minister within the walls of religion.	a. *The Inner Curtains:* Christ is pure and righteous; therefore, Christ fulfilled the symbolism of these inner curtains by being the perfect embodiment of purity and righteousness. "For he hath made him to be sin for us, who knew no sin; that we might be made the righteousness of God in him" (2 Co.5:21).
1) The design of cherubim was embroidered on each curtain (v.1). With a background color of blue, purple, and scarlet, the	d. God must be approached in reverence and awe and ever so carefully by men, even by the religious who are involved in His service.	b. *The Covering of Goat Hair:* Christ, being perfectly pure and righteous, was able to become the sin-offering for the sins of His people. The goat hair was probably black (see Song of Solomon 1:5).

THE FACTS CONCERNING THE SANCTUARY	WHAT IS TAUGHT BY THE SANCTUARY	HOW CHRIST FULFILLED THE SYMBOLISM
curtains were without doubt breathtaking. 2) The size of each curtain was about 42 feet long by 6 feet wide (v.2). Two groups of five curtains each were stitched together to make two sets of long curtains (v.3). 3) The loops and clasps to join and fasten the curtains together were made of blue material and sewn along the edges (v.4). A total of fifty loops was to be sewn on each curtain (v.5). The curtains were fastened together by making fifty gold clasps that were inserted through the connecting loops. This made the Tabernacle a single tent (v.6). b. The *second covering* was made of *goat hair.* These are the facts that apply to the covering of goat hair: 1) The number of the curtains was eleven (v.7). 2) The size of each curtain was about 45 feet long by 6 feet wide (v.8). Five of the curtains were joined together into one set and six curtains into another set. The sixth curtain was to be folded double at the front of the tent (v.9). 3) The loops and clasps fastened the curtains together, making the curtains a single covering for the tent or Tabernacle. Note how they were made: ⇒ Fifty loops were sewn along the edge of both curtains.		Therefore, Christ fulfilled the symbolism of the goat covering by taking the blackness of sin upon Himself. (See note, pt.2—Ex.26:1-4 for more discussion.) **"Who his own self bare our sins in his own body on the tree, that we, being dead to sins, should live unto righteousness: by whose stripes ye were healed" (1 Pe.2:24).** c. *The Covering of Ram Skin Dyed Red:* Christ willingly shed His blood for mankind. Therefore, the third covering of ram skins *dyed red* points to the sacrificial blood of Jesus Christ that was shed for man. **"For this is my blood of the new testament, which is shed for many for the remission of sins" (Mt.26:28).** d. *The Outside Leather Covering:* Christ is our protective separation from the world and from the coming wrath of God against the evil of the world; therefore, Christ fulfilled the symbolism of the outer cover. Just as the outer covering protected the Tabernacle from the elements of the world, Jesus Christ protects us from the world's perils and temptations and from God's terrible wrath against the sins of the world. **"Who gave himself for our sins, that he might deliver us from this present evil world, according to the will of God and our Father" (Ga.1:4).**

THE FACTS CONCERNING THE SANCTUARY	WHAT IS TAUGHT BY THE SANCTUARY	HOW CHRIST FULFILLED THE SYMBOLISM
⇒ Fifty bronze clasps were made for fastening the curtains together (vv.10-11). 4) The extra half sheet length of this first covering hung down at the rear of the Tabernacle (v.12). The goat hair curtain hung 18 inches over the sides of the Tabernacle. c. The *third covering of ram skins* symbolized the sacrificial blood. The ram skins had the wool removed and were then dyed red. Red, of course, is symbolic of the sacrificial blood. d. The *outside covering* was the covering of *leather or of seal skins.* It was the covering that kept the Tabernacle safe from the elements of the weather and the wilderness: the scorching sun, the torrential rains, the wind-blasted sand, and the wild animals. Moving from campsite to campsite, the Tabernacle obviously took a constant beating. The covering of leather protected the Tabernacle from the outside, from the elements of the world.		
B. The Tabernacle was a tent hanging over wood framing (acacia wood). Note the facts about the wood framing: a. The size of each framing board was 15 feet long by 2¼ feet wide with two pegs set parallel to each other for hooking to the base (vv.15-17). b. The framing consisted of the following items: 1) A wall, a frame of twenty boards on the south side (v.18). On the south side there	B. The Foundation of the Tabernacle tent: The Redemption and Stability of Christ a. The foundation of the Tabernacle was firmly planted... • in the shifting sands of the desert (a symbol of the world and its wilderness) • under God's direction and care as He led His people from campsite to campsite • in God's ability to save helpless men	B. The Foundation of the Tabernacle tent: The Redemption and Stability of Christ a. *The foundation of the Tabernacle:* Christ fulfilled the symbolism of the foundation of the Tabernacle. How? By dying upon the cross and redeeming man from his sins. By this act, Christ became the foundation of redemption for every believer. The silver in the Tabernacle was an ever-present reminder of

THE FACTS CONCERNING THE SANCTUARY	WHAT IS TAUGHT BY THE SANCTUARY	HOW CHRIST FULFILLED THE SYMBOLISM
was a foundation of forty silver sockets or bases, two under each board which were joined together by pegs (v.19). 2) A wall, a frame of twenty boards on the north side (v.20). Like the south side, the north side had a foundation of forty silver sockets, two sockets under each board (v.21). Each one of the silver sockets required about seventy-five pounds of silver. 3) A wall frame of six boards on the west (v.22). 4) A framing post of two boards for each corner (v.23)... • that was joined together at the bottom • that was joined together at the top, fitted into a single ring (v.24) • that had a total of eight board frames and a foundation of sixteen silver sockets, two under each board (v.25) 5) Fifteen durable crossbars (acacia wood). There were... • Five crossbars for the south (v.26) • Five crossbars for the north (v.27) • Five crossbars for the west (v.27) The exact design as to how these crossbars were arranged on each of the three walls is unknown. What is known is that the center crossbar ran from end to end in the middle of the frames (v.28).	b. The 15 crossbars served as a means of stability to the wood framing. Without the support of the crossbars, the Tabernacle would have been at the mercy of every contrary wind. The Scripture gives no reason why God wanted five crossbars for each wall. What we do know and can apply in a most practical way is the purpose of the crossbars: to give stability and support.	man's need for atonement: for reconciliation with God, for redemption. The foundation of the Tabernacle was a foundation of silver. This pictured a glorious truth: the foundation of the believer is redemption, reconciliation with God through His Son the Lord Jesus Christ. **"And thou shalt take the atonement money of the children of Israel, and shalt appoint it for the service of the tabernacle of the congregation; that it may be a memorial unto the children of Israel before the LORD, to make an atonement for your souls" (Ex.30:16).** **"Forasmuch as ye know that ye were not redeemed with corruptible things, as silver and gold, from your vain conversation received by tradition from your fathers; But with the precious blood of Christ, as of a lamb without blemish and without spot" (1 Pe.1:18-19).** b. Christ fulfilled the stability and support symbolized in the crossbars. Christ fulfilled the symbolism... • by being our support, our eternal refuge **"The eternal God *is* thy refuge, and underneath *are* the everlasting arms: and he shall thrust out the enemy from before thee; and shall say, Destroy *them*" (De.33:27).** • by holding us up, by sustaining us with His right hand **"Thou hast also given me the shield of thy salvation: and thy right hand hath holden me up, and thy**

THE FACTS CONCERNING THE SANCTUARY	WHAT IS TAUGHT BY THE SANCTUARY	HOW CHRIST FULFILLED THE SYMBOLISM
6) The crossbars were covered with gold and gold rings were made to hold the crossbars (v.29). The fifteen crossbars served as a means of stability to the wood framing.		**gentleness hath made me great" (Ps.18:35).** • by strengthening and helping us **"Fear thou not; for I _am_ with thee: be not dismayed; for I _am_ thy God: I will strengthen thee; yea, I will help thee; yea, I will uphold thee with the right hand of my righteousness" (Is.41:10).** • by delivering us **"And the Lord shall deliver me from every evil work, and will preserve _me_ unto his heavenly kingdom: to whom _be_ glory for ever and ever. Amen" (2 Ti. 4:18).** • by preserving us **"O love the LORD, all ye his saints: _for_ the LORD preserveth the faithful, and plentifully rewardeth the proud doer" (Ps.31:23).**

VI. THE SYMBOLIC LESSONS CONCERNING THE INNER VEIL, Ex.26:31-35; 35:12; 36:35-36; 39:34; 40:3, 21

THE FACTS CONCERNING THE INNER VEIL	WHAT IS TAUGHT BY THE INNER VEIL	HOW CHRIST FULFILLED THE SYMBOLISM
1. The facts: a. It was a veil of great beauty made with remarkable skill (v.31). Like the inner curtain, it was made of fine linen. The same striking colors of blue, purple, and scarlet were a part of this veil. The embroidered cherubim were also worked into this veil. b. It was hung with gold hooks on four posts of durable wood (acacia). The posts stood on four silver sockets or bases (v.32).	2. What the Inner Veil or Curtain Door taught: a. God is holy and righteous, far, far removed from man and his world—totally set apart and separated from the pollution and uncleanness of man. b. God must be approached ever so carefully—in reverence, awe, and fear. c. There is only one way to God, only one door into His presence. d. Fellowship and communion with God Himself is the supreme act of worship.	3. How Christ fulfilled the symbolism of the veil: • The _inner veil_ is rich in symbolism as it speaks of Jesus Christ. Christ fulfilled the symbolism of the inner veil. Christ and Christ alone is the way to God, the way to know God and to experience the presence, fellowship, and communion of God. Remember what happened to the inner veil of the temple when Christ died on the cross: it was torn from top to bottom, symbolizing that God

c. The purpose for the inner veil was basically to shield the ark of God from all else.
  1) The inner veil was to separate the Holy Place from the Most Holy Place (v.33). This symbolized the majestic holiness and righteousness of God, the light of His perfection which no man can approach.
  2) The inner veil separated the mercy seat from all else. The veil symbolized the holiness of God, separation from the presence of God (v.34). Note what was separated from the Mercy Seat in the Most Holy Place:
  ⇒ The Table of Showbread: was placed on the north side in the Holy Place (v.35).
  ⇒ The Lampstand: was placed opposite the table on the south side (v.35).
		Himself acted, took the initiative, and tore the veil. The heavenly veil that kept man out of God's presence was torn by Christ when He suffered and died on the cross. We now have eternal access into the presence of God. The door into God's presence is wide open.
		
		"Wherefore in all things it behooved him to be made like unto his brethren, that he might be a merciful and faithful high priest in things pertaining to God, to make reconciliation for the sins of the people" (He.2:17).
		"Seeing then that we have a great high priest, that is passed into the heavens, Jesus the Son of God, let us hold fast our profession. For we have not an high priest which cannot be touched with the feeling of our infirmities; but was in all points tempted like as we are, yet without sin" (He.4:14-15; see He. 6:19-20; 9:24; 10:19-20).

VII. THE SYMBOLIC LESSONS CONCERNING THE OUTER VEIL, Ex.26:36-37; 35:15; 36:37-38; 39:38; 40:5, 22

THE FACTS CONCERNING THE OUTER VEIL	WHAT IS TAUGHT BY THE OUTER VEIL	HOW CHRIST FULFILLED THE SYMBOLISM
1. The facts: a. It was an entrance of great beauty and craftsmanship (v.36). This curtain was identical to the inner curtain with one exception: there were no cherubim embroidered into the curtain. b. The hanging frame was slightly different from that of the inner curtain's hanging frame. 1) There were gold hooks and five posts overlaid with gold (v.37). The inner curtain was	2. What the Outer Veil or Curtain Door taught: a. A person cannot just rush into the presence of a holy God; he cannot show disrespect to a holy God. b. There is only one way into the deeper things of God. c. There is a deeper knowledge of God, much more to knowing and experiencing God's presence than just making sacrifice and receiving forgiveness of sins.	3. How Christ fulfilled the symbolism of the veil: • Jesus Christ fulfilled the symbolism of this outer curtain. With His shed blood, He invites men to come through the door and worship God. The way to a deeper knowledge of God, to the deeper things of God, is through the Lord Jesus Christ and through Him alone. **"And this is life eternal, that they might know thee**

hung on four posts overlaid with gold (see v.32).

2) There were five bronze bases or sockets for the posts (v.37). The poles for the inner curtain required only four bases of silver (see v.32). Note the change of metals for the bases from silver to bronze. Why? Most likely because sin offerings were made at the bronze Altar, and before a person can offer acceptable worship, he must deal with his sins. There at the bronze Altar, his sins were judged by God, and God's wrath was satisfied. This is the foundation of man's worship, the blood that cleanses a person from sin. Therefore, the foundation sockets for the entrance to the Tabernacle were made of bronze: all to symbolize the need for cleansing in order to worship God. Simply stated, until a man has been forgiven for his sins, he can never enter into the presence of God. Once blood has been shed, man is invited to come and worship God.

(Remember: offerings for sin were made at the brazen Altar in the courtyard. But there was more than this, more than forgiveness of sins, in knowing and worshipping God. There was worship in the Holy Place and even in the inner sanctuary of God's presence, in the Most Holy Place or the Holy of Holies.)

the only true God, and Jesus Christ, whom thou hast sent" (Jn.17:3).

"But of him are ye in Christ Jesus, who of God is made unto us wisdom, and righteousness, and sanctification, and redemption" (1 Co.1:30).

"But speaking the truth in love, may grow up into him in all things, which is the head, even Christ" (Ep.4:15).

"That I may know him, and the power of his resurrection, and the fellowship of his sufferings, being made conformable unto his death" (Ph.3:10).

"Therefore leaving the principles of the doctrine of Christ, let us go on unto perfection; not laying again the foundation of repentance from dead works, and of faith toward God" (He.6:1).

"As newborn babes, desire the sincere milk of the word, that ye may grow thereby: if so be ye have tasted that the Lord is gracious" (1 Pe.2:2-3).

VIII. THE SYMBOLIC LESSONS CONCERNING THE BRAZEN ALTAR, Ex.27:1-8; 35:16; 38:1-7; 39:39; 40:6, 29

THE FACTS CONCERNING THE BRAZEN ALTAR (THE ALTAR OF BURNT OFFERING)	WHAT IS TAUGHT BY THE BRAZEN ALTAR	HOW CHRIST FULFILLED THE SYMBOLISM
1. The facts: a. The Altar was made of acacia wood with the following dimensions: it was a square Altar that was 7½ feet wide by 7½ feet long by 4½ feet high.	2. What the Altar taught: a. Substitutionary sacrifice is necessary for the forgiveness of sins. b. There is no forgiveness without the shed blood of a sacrifice.	3. How Christ fulfilled the symbolism of the Brazen Altar: a. Christ is the Lamb of God.

b. Like the other parts of the Tabernacle, acacia wood was chosen for its hardness and for its durability. c. The Altar was made with a horn at each of the four corners, made of one piece. d. The Altar was overlaid (covered) with bronze. e. All of the utensils were made of bronze f. The Altar was to have a bronze grate g. The Altar had poles of acacia wood that were overlaid with bronze. These poles were then inserted into the four rings when the Altar was carried. h. The Altar was made hollow.	c. There is no way to approach God — to be saved — other than through the death of a substitute.	**"The next day John seeth Jesus coming unto him, and saith, Behold the Lamb of God, which taketh away the sin of the world!" (Jn.1:29).** b. Christ is the Lamb brought to the slaughter. **"He was oppressed, and he was afflicted, yet he opened not his mouth: he is brought as a lamb to the slaughter, and as a sheep before her shearers is dumb, so he openeth not his mouth" (Is.53:7).** c. Christ is our Passover sacrificed for us. **"Purge out therefore the old leaven, that ye may be a new lump, as ye are unleavened. For even Christ our passover is sacrificed for us" (1 Co.5:7).** d. Christ gave His life as a ransom. **"[I] give my life a ransom for many" (Mk.10:45).** e. Christ laid down His life for us. **"Hereby perceive we the love of God, because he laid down his life for us: and we ought to lay down our lives for the brethren" (1 Jn. 3:16).**

IX.   THE SYMBOLIC LESSONS CONCERNING THE WALLS OF THE TABERNACLE, Ex.27:9-19; 35:17; 36:20-34; 38:9-20; 39:33, 40; 40:8, 33

THE FACTS CONCERNING THE WALLS	WHAT IS TAUGHT BY THE WALLS	HOW CHRIST FULFILLED THE SYMBOLISM
1. The facts: a. A mandate had been given to build the courtyard (v.9). God had wanted to ensure the safety of the holy vessels of the Tabernacle by having His people	2. What the Walls taught: a. The walls of linen symbolized the righteousness and holiness of God. He is so righteous and holy, so white and pure, that He is set apart from the world.	3. How Christ fulfilled the symbolism of the Walls: • Christ is the righteousness of God. **"But now the righteousness of God without the law is manifested, being**

build a protective hedge around the Tabernacle.

b. The south side was built with these exact specifications (vv.9-10):
- 150 feet of linen curtains
- 20 posts that fit into 20 bronze bases
- silver hooks and bands attached to the posts

c. The north side was built with these exact specifications (v.11):
- 150 feet of linen curtains
- 20 posts that fit into 20 bronze bases
- silver hooks and bands

d. The west end was built with these exact specifications (v.12):
- 75 feet of curtains
- 10 posts set into ten bases

e. The east end was 75 feet long (v.13). Included in the east end was the one and only courtyard entrance. This entrance was flanked by two curtains. Note their specifications:
- Each was 22½ feet long
- Each was supported by 3 posts set into three bases (vv.14-15).

f. The entrance itself (v.16). This was the only door into the Tabernacle. The curtain was 30 feet long and was made of fine linen. This curtain was decorated, embroidered in blue, purple, and scarlet yarn. The same set of brilliant colors was used throughout the inner curtains of the sanctuary. This curtain was attached to four posts set in four bases.

g. The posts of the courtyard were connected by silver bands and hooks (v.17).

h. The Courtyard was 150 feet long by 75 feet wide with 7½ feet high curtain walls that were

b. When a person looks at God, he must see that God dwells in righteousness and holiness. When a person looked at the walls of the Tabernacle, he was to be reminded that God was holy.

c. When a person approaches God, he must approach Him in reverence and awe, adoration and worship. He must praise and thank God, that God allows him to enter His presence.

witnessed by the law and the prophets; Even the righteousness of God which is by faith of Jesus Christ unto all and upon all them that believe: for there is no difference" (Ro.3:21-22).

"For he hath made him to be sin for us, who knew no sin; that we might be made the righteousness of God in him" (2 Co.5:21).

"And that ye put on the new man [Christ], which after God is created in righteousness and true holiness" (Ep.4:24).

"And have put on the new man, which is renewed in knowledge after the image of him that created him" (Col.3:10).

made of fine linen. These walls were supported by bronze bases. i. The articles used in the work of the Tabernacle, including the tent pegs, were bronze.		

X. THE SYMBOLIC LESSONS CONCERNING THE DOOR OR GATE, Ex.27:16; 35:17; 38:18-19; 39:40; 40:8, 33

THE FACTS CONCERNING THE DOOR OR GATE	WHAT IS TAUGHT BY THE DOOR OR GATE	HOW CHRIST FULFILLED THE SYMBOLISM
1. The facts: Included in the east end was the one and only Courtyard entrance, but note: the entrance (door) to the Tabernacle was large, large enough to receive any person. a. The Door was on the east side. b. The Door was 30 feet wide and 7½ feet high. c. The Door was made out of fine twined linen woven together by needlework. This curtain was decorated, embroidered in blue, purple, and scarlet yarn—the same set of brilliant colors throughout the inner curtains of the sanctuary. d. The curtain was attached to four posts set in four bases.	2. What the Door or Gate taught: a. There is only one way to enter God's presence; there are not many ways as most men think and practice. b. God has to be approached. No person will ever live with God unless he approaches God.	3. How Christ fulfilled the symbolism of the Door or Gate: a. Jesus Christ is the door, the only door, that a man can enter to be saved. **"I am the door: by me if any man enter in, he shall be saved, and shall go in and out, and find pasture" (Jn.10:9).** b. Jesus Christ is the way, the only way by which a man can come to the Father. **"Jesus saith unto him, I am the way, the truth, and the life: no man cometh unto the Father, but by me" (Jn.14:6).**

XI. THE SYMBOLIC LESSONS CONCERNING THE ALTAR OF INCENSE, Ex.30:1-10; 35:15; 37:25-29; 39:38; 40:5, 26-27

THE FACTS CONCERNING THE ALTAR OF INCENSE	WHAT IS TAUGHT BY THE ALTAR OF INCENSE	HOW CHRIST FULFILLED THE SYMBOLISM
1. The facts: a. The Altar of Incense was made of acacia wood (v.1). b. The Altar of Incense was square: 18 inches by 18 inches by 3 feet high (v.2). c. The Altar of Incense had horns on each corner, carved from the same piece of wood (v.2). Horns are symbolic of God's power, strength, salvation, protection, security, sanctuary, and help.	2. What the Altar of Incense taught: a. The Altar was the place where sweet incense was offered up to the every morning and evening. The High Priest burned incense every morning when he tended the lamps and every evening when he lit them (v.7). This symbolized the critical importance of praying every morning and evening.	3. How Christ fulfilled the symbolism of the Altar: a. Christ is always praying, living and walking in an unbroken communion with God the Father. b. Christ intercedes for God's people. **"I pray for them: I pray not for the world, but for them which thou hast given me; for they are thine" (Jn.17:9).**

d. The Altar of Incense was overlaid with gold and had a gold molding (v.3). Just like the other holy pieces of furniture in the sanctuary, the Altar was covered with pure gold. e. The Altar of Incense had two gold rings attached to each side. The rings held the two poles used in carrying the Altar (v.4). f. The Altar of Incense had two poles made of acacia wood overlaid with gold (v.5). The Altar, like the rest of the Tabernacle, was designed to be moved. g. God told Moses to place the Altar just outside the inner curtain. It was opposite the Ark of the Covenant and its cover, the Mercy Seat (v.6).	b. The Altar of Incense had a permanent incense ascending up to the LORD (v.8). This symbolized two things. 1) There is the symbol of the permanent intercession of Jesus Christ. Jesus Christ is living forever—in the very presence of God—to make intercession for us. He died and arose from the dead for this very purpose: to stand before God as the great Intercessor for us. 2) There is the symbol that believers are to pray morning and evening, to pray always, to develop an unbroken communion with God, never to cease being in a spirit of prayer.	"Who is he that condemneth? It is Christ that died, yea rather, that is risen again, who is even at the right hand of God, who also maketh intercession for us" (Ro.8:34). "Seeing then that we have a great high priest [Intercessor], that is passed into the heavens, Jesus the Son of God, let us hold fast our profession. For we have not an high priest which cannot be touched with the feeling of our infirmities; but was in all points tempted like as we are, yet without sin" (He.4:14-15). "Wherefore he is able also to save them to the uttermost that come unto God by him, seeing he ever liveth to make intercession for them" (He.7:25).

XII. THE SYMBOLIC LESSONS CONCERNING THE BRONZE WASH BASIN, Ex.30:17-21; 35:16; 38:8; 39:39; 40:7, 30-32

THE FACTS CONCERNING THE BRONZE WASH BASIN	WHAT IS TAUGHT BY THE BRONZE WASH BASIN	HOW CHRIST FULFILLED THE SYMBOLISM
1. The facts: a. The size is not given. b. The builder made the Bronze Basin with a bronze pedestal (v.18). c. The Bronze Basin was placed between the Tabernacle and the Altar of Burnt Offering (v.18). d. The sole purpose of the Bronze Wash Basin was for the priests to wash their hands and feet (v.19). They were to wash when they entered the Tabernacle and when they approached the Altar to make a sacrifice. e. The warning was clear and blunt: the priests must wash or die (v.21). f. The importance of the washing and cleansing cannot be over-stressed: it was made a permanent law for all generations (v.21).	2. What the Wash Basin taught: a. A person *cannot enter God's presence* before he is cleansed and made pure. b. A person *cannot serve God* until he is cleansed and made pure. c. A person must be continually cleansed and made pure in order to *continually serve God*.	3. How Christ fulfilled the symbolism of the Bronze Wash Basin: • The Wash Basin was a symbol of Christ. God cleanses us and forgives our sins through the blood of His Son, the Lord Jesus Christ, through His death and His death alone. "Then Peter said unto them, Repent, and be baptized every one of you in the name of Jesus Christ for the remission of sins, and ye shall receive the gift of the Holy Ghost" (Ac.2:38; see Mt.26:28; Ac.5:31; 13:38; Ro.3:23-25). "In whom we have redemption through his blood, the forgiveness of sins, according to the riches of his grace" (Ep.1:7; see Col.1:14; Tit.2:14).

CHART 3

HOW CHRIST FULFILLED
THE SYMBOLISM OF
THE PRIESTHOOD

I. **THE SYMBOLIC LESSONS CONCERNING THE GARMENTS OF THE PRIESTHOOD**

    A.   THE SASH, Ex.28:4; 39:29

    B.   THE EPHOD, Ex.28:4, 6-14; 39:2-7

    C.   THE BREASTPIECE OR CHESTPIECE, Ex.28:4, 15-30; 39:8-21

    D.   THE ROBE OF THE EPHOD, Ex.28:4, 31-35; 39:22-26

    E.   THE GOLD MEDALLION OR DIADEM, Ex.28:36-38; 39:30-31

    F.   THE LINEN TURBANS AND TUNICS, Ex.28:4, 39; 39:27-28

    G.   THE LINEN HEADBAND, Ex.28:40; 39:28

    H.   THE LINEN UNDERCLOTHING, Ex.28:42-43; 39:28

II. **THE SYMBOLIC LESSONS CONCERNING THE ORDINATION OF THE PRIESTHOOD**

    A.   THE CEREMONIAL WASHING, Ex.29:4

    B.   THE JUDICIAL CLEANSING, Ex.29:10-14

    C.   THE TOTAL DEDICATION OF LIFE: THE SACRIFICE OF THE FIRST RAM AS THE BURNT OFFERING, Ex.29:15-18

    D.   THE CONSECRATION TO SERVICE: THE SACRIFICE OF A SECOND RAM, Ex.29:19-21

    E.   THE COMMITMENT TO GIVE GOD THE BEST: THE CEREMONY OF TWO WAVE OFFERINGS, Ex.29:22-28

I. THE SYMBOLIC LESSONS CONCERNING THE GARMENTS OF THE PRIESTHOOD

A. THE SASH, Ex.28:4; 39:29

THE FACTS CONCERNING THE SASH	WHAT IS TAUGHT BY THE SASH	HOW CHRIST FULFILLED THE SYMBOLISM
1. The Facts: • The sash for each priest was made of fine linen and multi-colored yarn	2. What the Sash taught: a. The multi-colored sash of fine linen was symbolic of truth, the truth of God's Word. It is comparable to the belt of truth in the armor of God that the believer is to put on (Ep.6:14). b. The Word of God enlightens and wraps together everything in the believer's spiritual wardrobe. c. It is the Word of God that holds everything together.	3. How Christ fulfilled the symbolism of the Sash: a. Jesus Christ fulfilled the symbolism of the Sash by being the Truth, the Living Word of God. **"Stand therefore, having your loins girt about with truth, and having on the breastplate of righteousness" (Ep.6:14).** **"Sanctify them through thy truth: thy word is truth" (Jn.17:17).** b. Jesus Christ is the One who holds everything and everyone together—all by His Word. **"For by him were all things created, that are in heaven, and that are in earth, visible and invisible, whether they be thrones, or dominions, or principalities, or powers: all things were created by him, and for him: And he is before all things, and by him all things consist" (Col.1:16-17).**

B. THE EPHOD, Ex.28:4, 6-14; 39:2-7

THE FACTS CONCERNING THE EPHOD	WHAT IS TAUGHT BY THE EPHOD	HOW CHRIST FULFILLED THE SYMBOLISM
1. The facts: a. The materials of the ephod consisted of gold thread that had been made from thin gold sheets cut into thin, thread-like wires (See Ex.39:3). The ephod also consisted of yarn that was blue, purple, and scarlet (v.6). The final type of material	2. What the Ephod taught: ⇒ The Ephod symbolized that the priest represented and carried the names of God's people before the LORD.	3. How Christ fulfilled the symbolism of the Ephod: • Jesus Christ is the One who represents and carries the name of believers before the Father. No matter what our burden, no matter how heavy or terrifying, we can cast it upon Christ. He will relieve us, strengthen us, and give

in the ephod was fine linen. b. The design of the ephod was spelled out with these exact instructions: 1) It was in two pieces, front and back, joined by two straps at the shoulder (v.7). 2) It had a sash or waistband made of the same materials as the ephod (v.8). 3) It had two onyx stones that had Israel's twelve tribes engraved on them (v.9). Six names were engraved on each stone in the order of their birth (v.10). Each stone was engraved just as a gem-cutter engraves a seal (v.11). The maker of the ephod mounted the stones in gold settings and then fastened the stones to the shoulder pieces of the ephod (vv.11-12).		us peace and rest from the burden. "Come unto me, all ye that labour and are heavy laden, and I will give you rest. Take my yoke upon you, and learn of me; for I am meek and lowly in heart: and ye shall find rest unto your souls. For my yoke is easy, and my burden is light" (Mt.11:28-30). "Who is he that condemneth? It is Christ that died, yea rather, that is risen again, who is even at the right hand of God, who also maketh intercession for us" (Ro.8:34). "Wherefore in all things it behooved him to be made like unto his brethren, that he might be a merciful and faithful high priest in things pertaining to God, to make reconciliation for the sins of the people. For in that he himself hath suffered being tempted, he is able to succour them that are tempted" (He.2:17-18).

C.   THE BREASTPIECE OR CHESTPIECE, Ex.28:4, 15-30; 39:8-21

THE FACTS CONCERNING THE BREASTPIECE OR CHESTPIECE	WHAT IS TAUGHT BY THE BREASTPIECE OR CHESTPIECE	HOW CHRIST FULFILLED THE SYMBOLISM
1. The Facts: a. The basic materials were the same as the ephod garment (v.15). b. The design was a 9 inch square, folded double, forming a pouch (v.16). On the breastpiece were attached four rows of precious stones which numbered a total of twelve (vv.17-20). Each one of these twelve stones was attached to a gold setting (v.21). The twelve stones represented the twelve tribes of Israel and were identified by engraving the names of the twelve tribes on the stones as a	2. What the Breastpiece or Chestpiece taught, the two-fold purpose: a. First, to symbolize that the High Priest represents and carries the names of God's people upon his heart, that he represents them before the LORD continually (v.29). b. The second purpose of the chestpiece was to hold the urim and thummim (probably two stones or lots) next to the High Priest's heart (v.30). This symbolized the High Priest seeking God's will for the people. Imagine the	3. How Christ fulfilled the symbolism of the Breastpiece or Chestpiece: • Jesus Christ is our great High Priest who represents and carries the names of believers upon His heart and before the Lord continually. This is a strong picture of the love of God: how much God loves His people. He loves us so much that He keeps us ever so close to His heart, continually before His face. "Before I formed thee in the belly I knew thee; and

seal (v.21). The chestpiece was then permanently attached to the ephod. The maker of the chestpiece made braided cords of pure gold (v.22). The chestpiece also had two gold rings which were attached to the top corners of the chestpiece—for the gold cords to go through. Then the cords were tied to the gold settings on the shoulder pieces of the ephod garment (vv.23-25). Two more gold rings were made and attached to the other two ends of the chestpiece—on the inside next to the ephod garment (v.26). The final two gold rings were made and attached to the ephod garment near the sash (v.27). To hold the breastpiece and ephod together, the rings of the chestpiece were tied to the rings of the ephod with blue cord. This blue cord held both garments securely together (v.28).

scene as the High Priest entered into the Holy Place. He was there on behalf of the people of God.

before thou camest forth out of the womb I sanctified thee, and I ordained thee a prophet unto the nations" (Je.1:5).

"Behold, God is mine helper: the Lord is with them that uphold my soul" (Ps.54:4).

"The LORD is nigh unto them that are of a broken heart; and saveth such as be of a contrite spirit" (Ps.34:18).

"I know thy works: behold, I have set before thee an open door, and no man can shut it: for thou hast a little strength, and hast kept my word, and hast not denied my name" (Re.3:8).

"But even the very hairs of your head are all numbered. Fear not therefore: ye are of more value than many sparrows" (Lu.12:7).

D.   THE ROBE OF THE EPHOD, Ex.28:4, 31-35; 39:22-26

THE FACTS CONCERNING THE ROBE OF THE EPHOD	WHAT IS TAUGHT BY THE ROBE OF THE EPHOD	HOW CHRIST FULFILLED THE SYMBOLISM
1. The Facts: a. It was a long, sleeveless, solid blue robe. An opening was made in the center of the robe for the head. The maker reinforced the opening with a woven collar so it would not tear (v.32). b. Pomegranates were made out of yarn in the colors of blue, purple, and scarlet (v.33). These pomegranates of yarn were attached to the hem of the robe with gold bells between	2. What the Robe of the Ephod taught, the symbolic twofold purpose: a. To sound forth the intercessory ministry of the High Priest (v.35). Before the High Priest would minister before the Lord, he would slip this robe over his head. After he was fully dressed in the priestly garments, the tinkling of the golden bells would mark his every step. The sound of the bells told the people where he was as he carried their names before	3. How Christ fulfilled the symbolism of the Robe of the Ephod: a. Jesus Christ is our great High Priest who sounds forth the intercessory ministry of the High Priest. His intercession never ends, never stops. **"But this man, because he continueth ever, hath an unchangeable priesthood. Wherefore he is able also to save them to the uttermost that come unto God by him, seeing he ever liveth to make intercession for them" (He.7:24-25).**

them. The pattern alternated the pomegranates and bells at the hem of the robe (v.34).	the LORD. As he ministered in their behalf, they could follow his intercessory ministry as he moved about the various rituals of worship. As he carried out a particular ritual, the people would obviously meditate and pray over the truth symbolized by the ritual. b. To sound forth that God had accepted the offering of the High Priest, that the High Priest had not been stricken dead (v.35). The sound of the bells let the people know that he was alive and ministering on their behalf. Every time the High Priest went into the Holy Place, there was always the chance that his offering would be unacceptable to God. When a Holy God is approached by an unholy offering, death is always the final consequence (always spiritual death; sometimes physical death).	b. As the great Intercessor, Jesus Christ offered Himself to God... • as the perfect offering, the Lamb of God • as the resurrected Lord and Christ, the One who lives forever more • as the perfect High Priest, the One who intercedes for man **"The next day John seeth Jesus coming unto him, and saith, Behold the Lamb of God, which taketh away the sin of the world"** (Jn.1:29). **"Wherefore God also hath highly exalted him, and given him a name which is above every name"** (Ph.2:9). **"Who** *is* **he that condemneth?** *It is* **Christ that died, yea rather, that is risen again, who is even at the right hand of God, who also maketh intercession for us"** (Ro.8:34). **"Therefore will I divide him a portion with the great, and he shall divide the spoil with the strong; because he hath poured out his soul unto death: and he was numbered with the transgressors; and he bare the sin of many, and made intercession for the transgressors"** (Is.53:12).

E.   THE GOLD MEDALLION OR DIADEM, Ex.28:36-38; 39:30-31

THE FACTS CONCERNING THE GOLD MEDALLION	WHAT IS TAUGHT BY THE GOLD MEDALLION	HOW CHRIST FULFILLED THE SYMBOLISM

1. The facts:
  The gold medallion was worn on the turban, the headdress cloth or cap. The gold medallion was most significant, the crowning piece of the priestly garments. Note the special instructions for the gold medallion:
  a. It was engraved with these words: HOLY TO THE LORD (v.36). It is
	2. What the Gold Medallion taught:
	There was a twofold symbol:
	• The Gold Medallion symbolized that the High Priest bore the guilt for the shortcomings of the people.
	• The Gold Medallion symbolized that the people must seek the acceptance of a holy God.
		3. How Jesus Christ fulfilled the symbolism of the Gold Medallion:
		
		a. It is Jesus Christ who bore the guilt for the shortcomings and errors of the people. Man needs a perfect Sacrifice. Jesus Christ is that sacrifice

important to note where this medallion was to be worn: on the forehead of the High Priest. What a great proclamation to wear such inspiring words as a testimony to the LORD: HOLY TO THE LORD. b. It was attached to the front of the turban by a blue cord (v.37).		"For Christ also hath once suffered for sins, the just for the unjust, that he might bring us to God, being put to death in the flesh, but quickened by the Spirit" (1 Pe. 3:18; see Tit.2:14). b. We must seek the approval of God by approaching God through Christ and Christ alone. "Jesus saith unto him, I am the way, the truth, and the life: no man cometh unto the Father, but by me" (Jn.14:6; see Ac.4:12).

F. THE LINEN TURBANS AND TUNICS, Ex.28:4, 39; 39:27-28

THE FACTS CONCERNING THE LINEN TURBANS & TUNICS	WHAT IS TAUGHT BY THE LINEN TURBANS & TUNICS	HOW CHRIST FULFILLED THE SYMBOLISM
1. The Facts: The turban and tunic (a long coat-like garment) were to be made of fine linen (v.39).	2. What the Linen Turbans and Tunics taught: • The turban and tunic (a long coat-like garment essentially covering the whole body) are symbolic of putting on God's righteousness. Those who minister in God's name must bear His righteousness. Anything less than God's righteousness is totally insufficient.	3. How Jesus Christ fulfilled the symbolism of the Linen Turbans and Tunics: • It is Jesus Christ who is the righteousness of God. "I put on righteousness, and it clothed me: my judgment was as a robe and a diadem" (Jb.29:14; see Is.61:10; 1 Co.1:30). "For he hath made him to be sin for us, who knew no sin; that we might be made the righteousness of God in him" (2 Co.5:21).

G. THE LINEN HEADBAND, Ex.28:40; 39:28

THE FACTS CONCERNING THE LINEN HEADBAND	WHAT IS TAUGHT BY THE LINEN HEADBAND	HOW CHRIST FULFILLED THE SYMBOLISM
1. The Facts: Linen headbands were made for the priests (v.28).	2. What the Linen Headband taught: • The linen headbands were, of course, worn on the head. They were symbolic of the believer's mind and will being subjected to God. The believer is to willingly submit his will, his thoughts, and his own personal agenda to God.	3. How Christ fulfilled the symbolism of the Linen Headband: • It is Jesus Christ who has established His Lordship over every thought, every idea, every scheme of man. "I beseech you therefore, brethren, by the mercies of God, that ye present your bodies a living sacrifice,

| | | holy, acceptable unto God, which is your reasonable service. And be not conformed to this world: but be ye transformed by the renewing of your mind, that ye may prove what is that good, and acceptable, and perfect, will of God" (Ro.12:1-2; see Ps.143:10; Ep.6:6).

 "Casting down imaginations, and every high thing that exalteth itself against the knowledge of God, and bringing into captivity every thought to the obedience of Christ" (2 Co. 10:5). |

H.   THE LINEN UNDERCLOTHING, Ex.28:42-43; 39:28

THE FACTS CONCERNING THE LINEN UNDERCLOTHING	WHAT IS TAUGHT BY THE LINEN UNDERCLOTHING	HOW CHRIST FULFILLED THE SYMBOLISM
1. The Facts: The undergarments were made of fine twisted linen (v.28).	2. What the Linen Underclothing taught: • The linen underwear was symbolic of covering the believer's spiritual nakedness. The person who is without Christ is exposed and shamed. We must all put on the Lord Jesus Christ and make no provision for the flesh.	3. How Christ fulfilled the symbolism of the Linen Underclothing: • It is Jesus Christ who covers man with His righteousness, protecting man from exposure and shame before God and man. "But put ye on the Lord Jesus Christ, and make not provision for the flesh, to fulfil the lusts thereof" (Ro.13:14; see Ro.6:6; Col.3:10; Tit.2:12).

II.   THE SYMBOLIC LESSONS CONCERNING THE ORDINATION CEREMONY OF THE PRIESTHOOD

A.   THE CEREMONIAL WASHING, Ex.29:4

THE FACTS CONCERNING THE CEREMONIAL WASHING	WHAT IS TAUGHT BY THE CEREMONIAL WASHING	HOW CHRIST FULFILLED THE SYMBOLISM
1. The Facts: The priests were presented and washed with water (a ceremonial washing): this washing was a onetime, once-for-all cleansing, the only time they were washed by Moses. Remember, Moses stood as the mediator be-	2. What the Ceremonial Washing taught: a. This washing symbolized spiritual cleansing, a onetime, once-for-all cleansing. It symbolized the moment of salvation and regeneration, of being eternally saved, and	3. How Christ fulfilled the symbolism of the Ceremonial Washing: • This washing speaks of what Christ has done for all believers. He has washed us and pronounced us "clean" (Jn. 15:3). Christ has made

tween the people and God until the ordination of Aaron. As mediator, Moses spoke and acted for God in appointing the priests.	the removal of uncleanness and sin (v.4). b. The person who serves God must be clean, morally pure, cleansed from all filthiness of the sinful nature and spirit.	us clean: He has regenerated us, eternally saved us. **"Having therefore these promises, dearly beloved, let us cleanse ourselves from all filthiness of the flesh and spirit, perfecting holiness in the fear of God" (2 Co. 7:1; see Ps.79:9; Is.1:16; 2 Ti.2:21; Js.4:8).**

B.   THE JUDICIAL CLEANSING, Ex.29:10-14

THE FACTS CONCERNING THE JUDICIAL CLEANSING	WHAT IS TAUGHT BY THE JUDICIAL CLEANSING	HOW CHRIST FULFILLED THE SYMBOLISM
1. The Facts: a. The priests laid their hands on the bull's head b. The priests slaughtered the bull before the LORD c. The priests applied blood to the horns and base of the Altar d. The priests took the bad—the flesh, skin, and waste—outside the camp to burn	2. What the Judicial Cleansing taught: a. The act of the priest's laying their hands on the head of the bull symbolized identification, transferring their sins to the animal. b. The slaughter of the bull before the LORD symbolized appeasement and substitution, the substituting of the animal to bear God's judgment. c. The taking of the bad outside the camp… • Symbolized that sin (the bad) had to be taken out of the camp, away from the worshipper. • Symbolized the sin offering: the taking away of sin by the sacrifice of one (Jesus Christ) for another.	3. How Christ fulfilled the Judicial Cleansing: a. God accepted the blood of the sacrifice as payment for the sins of the believer. God accepted the faith of the believer and counted him righteous (forgiven) when he identified with the sacrificed animal. b. God's wrath toward sin can only be appeased by a sacrifice. The only sacrifice that has ever satisfied God's eternal wrath was the Lamb who was slaughtered on the cross. c. It was Jesus Christ who fulfilled this symbol of taking the bad (sinful, evil) outside the camp. He fulfilled the symbol by His own death on the cross when He was *crucified outside* the walls of Jerusalem on Calvary. **"But God commendeth his love toward us, in that, while we were yet sinners, Christ died for us. Much more then, being now justified by his blood, we shall be saved from wrath through him. For if, when we were enemies, we were reconciled to God by the death of his Son, much more, being reconciled we**

		shall be saved by his life. And not only so, but we also joy in God through our Lord Jesus Christ, by whom we have now received the atonement" (Ro. 5:8-11; see Ro.5:6; Mt. 26:28; 2 Co. 5:21; Tit.2:14; He.9:14; 13:12)

C. THE TOTAL DEDICATION OF LIFE: THE SACRIFICE OF THE FIRST RAM AS THE BURNT OFFERING, Ex.29:15-18

THE FACTS CONCERN-ING THE FIRST RAM & ITS SACRIFICE	WHAT IS TAUGHT BY THE FIRST RAM & ITS SACRIFICE	HOW CHRIST FULFILLED THE SYMBOLISM
1. The Facts: a. The priests were to lay their hands on the ram's head (v.15). b. The priests were to slaughter the ram and sprinkle blood on all sides of the Altar (v.16). c. The priests were to cut the ram into pieces and wash the inner parts and legs (v.17). d. The priests were to burn all the parts on the Altar so the pleasing aroma would ascend up toward heaven (v.18).	2. What the sacrifice of the First Ram taught: a. The act of the priest's laying their hands on the head of the bull symbolized identification, transferring their sins to the animal. b. God accepted the person's sacrifice and dedication.	3. How Christ fulfilled the symbolism of the First Ram and its sacrifice: a. God accepted the blood of the sacrifice as payment for the sins of the believer. God accepted the faith of the believer and counted him righteous (forgiven) when he identified with the sacrificed animal. b. God accepted Christ's sacrifice and dedication on behalf of every believer. c. Christ gave His life willingly, unconditionally, that men might come to know the truth and spend eternity with God. "But he was wounded for our transgressions, he was bruised for our iniquities: the chastisement of our peace was upon him; and with his stripes we are healed. All we like sheep have gone astray; we have turned every one to his own way; and the LORD hath laid on him the iniquity of us all" (Is.53:5-6; see Is. 53:10). "Who gave himself for our sins, that he might deliver us from this present evil world, according to the will of God and our Father" (Ga.1:4; see Ep.5:2; Re.5:9).

D.   THE CONSECRATION TO SERVICE: THE SACRIFICE OF A SECOND RAM, Ex.29:19-21

THE FACTS CONCERN-ING THE SECOND RAM & ITS SACRIFICE	WHAT IS TAUGHT BY THE SECOND RAM & ITS SACRIFICE	HOW CHRIST FULFILLED THE SYMBOLISM
1. The Facts: a. The priests laid their hands on its head (v.19). b. The priests slaughtered the ram and put some blood... • on the tip of the right ear: setting it apart to listen (v.20). • on the thumb of the right hand: setting it apart to touch and do only righteous things (v.20). • on the big toe of the right foot: setting it apart to walk in the ways of God (v.20). • on all sides of the Altar (v.20). c. The priests mixed some blood and anointing oil and sprinkled the mixed oil and blood on the priests and their clothes (v.21).	2. What the sacrifice of the Second Ram taught: a. A person is to believe God, to trust that He accepts and forgives the person who truly believes and identifies with the sacrificed animal. b. The purpose symbolized full consecration to the service of God. • A person is to dedicate and sanctify (set apart) his ears to God • A person is to dedicate and sanctify (set apart) his fingers to do good • A person is to dedicate and sanctify (set apart) his feet to walk in the ways of God	3. How Christ fulfilled the symbolism of the Second Ram and its sacrifice: • Jesus Christ was fully consecrated to the service of God: He obeyed His Father perfectly. He dedicated Himself—His entire body—to do His Father's will. **"But that the world may know that I love the Father; and as the Father gave me commandment, even so I do. Arise, let us go hence" (Jn.14:31).** **"If ye keep my commandments, ye shall abide in my love; even as I kept my Father's commandments, and abide in his love" (Jn.15:10).** **"For as by one man's disobedience many were made sinners, so by the obedience of one shall many be made righteous" (Ro.5:19; see He.5:8; 10:9).**

E.   THE COMMITMENT TO GIVE GOD THE BEST: THE CEREMONY OF TWO WAVE OFFERINGS, Ex.29:22-28

THE FACTS CONCERNING THE TWO WAVE OFFERINGS	WHAT IS TAUGHT BY THE TWO WAVE OFFERINGS	HOW CHRIST FULFILLED THE SYMBOLISM
1. The Facts: a. The fat and choice parts were to be cut away from the ram of ordination (v.22). b. One loaf of unleavened bread, one cake, and one wafer from the basket (v.23) were to be taken by the priests. They were then to lift them up and wave them before the LORD as a wave offering (v.24). c. After waving them before the LORD, these	2. What the Ceremony of the Two Wave Offerings taught: • Note that only the choice parts were given to God. The two Wave Offerings symbolized that only the very best should ever be offered to God. Only the very best pleases Him. God accepts only the very best.	3. How Christ fulfilled the symbolism of the Two Wave Offerings: • Jesus Christ gave only the very best to His Father. Therefore, God the Father was well pleased with Jesus Christ in all things. Everything that Christ said, thought, and did was acceptable to the LORD. **"And lo a voice from heaven, saying, This is my**

items were to be burned upon the Altar as a burnt offering of pleasing aroma to the LORD (v.25).		beloved Son, in whom I am well pleased" (Mt.3:17).

items were to be burned upon the Altar as a burnt offering of pleasing aroma to the LORD (v.25).

d. The breast and shoulder of the ram were also to be lifted and waved before the LORD (v.26). God gave two specific reasons for this:

1) To sanctify—set apart as holy—the parts of the rams that belonged to the priests (v.27).

2) To stress that these parts were to be given to the priests when making fellowship offerings [thanksgiving or peace offerings] (v.28).

"While he yet spake, behold, a bright cloud overshadowed them: and behold a voice out of the cloud, which said, This is my beloved Son, in whom I am well pleased; hear ye him" (Mt.17:5).

"And there came a voice from heaven, saying, Thou art my beloved Son, in whom I am well pleased" (Mk.1:11).

"And the Holy Ghost descended in a bodily shape like a dove upon him, and a voice came from heaven, which said, Thou art my beloved Son; in thee I am well pleased" (Lu.3:22).

"For he received from God the Father honour and glory, when there came such a voice to him from the excellent glory, This is my beloved Son, in whom I am well pleased" (2 Pe.1:17).

OUTLINE & SUBJECT INDEX

DISCOVER THE GREAT VALUE of the Subject Index. The Subject Index gives you...
- A practical list of subjects that can be easily developed for preaching, teaching, or for personal Bible study
- Support Scriptures or cross references for the Subject
- A wealth of topics that will meet your own personal need

DISCOVER THE GREAT VALUE of the Index for yourself. Quickly glance below to the very first subject of the Index of *What the Bible Says About the Tabernacle*. It is:

AARON
Dedication of. **A**. as High Priest. pp.123, 250

Turn to the page and note the discussion. You will immediately see the GREAT VALUE of the INDEX.

OUTLINE & SUBJECT INDEX

To anoint the priests & sanctify them for the ministry. p.150
To anoint the Tabernacle & its furnishings. p.150
To anoint the Table & its utensils. p.150
To anoint the Wash Basin with its stand. p.150
To sanctify the Tabernacle & its furnishings; to make holy. p.150
Essential. God's **a**. No minister can serve God apart from God's **a**. p.124
Instructions for **a**. To **a**. with oil. p.124
Warning. The **a**. is not man's to give; it belongs to God. p.150
What God **a**.
People. p.150
Things. p.150

APPROACH - APPROACH-ABLE
Discussed.
Many do not pray because they do not understand how to **a**. God. p.215
The great lesson of the Tabernacle. pp.167-169
Facts.
We must be exact & careful in our **a**. & worship of God. p.167
To God.
Must be **a**. ever so carefully--in reverence, awe, & fear. p.67
Type - Symbol of. The Courtyard of the Tabernacle symbolized that God can be approached. pp.85, 91

ARCHITECT
Description of God. p.9
Why God had to be the Tabernacle's **a**. p.9

ARK
Meaning of the three arks mentioned in Scripture. pp.23-24

ARK OF GOD
Construction of.
Discussed. pp.22-23, 207
Instructions for construction. pp.22-23, 207
Set up. p.252
Facts.
Held the Testimony [the Ten Commandments]. p.252
Mentioned over 200 times in the Bible. p.23
Names of. p.23
Placement of. p.207
Purpose of. Four purposes listed. pp.28-30
Throne of. (See **THRONE**)

Type - Symbol of.
Christ fulfilling every picture of the Ark. pp.31-33
Divine instruction & guidance. The throne & presence of God. pp.30, 32, 177, 207, 252
God's law holding the Ten Commandments. pp.28, 32, 252
God's mercy covered the **a**. pp.24, 31, 178, 211, 252
God's special presence revealed. pp.28, 31, 177, 207, 252

ARK OF THE COVENANT OF GOD (See **ARK OF GOD**)

ARK OF THE LORD (See **ARK OF GOD**)

ARK OF THE LORD GOD (See **ARK OF GOD**)

ARK OF THE TABERNACLE (See **ARK OF GOD**)

ARK OF THE TESTIMONY (See **ARK OF GOD**)

ARMOR OF GOD
Discussed. p.240

ASSURANCE (See **SECURITY**)

ATONEMENT
Discussed. How the Tabernacle offering was to make **a**. for one's life. pp.146-148
Fact. Man needs the **a**. p.221
Meaning. pp.24-26

ATONEMENT COVER, The (See **MERCY SEAT**)
Meaning. pp.24-26

ATONEMENT MONEY (See **SILVER**)
Fact. Each Israelite man gave atonement money in the form of silver. pp.64, 146-147, 153

B

BADGER SKINS
Construction of.
Described. pp.62, 195
Discussed. pp.14, 195
Instructions for construction. p.62
Set up. p.251
Type - Symbol of. A picture of separation, of being protected from the world. pp.16, 62, 195

BASES (See **TABERNACLE**)

BELIEVER - BELIEVERS
Names - Titles.
Name is carried by the High Priest before the LORD. pp.102, 109-110, 235
Name is known by God. pp.102, 109-110, 235

BEZALEL
Described as.
A faithful man. Made everything the LORD commanded. p.228
Skilled manager. p.188
Discussed. His final glimpse of the Ark. p.252
Equipped. List. pp.161, 182
Fact. God filled **B**. with intelligence, knowledge, & skill in construction. p.182
Life.
Family heritage. pp.160-161
Tribe of Judah. p.161
Meaning of **B**. Under the shadow of God. p.160
Ministry of. Call.
God called **B**. by name. p.160
Overseer of the building of the Tabernacle. p.160
Spiritual experiences of. Filled with God's Spirit. pp.161, 182

BLOOD (See **JESUS CHRIST**, Blood of)

BLUE, Color of
Type - Symbol of. The heavenly character of Christ. pp.12, 71

BOAST - BOASTING (See **PRIDE**)

BODY OF CHRIST
Discussed. The Tabernacle is a symbol of the body of Christ. p.3

BRASS (See **BRONZE**)

BRAZEN ALTAR (See **ALTAR OF BURNT OFFERING**)

BREAD (See **SHOWBREAD**)

BREAD OF LIFE (See **SHOWBREAD**)

BREASTPIECE (See **CHESTPIECE; HIGH PRIEST**)

BRONZE
Fact.
Overlaid the Altar of Burnt Offering. p.83
The primary metal in the Courtyard of the Tabernacle. p.226
Type - Symbol of. The death of Christ. pp.12, 90-91

BRONZE ALTAR (See **ALTAR OF BURNT OFFERING**)

BRONZE WASH BASIN (See **WASH BASIN, BRONZE**)

BROTHERHOOD (See **UNITY**)

**BUILD - BUILDERS - BUILD-
ING (See TABERNACLE)**
Of the Tabernacle.
Bezalel was the superinten-
dent. p.160
God was the architect of the
Tabernacle. p.9
Oholiab was the assistant su-
perintendent. pp.161-162

BULL
Sacrifice of. p.125
Type - Symbol of. Christ as
the sin-bearer of the world.
pp.125-126

BURNT OFFERING
Discussed. Instructions given.
pp.125-127
Duty. To give all that we are
& all that we have to God.
pp.126-127
Meaning. p.126
Type - Symbol of.
Christ as the sin-bearer of
the world. p.125
God accepting the person's
sacrifice & dedication.
p.126

BUSINESS
Discussed. What it takes to
build a successful **b**. p.173

C

**CALL - CALLED (See DISCI-
PLE - DISCIPLES)**
Duty.
Demands faithfulness, per-
sonal responsibility. p.100
Demands great & careful
diligence. p.100
Requires a person to walk
worthy of God. p.100
Nature of.
A glorious call & hope.
p.100
A heavenly calling. p.100
A high calling, ultimate
goal for life. p.100
A holy calling. p.100
An eternal call. p.100
God always calls a person
by name. p.160
Limited. Unique, one of a
kind. p.101
Of God.
Every believer is **c**. to build
God's church here upon
the earth. p.174
Fact. No greater **c**. than the
c. of God. p.234
Source. God.
He always takes the initia-
tive & does the calling.
p.98
He calls & always equips.
p.161
Made possible because of
the gospel. p.100
No greater **c**. p.234

To what. (See **CALL**, Purpose)
To be representatives of
God, mediators between
God & man. p.99
To offer gifts & sacrifices
for sin. p.99
To pray & make strong inter-
cession for the people. p.99
To set the priests apart from
all other people so they
could serve God. p.99
To show compassion for
the ignorant & to people
going astray. p.99
To teach the people. p.99

**CANDLESTICK, GOLD (See
LAMPSTAND, GOLD)**

**CEREMONIAL WASHING
(See PRIESTHOOD;
CLEAN)**

CHERUBIM
Construction of.
Discussed. pp.26, 211
Overshadowed the Mercy
Seat. pp.26, 211

**CHEST OF GOD (See ARK OF
GOD)**

**CHESTPIECE (See HIGH
PRIEST)**
Discussed. pp.103, 236
Instructions for making **c**.
pp.103, 236
Purpose for the **c**. pp.103, 236
Type - Symbol of.
The High Priest, Jesus
Christ, representing &
carrying the names of
God's people upon His
heart continually. pp.103,
110, 236
The High Priest seeking
God's perfect will for the
people. pp.103, 110, 236

CHRISTIAN SERVICE
Duty. To build God's church
here upon the earth. p.174

**CHURCH WORK (See
CHRISTIAN SERVICE)**

**CLEAN - CLEANLINESS -
CLEANSING**
Duty - Essential. To be morally
cleansed by the Lord. p.124
Judgment of. Those who are
not **c**. p.192
Kinds.
Judicial. pp.125-126
Moral. p.124
Verses. List of. pp.149-150

**CLOTHE - CLOTHING,
SPIRITUAL**
Duty.
To be clothed with the
righteousness of Jesus
Christ. p.124
To put on holy clothes. p.124

CLOTHING
Chestpiece (See **CHEST-
PIECE**)
Discussed.
Aaron was to be dressed in
the priestly **c**. p.124
Sprinkling blood & anoint-
ing oil on the priests &
their clothes. p.128
Ephod. (See **EPHOD**).
Facts.
The High Priest's **c**. was to
be passed down to the
succeeding son. p.130
The ordination **c**. was to be
worn for seven days.
p.130
Gold Medallion. (See **ME-
DALLION, GOLD**)
List of garments. p.101
Making of. pp.234-240
Materials to be used. p.101
Purpose for. To minister in the
Holy Place. p.234
Robe of the Ephod. (See
ROBE OF EPHOD)
Sash (See **SASH**)
Tunic (See **TUNIC**)
Turban (See **TURBAN**)
Type - Symbol of. The priest's
c. Pictured the dignity &
honor due to the name of
God. pp.180, 234
Underclothing (See **UNDER-
CLOTHING**)

COME (See INVITATION)

**COMMIT - COMMITMENT
(See DEDICATION - DEVO-
TION)**
Call to **c**.
To give God the best.
pp.128-130

**COMMUNION (See FEASTS,
RELIGIOUS; FELLOWSHIP
MEAL)**

**CONSECRATION (See
COMMITMENT; CROSS,
DAILY; DEDICATION;
HEART)**
Discussed.
How the priests were to
sanctify & **c**. themselves.
pp.119-133
Meaning. p.127
Of whom - Of what.
The burnt offering of the
first ram. p.126
The repetition of the ordi-
nation ceremony. p.131
The sacrifice of the second
ram. p.127
Type - Symbol of. Full **c**. to
the service of God. p.127

**CONSTRUCTION (See TAB-
ERNACLE)**

COPPER (See BRONZE)

343

Pointed to the perfect demonstration of God's mercy & grace. p.252

The finished work of Christ. p.29

Type - Symbol of.
God covering the Law with His mercy. p.29
The finished work of Christ pp.29, 34-35
The mercy of God Himself. p.33

MIND
Duty - Essential. To subject one's m. to God. pp.114, 239

MINISTER (See DISCIPLE - DISCIPLES; MINISTRY - MINISTERING)

MINISTRY - MINISTERING (See BELIEVERS; DISCIPLES; MINISTERS for more discussion)
Duty in relation to God. Must be consecrated to service for God. pp.127-128

MIRROR
Fact. The Bronze Wash Basin was made with the m. given by the women. p.225

MISSION (See PURPOSE)

MODESTY
Discussed. Purpose of linen underclothing. pp.107-108, 115, 239

MONEY (See RICH - RICHES)
Type - Symbol of. The raising of m. for the Tabernacle offering symbolized the ransom paid for one's life. p.148

MORNING & EVENING SACRIFICES (See SACRIFICES - SACRIFICIAL SYSTEM)
Blessings of. p.133
Discussed. pp.131-133

MOSES
Ministry of.
Inspected all the work done on the Tabernacle. p.243
To anoint Aaron & his sons with oil. p.124
To build the Tabernacle. p.167
To dress Aaron & his sons. p.124
Washed Aaron & his sons. p.124
Obedience of.
Set up the Tabernacle--just as God commanded him to do. p.168

Spiritual experiences of.
Could not enter the Tabernacle because of the intense glory of God. p.255

MOST HOLY PLACE (See HOLY OF HOLIES)

N

NAKED - NAKEDNESS
Spiritual n. Linen underclothing.
Purpose. To cover the nakedness of the priests as they climbed the steps of the altar. p.108
Type - Symbol of. Covering the believer's spiritual nakedness. pp.115, 239

NAME - NAMES
The name of believers. (See BELIEVERS, Names - Titles)
Is carried by the High Priest before the LORD. p.235
Is known by God. p.235

NEW BEGINNING (See STARTING OVER; RESTORATION)
Discussed.
God is the God of new beginnings. p.249
Type - Symbol of. A brand new start. p.249

NEW YEAR
Discussed. The Tabernacle was assembled on the first day of the first month of a brand new year. p.249

NEWNESS OF LIFE (See NEW BEGINNING)

O

OBEY - OBEDIENCE
Duty in relation to God.
Moses did everything God commanded. pp.251-254
To give dignity & honor to God's call. p.234
To put into action the plan of God. p.188
Duty in relation to oneself.
Example.
Moses did everything God commanded him to do. pp.251-254
The people built the Tabernacle exactly as God commanded. p.242
Two lessons gleaned from the o. of Moses. p.254
Questions concerning o. pp.162-163

Results.
Affects all other commandments. p.163
When Moses o. the LORD & built a place for Him, God filled the Tabernacle with His presence & glory. p.256
When Solomon o. the LORD & built a place for Him, God filled the Temple with His presence & glory. p.256
When the Christian believer o. the LORD & builds a place for Him, God fills the heart of the believer with His presence & glory. p.257

OFFERING - OFFERINGS (See GIFTS; GIVING; STEWARDSHIP)
Discussed.
The abundance of o. pp.189-190
The raising of money for the Tabernacle o. pp.146-148
Why God wants our resources. p.175
Duty.
The church has a responsibility to meet the needs of a desperate world. p.176
Facts.
About raising money for the Tabernacle o.
Each one counted under the census was to pay one fifth of an ounce of silver. p.147
Not everyone brought his offering to the LORD. p.147
The amount of the offering was the same for rich & poor. p.147
The census was to include every person twenty years old & above. p.147
The people were to pay a ransom tax every census. p.146
Instructions on how to give an o. p.10
To be a cheerful giver. p.182
To be from a willing heart. p.181
Kinds of o.
Common things. p.181
Curtains. p.182
Gold jewelry. p.181
Oil. p.182
Silver & bronze. p.182
Spices. p.182
Stones & gems. p.182
The right kinds of o. p.176
The wrong kinds of o. p.176
Wave o. p.181

353

WORK FOR GOD
Discussed. The need to put into action the plan of God. p.188
Essential.
Everyone must surrender personal pride & work together. p.189
We must do our best to complete the work of God upon earth. pp.228-229
Fact. God will always supply what is needed to do His work. p.229

Source. All skills & abilities are from God. p.188

WORKS, GOOD (See **MAN; PERFECT - PERFECTION**)
Duty.
Must abide in God's Word. p.108
Must bear much fruit. p.108
Must forsake all & follow Christ. p.108
Must live a life that is godly & above reproach. p.108

WORLD
Warning. Against the dangers of the w. pp.196-197

WORSHIP
Duty.
To w. morning until night-- all day, every day. p.131
Entrance into. Christ invites men to come through the door & w. Him. p.68
Fact. Impossible to w. if God's law & Word are not close at hand. p.165

ACKNOWLEDGMENTS AND BIBLIOGRAPHY

Every child of God is precious to the Lord and deeply loved. And every child as a servant of the Lord touches the lives of those who come in contact with him or his ministry. The writing ministries of the following servants have touched this work, and we are grateful that God brought their writings our way. We hereby acknowledge their ministry to us, being fully aware that there are many others down through the years whose writings have touched our lives and who deserve mention, but whose names have faded from our memory. May our wonderful Lord continue to bless the ministries of these dear servants—and the ministries of us all—as we diligently labor to reach the world for Christ and to meet the desperate needs of those who suffer so much.

THE REFERENCE WORKS

Archer, Gleason L. Jr. *A Survey of Old Testament Introduction.* Chicago, IL: Moody Bible Institute of Chicago, 1974.

Baker's Dictionary of Theology. Everett F. Harrison, Editor-in-Chief. Grand Rapids, MI: Baker Book House, 1960.

Brown, Francis. *The New Brown-Driver-Briggs-Gesenius Hebrew-English Lexicon.* Peabody, MA: Hendrickson Publishers, 1979.

Cruden's Complete Concordance of the Old & New Testament. Philadelphia, PA: The John C. Winston Co., 1930.

Dake's Annotated Reference Bible, The Holy Bible. Finis Jennings Dake. Lawrenceville, GA: Dake Bible Sales, Inc., 1963.

Elwell, Walter A., Editor. *The Evangelical Dictionary of Theology.* Grand Rapids, MI: Baker Book House, 1984.

Encyclopedia of Biblical Prophecy. J. Barton Payne. New York, NY: Harper & Row, Publishers, 1973.

Funk & Wagnalls Standard Desk Dictionary. Lippincott & Crowell, Publishers, 1980, Vol.2.

Geisler, Norman. *A Popular Survey of the Old Testament.* Grand Rapids, MI: Baker Book House, 1977.

Good News Bible. Old Testament: © American Bible Society, 1976. New Testament: © American Bible Society, 1966, 1971, 1976. Collins World.

Good, Joseph. *Rosh HaShanah and the Messianic Kingdom to Come.* Pt. Arthur, TX: Hatikva Ministries, 1989.

Harrison, Roland Kenneth. *Introduction to the Old Testament.* Grand Rapids, MI: Eerdmans Publishing Company, 1969.

Josephus, Flavius. *Complete Works.* Grand Rapids, MI: Kregel Publications, 1981.

Kelley, Page H. *Exodus: Called for Redemptive Mission.* January Bible Study. Nashville, TN: Convention Press, 1977.

Kohlenberger, John R. III. *The Interlinear NIV Hebrew-English Old Testament.* Grand Rapids, MI: Zondervan Publishing House, 1987.

Life Application® Bible. Wheaton, IL: Tyndale House Publishers, Inc., 1991.

Lindsell, Harold and Woodbridge, Charles J. *A Handbook of Christian Truth.* Westwood, NJ: Fleming H. Revell Company, A Division of Baker Book House, 1953.

Lipis, Joan R. *Celebrate Passover Haggadah.* San Francisco, CA: Purple Pomegranate Productions, 1993.

Living Quotations For Christians. Edited by Sherwood Eliot Wirt and Kersten Beckstrom. New York, NY: Harper & Row, Publishers, 1974.

Lockyer, Herbert. *All the Books and Chapters of the Bible.* Grand Rapids, MI: Zondervan Publishing House, 1966.

———. *All the Men of the Bible.* Grand Rapids, MI: Zondervan Publishing House, 1958.

———. *The Women of the Bible.* Grand Rapids, MI: Zondervan Publishing House, 1967.

Martin, Alfred. *Survey of the Scriptures*, Part I, II, III. Chicago, IL: Moody Bible Institute of Chicago, 1961.

McDowell, Josh. *Evidence That Demands A Verdict*, Vol.1. San Bernardino, CA: Here's Life Publishers, Inc., 1979.

Miller, Madeleine S. & J. Lane. *Harper's Bible Dictionary.* New York, NY: Harper & Row Publishers, 1961.

Nave's Topical Bible. Orville J. Nave. Nashville, TN: The Southwestern Company. Copyright © by J.B. Henderson, 1921.

Nelson's Expository Dictionary of the Old Testament. Merrill F. Unger & William White, Jr. Nashville, TN: Thomas Nelson Publishers, 1980.

New American Standard Bible, Reference Edition. La Habra, CA: The Lockman Foundation, 1975.

New International Version Study Bible. Grand Rapids, MI: Zondervan Bible Publishers, 1985.

356

New Living Translation, Holy Bible. Wheaton, IL: Tyndale House Publishers, Inc., 1996.
NIV Exhaustive Concordance. (Grand Rapids, MI: Zondervan Corporation, 1990).
Orr, William. *How We May Know That God Is.* Wheaton, IL: Van Kampen Press, n.d.
Owens, John Joseph. *Analytical Key to the Old Testament,* Vols.1, 2, 3. Grand Rapids, MI: Baker Book House, 1989.
Pilgrim Edition, Holy Bible. New York, NY: Oxford University Press, 1952.
Ridout, Samuel. *Lectures on the Tabernacle.* New York, NY: Loizeaux Brothers, Inc., 1914.
Roget's 21st Century Thesaurus, Edited by Barbara Ann Kipfer. New York, NY: Dell Publishing, 1992.
Rosen, Ceil and Moishe. *Christ In The Passover.* Chicago, IL: Moody Press, 1978.
Slemming, C.W. *Made According To Pattern.* Fort Washington, PA: Christian Literature Crusade, 1983.
Soltau, Henry W. *The Holy Vessels And Furniture Of The Tabernacle.* Grand Rapids, MI: Kregel Publications, 1971.
———. *The Tabernacle The Priesthood And The Offerings.* Grand Rapids, MI: Kregel Publications, 1972.
Stone, Nathan J. *Names of God.* Chicago, IL: Moody Press, 1944.
Strong's Exhaustive Concordance of the Bible. James Strong. Nashville, TN: Thomas Nelson, Inc., 1990.
Strong, James. *The Tabernacle Of Israel.* Grand Rapids, MI: Kregel Publications, 1987.
The Amplified Bible. Scripture taken from THE AMPLIFIED BIBLE, Old Testament copyright © 1965, 1987 by the Zondervan Corporation. The Amplified New Testament copyright © 1958, 1987 by The Lockman Foundation. Used by permission.
The Hebrew-Greek Key Study Bible, New International Version. Spiros Zodhiates, Th.D., Executive Editor. Chattanooga, TN: AMG Publishers, 1996.
The Holy Bible in Four Translations. Minneapolis, MN: Worldwide Publications. Copyright © The Iversen-Norman Associates: New York, NY, 1972.
The Interlinear Bible, Vol.1, 2, & 3, Translated by Jay P. Green, Sr. Grand Rapids, MI: Baker Book House Company, 1976.
The International Standard Bible Encyclopaedia, Edited by James Orr. Grand Rapids, MI: Eerdmans Publishing Company, 1939.
The NASB Greek/Hebrew Dictionary and Concordance. (La Habra, CA: The Lockman Foundation, 1988).
The New Compact Bible Dictionary, Edited by T. Alton Bryant. Grand Rapids, MI: Zondervan Publishing House, 1967. Used by permission of Zondervan Publishing House.
The New Scofield Reference Bible, Edited by C.I. Scofield. New York, NY: Oxford University Press, 1967.
The New Thompson Chain Reference Bible. Indianapolis, IN: B.B. Kirkbride Bible Co., Inc., 1964.
The Open Bible. Nashville, TN: Thomas Nelson Publishers, 1975.
The Zondervan Pictorial Encyclopedia of the Bible, Vol.1. Merrill C. Tenney, Editor. Grand Rapids, MI: Zondervan Publishing House, 1982.
Theological Wordbook of the Old Testament, Edited by R. Laird Harris. Chicago, IL: Moody Bible Institute of Chicago, 1980.
Vine's Complete Expository Dictionary of Old and New Testament Words. W.E. Vine, Merrill F. Unger, William White, Jr. Nashville, TN: Thomas Nelson Publishers, 1985.
Webster's Seventh New Collegiate Dictionary. Springfield, MA: G. & C. Merriam Company, Publishers, 1971.
Wilson, William. *Wilson's Old Testament Word Studies.* McLean, VA: MacDonald Publishing Company, n.d.
Wood, Leon. *A Survey of Israel's History.* Grand Rapids, MI: Zondervan Publishing House, 1982.
Young's Analytical Concordance to the Bible. Robert Young. Grand Rapids, MI: Eerdmans Publishing Company, n.d.
Young, Edward J. *An Introduction to the Old Testament.* Grand Rapids, MI: Eerdmans Publishing Company, 1964.
Zehr, Paul M. *Glimpses of the Tabernacle.* Lancaster, PA: Mennonite Information Center, 1976.

THE COMMENTARIES

Barclay, William. "Daily Study Bible Series." Philadelphia, PA: Westminster Press, Began in 1953.
———. *The Old Law & The New Law.* Philadelphia, PA: The Westminster Press, 1972.
Barnes' Notes, Exodus to Esther. F.C. Cook, Editor. Grand Rapids, MI: Baker Book House, n.d.
Bush, George. *Commentary on Exodus.* Grand Rapids, MI: Kregel Publications, 1993.
———. *Exodus.* Minneapolis, MN: Klock & Klock Christian Publishers, Inc., 1981.
Childs, Brevard S. *The Book of Exodus.* Philadelphia, PA: The Westminster Press, 1974.

Cole, R. Alan. *Exodus*. "The Tyndale Old Testament Commentaries." Downers Grove, IL: Inter-Varsity Press, 1973.

Dunnam, Maxie. *The Preacher's Commentary on Exodus*. Dallas, TX: Word Publishing, 1987.

Durham, John I. *Understanding the Basic Themes of Exodus*. Dallas, TX: Word, Inc., 1990.

_____. *Word Biblical Commentary, Exodus*. Waco, TX: Word, Inc., 1987.

Ellison, H.L. *Exodus*. Philadelphia, PA: The Westminster Press, 1982.

Fretheim, Terence E. *Exodus, Interpretation*. Louisville, KY: John Knox Press, 1991.

Gaebelein, Frank E. *The Expositor's Bible Commentary*, Vol.2. Grand Rapids, MI: Zondervan Publishing House, 1990.

Gill, John. *Gill's Commentary*, Vol.1. Grand Rapids, MI: Baker Book House, 1980.

Hayford, Jack W., Executive Editor. *Milestones to Maturity*. Nashville, TN: Thomas Nelson Publishers, 1994

Henry, Matthew. *Matthew Henry's Commentary*, 6 Volumes. Old Tappan, NJ: Fleming H. Revell Co., n.d.

Heslop, W.G. *Extras from Exodus*. Grand Rapids, MI: Kregel Publications, 1931.

Hewitt, Thomas. *The Epistle to the Hebrews*. "Tyndale New Testament Commentaries." Grand Rapids, MI: Eerdmans Publishing Co., Began in 1958.

Huey, F.B. Jr. *A Study Guide Commentary, Exodus*. Grand Rapids, MI: Zondervan Publishing House, 1977.

Hyatt, J.P. *The New Century Bible Commentary, Exodus*. Grand Rapids, MI: Eerdmans Publishing Company, 1971.

Keil-Delitzsch. *Commentary on the Old Testament*, Vol.1. Grand Rapids, MI: Eerdmans Publishing Company, n.d.

Life Change Series, Exodus. Colorado Springs, CO: NavPress, 1989.

Maclaren, Alexander. *Expositions of Holy Scripture*, 11 Vols. Grand Rapids, MI: Eerdmans Publishing Company, 1952-59.

McGee, J. Vernon. *Thru The Bible*, Vol.1. Nashville, TN: Thomas Nelson Publishers, 1981.

Meyer, F.B. *Devotional Commentary on Exodus*. Grand Rapids, MI: Kregel Publications, 1978.

Napier, B. Davie. *Exodus*. "The Layman's Bible Commentary," Vol.3. Atlanta, GA: John Knox Press, 1963.

Olford, Stephen. *The Tabernacle, Camping With God*. Neptune, NJ: Loizeaux Brothers, 1971.

Pink, Arthur. *Gleanings in Exodus*. Chicago, IL: Moody Bible Institute of Chicago, Moody Press, n.d.

_____. *The Ten Commandments*. Grand Rapids, MI: Baker Books, 1994.

Reapsome, James. *Exodus*. Downers Grove, IL: InterVarsity Press, 1989.

Salmond, S.D.F.. *The Epistle to the Ephesians*. "The Expositor's Greek Testament," Vol.3. Grand Rapids, MI: Eerdmans Publishing Co., 1970.

Sarna, Nahum M. *Exploring Exodus*. New York, NY: Schocken Books Inc., 1986.

Strauss, Lehman. *Devotional Studies in Galatians & Ephesians*. Neptune, NJ: Loizeaux Brothers, 1957.

_____. *The Book of the Revelation*. Neptune, NJ: Loizeaux Brothers, 1964.

The Biblical Illustrator, Exodus. Edited by Joseph S. Exell. Grand Rapids, MI: Baker Book House, 1964.

The Epistle of Paul to the Ephesians. "Tyndale New Testament Commentaries." Grand Rapids, MI: Eerdmans, n.d.

The Interpreter's Bible, 12 Vols. New York, NY: Abingdon Press, 1956.

The Pulpit Commentary. 23 Volumes. Edited by H.D.M. Spence & Joseph S. Exell. Grand Rapids, MI: Eerdmans Publishing Company, 1950.

Thomas, W.H. Griffith. *Through the Pentateuch Chapter by Chapter*. Grand Rapids, MI: Eerdmans Publishing Company, 1957.

Wuest, Kenneth S.. *Ephesians and Colossians*. "Word Studies in the Greek New Testament," Vol.1. Grand Rapids, MI: Eerdmans Publishing Co., 1966.

Youngblood, Ronald F. *Exodus*. Chicago, IL: Moody Press, 1983.

OUTLINE BIBLE RESOURCES

T his material, like similar works, has come from imperfect man and is thus susceptible to human error. We are nevertheless grateful to God for both calling us and empowering us through His Holy Spirit to undertake this task. Because of His goodness and grace, *The Preacher's Outline & Sermon Bible*® New Testament is complete, and Old Testament volumes are releasing periodically.

The Minister's Personal Handbook and other helpful **Outline Bible Resources** are available in printed form as well as releasing electronically on WORDsearch software.

God has given the strength and stamina to bring us this far. Our confidence is that as we keep our eyes on Him and grounded in the undeniable truths of the Word, we will continue working through the Old Testament volumes. The future includes other helpful Outline Bible Resources for God's dear servants to use in their Bible Study and discipleship.

We offer this material first to Him in whose Name we labor and serve and for whose glory it has been produced and, second, to everyone everywhere who preaches and teaches the Word.

Our daily prayer is that each volume will lead thousands, millions, yes even billions, into a better understanding of the Holy Scriptures and a fuller knowledge of Jesus Christ the Incarnate Word, of whom the Scriptures so faithfully testify.

Y ou will be pleased to know that Leadership Ministries Worldwide partners with Christian organizations, printers, and mission groups around the world to make Outline Bible Resources available and affordable in many countries and foreign languages. It is our goal that *every* leader around the world, both clergy and lay, will be able to understand God's Holy Word and present God's message with more clarity, authority, and understanding—all beyond his or her own power.

LEADERSHIP MINISTRIES WORLDWIDE
PO Box 21310 • Chattanooga, TN 37424-0310
(423) 855-2181 • FAX (423) 855-8616
info@outlinebible.org
www.outlinebible.org - FREE Download materials

LEADERSHIP MINISTRIES WORLDWIDE

Publishers of Outline Bible Resources

Currently Available Materials, with New Volumes Releasing Regularly

- **THE PREACHER'S OUTLINE & SERMON BIBLE® (POSB)**

NEW TESTAMENT

Matthew I (chapters 1-15)	1 & 2 Corinthians
Matthew II (chapters 16-28)	Galatians, Ephesians, Philippians, Colossians
Mark	1 & 2 Thess., 1 & 2 Timothy, Titus, Philemon
Luke	Hebrews, James
John	1 & 2 Peter, 1, 2, & 3 John, Jude
Acts	Revelation
Romans	Master Outline & Subject Index

OLD TESTAMENT

Genesis I (chapters 1-11)	Judges, Ruth	Isaiah 1 (chapters 1-35)
Genesis II (chapters 12-50)	1 Samuel	Isaiah 2 (chapters 36-66)
Exodus I (chapters 1-18)	2 Samuel	Jeremiah 1 (chapters 1-29)
Exodus II (chapters 19-40)	1 Kings	Jeremiah 2 (chapters 30-52),
Leviticus	2 Kings	Lamentations
Numbers	1 Chronicles	Ezekiel
Deuteronomy	Ezra, Nehemiah,	Daniel, Hosea
Joshua	Esther	*New volumes release periodically*

KJV Available in Deluxe 3-Ring Binders or Softbound Edition • **NIV Available in** Softbound **Only**

- **The Preacher's Outline & Sermon Bible New Testament —** 3 Vol. Hardcover • KJV – NIV

- *What the Bible Says to the Minister* **— The Minister's Personal Handbook**
  12 Chs. - 127 Subjects - 400 Verses Expounded - Italian Imitation Leather or Paperback t

- **Practical Word Studies In the New Testament** — 2 Vol. Hardcover Set

- **The Teacher's Outline & Study Bible™ - New Testament Books**
  Complete 30 - 45 minute lessons – with illustrations and discussion questions

- **Practical Illustrations — Companion to the POSB**
  Arranged by topic and Scripture reference

- **OUTLINE New Testament with Thompson®** Chain-References
  Combines verse-by-verse outlines with the legendary Thompson References

- **What the Bible Says Series – Various Subjects**

  Prayer • The Passion • The Ten Commandments • The Tabernacle

- **Software – Various products powered by WORDsearch**

  New Testament • Pentateuch • History • Various Prophets • Practical Word Studies

- **Non-English Translations of various books**
  Included languages are: Spanish - Korean - Russian - –Chinese - Nepalese

— Contact LMW for Specific Language Availability and Prices —

For quantity orders and information, please contact:
LEADERSHIP MINISTRIES WORLDWIDE or Your Local Christian Bookstore
PO Box 21310   • Chattanooga, TN 37424-0310
(423) 855-2181 (9am – 5pm Eastern) • FAX (423) 855-8616
E-mail - info@outlinebible.org Order online at www.outlinebible.org

PURPOSE STATEMENT

LEADERSHIP MINISTRIES WORLDWIDE

exists to equip ministers, teachers, and laymen in their understanding, preaching and teaching of God's Word by publishing and distributing worldwide *The Preacher's Outline & Sermon Bible®* and related **Outline Bible Resources**, to reach & disciple men, women, boys and girls for Jesus Christ.

MISSION STATEMENT

1. To make the Bible so understandable – its truth so clear and plain – that men and women everywhere, whether teacher or student, preacher or hearer, can grasp its message and receive Jesus Christ as Savior, and...

2. To place the Bible in the hands of all who will preach and teach God's Holy Word, verse by verse, precept by precept, regardless of the individual's ability to purchase it.

Outline Bible Resources have been given to LMW for printing and especially distribution worldwide at/below cost, by those who remain anonymous. One fact, however, is as true today as it was in the time of Christ:

THE GOSPEL IS FREE, BUT THE COST OF TAKING IT IS NOT

LMW depends on the generous gifts of believers with a heart for Him and a love for the lost. They help pay for the printing, translating, and distributing of **Outline Bible Resources** into the hands of God's servants worldwide, who will present the Gospel message with clarity, authority, and understanding beyond their own.

LMW was incorporated in the state of Tennessee in July 1992 and received IRS 501 (c)(3) nonprofit status in March 1994. LMW is an international, nondenominational mission organization. All proceeds from USA sales, along with donations from donor partners, go directly to underwrite our translation and distribution projects of **Outline Bible Resources** to preachers, church and lay leaders, and Bible students around the world.